THE NEW
GERMAN SHORTHAIRED POINTER

Intensity, the mark of a keen hunting dog: Dual Ch. Sager v. Gardsburg.

Australian Ch. & Retrieving Trial Ch. Linstan Kathi (Ch. South Creek Baron ex Tainui Gerda.) Breeders, Linstan Kennels, Victoria. Owner, W. Morris, Victoria. For the Australian GSP, the privilege of competing for the Retrieving Trial title is a most valuable concession, providing encouragement to preserve the water-working abilities of the breed, so basic a part of original breed development. Kathi's dam, Tainui Gerda, was imported in-utero to New Zealand, later re-exported to Australia, where her water-work inheritance was proven in much of her produce. Her breeders, Mr. and Mrs. E. Beaumont of Stokes Valley, Wellington, brought first GSP to New Zealand.

The New
GERMAN SHORTHAIRED
POINTER

by C. BEDE MAXWELL

Fourth Edition
ILLUSTRATED

with line drawings
by Phyllis Kjerulff

1982 — 1st Printing
HOWELL BOOK HOUSE INC.
230 PARK AVENUE
NEW YORK, N.Y. 10169

Dr. Charles Thornton, in 1961, handed over his records and photos to the author. These are now in the American Kennel Club Library in New York City. *Photo: Shirley Miner.*

Copyright © 1982, 1975, 1965, 1963 by Howell Book House Inc.

No part of this book may be used or reproduced in any manner whatsoever without written permission from the publisher, except in the case of brief excerpts quoted in reviews.

Printed in U.S.A.

Library of Congress Cataloging in Publication Data

Maxwell, C. Bede, 1901–
    The new German shorthaired pointer.

    Bibliography: p. 320
    1. German shorthaired pointer.   I.   Title.
SF429.G4M3   1982   636.7'52   82-3059
ISBN 0-87605-157-3   AACR2

To the Great Pioneers,
DR. CHARLES R. THORNTON
JOSEPH BURKHART
WALTER MANGOLD
ERNEST ROJEM
whose breed strains dominate
the background of our best American dogs,

and further—modernly—to the memory of
RALPH A. PARK, SR., *first president (1964) of the GSPCA,*
whose practical, breed-protective aim is memorialized by an
achievement that may never again be duplicated,
the finishing of five American/Canadian dual champions,
four of them homebreds,

this NEW GERMAN SHORTHAIRED POINTER
is most respectfully dedicated.

Kennelmates and all three earned dual championships in both Canada and the United States—Arrak v. Heisterholz (German import), Gert's Dena v. Greif and Gert's Duro v. Greif. Owned by Ralph A. Park, Sr., Seattle.

Serakraut's Kraut (Ch. Serakraut's Exactly/Serakraut's Constellation). Breeder: Ann Serak, Wisconsin. Owner: Gary de Young, Wisconsin.

Contents

Acknowledgments   9

1. Origin and Early Development   13
2. 20th Century German Breed Pillars   33
3. Modern-Day Strains in Germany   47
4. The Early American Scene   73
5. Progress in American Breeding   89
6. German Shorthairs Out of the West   103
7. Nationwide into the '80s   115
8. The Field Competitive Shorthair   131
9. Field Trials for German Shorthaired Pointers in America   143
10. British and Commonwealth Shorthairs   167
11. Showing Your German Shorthaired Pointer   199
12. The A.K.C. Standard   214
13. Gait   244
14. Breeding Your German Shorthaired Pointer   249
15. Picking Shorthair Pups   309
16. German Titles, Vocabulary, etc.   313

Unanswerable proof that there were Shorthairs in this country long before the Thornton imports of the 1920s. This unidentified picture was picked up in an empty house in Dallas, Pennsylvania some years ago. The sole clue it offers is the name of the photographer on the back—Cobb, Binghamton, New York. Inquiry at the City Hall in Binghamton proved that Cobb was in business there from the 1890s to the early 1900s. The elegant quality of the dog is apparent and one reflects that he was a near-enough contemporary of the Hoppenrades.—*Lent by Richard S. Johns.*

Acknowledgments

SINCERE thanks are due to the many breeders who so generously made their cherished records available towards the compilation of this book. Far too many to be named individually, their contributions are made plain within the body of the text, for lacking these contributions there could have been, of course, no book at all.

In particular, though, our indebtedness must be acknowledged in respect to the contributions of the great pioneers. Dr. Charles R. Thornton, of Washington, made available his complete kennel records, pedigrees, photographs, journals. Mr. Walter Mangold, of Nebraska, also forwarded his German pedigrees and much information on pioneering experience with the breed. Mr. Joseph Burkhart, of Minnesota, went to a great deal of trouble to clarify historical puzzles, as did Mr. Rudolph Hirschnitz, of California. German Shorthaired Pointer breeders of the present day should never underestimate their indebtedness to these pioneers, in both the practical and the historical sense.

Thanks are due, also, to breeders of our time who were history-minded enough to keep informative files, and generous enough to make them available.

Many of those that for earlier editions provided valuable help are no longer with us, though the Sandbergs of "Kaposia," Don and Betty are still pillars of strength and encouragement, and Mrs. Earle Dapper's early-day support remains well-remembered. The quest for updatings for this new edition brings with it appreciation

9

of the kindness extended by, especially, Mrs. Maxine Collins, Chairperson of the GSPCA Year Book Committee, of Mr. Dean Kerl, past president, and Mr. Robert McKowan of the presidency of today, and of course, of the many, many wonderful contributors otherwise mentioned within the body of the text.

From overseas, the original assistance provided by then English K.C. Secretary, the late Mr. Charles Binney is endlessly to be recalled, as his unearthings from the files rescued material which even the pioneer Germans seem not to have had ready to hand. The officers of the two German Shorthaired Pointer Clubs of England have been sympathetically kind, with indebtedness here in the main to Mrs. M. Mills de Hoog (Wittekind) and Mr. David Layton of the famed Midlanders.

Out of Europe, original thanks are still within remembrance in terms, especially, of help from the Osterreicher Kurzhaar Klub (Vienna, Austria) through secretary Dr. Otto Fischer; from Klub Kurzhaar, Berlin, in respect especially of the earlier compilation of the Dr. Kleeman Auslese Prüfung results, year by year, from Herr F. Böllhoff, of Münster. Here too, time has taken toll, of which my good friend, Frau Maria Seydel is most deeply remembered for so much practical help given, including making available to me books otherwise unprocurable, most importantly Dr. Paul Kleeman's definitive work prepared in conjunction with the famed Herr v. Otto.

Now, in the 1980s, there is another acknowledgment of great importance to be made—to Professor Alfons Lemper, of Klub Kurzhaar (*Obmann für Prüfungswesen*) whose valuable and educational article, made available so generously, provided ongoing insight into the present-day status of the breed.

A wider geographical sweep, bringing in the enormous enthusiastic assistance of the Shorthair breeders within the several States of Australia has added to the score of acknowledged indebtedness. Perhaps before all to Lynn and Carolyn Butler for earliest encouragement and a wealth of breeder-comprehensive material covering much of the introductory processes that introduced the breed to New South Wales, as Mr. Jack Thompson of the *Dunfrui* strain had for earlier editions provided material concerning original introductions to Victoria. Perhaps, most readably of all, however, has been the explanatory material provided by Mr. Kevin Walshaw of

10

Canberra, ACT, with its descriptions of field trial and hunting styles, and type of game and terrain involved. Many hands beside have made contribution, acknowledged within the text and, for final mention, there was Mr. Westy Morris of Ruvalen Kennels, Victoria, who made available the most graphic photograph that any of us, anywhere, have seen of a working Shorthair—his Ch. Linstan Kathi tensed for her take-off.

To all who have helped, wherever our appreciation is registered, here or within the text, the grateful thanks of the Shorthair folk, of today and tomorrow.

—C. BEDE MAXWELL

Woodcock season in Pennsylvania! Featuring the star performer the locals called "Missus Woodcock". To her owner-breeder, Dick Johns, she was Inge v. Graben-brunch, last of her line of inbred Grabenbruchs. As for woodcock, Inge could find them, flush them, retrieve them—but she couldn't stand the taste of them. Pictured—Dick Johns, Inge and author C. Bede Maxwell.—*Lee Barnes*

The C. F. Decker painting of the German Pointer of the 1860s shows us still a tremendous strength of hound influence. He even retains his full length of hound tail with his heavy body. Breeders had managed to get his head up from the ground, and for that they named him the High-Running German Bird Dog. He was an early stage of utility dog development and interesting to compare with our pictures of Hector Foedersdorf and the Schweisshund.

Hector Foedersdorf, described as a "German Pointer", has been for decades in the care of the British Natural History Museum, England. His likeness to the Schweisshund in head and expression, and his endowment of long hound ears, is unmistakable. An interesting link between the Scent Hound basis and the eventual German Shorthair type development.—*C. Bede Maxwell*

1

Origin and
Early Development

THE popular modern utility sporting breed known
as the German Shorthaired Pointer was brought into being over a
term of years to suit the rapidly changing needs of 19th century
German hunting sport. Hunting privileges, long reserved for the
wealthy nobles, had become available to lesser men who owned or
rented their game preserves. Such men did not want to maintain
big kennels of specialized breeds, even had a saying that a man
who went hunting with three dogs had NO dog!

Yet it was clear that to enjoy sport with only one dog along it
would need to be capable in every sphere. It must point the game
its good nose had first allowed it to find, do this at reasonable distance for a man hunting afoot. It must retrieve fur or feather, from
land or water. It must have the will and courage to destroy predators, and tracking instinct to trail a blood spoor of a wounded
animal if necessary. No humane hunter would wish to leave touched
game to die miserably.

The intention to breed all these qualities into one dog demanded
work, time, breeder co-operation. The latter, of course, proved the

hardest to get, humans being humans. While all concerned agreed upon the qualities a versatile hunting dog would need, from the first there was widest disagreement as to how these could be secured and fixed in a true-breeding strain.

Breeders could use only material available—flesh-and-blood dogs that actually existed in the country. Mere pre-vision of some dreamed-of ideal paid no dividends in any practical sense. That some widely variant sources were co-opted is made clear by old records and pictures, the historically recorded and unrecorded experiments of such enterprising men as Hofjaeger Isermann, of Nordhausen, and many others.

Nowadays, Klub Kurzhaar (Berlin) admits frankly that early experimental German Shorthaired Pointer breeding produced stock that little resembled the breed type as fixed today, either shapewise, temperamentwise, even coatwise. In a letter of 1961, the Klub spokesman pointed out that early types bore about the same resemblance to present dogs as did Man's ancestor, the ape, to human beings of our time. Dr. Paul Kleeman, long time *Vorsitzender* (President) of Klub Kurzhaar, the third to hold the honor in the life of the Klub, the most knowledgeable authority to write of the German Shorthaired Pointer development, makes many references to pioneer activities—and squabbling!

The more practical breeders recognized that the dogs would most likely be produced by breeding selectively to performance, possibly the reason so many different strains, types, even breeds, were used. As a practical measure, the services of dogs that were actually available in the country were used. One group held to firm belief that Germany had once possessed an ancient sporting dog of all possible virtues and dedicated itself to reproducing its like. This group clung to outward physical indications believed to indicate inherited working qualities. They held these to be mainly long, rounded ears, a stopless profile. Dr. Kleeman's belief, as published, was that the historical paragon belonged to the realm of fairytale—a *Märchen*, he described it. He also reminded all that clamored for "such a dog as our fathers hunted with" that most of their fathers had been only thwarted onlookers. Their "social betters" had kept the hunting privileges jealously to themselves.

Germany's ancient dogs, as those of Europe, including England, were, by the old-time writings, endless variations on the theme of

14

the Old Spanish Pointer and the Hounds of St. Hubert. "Old Spanish" had fanned out first from Mediterranean lands at civilization's heels. St. Hubert's are believed to have reached the famed French monastery with the Crusaders returned from the East, these bringing to Europe not only new kinds of dogs, horses, modes of architecture, but even modes of thought, an everlasting influence. "Old Spanish" was much valued. Basic of all sporting breeds that stand to game, his instinct to hesitate momentarily before springing has, down the centuries, been sharply honed by sporting men to their finest tool. The St. Hubert's brought cold-trailing abilities. They stand as the progenitors of all scenting hounds now known to us, either in modern or historical representation.

Many ancient writers, artists, have left descriptions of "Old Spanish." The engravers show him with heavy head, jowl, deep flews, large sunken eyes, upthrust nose with a cleft "double" nostril. His bone was huge, his coat a little rough, but never enough to fuzz his outline. His tail was docked. His liver-and-white color scheme was also his gift to sporting breeds. Surely no beauty, he was nevertheless the pride of kings in his day, hunting to hawk or net. Pointing was his virtue, slow gait his vice. When firearms developed, were improved, when men could shoot down birds where they flew dark against the sky, sportsmen everywhere set out to liven "Old Spanish" with some cross-breeding.

The English went to Foxhound, gaining elegance and speed to make their new specialized Pointer a national pride. Foxhound colors prettied the sober liver-and-white, the lemon, orange, black fleckings and patchings, and even solid blacks and full livers. The solids, in our time, are extremely rare. The Germans long ago used the black to form one type of German Shorthaired Pointers, and Scandinavian countries still have some true-type solid blacks, while Australia's best known Pointer breeder of today also has such a bitch. That America has had solid livers is to be proved by an historical painting in the De Young Museum, San Francisco, in which such a one is running with the turnout of Mr. Ogden Mills, of California.

The French also livened "Old Spanish," securing stepped-up elegance in the production of beautiful pack hounds, especially, with diverse variation of St. Hubert stock. Widely distributed, these became basics of other breed developments. Those who think

THE OLD SPANISH POINTER, painted Stubbs (1724–1806).

Photo lent by L. L. de Groen, Australia.

Early German Pointers—the breed in transitional stage.

Photo lent by L. L. de Groen, Australia.

16

of scent hounds only in terms of Bloodhound or Basset heaviness and wrinkle should check historical pictures of the Talbots and other vanished tall French hounds—the Gascons, Normandys, etc., and even the Kerry Beagles (Ireland), pure French Talbot in origin and so maintained, a century and more, standing to 24″, with wrinkle-free heads—to prove how type could be changed and maintained. Kerry Beagles, as their photos show, had even that round ear the German pioneers craved, and straight profiles as well. The superb Talbot brace in the famed painting (now in Christchurch Museum, New Zealand) of the great British colonizer, Edward Gibbon Wakefield, a notable dog fancier in his day, also shows what could be done in terms of beautiful-headed tall hounds.

The 19th century French were well ahead of the Germans in breeding up good-looking, balanced hunting dogs from original clumsy material. Comparison of the 1871 experimental German Shorthaired Pointer, Feldmann I, with the 1865 prize-winning Gascon Hound, Genereaux, at the Paris Exhibition is in this respect interesting. This Genereaux will not look *too* strange to German Shorthaired Pointer folk, apart from his ears and tail. Balance-wise, he leaves Feldmann I for dead! E. v. Otto describes Feldmann I, bred by the Prince Albrecht zu Solms-Brauenfels, as *dreifarbig* (tricolor). Genereaux, following true to the Gascon Hounds, was blue-mottled. As it turned out, French breeders of the 19th century backed the wrong horse. Hunting with pack hounds went out of style in the practical sense with changing ways of life, fencing of properties, but the German Shorthaired Pointer's dog-of-all-work status has been upheld in popularity even to the present day.

Some among modern-day breeders here still argue strenuously from the firm, if wishful, belief within their own hearts that the background of the German Shorthaired Pointer is to be found only as "Old Spanish." *No* English Pointer, no, sir! No Hound, no! Some "authorities" have even engaged themselves with confidence in compartmentizing the breed heritage—so much percent Pointer, so much percent Bloodhound, etc. etc. Anyone could be so definite!

Dr. Kleeman points out that early-day German breeders had access to several types of pointing dogs, often as developed first in other countries. There was also a little native German "bracken," considered of little merit and hard to train. However, the hunting fraternity (*Jägerei*), the Hanoverian especially, had long favored infusion of English Pointer to improve the noses of their dogs. As Dr. Kleeman clarifies the squabbling for us, the opposition interest, obsessed with patriotic aspirations, wanted nothing English—not even dogs. These people could not be persuaded that to the required qualities of Pointer nose and style could also be added the utility qualities the Pointer admittedly did not have. Serious breeders admitted the deficiency of the Pointer in utility respects, but clung to a belief that weldings could be contrived. One faction, then, would seem to have argued along positive lines, the other along negative.

By 1879, when some widely divergent breed types had already appeared, the patriotic believers in an ancient German utility dog held strength enough in Committee to enforce their views. They denied the Stud Book to any dog lacking round ears, a stopless profile. All right, present-day "Old Spanish" fans, look away from *him* as the sole breed founder—his profile was anything *but* stopless! Look rather to inheritance from St. Hubert—say, such a browed profile as the now-vanished Talbots showed—along with other hound badges, such as that short roughness under the tail, and the slightly longer hair in back of the thighs, as these are still asked for by the American breed standard for the German Shorthaired Pointer.

Argument has long ranged as to whether the German Shorthaired Pointer does or does not owe to the Bloodhound. It must be accepted that modern German authority rejects any such notion entirely. The Germans have tried their best to kill the stubborn belief that was fostered first by English-writing "historians" of the breed. It has been officially spelled out for us. First, in 1951, in answer to California pioneer breeder, Rudolph Hirschnitz, Herr Rommeswinkel, long-term President of Klub Kurzhaar (Berlin) spelled it out all the way. NO BLOODHOUND! This breed had *nothing* to do with Kurzhaar inheritance! In 1961, the present writer enquired from Klub Kurzhaar whether there had been any change of thought. A spokesman for the Parent Club (Herr Rommeswinkel being now dead) was just as emphatic: *"There has never been any connection between our breed and the hound known in English as the Bloodhound.* True, the Kurzhaar in his work is set upon the *Schweiss-spur* (the blood trail) of wounded game. From this, doubtless, we hear so often that fairy tale of Bloodhound origin prevailing in America especially." (*Letter to the author, June 28, 1961.*)

"Généreaux," a Gascon Hound, won First Prize, Paris Exhibition, 1865. The French were first with tall, wrinkle-free sporting dogs.

Photo lent by L. L. de Groen, Australia.

Feldmann I, not reg., wh. 1871. An early experimental dog, owned by Prince zu Solms-Braunenfels of the Royal House of Hannover.

19

The misconception has, however, been so often repeated it is now held by most to be truth. Wherever interested folk have written of the German Shorthaired Pointer in English they seem to have culled from the same limited sources, each one repeating the other's error. Actually, the original mistake seems to have turned on one of those traps that lurk in translating language.

The German name for the Bloodhound as a separate breed IS *Schweisshund.* German writers on the German Shorthaired Pointer *do* specifically say that the foresters' working dogs were *Schweisshunde,* and that these were incorporated into the developing utility breed. However, dictionary definition of *Schweiss* is "scent, sweat, moisture, perspiration, exudation, and the blood-trail, as in hunting." *Any* dog that will follow *Schweiss* (scent in any form) is therefore a *Schweisshund*—even a police-tracking Doberman or German Shepherd. *Hund* means "dog," not necessarily "hound." If he works a trail, presto—he's a *Schweisshund.* But by no manner of means is he necessarily a *Bloodhound.* If the German language were written in the same way as English, the use of the capital letter would clarify the point—Bloodhound, as a separate breed, spelled with a capital *B,* and bloodhound, as a tracking dog, with a small *b.* The German language capitalizes all nouns.

However, if the Germans are firm in repudiating the heavy, wrinkled hound that the English know as a Bloodhound, they would never doubt that, as all Scent Hounds trace to the same St. Hubert origin, the Bloodhound shares with their own lighter-bodied, trail-keeping types of that earlier day the qualities inherited from their mutual ancestors. For this we may look in passing at a description of the *English* Bloodhound of the very time the Germans were making their new breed. It comes from one of the best of 19th century dog writers, "Idstone."

"They (the Bloodhounds) are for the most part—for tempers vary in dogs as in Christians—amiable, sagacious, faithful, obedient, docile. They are tremendously clever at tracking wounded deer and are, additionally, as a breed, tremendously fond of water. Theirs, too, is the gift of bell-like baying that distinguishes all hounds gifted with keen discrimination and delicate powers of scenting, holding to the line. They can retrieve most tenderly, and decidedly they propagate good scenting power, mate them to what you will." (*THE DOG,* "*Idstone," p. 59.*)

20

In that easily-recognizable catalog are counted out the exact qualities that the Germans wanted for their new dog; that came with the universal heritage of Scent Hounds through the ancient endowment. All over Europe, in one bodily shape or another, were good, nice-natured, working scenthounds (SCHWEISSHUNDE, yet!) with these virtues. All over Europe, they were being combined with this and with that. None of these virtues belonged to "Old Spanish," said to have been a surly fellow even at his temperamental best. As they were incorporated into the developing German utility dog they did not come from him. One thing, though, the *Schweisshunde* of the German foresters must have been spryer on their legs than the English Bloodhound of the time. "Idstone" writes that the Bloodhounds were so slow they were carried on horseback to where a trail began!

In compiling the history of any breed—or of anything!—there is always danger in following unquestioningly the tracks of the Other Guy. This is vividly stressed in other aspects of German Short-haired Pointer history besides that of the trap in translation that the Bloodhound belief represents. One rather startling example, long overdue for revision, was that discoverable in the unlikely location of the A.K.C. official publication, *The Complete Dog Book*. It would have electrified the German authorities, with their rigid breed control, strict stud books, to have read in the 1961 edition that "...about fifty years ago, German and Austrian sportsmen, looking with envy on the speed and dash of our American pointers, straightway started to cross their heavy German Pointer with our American or English pointer."

In newer editions of the A.K.C. book the statement has been removed. Nothing in the breed history, in fact, suggests that at any stage the German Shorthaired Pointer in his homeland was subjected to irregular cross-breeding with the American Pointer, nor that foreign breeders envied any of that breed's qualities, speed, dash or whatever. Parallel claim, made in 1942, in *How To Train Hunting Dogs,* by Wm. F. Brown, may have been drawn from this A.K.C. source (or the other way around!). On p. 21, Mr. Brown claims: "With the growth of popularity of (American) Field Trials, there was an infusion of the agile American Pointer to streamline the conformation of the Shorthair."

Both statements, unfortunately, appear to endorse officially a practice that, where provable, is of such irregularity as to render the produce of such cross-mating unregisterable, in Europe or here. As these books tend to fall into the hands of novices, it is not at all impossible that the dangerous mis-directions may be taken for gospel, inspiring like experimentation. In truth, though the Pointer *was* originally combined with other breeds to form the German Shorthaired Pointer a century ago, the latter has long, long since developed into a separate breed. Any belief that the re-introduction of Pointer (or any other basic breed) is merely "in the family" procedure is quite erroneous. To breed together a Pointer and a German Shorthaired Pointer in this age is to bring about a cross-breeding, a mongrelization.

In early years of importation here, hunting men buying from pioneer breeders such as Dr. Thornton, not understanding they were buying purebreds, sometimes did ignorantly crossbreed their German Shorthaired Pointers not only to "the agile American Pointer" but to the agile Springer, Setter, Coonhound, even to the agile Heinz in his many varieties. Dr. Thornton often received photos of mongrelized produce of his stock—to his horror! However, such dogs were unregisterable, dropped from sight. If, later, "with the growth of popularity of Field Trials" there *has* been "infusion of the agile American Pointer" it must of necessity have been secretly done. Registration of resulting stock could only be secured by fraudulent misrepresentation. The A.K.C. does not knowingly register German Shorthaired Pointers with American Pointer sires or dams. For that reason, and for the danger that novices may gain a wrong impression of what is or is not permissible or even wise, it is good that the serious error in the official Book and Standards has been withdrawn.

Back to the 1870's . . . Early experimentation in Germany produced at first some very undesirable, often awkward dogs, heavy-bodied, stumpy-legged. Progress, as in all the undertakings of man, had to be by trial and error. The stubborn patriots lost themselves entirely, chasing head and ear shape, though the more malleable saw merit in the direction given by their early-day patron, Prince Albrecht zu Solms-Brauenfels, of the Royal House of Hanover. He gave the breeders a direction best now to be translated into the familiar "Form Follows Function." He told them that the only way to develop the wished-for utility dog-of-all-virtues was to take and use only the dogs best performed in these requirements, not to worry at this early stage about outward appearances. These would with time take care of themselves. He gave a practical lead by his own experiments in breeding, producing some truly extraordinary-looking dogs, with what future influence on the breed we do not now know. Doubtless they too were basics.

Time proved the Prince's direction valid. Form *did* follow Function, eventually producing the dog known to us today. All manner of plums went into the pudding: hound, pointer, braque, with a dash of setter. All elements were eventually blended skilfully, culled, reblended to produce a competely new breed. It was then no longer—*nor is it now*—possible to re-introduce any of these components in the "raw" state without the irregularity screaming out for all to recognize, be the introduction sporting dog or hound.

The stubborn continued to ignore the Prince's direction. When the performance of the early-registered dogs, chosen by the appearance pattern, the head-and-ear deal, matched his worst forebodings, His Highness bowed out of the breed interest. Dr. Kleeman, in his famed breed monograph, *Deutsch Kurzhaar,* also shrugs off the early approvals of the Stud Book, including Hektor I, the first entry.

"Unenergetic, cold-blooded clods," he held them, and "anciently German" only wherein they in part resembled "Old Spanish." Their performance was as clumsy as their looks. He quotes a contemporary who held there was as much sport to be had hunting fleas across the back of a German poodle as in hunting birds with a German dog. Of the deliberations of the Klub he reports sourly: "Nature errs never—committees very often!" This, by the way, is as true now as then.

Prince zu Solms' directive, though, had not gone for nothing. There were breeders choosing their stock on grounds of ability, and there was much use of the English Pointer to improve that most important tool of all, the nose. From among such appeared, in 1881, Herr Julius Mehlich, of Berlin, working the first really well performed German Shorthaired Pointer, Nero 66. At a Pointer/Setter trial at Buckow, this brown, tick-chested, strong, fast, good-nosed dog made a fine showing, though the traditionalists took after him, full cry, for his lack of a "German head," calling him an English Pointer. Herr Mehlich seems to have given no argument, but in later years Dr. Kleeman specifically named Mehlich's strain

Meisterzuchter Julius Mehlich with his foundation dog, Nero 66 (Hoppenrade), in 1883.

Photo: Courtesy, Kurzhaar Blätter, *Germany*.

as Pointer-endowed, but for more than merely the evidence of Nero's head.

In 1883, Mehlich's Nero 66 was in the news again, tying first in the German Derby with the brown dog, Treff, always identified by two numbers, 1010 in the German all-breed registration, and 56 in the new Kurzhaar Stud book. The tie-placing is interesting, for these two brown dogs are the all-time breed pillars.

After that Derby, Herr Mehlich and Nero were guests at the hunting preserve of "Hoppenrade." A charming story, told in several places, German and Danish, tells of Nero taking off under the eyes of the host, Herr Smidt, after a touched hare. The dog was so long gone the party thought he had met with accident. Then—suddenly! —there was Nero, on the far side of a swift stream, the hare heavy in his jaws. Despite what had been a long, weary carry, Nero plunged into the swift water, battled across to bring the hare to Herr Mehlich. Herr Smidt was loud in admiration. "From this time on, you are no longer merely Nero 66—you are Nero v. *Hoppenrade!* And the name shall be given to all your descendants as well."

So was the famous strain name gained. Nero's descendants lent it luster, and it is paramount in early-day breeding, with Nero's granddaughter, Erra Hoppenrade, 382, having the honor to count No. 1 in the Gebrauchshunde-Stammbuch (the German Working Dog stud book) after her 1892 competition wins. Erra's dam, Cora 40, was litter sister to Sally, the dam of Treff 1010, and she shared Treff's sire, Boncoeur 30.

(Note. In some publications, Erra's name is erroneously given as Gora. Matching historical sources prove the No. 1 registration went to an Erra, 382; it may be that the mistake is based on confusion with the name of her dam—Cora.)

Nero 66 was dead within the year, a bitter 1884 loss to Herr Mehlich. That same year, his daughter Flora produced three browns to Hektor 64 (Treff ex Diana, wh. 1880). They were Waldin, 175, Waldo, 174, Hertha, 188. Dr. Kleeman sees the true turn of breed fortune in these, especially when Waldin made his mark against Pointer/Setter competition in an English-style field trial at Buckow. This best Nero grandson was known as "Kranzler's Waldin," an honor to his owner, A. Kranzler, of Berlin. Waldin won the admiration of the German Emperor, who enjoyed the dog's work on pheasant to such an extent that he commissioned a famed German artist, Sperling, to paint Waldin's picture.

In those years, Hoppenrade dogs placed a mortgage on Derby competition especially. Many of the names gained fame; Harras and Morell, Maitrank, were all great names in early breed history. Much credit seems to rest with the introduction Herr Mehlich made from the breeding of Herr Koch, of Bohnenwald, the bitch Holla (later Hoppenrade). She was the first full-ticked introduction to this strain of chest-ticked solid brown (liver), and is identified as being by Caro from Cora 180. Her quality must have been excellent, and this is luckily provable in the comments of a judge who put her up in London (England) as B.O.B. in 1887. Her sons, Morell (brown, ticked chest) and Maitrank (ticked and patched), are her memorials within the breed.

Photographs show a tremendous difference, typewise, between Morell and Maitrank—much, much more than one would expect from half-brothers whose sires were father and son, Morell being by Waldin, 175, and Maitrank by Waldin's son, Balsam Hoppenrade. However, some interesting scuttlebutt is recorded by Herr Sahre, in the 1962 Winter issue of *Kurzhaar Blätter,* the Klub Kurzhaar breed paper. He tells how the breed-master of Hoppenrade, one morning, when Holla was in full flush of season, found in her kennel the brown Pointer, Donner, who had chewed his way through the fence to reach her. On the same day, she was mated to Balsam. However, Herr Sahre points out that to expect that she entertained her enterprising caller all night without results is to expect rather much, though, actually, nothing had been witnessed. From this mating mix-up came the useful and prepotent derby-winning Maitrank Hoppenrade, wh. 1890, who resembles no other Hoppenrade dogs as their photographs come down to us, but who is recognized as a breed pillar of worth. In this early stage of breed formation, the irregularity (if any) could be absorbed, though many breeders noted Maitrank's virtues as only Derby.

Herr Mehlich died in 1893, his strain woven through the developing breed. Meanwhile, it is necessary to backtrack to Treff 1010. No great beauty in modern sight, this dog is the most solid taproot of all. He set his name all over, and most dogs trace to him. Not to be confused with all the other Treffs to be located in early pedigrees, he is always identified by his double numerical endowment.

Saul-Fuhrberg (reg.), Schweisshunde, a recognized European breed, much used by foresters modernly. Prinz zu Solms-Brauenfels owned many good ones. Saul bears close resemblance to GSP taproot, Treff 1010 (below).

Juno 192, wh. 1882, bred and owned by Hofjaeger F. Isermann of Nordhausen. This is the earliest photo so far found of a registered German Shorthaired Pointer bitch. She is in many basic pedigrees.

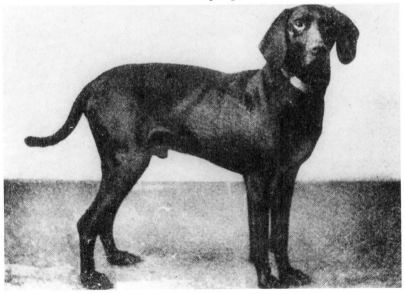

Treff 1010, ZK 56, wh. 1881. Most pedigrees in the breed trace to Treff (Wodan Hektor II was his grandson). Diversity of pioneer breed type is made plain in comparison of Treff with Juno.

His parents, Boncoeur 30 and Sally, the sister of Cora 40, are described for us also by Herr Sahre—Boncoeur 30, wh. 1878, as mostly brown, strong, but not inelegant, and of Cora 40 only her whelping date of 1879. Their location was in Thüringia.

Treff is everywhere to be found, but strongest perhaps in his v. Lemgo get. Founded by Professor Julius Engler, of Lemgo, based on his brown-ticked Juno v. Lemgo, 1315 (ex Wanda Brokemeier by Treu 93, a brown whose dam, Wanda 80, had a double cross of Hektor I), the most useful history of this strain so far encountered was that written (in Danish) in 1915 by Stationsforstander N.B. Buchwald, of Viborg, Denmark, published in the 1933 issue of the Danish Kurzhaar Klub magazine. Nor are v. Lemgo and Hoppenrade the only strains clarified in these history-rich publications of so much merit in compilation.

From a ticked son of Treff 1010, acquired by Prof. Engler, Wodan Hektor I v. Lemgo, 1275, wh. 1883, ex Diana v. Bünau, came Wodan Hektor II v. Lemgo, 1276, wh. 1888. This dog, of visible improvement in appearance, drew from Herr Richard v. Schmiederberg, judge, that this strain was "too handsome to be German!" But it was actually still a time when Form lagged behind Function. Registration numbers suggest many may have been bred, few retained. Such cull wastage attends upon the formation of any new breed, screening out unwanted characteristics. (As the Australians wrote of forming their cattle dog from radical crossing: "We bred a lot and we drowned a lot!")

Problems of experimental breeders can be visualized by comparing Treff's photo with that of Juno 192. Whelped 1882 to Treff's 1881, Juno is the earliest-dated bitch whose photo we have found. By an unidentified Feldmann from an unidentified Diana, owned by the bravely experimental breeder, Hofjaeger Isermann of Nordhausen, she shows as thick-headed, clumsy, Hektor-One-ish, the type that displeased Dr. Kleeman. Yet her mating to Treff 1010 underpins much contemporary breeding, and history knows her as the ancestress of Rubin Hoppenrade and the fine Hektor v. Pirna. The Danish breeding, where we first picked up her track, owes to her daughter, Bessie v. Jagerhaus, 254, mated to Marki, 322, the son of Waldin, 175, doubtless explaining breed-type improvement. Her great-grandson, Larron v. Sonderhausen, is one of Denmark's most important basics.

With Herr Mehlich's death in 1893, new names come to view—
v. Lemgo, v. Freudenthal, Holzweiler, Altenau, v. Freithof, Altenbach, v.d. goldenen Mark. The ear-and-head party saw its clumsy dogs outclassed. The zu Solms direction began to make sense. It became clear that Pointer nose *could* be kept, separated from unwanted Pointer characteristics such as aversion to trailing, dislike of water, jam-tail flight from, instead of at, predators. Utility qualities were secured from the good working dogs of the foresters, the *Schweisshunde*—but NOT bloodhounds!

Most good early-day dogs were brown (liver). It was long held the only permissible Kurzhaar color. Many were chest-ticked, as Waldin, 175, his son Morell, 444, and daughters; as Graf Hoyer v. Mansfeld, 867, as Trumpf Otto, 2129, a most distinguished one. The v. Lemgos, mostly ticked, carried the brown of Juno's sire, Treu, 93, as in the Wodan Hektor II v. Lemgo son, Nidung, 1288, and his good great-grandson, Waldo Waldheim, 178 B, ex Tellus v. Freudenthal's daughter, Hertha v.d. Maylust, 4622, a fine dam force, both these latter being ticked and patched.

Behind Nidung, wh. 1890, seems also to lie experiment. Stationsforstander Buchwald, in his v. Lemgo history, intimates that Nidung's solid-color dam, Frigga v. Berry, 1338, wh. 1886, owes to Irish Setter! In detail he describes her coat, rough and coarse, her body longish, standing over a lot of ground: "as an Irish hunter," as Herr Buchwald translates the familiar phrase. Frigga was owned and used as a matron by Professor Engler, but Hofjaeger Isermann bred her, her parentage given as Wanda, 149, and yet another unidentified Hektor, who may have been *it*. As long coat is recessive to short, and Frigga v. Berry, as pictured, is out of tune with accepted Kurzhaar shape, maybe Herr Buchwald has the right of it. However, her son, Nidung, proved a strong breed pillar.

The setter incross proved fairly persistent, lingering along the generations to pop up every so often with some longish-haired whelps, as Herr Sahre, in his fine breed summary of 1962, also notes (p. 573, *Kurzhaar Blätter*, Winter 1962). This proved to be especially the case in connection with the descendants of Golo Holzweiler, whom we will presently meet. So much so, that breeders often took care to advertise proudly that *their* stock was *"Golo-frei,"* that is, lacked Golo.

Waldo Waldheim, 178 B, wh. January 1900, links the centuries,

Tellus v. Freudenthal, wh. 1893, a son of Wodan Hektor II v. Lemgo, was known as "The Medal Dog." He is also a famed breed basic.

especially with his brown son, Caro Latferde, 245 D, wh. 1902. Caro sired roman-nosed Tell aus der Wolfsschlucht, 358 H, wh. 1907. Tell showed all desired virtues, including docility and style. Interestingly, the Germans rate docility high. Rightly, for lacking it, other qualities can be water over the dam. Tell is remembered too for long life, a familiar good in this breed. German Shorthaired Pointers well into their teens are not unusual. Since molding a good sporting dog takes time and money, longevity is a useful bonus.

From Tell we have K.S. Michel v.d. Goldenen Mark, 422 M, wh. 1911. His name backstops many American strains. His color, brown, came not only from Tell, but from his dam, Beye's Vilja v.d. goldenen Mark, 542 K, whose brother, Beyes Stopp, 683 K, channeled solid color on and down. By the 1920's, though, fashion was losing solid color. Old Jagdjunker v. Bassewitz, of Schwerin-Mecklenburg, his strain founded on Trumpf Otto, was asking sadly: *"Wo sind sie hin, die guten braunen Gebrauchshunde auf die wir mit Recht stolz waren? Sie sind verschwunden und vergessen!"* ("What has become of them, the good brown utility dogs of which we were rightly so proud? They are vanished and forgotten!")

Dr. Kleeman said, not so! In the Kurzhaar issue of *Deutschen Jager-Zeitung* of 1921, he points out that the good brown utility dogs of Schwerin, Trumpf Otto blood strong within them, were still a breed force. What the breeders had once in these still flourished. Color may have dwindled, but the qualities were there. Work must be done to restore the solids to their place in the breed. Dog breeds, as the world we live in, require all kinds to produce harmony and balance.

With K. S. Michel v.d. Goldenen Mark, we look directly back to Treff 1010. From brave experimentation of the 1870's/1880's, to the goodlooking, well-performed Sieger of 1911, thirty years had seen the new breed established. True to Prince Solms' forecast, Form had faithfully followed Function.

By the 1880s, heavy hound had yielded to elegance of streamlined construction. Hound profile and high earset remained the badge of origin. Morell Hoppenrade, a rare picture by the famous German artist, Sperling.—*Picture lent by Major and Mrs. Godsol.*

Golo Holzweiler, 123 c., wh. 1902. He was a most controversial stud, but to be found behind great dogs. His dishface may explain his ability to endow his get with wonderful scenting power.

2

20th Century
German Breed Pillars

A S important as it is interesting, is the chain of inheritance, among the many examined in these pages with relation to the influence exerted on American breeding, anchored on Golo Holzweiler, 123 c.

Wh. 1902, bred by Th. Rings, of Holzweiler, an active pioneer breeder, this dog's name soon becomes familiar to serious breed students. Historians seem unable to make up their minds whether to praise or damn him. His background is full of question marks, his utility qualities were about minus, and yet he is behind so many of the breed's best dogs! Dr. Kleeman said his blood was so mixed (heterogeneous) as to be difficult to blend into existing strains. Herr v. Otto saw him as less desirable as a type than as a means to secure it. Later historians repeat these opinions (often as their own!).

Some breed writers claim him to be Pointer-sired. His pedigree does not say so, but there he was, with his big head and his dished face that matches poorly with that roman-nosed profile of Wodan Hektor II v. Lemgo, to whom he carried back along several lines.

He tended to throw a percentage of stock with longish coats, which ties up with the Nidung line behind him. Yet he had good qualities —his nose, his constitution, his easy-keeper habit, maybe his setter-gentlemanly temperament. These things he gave his stock. His owner used him, and some of his friends, and with success. Some other breeders, strong in utility-bred stock, tried too, and though many failed with Golo, some had great success. For American interest, the most successful was Herr Gschwindt, whose famed Südwest line contributed much on this side of the Atlantic. It was founded on his Trudel Südwest, 226, wh. 1918, with eight crosses to Golo!

For specific step-by-step information on Golo's breeding we are again in debt to the Danish Kurzhaar Klub compilations. These take us to Wodan Hektor II v. Lemgo, and to Nidung. Golo's grand-dams (maternal and paternal) were German-registered Kurzhaar—Mary Holzweiler, 5349, and Spinne, 2499. His sire, Nimrod II Otzenrath (ex Spinne), was also fully registered in Germany. He, in turn, was by the brown, Nimrod Otzenrath, 3799, a Tellus v. Freudenthal son ex Morna v. Mansfeld, she a brown of brown parentage, Graf Hoyer v. Mansfeld and Janka v. Jägerhaus (granddaughter of brown Treff 1010). Golo's dam, Senta Holzweiler, 73 C (ex Mary Holzweiler) was by Greif Nidung Rheydt, 1367 (Nidung ex Erna v. Lemgo, 1320). With Erna we are right back to the pioneering spirit and experimental kennel of Professor Engler, where we might possibly expect to find some explanation for the dished face of Golo Holzweiler, 123 c. But too many years have gone by, dogs and people are dead, and the answers to our question can never now be given. So we must accept Golo, with whatever he carried, for he certainly cannot be ignored. Not only American dogs, but German and Danish are in his debt. The Danish take from him mostly through Ch. Rolf v. Freithof, sire of Ch. Hassan Freithof. And Südwest is certainly not the only famed German strain he backstops; count in Artus Sand's as well.

The careful extensions of these pedigrees, such as Golo's, available in the double-spread pages of the Danish club compilations, also provide the most valuable information concerning color. This has already been used by geneticists in compiling modern-day scientific color-inheritance research. Further, it constitutes a deep well of truth into which German Shorthaired Pointer researchers of today may dip, establishing the belief that some judges *and* all self-proclaimed galleryside "experts" could be on shaky ground in rejecting, merely out of hand, all clear-white-and-liver, pointer-patterned coats in German Shorthaired Pointers.

Most come down from the close inbreeding practiced by the pioneers. To reject dogs in the showring (or elsewhere) *merely* because of this color might possibly involve the purist in the rejection of some good, time-hallowed strains. In American breeding, show dogs, field champions, hunting companions, even Dual Champions, may well and legitimately, in certain throwback conditions, come up with this color scheme. However, it might also be considered that in some instances color may be trying to tell us of modern-day unpermissible experimentation, clumsily attempted. In that case, other characteristics, notably coat-texture, will be present for the judge to evaluate very carefully.

Early German breeders, especially around the turn of the century, often fussed about the possibility of some breeder having conducted an experiment with a new Pointer incross, knowing it could throw the breed inheritance awry. An interesting point, which needs to be brought to the attention of those few American "breeders" who may feel that further raw infusion of Pointer blood into their German Shorthaired Pointers may help them to win field trials, is that when the Germans used the Pointer in those formative years 'way back, from the first experimental breedings, they used it to gain *nose* and, in some cases, style. Never, at ANY time, did they consider the Pointer cross as useful to them to promote mere ability to *run*. They needed the *high nose,* took some risks to get it, but quickly counterbalanced the infusion to rid their developing breed of Pointer characteristics that did not belong in utility work—and from a so-called "Pointer" with a greyhound tail they would have fled in horror!

It should also be pointed out to optimists who are willing to "take a chance with throwing in a Pointer" (as it is phrased!) that they can use only such stock as is available to them here, and that stock is often, itself—since breed-type split, in the field-running type —at least doubtful in terms of simon-pure, long-term Pointer inheritance. So, in "taking the chance," unless they are VERY sure of what they are using, they could be getting still further from *nose,* for which *running* could prove a poor substitute in a field sport dog. Maybe the experienced breeders *do* know these things, and even which end of a Pointer to look at to gauge its likely status as purebred from all the way back. (*Note:* Writes that most famous of all Pointer men, William Arkwright: "The head is invaluable for showing character . . . but for the certificate of blue blood apply at the other end!") Novices, however, do *not* usually know these things, and as a large percentage of German Shorthaired Pointer ownership is most often novice, the risk needs to be spelled out here —as well as the danger of listening to often-equally-ignorant "old hands who know all about how to breed a good (running) German Shorthaired Pointer!"

By the early years of this century, any German breeders even suspected of "throwing in" a Pointer were subject to disapproval. One who had to weather such gales was Christian Bode, of Altenau, whose business in England interested him in Pointer *nose.* He built his line on Zeche, 2243 (Liebenberg, 694 ex Fauna unreg.), a brown Dr. Kleeman held basic. Her mate, Rolf Giersdorf, 5363, brown and white, was by Hektor-Wotan-Gutland, 1547, ex Toni Hardenstein, 3738. Hektor was a Wodan Hektor II v. Lemgo son ex a Morell Hoppenrade daughter. From Zeche and Rolf came Bessie Altenau, 69 c. When Bode bred his Bessie to his K.S. Flott Altenau, 12 F, who was her son and great-grandson, most historians note the "Pointerlet" look in the issue, Rino Altenau, 31 B, wh. 1907, though he did lack such embarrassment as Golo's dishface. Rino's best son, Rino Weisseritztal v.d. Wessnitz, 131 N (ex Hertha v.d. Burgerweise, 479 K), is behind many early imports here; also Artus Sand stock that came later, through the Artus Sand sire, Yelmos Gotz v. Kauffungen. From Bessie Altenau, too, came Lola Altenau, 642, whom Herr Sahre, in a 1962 *Kurzhaar Blätter,* described amusingly as good in the field, but reluctant to go in water unless the weather was *very* hot! Lola had American influence through her mating to K.S. Blitz v.d. Maylust, 147 J (Hektor v. Gerathal 2 C ex Frigga II v.d. Maylust). From this came Panther v.d. Maylust, making impact through his son, K.S. Edelmann Giftif, 68 Q.

In most breed history written in German, Edelmann Giftig's name sets the fur flying. His dam, Asta Giftig, was ex a litter sister of Rino Altenau. Most historians feel he brought temperamental faults. Herr Sahre considered his influence catastrophic. Yet, he was a Derby, Solms, Gebrauchshund-Prüfungs-Sieger. Sahre holds that this owed mostly to a first-class handler, and describes the dog's temperament as *"hochgradig nervenschwach und schreckhaft . . . vor dem kleinsten Geräusch oder ungewohnter Erscheinung prallte er seinem Fuhrer zwischen die Füsse!"* ("[he was] extremely weak-nerved and spooky . . . at the slightest clamor or unfamiliar circumstance he dived between his handler's feet!") (*Kurzhaar Blätter*, 1962, p. 575).

Such displays of temperament could not win German tolerance. Yet Edelmann Giftig, whose virtue was staunch, faultless pointing, could pass this virtue on, suggesting it was not merely the efficiency of that good handler. As he is firmly there in back of many great German dogs, and virtually ALL American basics, one wonders at this distance in time if the dog was *over*-trained, *over*-pressured. Over the years, in this and other breeds, one has seen dogs whose nerves had gone to pieces though they could rack up wins and get stock temperamentally healthier than they. Anyway, he is in strength behind such here as the basic imports to Montana, John Neuforsthaus and Seiger's Lore (1928); the 1931 Nebraskans, Claus v. Schleswig-Konigsweg and Jane v. grünen Adler; also the three famed 1932 newcomers to Minnesota, Arta v. Hohreusch, Bob v. Schwarenberg, Feldjager's Grisette. And one wonders of his strain name—*Giftig*. Translated, it means: "poisonous, venomous, pernicious, malignant, spiteful, angry"—words not in tune with breed temperament, as one knows.

Some German historians also point to irregularities behind famed Mars Altenau, through his sire, Hassan Altenau, 712. Whether scuttlebutt or history, it's too long ago to tell. Mars Altenau was a strong prepotent. Konrad Andreas, breed historian, remembers Mars as great-hearted, with grand nose, will to work, clever at trailing, but a fireball, needing strong handling.

Artus Sand, 1839 V, a little younger than Mars, carries the Golden Name in the breed. His dam, Ella Sand, 543 U, was ex Frigga Sand, 104 P, she a K.S. Michel v.d. Goldenen Mark daughter. Yelmos Gotz v. Kauffungen, 21 T, sire of Artus Sand, was by a K.S. Michel son, Lump Mauderode, ex Susl v. Kauffungen. That puts much solid brown (liver) behind Artus Sand, as Lump Mauderode was so, and K.S. Michel. It could be that from here stem the calm temperaments for which Artus Sand was famed.

All breed historians agree on the complementary qualities of

Artus-Sand

Geworfen am 23. April 1921

Eingetragen:
St. K. 1830V — D. G. St. B. 1638

Züchter:
Förster Lehner, Kienberg b. Nauen

Besitzer:
H. Heusser,
Kleinschmalkalden i. Thür.

Formwert: Vorzüglich

Vater: Yelmos-Götz von Kauffungen St. K. 21 T D. G.-St.-B. 1244	Lump-Mauderode 154 O	Michel von der goldenen Mark 422 M, 1027	Tell aus der Wolfsschlucht 358 H, 704	Caro-Latferde 245 D / Senta aus der Wolfsschlucht 210 E
			Beyes Vilja von der goldenen Mark 542 K	Treu-Schmarsow 151 G / Lotte vom Freithof 405 J
		Wach-Woge 102 K	Rino-Altenau v. d. Weßnitz 31 H, 700	Flott-Altenau 12 F / Bessie-Altenau 693 C
			Wach-Jo 305 G	Erwin von Lemgo 111 D / Hela-Mauderode 64 F
	Susl von Kauffungen 16 Q	Blitz von der Maylust 147 J	Hektor vom Gerathal 2 C	Hektor von Pirna 3532, 109 / Hertha von der Maylust 4622
			Frigga II von der Maylust 323 H	Treu II von der Maylust 257 B / Frigga von der Maylust 280 D
		Dina von Kauffungen 737 N	Wach-Wille 107 K	Rino-Altenau v. d. Weßnitz 31 H, 700 / Wach-Jo 205 G
			Thea von Kauffungen 683 H	Reckl-Iser 1160 D / Flora von Schacht 466 F
Mutter: Ella-Sand St. K. 543 U D. G.-St.-B. 1472	Rino-Weißeritztal v. d. Weßnitz 131 N, 1127	Rino-Altenau von der Weßnitz 31 H, 700	Flott-Altenau 12 F	Tasso-Altenau 32 D / Bessie-Altenau 663 C
			Bessie-Altenau 693 C	Rolf-Giersdorf 5363, 319 / Zeche 2243
		Hertha von der Bürgerwiese 479 K	Golo II-Holzweiler 160 F	Golo-Holzweiler 123 C / Lina-Holzweiler 256 B
			Frigga-Weidmannsfreud 368 E	Skat-Altenbach 5279 / Senta-Weidmannsfreud 80 C
	Frigga-Sand 104 P	Michel von der goldenen Mark 422 M, 1027	Tell aus der Wolfsschlucht 358 H, 704	Caro-Latferde 245 D / Senta aus der Wolfsschlucht 210 E
			Beyes Vilja von der goldenen Mark 542 K	Treu-Schmarsow 151 G / Lotte vom Freithof 405 J
		Erra-Cannstatt-Sand 489 H	Harras von Lauffen 486 H	Roland-Hektor II 484 H / Rätia von Chur 485 H
			Wally-Hoch-Karschau 488 H	Nimrod-Königsberg 487 H, 380 / Douna aus der goldenen Aue 2735

Mars and Artus, the fireball and the calm. Mars produced the sons, Artus the daughters. Dr. Kleeman could never seem to over-praise Artus Sand daughters. We find one, Asta Mauderode-Westerholt, 69 Z, mated with Mars' son, Rino Forst, 1685 U, wh. 1920, to produce great bitches. One, Edda Mauderode-Westerholt, 702 C, wh. 1928, makes almost all pedigrees now through her son, K.S. Kobold Mauderode-Westerholt, 124 F, wh. 1930. Kobold's sire, K.S. Magnet v. Ockerbach, 388 D, wh. 1928, was also Mars-Artus weld. His dam, Eule v. Runenstein, wins from Dr. Kleeman an accolade as the best Artus Sand daughter. His sire, Junker v. Bomlitztal, 1271 Z, came from Mars through Prince v. Schlosshof, 556 Z.

The international influence of K.S. Kobold is enormous. Brought early to America was his son, Donn v. Sulfmeister (ex Willa v. Wilsederberg). Imported by Dr. Thornton, Donn sired Timm v. Altenau (sire of 15 Am. Champions) and Fritz, sire of prepotent winner, Ch. Davy's Jim Dandy—two (only) reasons why Donn v. Sulfmeister could be named sire-most-neglected-by-breed-historians here.

K.S. Kobold's best German son could be K.S. Bodo v.d. Radbach, 190 H, wh. 1932 (ex K.S. Hussa v.d. Radbach), 571 e, by Hasso v. Nibelungenhort, 918 (ex Richa v.d. Radbach). For American interest, Hussa's "B" litter of 1932, including Bodo, was followed by her "C" in 1933. The sire was Kobold's own, K.S. Magnet v. Ockerbach, ex Artus Sand's best daughter, remember? From this litter, Dr. Thornton imported in 1935, Cosak v.d. Radbach, 257 i. This scion of Germany's proudest breeding spent most of his life in Bitter Root Valley, Montana, siring hunting dogs sold for modest prices; that is, when he wasn't thrilling the living daylights out of the doctor with his way of working a pheasant, or retrieving a hare against tough odds.

American breeders missed the chance Cosak represented, maybe because of the error in his FDSB registration, which seemed to get into more hands than his A.K.C. one, which is correct. As 240355, the FDSB registers him as ex a Russa v.d. Radbach, a meaningless name. His stemming from the great German Siegerin, status as three-quarter brother to famed Bodo, is lost in a typing error! Yet, consider what he represented, blending K.S. Hussa with Eule v. Runenstein, the best Artus Sand daughter! No wonder Dr. Thornton preserved lasting respect for "Old Coxie" (Cosak), the great working heart of him, the retrieves over miles and over mountains. And what a sad little notation in one of the doctor's Kennel Journals when "Coxie" left him for the East where, so far as these records go, the trail fades. Anyone know the end of the story?

Fortunately all his good was not wasted. He is behind Dual Ch. Valbo v. Schlesburg, also behind Sieglinde v. Meihsen, dam of the breed's first B.I.S., Ch. Sportsman's Dream. That the registration error was belatedly caught follows on Dr. Thornton's gift to this compiler of all his records. Perhaps now some breed enthusiasts will look up pedigrees and set an old wrong right.

Exceptionally strong in America is the impact of the Mars Altenau son, Heidi Esterhof, 342 (ex Cora v. Merkenich-Esterhof, 422 S). His get from Vita v. Wienbiet, 152 V (she an Edelmann Giftig granddaughter) included, in 1923, K.S. Tasso, Bob, Zilla—all v. Winterhauch. Tasso sired Seiger's Lore, imported here and represented in many Western pedigrees, especially through her Brickwedde descendants (by imported Artist v.d. Forst Brickwedde). Bob v. Winterhauch literally supports the Minnesota breedings from Joseph Burkhart's three imports. Of these Feldjager's Grisette was a Bob daughter. Arta v. Hohreusch and Bob v. Schwarenberg were half-brother and sister by Bob's son, K.S. Benno v. Schlossgarten. Zilla is the grand-dam of Hallo Mannheimia (K.S. Frei Südwest ex Cita Mannheimia), whose importation to New York and mating with Arta v. Hohreusch resulted in the siring of Treu v. Waldwinkel, one of this country's all-time prepotent sires.

K.S. Benno v. Schlossgarten made himself a great name in Germany. Through his daughter, Arta v. Hohreusch, he made himself a great name here as well. As the dam of Treu v. Waldwinkel, and also of Ch. Fritz v. Schwarenberg, not to mention several fine bitches, and some useful sons who crop up in the pedigrees very nicely, Arta conditions us to expect a good dog wherever she appears in multiple representation in any pedigree. A beautiful bitch sired by a beautiful dog, she is behind some of our very best, including Dual Champions, emphasizing that conformation, after all, is what a dog stands on, runs with and by. It is NOT something to find *here*, while the dog stands over *there*, as some seem to believe. Taken care of, good conformation keeps breeders in business. Permitted to degenerate, it runs them out as surely as rain falls down, not up. So with Arta's good qualities. Taken care of, they still

40

K.S. Benno v. Schlossgarten, 49 B, wh. 1926, a beautiful German dog that supports pioneer Minnesota breeding through imports.

K.S. Kobold Mauderode-Westerholt, 124 F, wh. 1930, a strong German stud force with great influence in America.

ornament the breed. Where they have been swamped with rubbish, not even she can overcome the wrong done.

Scotland's poet, Robert Burns, was writing of a personal enemy, not of dog-breeding, but it fits, by golly, it fits:

"Bright ran thy line, O Galloway,
Thro' many a far-famed sire.
So ran the far-famed Roman way,
And ended in a mire."

The years just before World War II saw the full flowering of many great strains of Kurzhaar in Germany. Some were later swamped and lost in the fiery tide, but many survive, and the best have representation here. Südwest, Beckum, Grabenbruch, v.d. Radbach, Waldhausen, Seiger's, v.d. Forst Brickwedde, Jägers, Pöttmes, Seydel's, v.d. Schleppenburg, v. Blitzdorf, were but some among the many supports for the breed edifice built in this country.

Südwest, one of the oldest, influenced many German strains, as well as pioneer establishment here, through the K.S. Frei Südwest son, Hallo Mannheimia, bred and exported through Herr Carl Seidler, still a force in the affairs of Klub Kurzhaar, as well as a well-known international breed judge. In Germany, a long stream of Siegers carried the name of Südwest, and some are intertwined also with the Grabenbruchers of Herr Peter Kraft, another source of Sieger gifting. Herr Seidler also had great success with K.S. Kora v. Grabenbruch, though his greatest breed pride in his life, as he still happily writes us, was his great Flott v. Dubro (Mannheimia). From Grabenbruch's wide acres, too, came America's first Sieger import, little Sepp v. Grabenbruch (K.S. Odin v. Weinbach ex Leda v. Grabenbruch, he a son of the great Reichs-und-Welt Sieger, Heide v.d. Beeke, she a K.S. Frei Südwest daughter).

Beckum is also extremely well known here, and perhaps the more so for the not entirely ethical habit of some American breeders of "borrowing" famous German strain names for locally bred dogs. To trace Beckum to its sources would entail overturning most of German breed history. Max Jürgens, of Munster, obviously established his breeding practice in the 19th century. Old pedigrees tell the story. It is perhaps as well told as anywhere in the pedigree of Lore Beckum, 58 g, wh. 1931, the foundation bitch of the Blitzdorf strain. Herr Böllhoff, the master of Blitzdorf, has made this pedigree available to us here. It takes us back by way of Lore's sire, Horst Beckum, 55 g, generation after generation—Freya Beckum, 379, Diva Beckum, 300 Z, Bessi Beckum, 186 X, Troika Altenau Beckum, 1013 U—right to the far edge of the pedigree paper. Bessi Beckum is graphed in the same line with Golo Holzweiler (wh. 1902). Bessi's dam, Troika, is in the same line with Golo's sire, Nimrod II Otzenrath. It's a long, long way. . . .

Lore Beckum's pedigree teaches us much concerning the German background of other strains here. Her sire, Horst Beckum, was by Zeus v.d. Bode, 720 c. He shares *his* sire, Taps Harrachstal v.d. Bürgerweise, with John Neuforsthaus, the first good stud in the breed to come to America. The dam of Zeus v.d. Bode, was a full sister to Pack v.d. Bode (Edelmann Giftig ex Kitty v.d. Bode), who counts so strongly behind the first imports to Nebraska.

From the old strain of Max Jürgens, we also have imported K.S. Franco Beckum, 1147 W, wh. 1947. Franco's dam, Viktoria Beckum, draws much as does Lore of the Blitzdorfers. Her sire, Monarch Beckum, was by Horst Beckum ex Rita v.d. Radbach. Franco, also an Amerian champion, is sired by a successful dog in K.S. Adel v. Assegrund (Junos v. Heidebrink ex Pierette Roggenstein), one that had great successes under the care of Herr H. F. Seiger. Pierette Roggenstein, a K.S. Markus Freising granddaughter, was by Seiger's Prinz. The Seiger strain has sent several useful dogs here, commencing with the in-whelp bitches, Seiger's Lore and Seiger's Holla II, brought in by Dr. Thornton. K.S. Seiger's Adel (K.S. Franco Beckum ex a sister to K.S. Adel v. Assegrund, Adda) has made more recent contributions. Here came his son, Harro v. Klostermoor (ex the K.S. Axel v.d. Cranger Heide daughter, Wiesal v.d. alten Postweg, 847 A); also the Michigan import of Carl Schnell, his Eros v. Scheperhof, 220 C (ex Delta v. Scheperhof, 292 A, she by K.S. Franco Beckum ex Seiger's Toska). K.S. Adel is well represented in Germany by such good ones as K.S. Duro v. Braumatal that made such an impression recently on the American breeder-judge, Bob Holcomb, who saw him in competition over there, reporting him as excelling in class and style, with drive and nose.

The Seiger strain is still to the fore, even after more than 30 years of active participation in German activities. Seiger's Para, a 1960 Spitz (which means top-rated, by the way, not a representative of quite another breed; *Spitz*, in German, means the apex, the top-dog), proved herself outstanding. Seiger's Tarantella, aunt to Para, was best bitch in the Kurzhaar Zuchtschau in Hannover, 1959. A year earlier, Seiger's Saltus was carrying the flag for this strain that, like the brook, seems likely to go on forever.

Which, in a way, brings us back to Lore Beckum. She whelped a daughter to a fireball, K.S. Don v.d. Schwarzen Kuhle, 209 f. Temperament came to Don honestly through his grandsire, Heidi Esterhof, the son of Mars Altenau. The daughter was most handsome. She was Adria v. Blitzdorf, 1487 m, first to carry this now-famous strain name into the pedigrees, and her breeder was Herr F. Böllhoff, present-day vice president of the Kurzhaar Klub for West and North Germany. Adria is behind all modern Blitzdorfers, including the Kleeman second-place dog of 1953, K.S. Pol v. Blitzdorf, 220 A, wh. 1951. Adria is the grand-dam of Pol's sire, Lux v. Blitzdorf and the dam of Freya v. Blitzdorf, 197 t, who whelped him. The 1958 Kleeman-Sieger, K.S. Zeus v. Blitzdorf, carries a like inheritance, being ex a litter sister to K.S. Pol. Bringing the story further along, the 1961 Kleeman-Sieger was also a Blitzdorfer, K.S. Elch v. Blitzdorf, 90 H, wh. 1958, and behind him in this same exacting competition for that year was K.S. Falk v. Rothenberg, 531 I, wh. 1959, who is by K.S. Zeus v. Blitzdorf ex a very sharp daughter of Ulk v.d. alten Postweg.

Americans know K.S. Pol v. Blitzdorf best as the sire of imported Dual & Nat'l. FT Ch. Kay v.d. Wildburg, 1959 Am. Field National winner and runner up for 1961. Kay was wh. 1956 (ex Cora v. Wesertor, whose background runs K.S. Axel v.d. Cranger Heide ex Fitz v. Tann). K.S. Axel is by a Moritz v.d. Postweg son, and Fitz is a K.S. Quandu v.d. Schleppenburg daughter. K.S. Quandu is also a Kleeman dog, his sire, Seydel's Gin, from a famous strain presently to be discussed. Further of interest is that the v.d. Wildburgs are carried on by one of the few old-time breeders still active in Germany. This is Oberförster Gummer, of Hemsloh-über-Diepholz, who for 30 years and more has bred and campaigned a single litter each year. His greatest may have been the 1953 Kleeman-Sieger, K.S. Eros v.d. Wildburg (K.S. Quandu v.d. Schleppenburg ex Drossel v.d. Wildburg, daughter of K.S. Axel v.d. Cranger Heide).

Kay v.d. Wildburg came to America in his Derby age, which means before he was subjected to any training pressure to conform to the German requirement to drop to shot, game, etc., thereby avoiding

44

K.S. Vito v.d. Radback, 1456 C (K.S. Pol v. Blitzdorf ex Resi v.d. Radback), wh. 1953.

the confusion that bedevils mature, trained German dogs that come here and are required to conform to different requirements here—often none too successfully. Kay did very well under the expert handling of Richard S. Johns, of Pennsylvania.

Another K.S. Pol v. Blitzdorf son was the post-war-years star, bred by the famous Herr Bleckmann, K.S. Vito v.d. Radbach, Kleeman-Sieger of 1955. No more famous, long-enduring name than v.d. Radbach exists in the world of the German Shorthaired Pointer, and the tally of champions stemming from this strain is by now beyond count. Only Herr Bleckmann himself could possible say how many times he has swung through and through the alphabet to name his litters bred. K.S. Vito's dam, Resi v.d. Radbach, was a K.S. Adel v. Assegrund daughter, ex Ondra v.d. Radbach. As Bodo made v.d. Radbach history before World War II, so did K.S. Vito in the mid-1950's, when the German breeders were getting into gear again after the loss and frustrations of the terrible years between. It was the worst of fortune that this beautiful dog should have met with death in a hunting field accident soon after sale to a breeder in Austria.

Several Vito descendants are here, perhaps as interesting as any being a quality daughter, the solid liver Centa v. Bornfeld, 477 H, wh. 1958, imported in 1961 by California breeder Don Miner, of Saratoga. In whelp to K.S. Arco v. Niestetal, 181 G, a Kleeman finalist of 1959, Centa had much to give here. Her dam line is a double cross of famed Heide v.d. Beeke, and her grand-dam, Seydel's Senta, 572 y, was a daughter of K.S. Seydel's Hella, the import closely resembling that famed Siegerin in type. Centa brought a sparkle to the eyes of Field Trial buffs as she went strutting by, an elegant, livewire lady, and a credit to Vito, her pa.

Also well-known in America, and usefully proved at stud, is K.S. Ulk v.d. Radbach, ex Ruth v.d. Radbach, full sister to Vito's dam, Resi. Owned by Dr. Kenworthy, of Vermont, Ulk was replaced in

Germany by his son. K.S. Benn v.d. Gottesstiege who, in turn, sired Arco v. Niestetal to whom Centa v. Bornfeld (above) was mated before export. K.S. Benn v.d. Gottesstiege is a good dog, as is his son, Arco, who in the Hannover Zuchtschau of 1959 took the Best Male award. Bred by A. Klinge, owned by Frau A. Poggenpohl, of Hannover-Bothfeld, whose late husband was an active pillar of breed interests in Germany, Arco is handled by Oberförster Heinz Burk in all his competitive outings. Heinz Burk, who bred Benn v.d. Gottesstiege, was well-established as a breeder when, in 1945, he was driven from his home by the Russian advance in Germany. As a refugee, all his dogs lost, he reached the West, where he made a fresh start, counting it luck that he managed to secure again a bitch of his former breeding that chanced to be located on the right side of the divided territory line.

Similar fortune did not attend all German Shorthaired Pointer breeders on the "wrong" side of the political wall. The Klub Kurzhaar mourns many good people and many fine strains of prewar vintage that are lost to it completely.

Kurzhaar-Sieger Magnet v. Ockerbach, famed German stud with great influence on the breed. His forehand construction and balance are illustrated here.

3

Modern-Day Strains
in Germany

A FULL-SCALE history of German breeding is beyond our scope. Here the aim is merely to examine some of the strains that have made major contributions to American bloodlines. It involves a hop-skip-jump technique, strain to strain, year to year. Few are the strain names that do not find some mention, somewhere, in the pedigree of one or another of the many imports.

Waldhausen we know for the impact of Treff v. Waldhausen, 422 Z, wh. 1924. The strain name is much respected, long-established. On January 12, 1962, the German breeders combined to congratulate the master of the v. Waldhausens, Cyriak Grohe, on the occasion of his 90th birthday, wishing him many years of good health. This great dog of his strain, Treff, later in the proud ownership of Herr H. F. Seiger, held a First in the Solms, the Shield of Honor at the International Exhibition at Hannover in 1929. His fame at stud was made through his son, R.S. & W.S. Heide v.d. Beeke, and his direct American influence is through his get from the imports, Seiger's Lore and Seiger's Holla II, brought in whelp to him. Holla's son, Kamerad v. Waldhausen, wh. 1934 in Montana, proved very prepotent, though with limited opportunities of his time. He was sired in Treff v. Waldhausen's last year at stud, the next-to-last litter, to be precise. The last (also in 1934) got Heide v.d. Beeke ex Diana v. Landsherrn, 867 h.

Heide v.d. Beeke must have been extensively used at stud and his batting average, if one may use the term, must have been high. Few extended German pedigrees now will lack his name. That he is still held in high regard there—he and his Waldhausen strain background—is established by the use of his picture in 1959 on the cover of *Kurzhaar Blätter*, the official magazine of Klub Kurzhaar (Berlin). Though many years dead, Heide v.d. Beeke's influence warranted this posthumous distinction.

The late 1930's, too, was the time of K.S. Marko v. Schaumberg, 1639, son of K.S. Kobold Mauderode-Westerholt, ex K.S. Kascha v. Schlossgarten, 1171. Marko interests American breeders through his son, Markus Freising, 1668, ex Juno Freising (by Furst v. Fuchspass). Not only is this dog solidly behind the "A" litter of the Assegrunds, and so behind K.S. Franco Beckum, but he is also the sire of one Berta Spiessinger v. Pfaffenhofen/Ilm DK 1166 (ex Gera v.d. Forst Brickwedde, 613 p). Berta, as all who have taken cramp from writing her name so often well know, is the dam of the fantastically propotent Austrian import, Field Ch. Greif v. Hundsheimerkogel, whose story is for the American chapters rather than for here.

The little ones of the late J. Meyerheim, the Pöttmes, constitute another strain usefully introduced to this country. Rudolph Hirschnitz, of California, and the late Wm. Ehrler, of the Rheinbergs in Michigan, had regard for these, and brought in several. They were all exceptional performers, capable for anything, and their tiny size was in direct opposition to the bulk of their breeder. Inbreeding closely but cleverly, Herr Meyerheim named his bitches along the way in numerical order, *Siebte, Achte, Neunte,* (Seventh, Eighth, Ninth), etc., reaching his apex (Spitz) with the solid liver, K.S. Elfte Pöttmes (the Eleventh). This strain ran strongly to solid liver.

So, too, does the famed strain of Seydel's, established also in the 1930's by Dr. (of medicine) Carl Seydel and his devoted wife, Maria, of Recklinghausen-Süd. The Seydel's strain wields great breed influence in Germany, but dogs sent here have in many cases been prey to exasperating accidental misfortunes. However, it is in terms of sheer human interest, as well, that the strain merits discussion here.

Now the question is, who was that first Herr Seydel to show a German Shorthaired Pointer? The year was 1887, the place was Barns Elms, London, an English K.C. show. The occasion was the only one in which GSHPs have been exhibited in England before the post-World War II years. The dog's name was Adda (Uncas-Aunsel). Frau Maria, in her day, said she had no idea who the gentleman was—maybe a relative of her late husband. Yet, also coincidentally, Dr. Seydel always wanted a brown German Shorthaired Pointer, and when he acquired one the pick pup of her first litter became Seydel's Adda! The story may never be finished for us. . . .

The dog that Dr. and Frau Seydel first acquired, a puppy, was Hella v. Böhmerwald-Gothnersitz, 186 1 (Aspodlesi 727 ex Flora v. Lindenschlösschen, 185 1). Hella capped a fine show career with a Welt Siegerin title at the Paris Exhibition of 1937. It was a wonderful win for such newcomers to the breed, but then Dr. and Frau Seydel discovered that to make her mark in Germany, Hella must do some winning in the Field. The doctor was professionally too busy to undertake her training. As a pet, she was too precious to be sent to any handler. Frau Maria learned Field Trial training along with the dog. It was tough going at first, but together they made the grade. Hella founded the famous strain, and Frau Maria became a famous handler.

Hella was bred to that same fireball, K.S. Don v.d. Schwarzen Kuhle, 209 f (Wodan Peppenhoven 1222 Z ex Hertana Päpinghausen, 26 Y, she a Mars Altenau granddaughter through Heidi Esterhof), whom we've already met as the sire of Adria v. Blitzdorf. The Seydel litter produced from brown Hella, six ticked, four brown (liver). The four were retained for the kennel. Careful line-breeding from three especially, Adda, Arno, Asta, made a tremendous contribution to the revival of the color of the pioneer basics. Researchers have since had pleasure in tracing back the solid-color inheritance that came strongly into Seydel's strain and has influenced so many great German strains onward till our present time.

The first Hella brought the color in her gift, through her sire line, through Wallo Eichsfeld, 334 M. Her dam line also goes clear back to brown in Trumpfdame Canzoe, 665, wh. 1889, a daughter of Carokönig, a good one in his day, a son of Waldin, 175, who of course was of the time when all the best dogs were famously brown, all carefully in tune with the model proposed by the important Hoppenraden. Wallo Eichsfeld's background of Beyes Stopp, 683 K, is also famously brown. His sister, Beyes Vilja v.d. goldenen Mark, is often mentioned in these pages when discussing the prepotency of her son, K.S. Michel v.d. goldenen Mark.

Adda and Asta were mated to a solid-color, 12-year-old K.S. Bill v. Hirschfeld, he by K.S. Wehrwolf v.d. goldenen Mark, 465 Z, ex a K.S. Michel daughter, Frigga Sand, 581 Y, also met already as the grand-dam of Artus Sand. Asta produced Seydel's Betty, 688 o, a very well-performed one. Betty whelped to Jäger's Naso, 1265 (by K.S. Frei Südwest) the famed K.S. Seydel's Hella. Adda, so beautiful, and a favorite of Dr. Seydel's, was in her day pronounced by Dr. Kleeman to be a very model of the breed. Her first litter produced a later-successful stud in Seydel's Gin. Of her second, she died whelping under the hail of bombs in a wartime raid in 1943. Coincidentally, the owner whose great pride she had been lost his life the same year. Dr. Seydel, critically injured during a bombing raid on an army train in which he was riding, on New Year's Eve, 1943, sacrificed personal attention to his own hurt to work with the wounded, and this cost him his life.

K.S. Seydel's Hella pleased the critics in her day, and has been described as the embodiment of feminine elegance in movement and deportment, her head with its dark eyes described as ideal.

Seydel name and fame does not begin or end with the two Hellas. Many good dogs have carried the strain name: Lotti, Claus, Moni; Seydel's Hill (brother to K.S. Hella), who is the grandsire of Moritz v.d. alten Postweg, 263 v, an elegant dog owned by Herr Ludwig Schürholz that sired his K.S. Axel v.d. Cranger Heide, 1994 w. K.S. Seydel's Troll, 1003 y, ex Moni, is a Moritz grandson, also through K.S. Axel, and is himself a Kleeman-Sieger (1951). Seydel's Gin also sired a Kleeman-Sieger, Quandu v.d. Schleppenburg. So it has gone, past and present, with the tireless lady still working her Shorthairs till the year of her death, 1970.

In Germany, the breed ideal never moves away from that of the competent working but elegant dog, of conformation to fit it for

Frau Maria Seydel made gift of this picture of her great ones. Old Seydel's Hella, the most famous of the strain, is the anchor gal on the right.

the showring if required. A famed German sports writer, Konrad Andreas, has commented: "There is no doubt that some hunters do not care whether a dog is or is not beautiful, so long as it is good at its work. This is no new thing to hear! It is certain that even the most beautiful shell is worthless if the kernel beneath is no good. However, in dogs it is well known that the one quality never does disqualify the other. We find in our Kurzhaar continually that our most beautiful dogs are also our very best to work." (*WALD UND WILD, October 1948*)

No worthwhile German breeder ever thinks that a sporting dog is likely to be better at work for being poorly constructed. Those in this country who proclaim (surely it is a *pose!*) that to breed for good looks in a dog is to cancel out its working qualities may, for all we know, merely be whistling bravely down the long, dark, sad lane of their own inability to breed a dog of good conformation. Their aim, then, may be to make necessity appear a virtue of choice. Unfortunately, such a complex, boldly and brassily expressed, as complexes tend to be, can often become accepted as truth by novices. Such indoctrinated novices can go into breeding ventures believing that there is neither virtue nor health in the breed Standard. Yet the wonderful tally of the German Shorthaired Pointer Dual Champions that keeps on building in our time proves how wrong is any such belief that a good-looking dog cannot work. It is a myth fostered by the ignorant, the frustrated, the unfortunates with only poor-type dogs in their ownership. And how the German breeders would despise such—they, who refuse to breed to even the *best* working dog if it should possess some discernible fault of conformation!

The ultimate ruin that can be imposed by the belief that poor conformation is anything but bad has been demonstrated in other breeds. The law of diminishing returns, operating for a few generations, is what put many one-time Pointer and Setter men into German Shorthaired Pointers in the first place. To a breed they found still unspoiled, some of them brought, however, the exact undesirable scale of values that ran them out of their previous breeds. The Germans, as well as the British, have always been much wiser. The honor of the Championship title, and all the privileges of the breeding pen that go with this, are reserved to dogs that can prove themselves desirable in both the performance and the conformation sense. Truly, as experience has proved to the hilt, and as Konrad Andreas phrases it, there is no reason to believe that one quality will cancel out the other.

As Heide v.d. Beeke in his day, so in his day was K.S. Axel v.d. Cranger Heide, 1994 w, seldom lacking in present-day pedigrees. Owned by Herr Ludwig Schürholz, of Hervest-Dorsten, and campaigned with the careful enthusiasm of this experienced breeder, Axel is ex Dora v. Schloss Dorneburg, 2204 t, wh. 1947. According to the description preserved by those who wrote of him in his prime, K.S. Axel was a somewhat smallish dog, but of great elegance, and possessed of a wonderful front-end flexibility (which, of course, means good shoulders). He was fast, obedient, quick to find, and his manners were excellent. Those who had known Mars Altenau many years earlier often commented that K.S. Axel greatly resembled the earlier breed pillar.

In 1952, the *Deutsche Hund-Zeitung* gave to K.S. Axel the top spot in German Shorthaired Pointers over the earlier two years of competition in Germany. His distinguished get is too numerous to spell right out here, but for American interest he will be found behind many present-day imports. As the sire of K.S. Gernot v.d. Heidehöhe, a Kleeman-placed dog, we have him behind the Illinois-owned import, Mr. R. C. Bauspies' Dual Ch. Alfi v.d. Kronnenmuhle (ex Heide v.d. Emmstadt). Dual Ch. Alfi is happily the dam of a Dual

Ch. bitch in Miss B'Haven v. Winterhauch (by Dual Ch. Captain v. Winterhauch), for this time a record, a Dual with two Dual parents. (Where, asks my novice, *do* the good ones come from? Answer: They come from other good ones!) K.S. Axel is also the grandsire of K.S. Arco v. Niestetal (already mentioned). In Germany, Axel has sired Drossel v.d. Wildburg, dam of the Kleeman-Sieger, Eros v.d. Wildburg; K.S. Amor v.d. Beeke; K.S. Seydel's Troll; K.S. Bosco v.d. Ilenburg—all Kleeman stars, as is seen in the table further along. This makes plain his great prepotency.

Contemporary with K.S. Axel v.d. Cranger Heide, and indeed quite often in competition with him in the field, was another very proud German stud force of those same earlier 1950's. This was K.S. Quandu v.d. Schleppenburg, 728 x. As the Kleeman-Sieger for 1950, he was a certain pride for his owner, Apotheker Leueu, of Lübbecke. Sired by Seydel's Gin ex Here v.d. Schleppenburg, 1108 c, this Sieger carries a name also become familiar here. His work on birds has been described by a lyrical observer as poetry, his movement as a song. In America, the strain has his best representation through the solid-colored dog, Field Ch. and National Ch. of 1959, Oloff v.d. Schleppenburg, owned in Illinois by Roy J. Thompson. His breeding is by Chick v.d. Schleppenburg ex Gerda v. Stau.

K.S. Gernot v.d. Heidehöhe, 5887, the K.S. Axel v.d. Cranger Heide son ex K.S. Bärbel v.d. Heerstrasse, is also of importance, as just mentioned in connection with Dual Ch. Alfi v.d. Kronnenmuhle. In Germany we find him often in the pedigrees, especially through his mating with the Diana-Siegerin of 1954, K.S. Aeskulaps Wiesel (by K.S. Widu v. Braumatal). This strain of Aeskulaps is represented also by many good modern-day dogs in Germany. The Siegerin's individual reputation is continually enhanced by her descendants, especially through her 1955 daughter, Aeskulaps Frigga, the dam of K.S. Arco v. Niestetal, resultant from the above-mentioned mating with K.S. Gernot v.d. Heidehöhe.

K.S. Widu v. Braumatal, in his own right, was also an excellent performer, and this strain name is also well-represented in America nowadays, put forward by imports of the 1960's, sired by such as Duro v. Braumatal and K.S. Lümmel v. Braumatal. Lümmel, a well-regarded performer, is one of the stud strengths of the v.d. Steilkuste establishment of Herr Eggersh, of Bargloy, and has some of his

Axel v. Wasserschling. This prepotent dominated GSP breeding for almost a decade in Germany. His get and grandget were exported worldwide. Owner, Gustav Machetanz, Dortmund.

get already established here in the Pacific Northwest. Also with long association here is the strain of v.d. Forst Brickwedde, of Herr R. Schulte, of Brickwedde über Bersenbrück. The history-minded will immediately think of the pioneer import, Artist v.d. Forst Brickwedde, and Alfred Sause's Ch. Dallo v.d. Forst Brickwedde. In present-day representation there is imp. Ebing v.d. Forst Brickwedde.

Modern German pedigrees also carry the names quite frequently, as Herr Schulte conducts a very extensive operation, and has done so for many years. His K.S. Quandus v.d. Forst Brickwedde is one of the names to catch the eye in any scanning of English pedigrees of the present day, too. Most strongly, the strain seems to be modernly indebted to K.S. Amor v.d. Beeke (K.S. Axel v.d. Cranger Heide ex Toska v.d. Beeke).

The postwar years saw the emergence of new names. The strain name with most impact has been that of Wasserschling. Herr Gustav Machetanz, out of East Germany ahead of the Russians, built up his strain to eminence as out of the Westfalen area and its environs to nationwide, even world-wide recognition. As from the Siegerin Thea v. Wasserschling, who took second place behind K.S. Aeskulaps Wiesel, from another famous strain, in the 1954 Diana Prüfung, to the sturdy solid liver stud, Axel v. Wasserschling, the build-up was tremendous. The German Shorthair scene, in its native land, *needed* in the immediate postwar years, such a dog as Axel. Catching

54

the eye and the interest of the knowledgable Herr Bollhöff of the Blitzdorfers, and actively praised by this breeder-judge, Axel, sound, solid, strong, over a space of several years, and into his old age, came to dominate the breed to such an extent that by the later 1960s, the breeders were made aware of an unexpected difficulty—the scarcity of outcross blood. The search for "Axel-frei" bloodlines became urgent.

Why the need for the services of sound, solid, strong Axel? Mainly, for the circumstance in which postwar German breeders found themselves—the war years had taken away their great dogs of the 1930s, and cessation of breeding had left virtually nothing to replace them. The search for good breeding stock was an agonizing one as the clubs were with all manner of difficulties, political as well as practical, reformed. In 1971 the *Frankfurter Jagdklub* published a magnificent 50-Year Jubilee Journal (1921–1971) in which the history of this body is accurately traced. The portion that deals with the resuscitation of the Jagdklub in the post WWII years illuminates the difficulties. Under Occupation, meetings were prohibited —no trials, no hunting, no permitted ownership of guns. Even the beer lacked; too often *gemütlichkeit* had to be fueled by water—only!

With the lifting of the tightest restrictions, the Frankfurter Klub, as others in the land, began to gather and assess the local dog stock, the survivors. "Das Hundematerial liess allerdings in Form and Gebäude zu wünschen übrig. Die Hunde waren grössenteils zu leicht und hatten kurze spitze Fänge. . . . Zur DK-Sonderschau im Rahmen der Hundeausstellung auf dem Frankfurter Schlachthof am Aug. 1947 waren 35 Hunde (15 Rüden und 20 Hündinnen) erschienen, wovon 4 Rüden und 3 Hundinnen mit 'vorzüglich' ausgezeichnet wurden." (*Ersten Frankfurter Jagdklub* 1971, pp. 23/24.)

(*Trans:* "The dog material left everything in shape and build to be desired. The dogs for the most part were too light-framed and had short, pointed muzzles. . . . At the Shorthair-Specialty in the Frankfurter Schlachthof, Aug. 1947, of 35 entries, 15 males, 20 bitches, only 4 males and 3 bitches gained award of "Excellent.")

The situation in Frankfurt was mirrored across Germany. The search for breeding stock of type and substance was rigorously pursued. Nor, indeed, was Axel the only stud with these qualities to convey, but he was the most promoted, and so the most used. Over the years since 1947, German breeders have labored to build the breed up to required substance and type excellences, and considerable success has attended these efforts, but there remained far too much of the substanceless, short-sharp muzzled rubbish, still being screened out as late as the end of the 1960s. By then, however, the breeder-care had provided increasing stock of good dogs, widening the blood pool so that one-stud dominance has become a thing of the past.

THE KLEEMAN-AUSLESE PRUFUNG

In line with their most admirable intention of perpetuating within the Fancy the names of those who have done their breed great service, the Kurzhaar breeders of Germany named their most exacting Trial for that genial man of great knowledge, Dr. Paul Kleeman, so many years their Klub President. No German dog can carry a title prouder than that of Kleeman-Sieger or Siegerin. The exclusive roll-call of those so endowed may in a very literal sense comprise the roll-call of the modern-day breed's greatest representatives.

First established in 1939, at Aschersleben, the Kleeman-Prüfung was at that time rather less of a working Trial than it is in present-day practice; rather, it was in the form of an exhibition of Stud Dogs in the Field. From 1949 on, however, new rules brought it closer to its present form. These rules have been further revised—in 1953, and since then. Requirements and qualifications continue to tighten, year by year.

No German Sieger—as no English Champion—ever comes by his title easily, or by default when the good dogs stay home; he has to work for it. Since 1953, a Kurzhaar Sieger must qualify in running well in a Kleeman Search. It must also have First Prizes in the Derby and Solms, and at least a Second in a *Verbandsgebrauchsprüfung* (Klub Utility Search), or else a Derby or Solms First, plus a First in the *Verbandsgebrauchsprüfung*. Later, the aspirant must add its *Verlorenbringenprüfung* on the trail of wounded hare (*krankgeschossenen Hasen*) that the dog has not previously seen (*geäugt*). It comprises finding and retrieving such lost game. When a dog has successfully competed so over a required distance of 400 m., under two recognized judges, he gains his award of Vbr. (*Verlorenbringenprüfung*), an endorsement found on many of the German pedigrees that reach here with imported dogs. The exacting tests match oddly with the opinion of some quite prominent American handlers, especially, who claim in print or in correspondence that the German Shorthaired Pointer is by inheritance no worthwhile tracker, retriever, or water dog!

K.S. Rauck Mauderode Westerholt, 739 h 4658. One of the four K.S. Kobold Mauderode Westerholt sons to head the placings in the first-ever Dr. Kleeman Auslese Prüfung of 1939.

Ch. Bama Belle's Feather of Eb (wh. 2/28/78, Ch. Robin Crest Achilles ex Ch. Jonmar Color Me Cocoa, CD). Breeders, Patricia A. Tear and Paul B. Averill. Owners, Wade H. and Gale Parsons, Florida. This successful show bitch is separated by half-a-century from K.S. Rauck Mauderode Westerholt, she down from much Thornton inheritance, on her sire's side especially, through her great-grand-dam, Ch. Montreal Belle, who comes by way of Timm v. Altenau from Donn v. Sulfmeister, imp., also a Kobold son. That genes are forever has seldom been so spectacularly depicted.

K.S. Cent v. Hege Haus—434 Y/75. At the Kleeman Auslese Prufung, Germany, 1980.—
Photo lent by *Prof. Alfons Lemper*, Klub Kurzhaar.

Handsome tailored clothes are worn by hunting men in Germany. Pictured at Kleeman-Auslese-Prufung, Kehl-am-Rhein, Germany.—*C. Bede Maxwell*

Post-WWII resumption of classic Kleeman springtime Field Trial participation was upon an annual basis as from 1949 to 1968. Change was then made in terms of the biennial, making yearly alternation with the become-popular IKP (*Internationale Kurzhaar Prüfung*) which drew the cream of European Shorthairs also into a biennial event, this one staged in autumn and moving country to country in terms of venue.

Kleeman judging and evaluation of entrants continued to be identified with the search for best breeding prospects and overall, the top Kleeman stars tended to make their presence felt over successive years at stud and in the whelping box. However, it also proved to be true that nature did not always make concession to human judgment, for it is also true that some very important producers do not carry the Kleeman title. Notably here, Axel v. Wasserschling, the breed's top modern producer, he having been "included out" by Judge Carl Seidler in 1962, his water and field work leaving him among the *"nicht bestandens."* Carl Seidler has long gone to his rest but Axel's name remains literally indivisible from modern breed history and it has been quoted in scholarly breed articles that when Axel's performance had been adversely judged in terms of Kleeman requirements, his young Derby and Solms-performing get was already making his name to the pattern of that of the fictional Abou Ben Adhem of our school book days, he whose name led all the rest.

That Klub Kurzhaar stalwarts were faulting the post-war breeding stock by the measure of the proven greats of the 1930s, the apex-years of the breed ended by war, was no secret into the 1970s, and search for quality breeder stock was never-ending. By mid-1970s, it became matter for consideration that many prospectively-useful studs, after their brief years in competition, retired as hunting or forester's dogs to the far reaches of the Reich, often at considerable travel-distance from the location of bitches that could benefit from their attentions. Operative, to a disturbing degree, to be considered as by distance wasted, were many good dogs denied breeder privileges—Out of Sight tended to become Out of Breeder Mind, European dog competition having no equivalent for the desperate straining after records that keep many U.S. dogs expensively before the public.

Basco v. Hellen Kamp 958 T 170. Owner, E. H. Busch, Germany.—*Photo lent by Prof. Alfons Lemper.*

K.S. Groll v. Südstrand, Dr. Kleeman Auslese Prüfung, Germany—1980.— *Photo lent by Professor Alfons Lemper, Klub Kurzhaar.*

Graf v. Rietberger Land 1231 7.70 (Rigo v. Hegehaus ex Edda v. Rietberger Land). Owner, Dr. Fl. Kluge, Birkenhof, Germany.—*Photo lent by Prof. Alfons Lemper.*

Presently was brought into Klub Kurzhaar notice a proposal to bring together, from those far reaches of the country, the cream of the living and active studs. Klubs at all points of the compass were invited to send a couple of representatives—their local best!—to a Stud Dog Show (*Zuchtrüdenvorstellung*) that breeders could comfortably reach for attendance and benefit by the opportunity to see in the flesh good studs otherwise destined to be neglected by the sheer factor of distance and comparative inaccessability. Held in December of 1976 in Dinklage, the event drew more than 300 breeders from across the country, and through the generous and ongoing kindness of Professor Lemper of Klub Kurzhaar, a detailed report on the 17 attendant studs was made available for this present revision of the American book, so serving to update the breeding situation in present-day Germany, the studs being of ages as from whelpings 1969 thru 1974. Critiques were exhaustive, provided by top-rated judges, and frankness was the order of the day, reports including good and bad, warts and all, and emphasizing the type of bitches that could be expected best to combine with the studs in all their diversities.

Review of the attending studs, published in catalog order and sequence of whelping dates makes a magnificent overlook of present-day influences and trends. The critiques are here much condensed from original size.

1.   BLITZ V. WESERMOOR: *Klub Schleswig-Holstein:* wh. '69: Medium-size tickpatch, whose background is K.S. Arco v. Niestetal, the Braumartels, K.S. Jucker v. Birkenbach. This a strongly endowed hunting man's dog.

2.   ARTUS V. SONNENFELS: *Klub Rheinland:* wh. '69: solid liver, a K.S. Pollux v. Bederkesa son, which meshes a strong Axel v. Wasserschling influence with Jucker v. Birkenbach. Again a dog well-proven in practical hunting character (reason, after all, for the breed's existence.)

3.   K.S.('72) EX V. KRUCKENMOOR: *Klub Nordmark:* wh. '69: Big-framed tick-patch, reported as having already exercised strong stud influence in his district. Comment included observation that he did not stamp his own good type, so was best matched with suitable bitches. A K.S. Zeus v. Blitzdorf son.

4.   K.S.('72) Arco v.d. Vohrener Höhe: *Klub Rheinland:* wh. '69. Solid liver, reported as a remarkable tracking dog, excelling in Schweisshund work. Shows sharpness of temperament but does not display this in work. A Pat v. Hanstein son —Pat also a sharp dog!— which is back to Axel v. Wasserschling, and his dam a Maniz v.d. Forst Brickwedde daughter. His working capabilities were of greatest value, but the review cautioned that his matings should be to the bitches of steadiest temperament. *("Die Hundinnen solten aber nervlich absolut sicher sein.")*

5.   Basko v. Hellenkamp: *Klub Hanover:* wh. '70: This one took all eyes as that rare article in post-war German breeding, a stud that was by inheritance completely *"Axel-frei,"* that is, carried none of the most-distributed bloodline. A most elegant solid liver, Basko carried instead of the K.S. the title of *Weltsieger,* a show award. Owner-pride must have rested in the circumstance that not only was Basko chosen, but three of his sons had been nominated by different Klubs for this same assemblage. His sire, Nurmi v. Blitzdorf, goes back to Axel v. Heidebrink, and it much pleased this compiler of this translation that Basko's dam was a daughter of "the dog she would have liked to bring home with her from Germany in '68—Caesar v. Bomberg."*(GSP News.)* No temperamental problems with this one.

6.   K.S. ('76) Don v. Stadum Nord: *Klub Schleswig-Holstein:* wh. '71: Solid liver. Amateur handled and so not under complete control this son of much-beloved K.S. Issos v. d. Muritzbucht, was again one in debt to Axel v. Wasserschling, also in the breeding of his dam. Described as a dog of initiative and good sense, sharp and *Mannsharp,* could structurally be improved in underline and would be best served by bitches strong in this feature.

7.   Amor v. Honnenholz: *Klub Westfalen:* wh. '71: Kleeman 1976 "bestanden"(qualified). Black/white/ticked–*Schwarzschimmel,* color increasingly evident in German breedings. Owned by famed Gustav Machetanz of Wasserschling, which may have had to do with judges' comment that Amor was "in no need to be made any wider known than already he is." However, it *was* for a great many attending breeders the first opportunity to see this distinguished son of K.S. Quell Pöttmes in the flesh. His dam, Senti v. Richtsbergen was an Ex v. Osterbach daughter. which of course is back to Axel and Wasserschling. A well-performed dog without noticeable fault but with get inclined at times to the delicate and small.

8.   K.S.('74) Caesar v. Uphuser Kolk: *Klub Nordwest:* wh. '71: An elegantly compact, medium-sized tick-patch. Of his 4 great-grand-

The plight of the departing dog at rear was for many years common to all German Kurzhaar that could not pass conformation examination the night before a Field Trial with a rating of either Excellent (*Verzuglich*) or Very Good (*Sehr Gut*). Dogs rated Good, Adequate or Poor were simply not allowed to compete in the Trial. This picture, taken at ring-entrance at the 1968 Kleeman, shows such a dog rejected by the conformation judges for inadequate size, substance and poor ("needle-nosed") headpiece. The Public Address System broadcast the verdict of the judges—always three judges and a veterinarian. At front, the next dog to be examined waits his turn (not show-stacked). Passing the examination, this one later did well in the Trial. As of 1981, the extreme harshness of the exclusion rule has been modified in that a dog that can command a "Good" (*Gut*) rating will at least be permitted to take part in the Trial to qualify, if successful, for a Prize I or II—but cannot receive or be credited with the actual award.—Photo, *C. Bede Maxwell*

parents, 3 were "named Axel v. Wasserschling" and the 4th was an Axel son—His sire, K.S. ('70) Vock v. Wasserschling. His field qualities were counted remarkable, his head could not be bettered, and he was proven to pass along his qualities which included exceptionally good waterwork.

9. K.S. ('76) ARRAK V. ETZELBERG: *Klub Hanover:* wh. '72: Again a black-white-ticked, judicially assessed a splendid working and tracking dog with the so-desired high nose and elegant manners: a successful sire. By Ex v. Osterberg by a dam through K.S. Pollux v. Bederkesa, K.S. Jucker v. Birkenbach to Amor v.d. Beeke. He was also described as best provided with bitches of size and substance.

10. CASER V. HOLTDAM: *No Klub identification:* wh. '72. Tick-patch. described as outstanding in the ring and having "air of a *Fremd-Product*" ("out of country breeding," which is not identified.) His sire side was Braumatal, his dam line Patria Zurich. Described as handsome, quiet, fine-nosed, with best field manners but no speedster moving with a somewhat heavy rolling gait. A utility dog of highest quality of inestimable value where substance, quiet, sharpness required.

11. ARTEMIS DONALD: *Klub Normark:* wh. '72. Kleeman *"bestanden"* 1976. Black/white/ticked. A high class stud, better than his pictures suggest and better than he often appears in the ring where he is the aggressive stud dog. Outside the ring this is no longer in evidence. A fireball, field and water accomplished, sharp, with definite indication of *Mannsharp.* (NOTE: a quality much valued by foresters who count on protective instincts of their working Shorthairs in possible emergency. CBM) His sire line back to Maniz v.d. Forst Brickwedde, his dam line to K.S. Arco v. Niestetal and Jucker v. Birkenbach.

12. K.S. ('76) BILL V.D. HERRENMÜHLE: *Klub Artland-Emsland:* wh. '72. Proudly presented by his Klub for good impression made by his early get in Derby competition- 8 First Prizes made it the best litter of the year. A quiet, comfortable, uncomplicated dog for hunting, also did well in hands of amateur handler. His sire, Grimm Donaria, has shown within recent years field manners and nose qualities among his endowments. Bill's dam, Anja v.d. Herrenmühle, through Pleck v. Bederkesa. A dog to deliver all qualities a hunter could desire.

13. JUNKER V. GOLDBACH: *Klub Westfalen:* wh. 1973. solid liver, one of the sons of Basko v. Hellenkamp (No. 5, this tabulation). His dam, a Bill v.d. Wildburg daughter, Fee v. Goldbach, an Ex v. Osterberg granddaughter, so again it is back to Axel v. Wasserschling. At-

tractive dog of good line and well-performed under amateur handling. An experienced judge made comment that he had been trying to fault this one on construction but to date without success. Further Judge's comment: A DOG SUCH AS WE WOULD WISH THE BREED TO BE. He should have his chance at stud.

14. DINO V. MUHLENBACH: *Klub Westfalen:* wh. '73: tick-patch. Described as one of the noblest in the ring, head and body line qualities. He was another of the sons of Basko v. Hellenkamp. His dam had repute as a notable *Verlorenbringer* (tracker/retrieving) Nio v. Wasserschling, her breeding Axel/Norma v. Bederkesa. A sharp and useful dog, though field not overwhelmingly his strength. This perhaps accounted for by his being continually worked in deep forestland, and this did not help him in Kleeman competition either. Works with half-high nose and made much use of for scenting work, which accounts for his steadiness and quiet. His get does well in Field.

15. ARCO V. NIERSTAL (not to confuse with K.S. Arco v. Niestetal) *Klub Rhineland:* wh. '73. The model of the field dog with speed and high style, but not in performance wide going, which cost him his first in the Solms. Excellent in water and strongly owes to Axel v. Wasserschling.

16. JAGER V. NIESTETAL: *Klub Niedersachsen:* v. Schaumberg-Lippe: wh. '74. Attracted much attention with his very light black-white, patterned jacket. "He stands on the lower border for size, needs more, and more breed type. By a nephew of K.S. Quell Pöttmes and the strong good-looking Comet Donaria in his double grandfather. Also has three times Axel v. Wasserschling and twice Axel's sister, Adda v. Wasserschling. Strong in field and water, and a vehicle for desired lightening of color but bitches sent him should have sufficient substance.

17. CENN V. FEUERTEICH: *Klub Braunschweig:* wh. '74: Handsome solid liver with ticked breast flecking—which was held to operate against his throwing solid colors. His background is *show*, and counts as a Weltseiger sire to a Weltseiger dam: his sire, Basko v. Hellenkamp is top-rated show dog; his dam, Heike v. Weserland, is rated top show bitch. As observation, the commentator remarks that the children of such proper-seeming arrangements don't always prove that breeding is easy. But Cenn, third of Basko's get in the show this day, is described as good-headed, well-built, with excellent rear quarters. His dam, a Pat v. Hanstein daughter to a double Axel v. Wasserschling grandget. He and his sisters demonstrated good field and track work, his outstanding forward thrust much praised.

DR. KLEEMAN AUSLESE PRÜFUNG
Germany's world-famous Breeder-search Field Trial

1949 (Krefeld, Rhineland) (Bestanden 5)

1. K.S. QUANDUS V.D. FORST BRICKWEDDE, 5940. Kleeman-Sieger.
2. K.S. AXEL V.D. CRANGER HEIDE, 1994 w
3. JÄGERS WEHRWOLF, 2477 t
4. KEMNAS CHICK, 289 w
5. K.S. FRANCO BECKUM, 1471 w

1950 (Krefeld, Rhineland) (Bestanden 5)

1. K.S. & V.S. QUANDU V.D. SCHLEPPENBURG, 728 x. Kleeman-Sieger.
2. BODO V. HEIMELSBERG, 742 w
3. K.S. AXEL V.D. CRANGER HEIDE, 1994 w
4. ARTUS V.D. WEDELER, 956 w
5. ARKO V.D. WEDELER, 954 w

1951 (Frankfurt a. Main) (Bestanden 4)

1. K.S. SEYDEL'S TROLL, 1003 y. Kleeman-Sieger.
2. TAPS V. ALTEN POSTWEG, 1514 y
3. GREIF V.D. BRUNAU, 766 y
4. XANTIPPE SUDWEST, 1486 y

1952 (Peine) (Bestanden 4)

1. K.S. ARMOR V.D. BEEKE, 1206 z. Kleeman-Sieger.
2. CLAUS V. WEIDENHOF, 1430 x
3. K.S. GERNOT V.D. HEIDEHÖHE, 588 z
4. K.S. LIPPERT'S ARGO, 1893 w

1953 (Frankenthal/Pfalz) (Bestanden 9)
(This year, the bitches were judged separately from the dogs.)

a. *Dogs.*

1. K.S. EROS V.D. WILDBURG, 529 A. Kleeman-Sieger.
2. K.S. POL V. BLITZDORF, 220 A
3. K.S. RAUCK V. ALTEN POSTWEG, 991 y
4. K.S. BILL V. BRAMBERG, 540 z

66

b. *Bitches.*

1. K.S. Banja v. Galgenacker, 34936 (Switzerland). Diana-Siegerin.
2. Carla v.d. Wedeler, 1216 z
3. K.S. Bona v.d. Schleppenburg, 837 z
4. Jolanthe Sudwest, 1191 y
5. Zilla v.d. Schwabenburg, 611 z

1954 (Buckeburg) (Bestanden 4)

1. K.S. Arco v. Braumatal, 504 z. Kleeman-Sieger.
2. K.S. Bosco v. Ilenbeck, 449 B
3. Seiger's Edler, 213 C
4. Grimm v. Pappelhof, 396 z

1954 Diana-Prufung (bitches). (Krefeld) (Bestanden 9)

1. Aeskulaps Wiesel, 625 A. Diana-Siegerin.
2. K.S. Thea v. Wasserschling, 421 A
3. Herta v.d. Matena, 243 A
4. Jägers Fritzi, 408 A
5. Grille v.d. Grossen Tulln, ÖHSt.B (Austrian Studbook) 1866
6. Blanka v.d. Schwabenburg, 1855 B
7. Anka v. Sonnenweg, 899 y
8. Xilli v. Alten Postweg, 784 B
9. Cita v. Dammerwald, 1366 B

1955 (Frankenthal) (Bestanden 6)

1. K.S. Vito v.d. Radbach, 1456 C. Kleeman-Sieger.
2. K.S. Jucker v. Birkenbach, 679 C
3. Zorn v. Waterkotten, 1417 C
4. Falk v. Langertstein, 677 B
5. Adel v. Rhönforst, 629 z
6. Ingo v.d. Metena, 136 C

1957 DR. KLEEMAN and DIANA-AUSLESE PRUFUNG (both sexes) (Bad Lippspringe) (Bestanden 7)

1. Erra v. Wesertor, 1143 D. Diana-Siegerin.
2. K.S. Coralle v. Brauwinkel, 498 E

3. Freya v. Kohlwald, 1150 D
4. Benn v.d. Gottesstiege, 579 E
5. Marga v. Brikenbaum, 559 E
6. Vasall v.d. Radbach, 1455 C
7. Xella v.d. Radbach, 1580 D

1958 (Seligenstadt bei Aschaffenburg) (Bestanden 5)

1. K.S. Zeus v. Blitzdorf, 322 E. Kleeman-Sieger.
2. K.S. Lümmel v. Braumatal, 301 F
3. K.S. Bitta v.d. Gottesstiege, 586 E
4. Seiger's Saltus, 77 G
5. K.S. Aeskulaps Gemse, 83 F

1959 (Wallerstein) (Bestanden 5)

1. K.S. Lackl v.d. Forst Brickwedde, 729 F. Kleeman-Sieger.
2. K.S. Orlanda v. Gartenschlag, 1311 G
3. K.S. Axel v. Heidebrink, 241 F
4. K.S. Arco v. Niestetal, 181 G
5. K.S. Cora v.d. Babilonie, 1407 E

1961 (bei Kassel) (Bestanden 3)

1. K.S. Elch v. Blitzdorf, 90 H. Kleeman-Sieger.
2. K.S. Falk v. Rothenberg, 531 I
3. K:S. Donna v. grunen Deich, 456 G

1962 (Stadhagen) (Bestanden 9)

1. K.S. Conni v. Moorachütz, 888 I/59
2. K.S. Blitz v. Klosterfield, 950 I/59
3. K.S. Edda v. Wilseder berg, 921 H/58
4. K.S. Seiger's Para, 161 J/60
5. K.S. Assan v. Böhnenhof, 212 J/60
6. Jucker v.d. Selde, 899 H/58
7. Imme v. Hanstein, 1275 G/57
8. Orion v. Gartenschlag, 1310 G/57
9. K.S. Eva Sand, 308 H/58

K.S. Zeus v. Blitzdorf, 322 E, wh. 1955, Kleeman-Sieger for 1958. Many of his get found their way to America.

1964 (Speyer) (Bestanden 9)

1. K.S. SEIGER'S MUNGO, 173 L/62
2. FLECK V. GARTENSCHLAG, 975 K/61
3. K.S. ARNO VON SOLZ, 308 K/61
4. BURSCH V. BIRKENBACH, 1696 J/60
5. K.S. POLLUX V. BEDERKESA, 516 K/61
6. ARKO VOM NORDHOF, 1841 J/60
7. CAHN V. OSTERBERG, 451 L/62
8. BIRKE VOM GRÜNTAL, 1898 K/61
9. BIENE V.D. BUCHENHEIDE, 875 K/61

1966 (Bosau) (Bestanden 21)

1. K.S. MINGO V. HEIMERSHEIM, 2014 M/63
2. ONKO V. TODTENSEE, 921 M/63
3. K.S. JANUS DU RAPIDO, LOF 2522
4. ISSOS V.D. MÜRITZBUCHT, 1995 M/63
5. MOHR V. WASSERSCHLING, 364 N/64
6. K.S. MASCOTTE V. WASSERSCHLING, 368 N/64
7. SCHELL VON BEDERKESA, 533 N/64
8. ARTEMIS ERF, 1966 M/63
9. AXEL V. BLOMBERG, 156 L/62
10. BARON V. SIEBENBERGEN, 2061 M/63
11. EX V.D. HÜNENBURGWIESE, 733 L/62
12. K.S. SEIGER'S TENNO, 1928 N/64

13. K.S. IVOS V. WASSERSCHLING, 661 M/63
14. PIA V. HANSTEIN, 1224 L/62
15. CILLA V. DROSTENHOF, 854 M/63
16. K.S. ANJE V.D. PORTA, 608 M/63
17. MAJA V. KLOSTERMOOR, 1803 J/60
18. LAIA DE LA MOTTE, SHSB 115 951
19. K.S. ARTEMIS BOLZ, 1344 K/61
20. EX V. OSTERBERG, 1006 M/63
21. DURO A.D. SCHOTTENGASSE, 483 L/62

1968 (Kehl-am-Rhein) (Bestanden 10)
1. K.S. ERRA V. SIXENHOF, 24 N/64
2. K.S. AMBER DONARIA, 205 N/64
3. K.S. BIRKE AUS DER PORTA, 975 O/65
4. K.S. CARA V. HOHENFELD, 647 N/64
5. ALPHA V. GODDBACH, 510 P/66
6. K.S. ANKE V. ICHENHEIM, 1306 N/64
7. K.S. TASSO V. GARZINER GRUND, 503 O/65
8. K.S. PAN DE LEMANIA, LOF 8488
9. MARK V. WASSERSCHLING, 361 N/64
10. KOX V.D. MÜRITZBUCHT, 161 P/66

1970 (Bad Lippspringe) (Bestanden 8)
1. K.S. QUELL PÖTTMES, 735 Q/67
2. K.S. AXEL V. BÜGELHOF, 69 Q/67
3. K.S. GRAF V. LINDENKREUZ, 739 P/66
4. K.S. VOCK V. WASSERSCHLING, 790 P/66
5. K.S. FIESTA DONARIA, 625 Q/67
6. BILL V.D. WILDBURG, 167 Q/67
7. MASSCOTTE V. MOORSCHUTZ, 578 Q/67
8. VINA V. WASSERSCHLING, 793 P/66

1972 Dogs: (Bestanden 14)
1. K.S. ARCO V.D. VOHRENER HÖHE 726 S/69 18196
2. K.S. RODO V. HEIMERSHEIM 978 R/68 17191
3. K.S. EX V. KRÜCKENMOOR 684 S/69 17930
4. K.S. XERXES V.D. RADBACH 700 R/68 15991
5. ARTUS V. SONNENFELS 616 S/69 18540
6. DAX V. AMTMANNSLOCH 360 T/70 18503

7. SANDOR v. HEIMERSHEIM 1803 S/69 18034
8. BINGO v. GRÜNBERGERH
9. AMOR v. MAXHOF 1650 Q/67 15790

Bitches:

1. K.S. UNDA v. HEGE-HAUS 538 T/70 17784
2. K.S. ALPHA v.d. ERLENKLINGE 1140 S/69 18227
3. K.S. HANNI v. SIXENHOF 362 R/68 17648
4. LADY v. LINDENKREUZ 308 R/68 17122
5. CARA v. GOLDBACH 673 R/68 17500

1974 Dogs: (Bestanden 13)

1. K.S. PAN v. OSTERBERG 1706 T/70 18975
2. K.S. FARKO v. FASANENPFAD 1888 U/71 19861
3. K.S. BASKO v.d. SCHILLERSGRUND 1020 U/71 20302
4. GRINGO v. WASSERSCHLING 2473 S/69 17818
5. INGO v. SIXENHOF 123 U/71 18739
6. CAESAR v. UPHUSER KOLK 1703 U/71 20395

Bitches:

1. K.S. GITTI v. PFAFFENBERG 1121 T/70 19139
2. K.S. BIANCA v.d. ERLENKLINGE 1667 U/71 19835
3. DIANA ROTHENUFFELN 450 V/72 20301
4. DIANA v. BÜGELHOF 2460 U/71 19887
(BELLA v. JOLLETAL 1468 V/72 19928 is listed as not permitted to take part in Trial as she failed in the conformation examination beforehand)
5. JUTTA v. GUNTAL 1956 S/69 19123
6. CENTA ROTHENUFFELN 802 U/71 19125
7. EDDA v.d. WÖLPENWIESE 560 V/72 19898

1976 (Bestanden 14) (No separation of sexes in listing)

1. K.S. BUCK v.d. ERLENKLINGE 1665 U/71
2. K.S. BILL v.d. HERRENMUHLE 1958 V/72
3. K.S. DON v. STADUM-NORD 218 U/71
4. K.S. FANNY v. HEISTERHOLZ 2203 T/70
5. K.S. ARRAK v. ETZELBERG 555 V/72
6. BESSIE v. BOXBERG 1502 V/72
7. CENTA v.d. HERRENMÜHLE 1269 X/74

8. DROSSEL v. HOLDERSTRAUCH 461 W/73
9. ARTEMIS DONALD 965 V/72
10. DAGO ROTHENUFFEIN 445 V/72
11. ASTRID GREWELEHAU 1532 T/70
12. AMOR v. NONNENHOLZ 1650 U/71
13. GUNDA ROTHENUFFEIN 475 W/73
14. DRAUF v. PREGELUFER 281 4/73

1978 (Bestanden 22) (No separation of sexes in listing)

1. K.S. ALF v. HÜNENBRINK 1172 X/74
2. K.S. BIRKO v. LIEDBACHTAL 1720 U/71
3. K.S. BLÜCHER v. HEGE-HAUS. 285 Y/75
4. K.S. CONDOR v. EIDERMUHLE 1021 Y/75
5. K.S. FESTA vom PREGELUFER 282 Y/75
6. K.S. JUPP PÖTTMES 1843 W/73
7. K.S. XILLA vom OSTERBERG 2059 Y/75
   NOTE: This year's Kleeman drew a very large entry. 51 were entered. 46 actually competed. The above 7 secured their K.S. (Kurzhaar Sieger title) and 15 secured a pass.

1980
Dogs:

1. K.S. DON v.d. EIDERMÜHLE 330/77
2. K.S. DUX v.d. NIEDERELBE 487 Y/75
3. K.S. REMO ROTHENUFFEIN 1043 Y/75
4. K.S. BLITZ vom TEGHOF 228/77
5. K.S. FRÖULICH von der ROTEN SCHANZE 1395/77
6. K.S. ENGHOLMS BASKO 628/77
7. K.S. GROLL vom SUDSTRAND 683 Z/76
8. K.S. CENT vom HEGE HAUS 434 Y/75
9. K.S. AXEL SUDHFELD 1213 Z/76
10. K.S. ULK von der GUNGELSHÄUSER HEIDE 574/77

Bitches:

1. K.S. ENGHOLMS BLANCA 632/77
2. K.S. ILKA vom SONSFELDER MEER 1728/77
3. K.S. JAGA von der HANSABURG 1203 Z/76
4. K.S. MONA vom NORDHOF 206 Z/76
5. K.S. JENNY vom NORDHOF 1168 Y/75
6. K.S. ADDA vom NACHTIGALLENWALD 785/77
7. K.S. ANNE von HEIMERSHEIM 1629/77

4

The Early
American Scene

THE first German Shorthaired Pointer to be registered by the A.K.C. (1930) was imported Greif v.d. Fliegerhalde, wh. 1928. Actually, many specimens had reached the country before that time. FDSB already had many registrations on file, and old family-album snapshots survive to prove that quite a few hunting and pet dogs of earlier years that found their way here, unregistered, were German Shorthaired Pointers too.

There is no question, though, that the first true establishment of the breed was effected by Dr. Charles R. Thornton, then of Missoula, Montana. The time was 1925. Dr. Thornton, whose favored relaxation from medical cares was the harrying of upland game with his setters, had been accidentally attracted to the German breed by the chance reading of a magazine article featuring the Hohenbruck strain (*Zwinger Hohenbruck*) of Herr Edwardt Reindt, of Bruck-an-der-Leitha, Austria. These all-purpose dogs, thought the doctor, matched beautifully with his own father's teaching, remembered from his Ohio boyhood—a dog is worth keeping only for what it can DO. He passed the magazine article over to his wife

Senta v. Hohenbruck, FDSB 125225, wh. 1924 (imp. Austria), arrived in U.S. 1925, whelped the first German Shorthaired Pointer litter in this country. Senta was imported by Dr. Charles R. Thornton of Montana.

with the observation that if these dogs could be bought for anything reasonably less than the earth, he was going to import himself a few.

Hohenbruck, for all the years since then, has been to students of the breed here no more than a name. The elderly Herr Reindt, with whom Dr. Thornton did business, is long dead. The strain has passed from existence. Yet, in its long-enduring day, it was of considerable prominence in Austria. Through the interest of Dr. Otto Fischer, of present-day Austrian Klub Kurzhaar (Vienna), there has recently been furnished to us an old broadsheet of Herr Reindt's kennel advertising. This establishes the strain foundation date as 1894. It is bordered on both sides with pictures of Hohenbruck dogs, and filled with references from satisfied buyers. Topping the list of these references—and the only one written in English, the rest of course being in German—is that dated 1928 and signed "Charles R. Thornton. " In it, he praises the cleverness and sense of his imported Senta v. Hohenbruck.

This historic bitch, wh. 1924 (Rih v. Hohenbruck ex Susi v. Hohenbruck) came to Missoula in whelp. A male that should have come with her was killed by a car the day of shipment. Her litter was the first German Shorthaired Pointer litter known to have been

74

whelped in America. The timing was neat—July 4th, 1925, she produced it: *Siebenköpfigen* (seven-headed) as the German breeders count, by heads rather than noses. Six survived to be given the collective name of "Everyuse" by Dr. Thornton for his faith in their utility qualities in prospect. They were, otherwise, Frisky, Smarty, Pep, Queen, King and Bob—as well as all the colors there are: solid liver, ticked, clear white and liver.

It is unfortunate that breed students can get tangled up in respect to this historical bitch. Twenty years later, another Senta v. Hohenbruck, A-933184, wh. Oct. 1945, by Ch. Hans v. Waldwinkel ex Pointa v. Hohenbruck, was registered with the A.K.C. by a Wm. Connolly, of Iowa. The recurrence of the name has already confused some breeders who have found it in their pedigrees. Perhaps this will now make all clear. . . .

Dr. Thornton's interest in donating his records for the compilation of this new book enables a clear picture to be gained of his importations from 1925 on. The pedigrees, as preserved, also represent a mine of information concerning great German bloodlines of

This painting, treasured by Dr. Thornton, depicts his first two import studs, huge Treu v. Saxony and tidy John Neuforsthaus. Many oversize GSP can be traced to Treu. In Bitter Root Valley, Mont. *Photo: S. Bede Maxwell.*

the past. Even the merest scanning makes clear what quality came to Montana in those early years. It was the cream of German bloodlines, the produce of all-time historically acclaimed studs, mostly through bitches brought in whelp. Almost before he knew it, as the doctor now relates, he was involved out in Bitter Root Valley with a thousand-acre farm to grow the crops tilled by registered Belgian horses to feed the registered brown Swiss cows to make the milk to feed the pups to fill the pens and boost the strain that Charles built!

First, there was the trouble of getting a good stud. The first replacement for the one killed came here old and sterile. The next, Treu v. Saxony, was a beautiful-headed dog of eye-catching, light ticked color, a great-limbed one of distinction. But he weighed 90 pounds—in condition! Poster handsome as he was, with a dramatic style in the field, such a big dog could not please Dr. Thornton, who well understood the preference of American hunters for smaller dogs than this. He used Treu a few times only, waiting for another stud to come. Senta v. Hohenbruck produced a 1926 litter to Treu; two bitches from this crop up still, in Western breedings especially: Belle of Montana and Senta's Vonnie. Senta v. Hohenbruck's imp.-in-dam daughter, Queen of Everyuse, an almost-white dog herself, also had two Treu litters (1926-27), registered as "v. Grassthal" —of which Marie, Girl, Bell, Trinket and Schoenheit were retained as broods. Those are also quite easy to locate in pioneer pedigrees. Following the wide distribution of stock from Dr. Thornton's kennels, it is quite possible that many big, pictorially handsome, light-ticked, good-headed German Shorthaired Pointers of today reach back to big Treu.

Dissatisfaction with the size of Treu set the doctor later to weighing and measuring his entire kennel stock. Fortunately, he recorded these statistics at the time on each separate registration certificate. These have interest nowadays as they pinpoint so exactly the size of the pioneer imports from the great German kennels of the time, correcting a somewhat general present-day impression that all dogs of that period were monsters. All quoted here are either direct imports or first-generation get from imports.

| Artist v.d. Forst Brickwedde (imp.) | d. | 23¾ inches | 56 lbs. |
| Gero v. Buchwald (imp.) | d | 23½ " | 65 lbs. |

FRITZ V. BITTERWURZEL	d	23½	"	64 lbs.
WANDA V. OTTERSTEIN (imp.)	b	23½	"	54 lbs.
PEYDA V. WESERSTRAND (imp.-in-dam)	b.	23¼	"	55 lbs.
SEIGER'S LORE (imp.)	b	22½	"	55 lbs.
VOGELEIN V. BITTERWURZEL	b	22½	"	50 lbs.
KOENIGIN V. WESERSTRAND (imp.-in-dam)	b	22½	"	44 lbs.
BELLE OF MONTANA (by Treu)	b	22½	"	65 lbs.
SILVA V. WESERSTRAND (imp.)	b.	22¼	"	57 lbs.
KINDCHIN V. BITTERWURZEL	b	22	"	43 lbs.
PEGGY V. BITTERWURZEL	b	21¼	"	59 lbs.
NANCY V. HOHENBRUCK	b	21¼	"	59 lbs.
DIANA V. OTTERSTEIN (imp.)	b	21	"	48 lbs.
GRILLE V. WESERSTRAND (imp.-in-dam)	b	20¾	"	44 lbs.

Such statistics match interestingly with the average size of present-day German imports, apparently making the point that the size over there has remained quite constant over the past 30 years or more.

The replacement for Treu v. Saxony was the 1926-wh. John Neuforsthaus, 322 b, (Taps Harrachstal v.d. Bürgerweise, 1474 U, ex Helga v. Neuforsthaus, 508 Y). His sire line stemmed v.d. Maylust, his dam was deep in debt to Edelmann Giftig, via Edelman and Horst Giftig as well, half-brothers these ex Asta Giftig (Waldo Bilin Schönerlinde, 441 F, ex Thyra Altenau, 67 H). As for size, though John does not figure in the surviving measurements of the kennel, in a beautiful on-point painting in Dr. Thornton's present-day home, he backs Treu v. Saxony's spectacular find and is, in size relation, to the big fellow as a cruiser to an aircraft carrier!

John and Senta, who worked so well, who bred the good stock, who helped school all the pups, figured most vividly in the memories that brightened the heart of the fire many days for Dr. Thornton. Senta—who could beat a duck at its own game in iced-over river slush. John—who could do everything, even herd cattle, so that on one occasion, by baiting a vicious bull, he saved a yardman's life! John's son was another in the same pattern—Fritz v. Bitter-wurzel (by the way, Bitterwurzel was Dr. Thornton's German rendering of Bitter Root!). As "Little Fritz," the doctor recalls him: "Clever little Fritz," and the tales of his cleverness are endless. Look through your pedigrees; he can so easily be there.

Four pioneer stud dogs imported to Missoula, Montana by Dr. Charles Thornton. Their order has been mislaid, but Dr. Thornton identified them as Artist v.d. Brickwedde, Donn v. Sulfmeister, Cosak v.d. Radback and John Neuforsthaus. No other identifying authority exists.—Photo, *Dr. Charles Thornton*

Among the great-strain representatives that reached Montana between 1925-30, were Diana and Waldo v. Otterstein (Treff II v. Reulbach ex Cilly v. Zampital); Seiger's Lore (K.S. Tasso v. Winterhauch ex Seiger's Halli); Seiger's Holla II (Fuchsfelds Dolling ex Herta Winzler)—both these in whelp to Treff v. Waldhausen, the sire of R.S. & W.S. Heide v.d. Beeke. Sylva v. Weserstrand was another of this procession of in-whelp bitches (Hallo v. Weserstrand ex Kleinchen v. Hastedt), as was Senta v. Lob (Reck Konigsbrunn ex Tika v. Lob). Studs included Artist v.d. Forst Brickwedde (Treff Kalthoff ex Cora Ahlert); Arco v. Lillianberg (Prinz v. Schlosshof ex the Blitz Mülligen II daughter, Iris v. Dubro); Gero v. Buchswald (Blitz Mülligen II ex Carmen v. Buchswald); Donn v. Sulfmeister (K.S. Kobold Mauderode-Westerholt ex Hella v. Wilseder Berg); Cosak v.d. Radbach (K.S. Magnet v. Ockerbach ex the famed Siegerin, Hussa v.d. Radbach).

There are quite a few breed "experts" nowadays who affect the pose of shrugging away all mention of "Thornton breeding." It takes little probing to find such people seldom have the least notion of what "Thornton breeding" actually was. Such "experts" gloat happily over the exact same German great names where these chance to lurk behind any dogs *they* own.

In brief, "Thornton breeding" embraces half-brothers and sisters to Reichs-und-Welt Sieger Heide v.d. Beeke; a three-quarter brother to K.S. Bodo v.d. Radbach; the Prinz v. Schlosshof inheritance of cleverness and sharpness; the heavy leverage on the strains of Mars Altenau, Artus Sand, Edelmann Giftig. No one can shrug away breeding of that order, nor was it subsequently bettered by anything brought in elsewhere at later dates. What is, of course, as true as it is regrettable, is that in the then-prevailing state of the breed market, it was necessary to let the produce of these great German bloodlines go out to hunting men who so often had not the least idea what to do with it. Dr. Thornton preserved, and passed on to us here with unhappy comment, many photos that have reached him through the years—produce of dogs he has sold. Many are obvious crossbreds—half-Pointers, Setters, Springers, Retrievers, Coonhounds.

Where this imported blood was, however, valued at its worth and carefully bred from, grand results accrued. Most American strains of today owe their fair share to "Thornton breeding" if the generations are back-tracked far enough. And in our own day, one of the last of Dr. Thornton's direct breeding is that great matron, Ch. Yunga War Bride (5 chs. including 4 Duals) wh. 1951, from his own damline, long preserved. Dr. Clark Lemley, of Michigan, breeder and owner of the strongly-Thornton-influenced Dual and Nat'l Ch. Dandy Jim v. Feldstrom, says with truth: "We, now rightly to be called the Old Timers of the breed, know what we owe to Dr. Thornton's importing enterprise of those founding years."

Actually, it is hard for novices to recognize "Thornton breeding" in their extended pedigrees, for this kennel was never endowed with a distinctive name. Dogs carried all manner of endowment. However, where, in a far-taken pedigree, there occur American-whelped Hohenbruck, Waldhausen, Brickwedde, and Altenau especially, "Thornton breeding" is presumable. The operative words are "American-whelped." Famed German strain names are arbitrarily lifted all over in this country, and imports are seldom tagged as such.

An A.K.C. spokesman recently explained that when a dog is registered, the country from which it is imported is included on the face of the certificate. "If people don't choose to use this information later when showing their dogs or signing papers in connection with it, the matter is beyond our control," he added. Yet, and in all respect, it could be held that confusion of status as between import and homebred is as surely an error of particulars as a wrongly-stated date of whelping or a miscalculation of wins. That such errors as the latter are thoroughly subject to control is well understood by all who breed and/or exhibit dogs.

The pedigree services, in many ways very efficient, also tend to ignore the status of importation. Recently sighted was a pedigree, professionally-compiled, of a most prepotent, present-day stud. His fourth generation is 100 per cent German dogs. His third, with the exception of one son of imports, is all import. Yet, for all the serious-minded student could gain to the contrary from this handsome compilation, all his forebears could have been whelped in the lobby of the Empire State Building. This would matter less if, at the same time, there did not exist the local practice of appropriating famous German strain names. Herr Bleckman, of the famed v.d. Radbachs, is not the only German breeder who wonders what protection he could invoke against the wide, unauthorized filching here of his name property.

Importing and breeding from good dogs was not Dr. Thornton's only responsibility in those early years. He was also concerned with the necessary promotion and publicity. The matter of breed recognition, official sanction from the A.K.C., was another concern to occupy him quite seriously. That, of course, involved the matter of the name by which it was to be known. As the doctor recalls, the first intention of the A.K.C. was to recognize the breed as the "German Shorthair." He held out against this, taking the view that it should be known as "German Shorthaired *Pointer*," that the shorter name could mean just *any* shorthaired German dog.

One may look back now and wonder whether the adoption of the word "Pointer" was actually in the best interests of the breed—something that could not have been discerned in that earlier time. Historically, new breeds have not always benefited by being bracketed together with those longer-established in the like field. Shakespeare to the contrary, there is much in a name where dog breeds are concerned, chiefly because of the ready triggering of the association of ideas. Belgian Sheepdogs carelessly judged in many cases as German Shepherds is one instance. Brittany Spaniels, faulted by Springer or Cocker standards too often, is another.

The Germans, who commenced by knowing their breed as *"Deutsche Kurzhaarige Vorstehhund"* (literally, German Shorthaired Pointer), must have dropped the last word just as soon as they perceived the significance and dangers in association therewith. By 1938, Dr. Kleeman and Herr v. Otto had settled for the shortened version, entitling their famed breed monograph simply *"Deutsch Kurzhaar."* In their opening paragraph they analyze the names by which the breed is known throughout Europe—mostly in some form and translation of "German Braque." (French: *Braque Allemand.* Italian: *Bracco Tedesco.*) Officially, under the rules of the European Canine Governing Body, the F.C.I. (Federation Cynologique Internationale) it is also known as German Braque.

English "Dog World" explored the matter very thoroughly in 1958, (March 14 issue) when the newly-awakened interest in this breed began to be apparent in that country. The famed English sporting dog authority, Frank Warner Hill, started the ball rolling. He invoked the opinion of some Continental experts. The first quoted opinion came from Herr Waldemar Marr, a German sporting dog authority of note: "I see that the problem of what to call in England the so-called German Shorthaired Pointer is still not solved. I advise the English K.C. to call the breed the German Shorthaired Gundog. 'Vorstehhund' was the name of the breed about 35 years ago. Now, the title 'Vorstehhund' (Pointer) has been abandoned in Germany and they call the breed 'Kurzhaar.' I think the English could call the German breeds German Shorthaired Gundog, German Long-haired Gundog, and German Wirehaired Gundog." (WALDEMAR MARR, Berlin.)

The Italian sporting dog expert, Signor Zavaterro, also consulted on this occasion, made clear that he went along with the F.C.I. name-endowment of "German Braque," adding: "To call a breed a German Pointer when it is not a Pointer at all is indeed a grave error. The Shorthaired German Pointer (in Germany) is now called *Kurzhaar,* and the club the *Deutscher Kurzhaar Klub.* . . . As a practical shooting dog the Kurzhaar is an excellent worker . . . an excellent bird dog, very steady at point, a good backer, and with many other excellencies of a good gundog."

In "Dog World" of June 8, 1962, Frank Warner Hill again granted space for the airing of this discussion, adding as his opinion that "these great all-round gundogs are definitely not Pointers in the accepted sense of the term in this country. Their owners acknowledged this originally in applying to the Kennel Club for the name of 'Pointer-Retriever' for their breed. It was obvious that this trespass on a specialist breed could not be allowed to stand, and so as almost a last resource the name of German Shorthaired Pointer was adopted."

Referring to the careful re-classification the English Kennel Club has recently granted the breed, including its own special type of competition for Field Trials, Mr. Warner Hill makes plain the realistic approach of the English to the employment of the breed: "German Shorthaired Pointers by this or any other name (are) in the original strong, powerful dogs used for all types of hunting, and as this they can command a niche of their own in the Gundog world, but must be kept separate in appearance, work, and general characteristics." Adding that there might be a case made for finding a name along the same lines as those given the Vizsla, the Weimaraner, Mr. Hill adds: "You cannot call a dog a Pointer when this is only a third of his work, the other two-thirds being hunting and retrieving both in and out of cover. The original description of the breed, as an ideal, was one that would work in all conditions of weather and cover, would hunt, point, retrieve tenderly on land or in water, track wounded game, act as guard against poachers. To achieve these things, size and substance must be preserved— and don't try monkeying around with any English Pointer crosses. . . ."

Here, of course, one comes upon the bitter kernel of a hard nut for the cracking. In arbitrarily dubbing the breed a Pointer, there is issued to the unthinking, the ignorant, a strong incentive to "try monkeying around with English Pointer crosses." The English, with their long-time reputation as breeders of every kind of livestock from horses to canaries, know the pitfalls that can be dug. They have, themselves, formed in their time so many of the well-known dog breeds of the present age, as well as improved many others besides. They know very well that when a breed has been finally formed from radical basic crossing of diverse breeds, it is impossible, at a later stage, to re-introduce any of the "basics" without causing trouble. The "basic," as a matter of fact, has become wholly alien, and its reintroduction to the new breed is nothing short of cross-breeding again. The German Shorthaired Pointer, long since "fixed" as a separate breed, can no longer with safety re-absorb English Pointer crosses any more than it can absorb Schweisshund, or whatever form of scenting hound the 19th-century breeders borrowed from the German foresters.

This, then, is at least one of the dangers the English breeders of long experience discern in the name of the German breed as it is now recognized. For this reason, to take it outside the sphere of possible "monkeying," some of their wisest people are giving the matter great thought. They have even asked that the Americans also give consideration to helping them solve the problem. It will be interesting to see if, in the final analysis, anything comes of the intention to re-name the breed there, and whether, for goodness' sake, the English eventually range themselves with the Germans, and adopt the name the A.K.C. had here proposed in the first place, more than thirty years ago.

* * * * *

The second base for German Shorthaired Pointer breeding in America was also in the West, at Bennington, Nebraska. Here, in

1931, two hunting partners, Walter Mangold and Ernest Rojem, imported a dog and bitch. Both had had experience with the breed overseas. During World War I they had served on opposite sides, Rojem with the German army, Mangold with the American army. After the war, they met in Nebraska, the state running over with game—pheasant, prairie chicken, quail, grouse. Population pressure has now driven the game away, but just after the war the young men had great sport. Rojem's brother, Peter, living in Germany, was commissioned to find them a good pair of *Kurzhaar*. After long search he found in Schleswig-Holstein a six-months-old, Claus v. Schleswig-Konigsweg, wh. 1931, paying 80 marks for him. It took longer to find Jane v. grünen Adler, 341 l, and at two years old and trained she cost 180 marks. Claus was by Golo v. Gottorp, 754 c, ex Arna v. Altenberg, 606 h. Jane was by Horst Fürstermoor, 924 Y ex Toni v. grünen Adler, 661 U.

It took money, time, and some string-pulling to get them out of the country. Then, as now, the Germans tried to keep their best dogs in the country. Both were royally bred. Claus' sire, Golo v. Gottorp, was an Artus Sand son ex Karin Fürstermoor, 925 Y, she a Pack v.d. Bode daughter ex Ulme v.d. goldenen Mark, both stemming from Edelmann Giftig, the sire of Pack. Here, again, is an important basic pedigree subjected to compilation error. As Claus v. Schleswig-Konigsweg touches so many moderns, it is worth correcting. He was registered with FDSB, United K.C., A.K.C. Only the latter records his particulars correctly, and this compiler has sighted many pedigrees in which the error in the other two is carried along. His name (in these) is wrongly spelled, his sire's name is wrongly spelled, and he has been awarded an entirely different dam, recorded as Lena v. Schlenbarge. This must have been plucked from the air, as there is no bitch of that name in any part of his authentic German *Ahnentafel* (pedigree) here in our hands. The error is the more in need of correction in that Golo v. Gottorp, as an Artus Sand son, has merit. Misspelled, his name is a nothing. This strain name, by the way, still functions in Germany, registering dogs right into the late 1950's and beyond.

"Claus was a great dog for us," Walter Mangold writes. "It was tough getting the breed going, though—perhaps it was still a little close to war days in a small community. Dog judges showed prejudice, too. At one water trial, a judge looked at Claus standing beside me, asked: 'Can HE swim?' After several dogs failed to retrieve a dead duck in heavy waves, Claus swam out to a sandbar in the river, raised his head high for the scent, then swam directly to retrieve the duck. The crowd went wild with excitement when he was seen to catch the scent! He didn't waste time swimming circles, either, like some of the better-known water breeds did on the day. Funny—I didn't see anything of that judge later in the day, the one who asked me if Claus could swim. . . .

"He had the rugged constitution needed here, summers over a hundred, winters to thirty below, snow drifted to twelve feet and more quite often. We sent him through floating ice after duck. And he was a fireball on land, not even sand burrs stopped him. He was a gentle dog, too. As postmaster, I had him with me at the office. Children coming in for mail rode around on his back. But he was a good guard too, and no stray dogs ever bothered him twice. He got us lots of good dogs that were widely distributed, and lived to be very old. We buried him in what was native hay land east of here, but it's all built over now that we're the center of U.S.A."

In examination of pedigrees, and tracing beyond the conventionally-given four generations, this compiler is forever coming up with Claus v. Schleswig-Konigsweg—in such as the wonderful producer, Little Gretchen's Brownie, dam and grand-dam of National Field Trial champions; as Dual Ch. Wag-Ae's Snowflake, with her fine produce of bench and field champions, and dozens upon dozens more beside. Lance McGilbrey, of Columbia River, who purchased his first German Shorthaired Pointer from Walter Mangold while living in Nebraska, owes to old "Claus-can-HE-swim," and maybe *you,* Mr. Breeder, owe to him too. Go look to see. . . .

* * * * *

By 1932, the tide of importation flowed strongly into the mid-West. In St. Croix Falls, Wisconsin, a dedicated breeder sat nights over his homework, German field and show reports. This was Joseph Burkhart, one-time German gamekeeper. He made his choice on the basis of line-breeding to a fine-performed German bitch, Wandadora. Her son, by K.S. Benno v. Schlossgarten, her grand-daughter also by Benno, were partnered by a bitch by Benno's own sire, Bob v. Winterhauch, the Heidi Esterhof son. They were

Bob v. Schwarenberg, (K.S. Benno v. Schlossgarten ex Wandadora);
Arta v. Hohreusch (K.S. Benno v. Schlossgarten ex Afra v. Schwarenberg); Feldjager's Grisette (Bob v. Winterhauch ex Edith v. Karlbach, a Junker v. Bomlitztal daughter ex Wanda v. Karlbach).

Impact of the three on American breeding is beyond hope of
exact assessment. It is difficult to find strains from which they are
totally absent. Maybe only the modern Danish imports exclude
them to any degree, and this may not last indefinitely. There is
just too much Minnesota breeding around for it to be kept forever
out of a breeder's planning.

Joseph Burkhart not only chose well, he gained the confidence
of people who bought from him, he taught them how to line-breed,
saving what they had. A fully-extended pedigree of such as, say,
Joseph Burkhart's own personal dog for so many years, Ch. Thalbach Waldwinkel Mark, is a model of practical application of line-
breeding practice to prepotent basics. Mark's fourth generation
could be the most "family" compilation outside that of the Fletcher
Christians on Pitcairn Island! Joseph Burkhart's teaching was as
direct as it was brief. Breed *only* the best *to* the best, not merely
male to female.

In the dedication to continuity that such ownerships as this represent, the backbone strength of any breed is to be found.

Of the three imports, the palm must surely go to Arta v. Hohreusch. Feldjager's Grisette, much plainer looking, proved out her
bloodlines, but not to the extent that Arta did. Bob v. Schwarenberg died of heat stroke less than two years after his importation.
Fortunately, Arta, his half-sister, had whelped him two litters before
then. Dr. Berg, a good friend of Joseph Burkhart's, took the pick
bitch of the first litter, naming her Berg's Choice. Go on, look into
your pedigree—see if you can't find her easily. She was good. From
the second litter, the late Jack Shattuck picked a dog on the very
day that Bob v. Schwarenberg died. Jack Shattuck named his pup
Fritz v. Schwarenberg.

Too many of the litters, like those of Dr. Thornton, went to hunting men, many of whom didn't even bother to register their pur-
chases. Feldjager's Grisette justified herself with Bessie v. Winterhauch (by Ch. Fritz v. Schwarenberg), but it is surely Arta that
supports the entire strength of Minnesota breeding. After her
litter that included Ch. Fritz v. Schwarenberg (the balance was all

but wiped out by distemper, which in those days was not under control as it is now), she was sold to New York, where she had recently had imported for her a son of K.S. Frei Südwest, Hallo Mannheimia, from the breeding of Herr Carl Seidler, of Mannheim. It was a stipulation that Arta be bred to this dog, and that Joseph Burkhart have his choice of a pup. So he came to be possessed of Treu v. Waldwinkel. As the dam of Fritz and Treu, Arta's influence has to be conceded.

"And one old dog I have these days," Joseph Burkhart had written to then-novice breeder, Don Miner, of California, in 1947; "Eleven years old is this old dog now, and he has the record of being the sire of more champions than any living Shorthaired Pointer that we know of, though he himself was never entered in any show. . . ."

That was Treu v. Waldwinkel. . . .

"Treu v. Waldwinkel?" mused that other tower of breed knowledge, Hjalmer Olsen, of Georgia, the master of the Fieldborns. "How *very* much all we breeders owe to old Treu. . . ."

Before Treu though, remember, there had first to be Arta!

Treu v. Waldwinkel, whose record of prepotency has kept him with the top flight of studs in the U.S. (By Hallo Mannheimia, imp. Germany, ex Arta v. Hohreusch.)

Am/Can. Dual Ch. Arrak von Heisterholz (imp. Germany) was named Northwest Shooting Dog of the Year in 1963 and 1964. Owner: Ralph Park, Sr., Washington.

Am./Can. Field Ch. Lutz von dem Radbach (imp. Germany), (Xot von dem Radbach ex Fitz von dem Radbach). Breeder: Ernest Bleckman, Germany. Owner: T. L. Whitcomb, Washington. Lutz's life was very short, and the loss to breeders may be gauged by the circumstance that of his 15 champion get, four were Dual Champions! It represents a percentage that likely no other stud can match.

5

Progress in
American Breeding

BY 1938, breed strength was gathered mainly in the Minnesota-Wisconsin areas with a lap-over into Michigan. This permitted making application to the A.K.C. for Parent Club status. First officers were Jack Shattuck, Jr., D. R. Lugar, J. MacGaheran, Beckwith Mayer, Joseph Burkhart, Henry Radle, H. J. Loring, H. B. Klein, G. Noltimier. Their first problem concerned a name for the club. The A.K.C. rejected the first proposal—The German Shorthaired Pointer and Retriever Club of America, Inc., exactly as the English K.C. was later to reject the same proposal from breeders in that country. Official view would seem to be that as pigs is pigs, so Pointers is Pointers. They cannot be Retrievers too. The plain fact, of course, is that they *are* Retrievers too.

Looking back, one wonders why the superb retrieving abilities of the breed have never gained official recognition here; why no opportunity exists for a German Shorthaired Pointer to prove himself competitively at retrieving skills and win points for it. At least, if the English K.C. denied the use of the double-barreled name, they have provided the means for exercising the ability. It may well be that the early-day insistence on recognition as a Pointer clouded the issue as to utility abilities. It may also be that at that time many people, newly-recruited to ownership of the German breed here, ill understood those potentialities that the ordinary hunting man had so quickly discovered. A contributing factor to misunderstanding of the breed aims may also have been the sad circumstance—still prevailing—that no one has ever provided German Shorthaired Pointer owners with training manuals fitted to the performance of their breed. The novice who wants to train his dog has to buy the books catering to Pointer/Setter performance and, inevitably, and unfortunately, as he reads, so he tailors his views as to what his dog should do. Lastly, many recruits to German Shorthaired Pointers came directly from Pointer/Setter activities. They brought with them their own measure of a Field Trial dog— a Bird Dog. They had known no other, and rather than change their viewpoint and training practices, they set out to change, to the best of their ability, the dog. People with such views were not likely to besiege the A.K.C. to provide a type of competition suited to the particular skills of the breed into which they had now insinuated themselves. Their ideal measure of performance remained as it had always been, and many of them worked hard to thrust it upon their associates in competitive activity.

The Parent Club application for a Charter, then, was eventually granted to The German Shorthaired Pointer Club of America, Inc. First responsibility was that imposed by Article IV (Sec. 5) of the Constitution and By-Laws of the A.K.C., ". . . that it was the duty and privilege of each Parent Member Specialty Club to define the true type of the breed of purebred dogs which it was organized to promote and improve." That meant a Standard to be compiled. Adapted from the German, with slight variation, it was officially approved in May, 1946. It has not since then suffered any revision, as have so many other Standards, especially over the past ten years. Yet the Parent Club, in its beginning, had recognized that such a revision could become necessary. The Amended Articles (1945) hold, as an added objective, "the need to improve the definition of the Standard for the true type of German Shorthaired Pointers from time to time, and to establish uniform methods of judging, either at Field Trials and/or Bench Shows."

As it is no secret that many Regional Club members would like to see the Standard gone over, it would seem that the Amended Articles of 1945 provide the basis for firm demand along such lines.

The Parent Club was first with Field Trial competition for the breed, promoting this first at Anoka, Minnesota, then at Ft. Snelling, also in Minnesota. So it presently became possible for German Shorthaired Pointers to work towards their Field Trial titles and the coveted Dual title, Field and Bench. As more and more Regional Clubs were formed across the nation, additional venues were provided.

The first A.K.C show championships (1936) were gained by Becky v. Hohenbruck (Trill v. Hohenbruck ex Lotte v. Hoellenthor) and Baron v.d. Brickwedde (Artist v.d. Brickwedde, imp., ex Dixie Queen Buchwald), Thornton-breds. First to make true gallery impact, though, was Ch. Fritz v. Schwarenberg (Bob v. Schwarenberg, imp., ex Arta v. Hohreusch, imp.). Championship honors never fell to old Treu v. Waldwinkel. His day was before that of Field Trials for his breed; and youthful curiosity in respect to the workings of a wolf trap disqualified him for show.

Ch. Fritz was widely campaigned, publicizing his breed in all ways his owner, Jack Shattuck, Jr., of Minneapolis, could contrive. Morris & Essex and Westminster are among his B.O.Bs, and he took four years in a row at Chicago International, including the first Breed Specialty held there. He is still a medium of breed publicity, by the way, posing for German Shorthaired Pointer conformation in the A.K.C. *Book of Standards* (Plate 2). His life was useful and long, Jack Shattuck reporting him still in great heart at age eleven, still a tireless hunter, with more than 3000 pheasants shot over him. He founded the long-enduring v. Schwarenberg strain here, and sired the first bitch of the breed to get her Dual (1949) in Dr. Zahalka's Schatz v. Schwarenberg (ex Helga v. Schwarenberg).

Contemporary with Ch. Fritz was another fine breed publicist in Ch. Sportsman's Dream, bred by Rudolph Hirschnitz, then of Wyoming, and owned by V. E. Lantow, of Denver, Colorado. Ch. Sportsman's Dream gained at least one honor that eluded Ch. Fritz—an all-breed B.I.S. It was the first for the breed, and taken at San Diego, California, in 1940. The judge, Col. E. E. Ferguson, recalled him as "a most exceptional dog of his time, so much so that if he were showing now he would compare well with our top winners in the breed. Coincidently, my B.I.S. at a 1960 show was later reported to me as a Sportsman's Dream grandson (Ch. Huntsman's Drumfire) proving that the dog of twenty years ago was not only good in himself but able to influence his breed."

Ch. Sportsman's Dream was sired by the Hirschnitz import, Astor v. Fischtal, 1736 k (Flott Teutoberg gen Ingo, 322 g ex Erna Teutoberg, 297 k), ex the American bred Sieglinde v. Meihsen, a granddaughter of Cosak v.d. Radbach, imp. Importing as early as the mid-1930's, Rudolph Hirschnitz also qualified as a breed pioneer. His experience was drawn upon during the earliest institution of field trials in California, in which he took interest to the end of his life. Sharing his German correspondence solved for me many problems of compilation, placing me deeply in debt for historical matter from his files and for advice as to where more might hopefully be sought.

Jack Shattuck's next star was to become a legend: the solid liver dog, Rusty v. Schwarenberg (Mars v. Ammertal, imp. ex Vicki v. Schwarenberg). As the first Field Trial Champion, the first Dual in his breed (1947), Rusty stemmed dam-side from the Burkhart imports, Arta v. Hohreusch and Feldjager's Grisette, his grand-dams. His sire, Mars v. Ammertal, also solid liver, was said to be a very good worker, an efficient cold-trailer, a little dour of temperament. As a phenomenal dog of any time, Rusty's record includes two Westminster B.O.Bs, three Breed Specialties, and an ability to switch from Field to Show and back again. The day after winning the 1944 Breed Specialty, he went out to win a First in an Open All Age Stake in the field. Competing often against Pointers and Setters, worked from a horse, his useful performances on such occasions did much to break down Pointer-men's prejudices against his breed; not that he was ever one to hug the horizon—merely that he gave useful performances practical men could evaluate.

Jack Shattuck, Jr., deserves to have his memory perpetuated by the breeders here. Not only did he campaign good dogs widely to advertise the breed, but he gave a great deal of time and energy to publicity work as well, though his health condition made exertion difficult for him. He was still young when serious disability overtook him. "A broken hip won't heal right," he wrote Don Miner, of California. "Now I can hardly walk . . ." In those final years of pain he had Dual Ch. Rusty with whom he could re-live old triumphs, the dog pre-deceasing him by only a few weeks in 1952.

It ought to be possible to give consideration to the possibility of perpetuating the memory of the outstanding breed pioneers in the same way as the Germans have done. They name their proudest competitions for those to whom the breeders are indebted, such as Prince zu Solms-Brauenfels and Dr. Kleeman. Obvious nominations in this country for such honorable recognition would certainly include Dr. Thornton, Joseph Burkhart and Jack Shattuck, Jr. It is not a right thing that the names of good men be allowed to slip away from knowledge of the breeders and owners of the future.

It is not possible to list by name all the Minnesota-Wisconsin breeders of the period. Many founded strong strains with good dogs. Among such count the late Dr. E. W. Berg, Henry Radle, Dr. and Mrs. H. Zahalka, Fr. Gerald Baskfield, the late W. A. Olsen, Hjalmer Olsen, and Joseph and Magdalina Deiss, all making the wisest use of the good breeding material Joseph Burkhart put into their hands. Their breeding activities formed an intricate mesh from the original imports and their descendants, harping heavily on the thread of Treu v. Waldwinkel.

Thus the Zahalkas followed up their Dual Ch. Schatz v. Schwarenberg with the handsome Ch. Searching Wind Bob (Treu v. Waldwinkel ex Maida v. Thalbach, his granddaughter). Bob, in turn, sired Searching Wind Topper (ex Fieldborn Katzie Karlbach) with whom his breeder-trainer, Hjalmer Olsen, completed the Dual in 1951. From Ch. Searching Wind Cita (Treu v. Waldwinkel ex Dual Ch. Schatz) came six champions, three sired by her half-brother, Ch. Searching Wind Bob, and three by Heinrich v. Karlswald (Treu v. Waldwinkel ex Senta v. Karlbach). All within the mesh pattern. . . .

With far fewer stud opportunities than fell to better-publicized dogs of his time, Treu v. Waldwinkel's record of champions sired, plus the produce of his prepotent daughters and granddaughters, must be viewed with respect. Of Treu's female descendants, Fr. Baskfield's Maida v. Thalbach (Ozzie v. Schwarenberg ex Bibi Winterhauch, she a Treu daughter ex Bessie v. Winterhauch) is also a standout. In addition to Ch. Searching Wind Bob, she produced Ch. Thalbach Waldwinkel Hans to Treu, this one becoming the base of the late W. A. Olsen's strain, the Waldwinkel taken proudly from old Treu. Ch. Thalbach Waldwinkel Heide (by Tell v. Thalbach) was a Maida one that did well for D. K. Johnson, and

Ch. Thalbach Waldwinkel Mark was Maida's son by Ch. Glanz v. Winterhauch (Treu v. Waldwinkel ex Bessie v. Winterhauch). Mark, who made a good winning record, lived on to an extreme old age with Joseph Burkhart, and it was a sad letter that reached us here, while this book was being compiled, telling that Mark, last direct link with the pioneer imports, was dying of leukemia in his thirteenth year.

Bessie v. Winterhauch, a singleton effort of Feldjager's Grisette to her mating with Ch. Fritz v. Schwarenberg, was owned by a close friend of Joseph Burkhart's, Henry Radle, who mated her to old Treu (who but!) to produce the future champion, Fritz v. Schlossgarten. With Fritz, Hjalmer Olsen got under way with this breed, winning the first Field Trial, he notes, promoted for German Shorthaired Pointers, held at Solon Springs, Wisconsin, April, 1940.

No one associated with German Shorthaired Pointers has won more lasting respect, from a wider cross-section of fanciers, than has Hjalmer Olsen, now of Cordele, Georgia, growing no younger, for sure, but still vitally interested in the progress of the breed—still able to rap the knuckles of the lunatic fringe when he deems their activities not in the best interests of German Shorthaired Pointers en masse. Frankly, and in print (*Dog World,* May, 1958), Hjalmer Olsen tells us that his true love is the English Pointer, doubtless the breed on which his first enthusiasms were built. However, he makes it abundantly clear that Pointers is Pointers and German Shorthaired Pointers are something else again, understanding the breed to which he has devoted so many practical-minded years as a breeder, importer, judge.

With the name of Hjalmer Olsen, too, is earliest associated that of a Thornton-bred he acquired as a pup, handled to within a few points of its title, and sold then to William Ehrler, of Michigan. This was Timm v. Altenau, who never actually finished, but who holds a place in breed history through having sired fifteen champions—for many years the record till Austrian import, Field Ch. Greif v. Hundsheimerkogel came to say move over, please! Timm was by the K.S. Kobold Mauderode-Westerholt son, Donn v. Sulfmeister, imp. His dam was also Thornton-bred, Dreizenheim v. Brickwedde (Artist v.d. Forst Brickwedde, imp. ex Seiger's Lore, imp.). Timm v. Altenau produced six of his champions from Distel v. Rheinberg (Tell v. Schoenwalde ex Wanda Gale Altmark); four from Distel's older sister, Dixie v. Rheinberg; three ex Tillie v. Rheinberg, his daughter ex Distel. There was another ex Distel's dam, Wanda Gale Altmark. The only champion outside the family pattern was Hjalmer Olsen's own Ch. Loal's Dot, ex Zest v. Horstig.

Wanda Gale Altmark, supporting the edifice on the female side of this fantastic production, was a granddaughter of the Thornton import, John Neuforsthaus, ex Marie v. Grasstal, already in these pages mentioned as a daughter of that big handsome Treu v. Saxony —remember? Wanda also has influence through her non-champion son by Timm v. Altenau—Duke v. Rheinberg. He sired future Dual Ch. Valbo v. Schlesburg, owned by Carl Schnell of Fraser, Michigan, long-time still active breeder there. Valbo's striking good looks may have owed something to big boy Treu, but here we consider him rather for winning the first A.K.C. Field Trial Championship in Michigan in 22 exciting days, at fifteen months of age. He was also the first Field Ch. handled by Russell Dixon! Dual Ch. Valbo v. Schlesburg's pedigree is an interesting one to reproduce here, presenting, as it does, most of the Montana and Nebraska imports we have discussed. This, of course, was still the time when so many owners strained after dogs that worked as well as they looked, that looked as well as they worked.

Those who have come with us so far through these pages will readily identify all the imports, while noting that none are indicated in any way as such. This could be usage, but one hesitates to describe it as good usage.

Carl Schnell had success also with his Ehrler-breds from Timm v. Altenau, finishing four: Bella and Hilda v. Rheinberg, Sweet Tillie Too, and Rita v. Altenau. Rita made 1948 a bonanza year, many B.O.B., Group placings, and the breed Specialty best under Jack Shattuck, Jr. Ch. Alsedda (Timm v. Altenau ex Tillie v. Rheinberg) gave Dr. Clark Lemley, of Detroit, his early successes.

Here, too, bowed in Del Glodowski, of Sturtevant, Wisconsin. His Baron v. Strauss, a Dual Ch. of 1953, also stems from the pioneer imports, his sire vintage Burkhart, his dam line chock-full of Thornton, being anchored on Sieglinde v. Meihsen, the dam of Ch. Sportsman's Dream. Sieglinde was by Monte v. Kissell, a son of the Thornton imp.-in-dam, Kamerad v. Waldhausen, by Treff v. Waldhausen (Germany) ex his half-sister, Weisse v. Brickwedde (Artist v.d. Forst Brickwedde ex Seiger's Lore, both imports). Sieglinde's dam, Judy v. Burg, was by Cosak v.d. Radbach, imp., ex Nancy v. Hohenbruck (ex Senta v. Lob, imp.). That Sieglinde is a combination of the forces producing the great German dogs, K.S. Bodo v.d. Radbach and R.S. Heide v.d. Beeke, makes sense of the excellence of her descendants and something else again of the dictum of those who, on the basis of no knowledge at all, elect themselves to dispose contemptuously of "Thornton breeding."

This brief analysis should interest Colorado folk who owe to Ch. Sportsman's Dream and also currently to that dog's grandson, Dual Ch. Baron Turn and Taxis, owned by Mr. W. Barth. Also, it concerns all with descendants of Dual Ch. Baron v. Strauss, among which count his sons, Ch. Otto v. Strauss, Field Ch. Spiker and Mort v. Strauss. In the next generation is Dual Ch. Strauss' Working Boy (by Otto) and the National (A.K.C.) Field Ch. of 1960, Field Ch. Duke Strauss III (by Spiker), plus the bonus that Field Ch. Fritz v. Strauss also represents.

Burkhart basics built up the Oak-Crests of Joseph and Magdalina Deiss, of Minnesota. Joseph had worked with German Shorthaired Pointers in his native Germany, and was not long without one here, finding his first really good one in a litter sister to Dual Ch. Rusty v. Schwarenberg. This was Ch. Cora. Mated to Fr. Baskfield's Ch. Glanz v. Winterhauch, she rewarded them with Ch. Cora's Penny of Oak-Crest. Liking her, they presently sent Glanz another Arta v. Hohreusch granddaughter (as Cora had been) in Chimes Girl (Mars v. Ammertal, imp. ex Berg's Choice). This was sound linebreeding. It produced their Ch. Oak-Crest's Rick v. Winterhauch, who put to such good use his heritage, which is Arta-plus-Arta-plus Arta, that he is now honored with ten American champion get, including three Duals and that resplendent B.I.S.-winning bitch, Ch. Oak-Crest's Cora v. Winterhauch.

The pedigree of Ch. Oak-Crest's Rick is worth reproducing in full. By that old proverb holding that an ounce of seeing is worth a ton of hearing, it is an outstanding example of how the Minnesota breedings were carefully contrived, a lesson to the followers of the haphazard, and shows at a glance most of the dogs discussed in these pages.

Mrs. Deiss tells a grand yarn of their involvement with the breed. "We always had *two* German Shorthaired Pointers, even when we lived in the city," she reminisces. "To 'keep a few more,' as one says,

```
                                                    ┌ Frei Sudwest -
                                  ┌ Hallo Mannheimia, 924,177
                                  │                 └ Cita Mannheimia -
               ┌ Treu v Waldwinkel, A-230,208
               │   Sire of 10 Champions
               │                  ┌ Benno v Schlossgarten -
               │                  │
               └ Arta v Hohreusch, 894,328
               │   Dam of 1 Champion
               │                  └ Afra v Schwarenberg -
  ┌ Ch. Glanz v Winterhauch, A-494,473
  │   Sire of 3 Champions
  │                               ┌ Bob v Schwarenberg, 885,741
  │                               │   Sire of 1 Champion
  │            ┌ Ch. Fritz Schwarenberg, A-173,976
  │            │   Sire of 7 Champions
  │            │                  └ Arta v Hohreusch, 894,328
  │            │                      Dam of 1 Champion
  └ Bessie v Winterhauch, A-279,248
  │   Dam of 2 Champions
  │                               ┌ Bob v Winterhauch -
  │                               │
  └ Feldjagers Grisette, 894,329
      Dam of 2 Champions
                                  └ Edith v Karlbach -
```

Ch. Oak-Crest's Rick v Winterhauch,
German Shorthaired Pointer (male)
Sire of 11 Champions   S-224,872

```
                                  ┌ Ajax Frankfurt (Main) -
               ┌ Heros v Ammertal -
               │                  └ Hansa v Schertelspitz -
  ┌ Mars v Ammertal, A-413,778
  │   Sire of 6 Champions
  │                               ┌ Hasso v d Schwarzwaldecke -
  └ Asta v d Rohrhalde -
                                  └ Ella v Ammertal -

Chimes Girl, A-676,166
  Dam of 1 Champion
                                  ┌ Benno v Schlossgarten -
               ┌ Bob v Schwarenberg, 885,741
               │   Sire of 1 Champion
               │                  └ Wandadora -
  └ Berg's Choice, A-259,273
      Dam of 1 Champion
                                  ┌ Benno v Schlossgarten -
               └ Arta v Hohreusch, 894,328
                   Dam of 1 Champion
                                  └ Afra v Schwarenberg -
```

we moved out onto seven acres. Before long we had *seventeen* German Shorthaired Pointers and had to make a choice which would quit eating, the dogs or the family. So, to ease the strain, we took a few boarders. Soon we had seventy dogs to take care of, plus our own breeding stock, plus the twenty-thirty puppies always in my care. By 1959 this was getting to be rather much. We sold the kennels and now we are where we started, we have *two* German Shorthaired Pointers." It is not by any means an unusual history of dog involvement.

The pride of Oak-Crest's earlier days was at one time Ch. Schatz v. Konigsheim, Ch. Cora's son by Ch. Fritz v. Schwarenberg. Sold as a pup, he was donated by his owners to the K9 Corps in World War II. His litter mate was killed on Saipan but Schatz came home, was de-trained for civilian life and restored to his owners. Maybe the de-training didn't take. There were incidents. He was returned to Mr. Deiss in hope something could be done with him. It took a year of patient training to make Schatz trustworthy again. Then, being six years old, he went to his first show, finishing smartly with three five-point majors. Thereafter, as Mr. Deiss' most dependable hunting and tracking dog, he lived out the useful life of a worker into his twelfth year.

This period also saw the first German import to gain an American championship in Alfred Sause's Ch. Dallo v.d. Forst Brickwedde, a Westminster and M.&E. Best of Breed. His sire, Artus v. Hasetal (Furst v. Fuchspass ex Cora v.d. Brickwedde, an Artus Sand grand-daughter) was also the grandsire, through his daughter, Gerda v.d. Forst Brickwedde, of Berta Spiessinger v. Pfaffenhofen/Ilm, dam of the top American producing sire, Field Ch. Greif v. Hundsheimer-kogel. Dallo's dam was a daughter of that fireball, K.D. Don v.d. Schwarzen Kuhle, who played such a big part in the foundation of the Seydels and Blitzdorfer strains in Germany.

Dallo was killed in a hunting accident, but his owner, Alfred Sause, has been connected with other good dogs, including Pheasant Lane champions Schnapps and Tomahawk. Dallo's direct breed influence is perhaps most usefully through his daughter, Ch. Katinka of Sycamore Brook, C.D. who, in the ownership of the Johns broth-ers, of Benton, Pennsylvania, produced two Dual Champions, Val-kyrie and Junker v. Grabenbruch, the home-owned Valkyrie finishing in 1952 and Junker, owned by Mr. J. Lurba, in 1955. Both are by

Field Ch. Kaposia's Chief of Oak Crest, pictured on his 13th birthday in 1965. This fine old personality dog was representative of the solid early-day type of solid livers within this breed, and faithfully passed along his inheritance. Breeders: J. and M. Deiss, Minnesota. Owners: Don and Betty Sandberg.

Ch. Oak-Crest Cora v. Winterhauch, the first bitch in the breed to take a BIS (1956). In addition to compiling a phenomenal show record, she is the dam of six champions.

Johns' Dual Ch. Blick v. Grabenbruch, who finished, in 1951, the first German Shorthaired Pointer Dual on the East Coast. His parents were the imports, K.S. Sepp v. Grabenbruch and Nanny v. Lückseck.

Sepp was the first German Sieger brought here, coming at the end of the war from the kennels of that breeding genius, Peter Kraft, of Hof Grabenbruch, Rhine-Hessen. It has always been hard to get good dogs out of Germany, and the Grabenbrucher's, like all kennels after the war, was down in numbers. It took Richard Johns a year of coaxing to get Sepp for America. Johns had noted that the vast flat fields, the partridge and pheasant country of Sepp's birth, were suited to the production of a wider-going, faster type of dog, and felt that Sepp, with speed, nose, and intensity on point, had something American strains could use. History would seem to support this very reasonable assumption.

It is one of the paradoxes of dog registration, from country to country, that Johns had trouble persuading the A.K.C. that this German Sieger from the famous kennel was registerable. As the matter stands, Sepp is FDSB, but not A.K.C., registered. However, his descendants, including his Dual champion grand-get, are all A.K.C. registered, achieving this through their sire, Dual Ch. Blick v. Grabenbruch, who was rendered acceptable on the basis of points won in competition. This brief explanation may help those whose

Timm v. Altenau (Donn v. Sulfmeister, Ger. imp. ex Dreizenheim v. Brickwedde). More than a score years after his death, this Thornton-bred still exercises influence. Breeder: Dr. Charles R. Thornton. Owner: Wm. Ehler, Mich.—*Photo, Hjalmer Olsen (lent by Mrs. C. Carlson.)*

research on Grabenbruch dogs here carries them back to the A.K.C. intimation that they have no record of K.S. Sepp.

Sepp's breeding, therefore, should be placed here on record for the sake of reference, apart from its worth. His sire, Reichs-Sieger Odin v. Weinbach, is a son of R.S. & W.S. Heide v.d. Beeke ex Mauki v. Schlossgarten, she a granddaughter of K.S. Bill v. Hirschfeld (solid liver) and Argus v.d. Weihermuhle, a well-known and well-performed son of Artus Sand. Sepp's dam, Leda v. Grabenbruch is ex a K.S. Benno v. Schlossgarten daughter, her sire a K.S. Frei Südwest son ex Asta v. Angetal (by Treu Südwest ex Jutta Mannheimia).

Sepp was small, and contemporary reports do not particularly praise his good looks, but he was full of terrific drive and burning desire to find game. He has been described as "a hunting demon." It was unfortunate that a virus carried him off so early, but his qualities were obviously preserved for the future in his son, Dual Ch. Blick v. Grabenbruch, with his get including three Duals.

Blick lived the long life of the best German Shorthaired Pointers, long his owner's grouse and woodcock dog. His daughter, Dual Ch. Valkyrie v. Grabenbruch, a Dual at two-and-a-half, was also a good winner on the bench, including a M.&E. and the Eastern breed Specialty. In Gundog competition against Setters and Pointers at the famed Jockey Hollow Club, Valkyrie shone in 1954-5 and also topped similar competition in the first "shoot to kill" stake in Delaware.

Developed entirely on grouse, few dogs ever attained to better knowledge of this wily quarry, her owner, Dick Johns, reports. Mated to Ch. Tell v. Grabenbruch (by Int. Ch. Franco Beckum imp. ex Adda v. Assegrund, imp.) she produced Kenwick's Diana Beckum, dam of the 1957 Nat'l Field Trial Ch., Field Ch Bobo Grabenbruch Beckum, owned by Dr. Wm. Schimmel of California. To bring the story a generation further, Bobo's get now includes the winner of the 1961 A.K.C. National, Field Ch. Von Saalfield's Kash, owned by Walter Seagraves, of California, and many other distinguished get, welcoming his first Dual champion in 1964, the elegant Bee's Gabby v. Beckum, owned by D. Briggs of California and handled by veteran trainer, J. Huizenga. Gabby's dam line brings in further strength in a strong background of the famous "Dixon" strain from Michigan.

Field Ch. GREIF V. HUNDSHEIMERKOGEL (imp. Austria)
Amazingly versatile, this great stud of modern times died in 1958.
He is shown here with his trainer, Stanley Head of California.

6

German Shorthairs
Out of the West

M IDWEST Shorthairs certainly made first mark in
organized competition, though the Far-Westerners lagged not so
very far behind. Original Thornton imports, however, went wholly
into the hands of Northwestern hunters, making their way down
eventually to California as their reputation carried. There was min-
imal interest in showing, and Field Trials were not yet in being.
The post-war years, with the re-contouring of the rice fields, especially, with the new machinery the Seabees had brought back
home, saw greatly increased use of the breed and expansion of
numbers. "Strong dogs," recalled the late Geoff Zander, one of the
pioneer California users, "able to work to their chests in water—
undoubtedly the pattern then favored by the Germans in their
homeland. It was an entirely different ball game those years—
upland game very thin on the ground, pheasants by no means then
properly acclimatized, so we hunted for the most part on duck.
Did the Shorthairs suffer with their short coats, sitting in the blinds?
Never had reason to think they did—the Germans made a lot of
talk about having bred water-resistant jacketings, saying seals don't
have fringes either. But we did try not to keep them sitting too
long wet and cold."

Bearing worse than wet and cold on the smooth-jacketeds was the work in rice stubble, sharp as glass, dogs coming in with faces swept bare of hair; bitches with severely chafed teats—and the man neglecting to pitch-pine his dog's feet before the start didn't have it working for him very long. But there were also owners, as Geoff Zander pointed out, that appreciated no burrs to pick at day's end.

There was some scattered comment about these being German—enemy-breds, the war still so close, but names were just names and what the hunters' dogs were called was seldom in tune with the jawbreaker names on the papers—of those that had papers! Interest in pedigree came later, the time when competition took hold in showing—the day of Johann v. Schwarenberg, Brown Ace, Little Gretchen's Brownie and that pride of Ted Werner's Iron v. Schwarenberg—all early before the show-going public, gaining at least breed recognition in the rings. Previous editions of this work have named so many—good dogs beyond any doubt, bred it is to be remembered from parent stock drawn from Germany in those pre-war years that in that country are still regarded—poignantly!—as the apex years of the breed. No space here to re-tell . . .

Thrust in easterly direction, crossing the Rockies, came later. Then there was Ch. Flash v. Windhausen, of Utah, owned by the Carl Nussbaums, going to New York and taking breed and a group placing at Westminster! Ch. Alnor's Brown Mike, carried to New York by an airline pilot and his family, was another from the West to make a name in Eastern shows. Meanwhile . . . well, back west, the far north side of the Columbia River, a little town, there was a big man, Lance McGilbrey, breeding big handsome Shorthairs and taking them to shows, produce down from his pheasant dog, Tillie. When he realized he had a strain, he named it after the river, and the credit he insisted on giving to Tillie, despite the clear observation that the young-'uns all looked like their sire, Ch. Pheasant Lane's Stormalong, whopping big tick-patch son of a dog with reputation already made, Ch. Davy's Jim Dandy.

Tillie—Columbia River Tillie!—not size, not jacketing her contribution, but prepotency! She was sixteen years old when this compiler took her photo—Nebraska-bred from Claus-v. Schlesweg-Konigsweg, making her strong contribution to Jim Dandy's stemming from a grandson of imported Donn v. Sulfmeister the K.S. Mauderode—Westerholt son. Nor was Stormalong the only prepotent at benefit from Jim Dandy's background—count also Dual

& Nat. Field Trial Ch. Dandy Jim v. Feldstrom, owned by Dr. Clark Lemley of Michigan, a notable breed supporter in both local and national sense. His top dog, the Dual/National winner, siring four Duals, has carry-on impact into present times, his most notable mate Am/Can. Ch. Susanna Mein Liebchen, owned by Maxine Collins, also of Michigan.

So much one would wish to cram into space that isn't there! However, not to neglect the crystal-ball pronouncement of a Midwesterner of the period that "there have never been good dogs come out of the West and, what's more, there never will be!" To pick up which gauntlet came H.V. Garrard's California-bred, Duchess of High-Hasit, to the historic Fort Snelling Trial Grounds to carry off the Limited Stake in the new-formed Parent Club's first Field Trial! And came Little Gretchen's Brownie to qualify for the honors at the Amateur Pheasant Club of America date before taking herself home to California to whelp 1957 GSPCA National FT Champion in Traude v. Wengenstadt. It was also the time when the far West welcomed its first Dual—Riga of Hohen Tann, of Washington, she ex a German import, Bella of Hohen Tann mated to another sprig of Pheasant Lane, Ch. Bill's Linzer Boy.

So many of the pioneer breeders of the Far West are gone, but also, happily many remain, notably Mr. Jake Huizenga, of Salinas (Oxton); Mrs. Mildred Combs (now Revell) of Cotati (Weidenbach); Miss Irene Pauly, of Sonoma (Erdenreich), all with three decades-plus in the interest. Mrs. Revell reached top point of pride with her Ch. Weidenbach Bridget in the early '70s, fighting those good battles with Ch. Gretchenhof Columbia River and winning her share. Goodness, only the other day, another good young Weidenbach bitch took her final points under this compiler at Reno, name of Annaliese.

Miss Pauly's connection with the breed has been productive not only in terms of breeding activities and competitive engagements, but in hard work to further the establishment of the Parent Club, plus becoming organizer and custodian for years of the on-going Championship File which is one of the Parent Club's most valuable offshoot possessions. In more recent years, the File has been under the care of Carolyn Muterspaw, also of California, she handing over in 1981 to a new-formed Parent Club Committee. Considering the circumstance that in all national dog clubs, committees are formed of members scattered geographically and subject to continual change, one recalls uneasily the hope that this item—which is by now of very considerable bulk as well as value—is blessed with the boon one wishes also every dog whelped—a Good Home.

Central California, in short space of years, brought into being some very strong strains, mostly in the hands of hunting devotees that over years moved into Field Trial interest when this became established. Count among such the E.E. Hardens, of Salinas, and Jake Huizenga and wife Sally with their "Oxtons," Don and Shirley Miner with the "Von Thalbergs," all of which have had wide influence, both in the supportive and the practical aspects of the sport and which, as a body, had most to do with the preservation of the heritage of Field Ch. Greif v. Hundsheimerkogel.

A backyard dog—first of his get to make impact was Bob Holcomb's Field Ch. Yunga v. Hundsheimerkogl. and a half-sister Field Ch. Karen v. Greif. The backyard was that of a hunting buff, uninterested in any form of competition, Dave Hopkins of Watsonville CA. Huizenga sent his Schwarenberg-bred, Ch. Yunga War Bride—and four Duals came of the two matings. The half-brother sister pair produced a litter that presently put into the faraway yard of Ralph A. Park, Sr., of Seattle, a smallish, solid liver, registered as Gretchen v. Greif. First ever to gain the Am/Can. Dual titles, she has also had great impact in the breed.

At Saratoga, into that Californian scene, and after a mating to the Hopkins' backyard import, Don Miner's hunting bitch, Von Thalberg's Katydid (a Yunga daughter), dropped one that Don named after his first-ever-owned Shorthair, Fritz—Von Thalberg's Fritz II. And about the same time got to wondering what in heck did "Hundsheimerkogel" mean? Well, not even the Secretary of the Austrian Klub Kurzhaar, wherewith the dog was registered, has been able to translate—the owner, Viktor Rohringer, of Vienna, was dead. But the name—continued the Secretary—came up in the very best Austrian breedings always—the Czech influence?

Owner Dave Hopkins wasn't interested much in the Austrian. He had his long-proven hunting dog and the import stayed home in the yard, exercising a considerable charm—later recognized as a strain characteristic—upon Mrs. Hopkins and getting into trouble chasing chickens yet! Sent for cure to trainer J. Stanley Head, the next development was Head's insistence that the dog was a top field trial prospect—yes, at six years old, yes it was! Owner Hopkins

106

remained uninterested. But one day—one day!—the favored hunting dog fell ill and Hopkins went off with his "spare tire"—to waken Stan Head a few days later, 3 a.m., a phone call from hundreds of miles, to announce with a considerable awe: "Stan! I got me a *dog*!" So the Field Trial okay was given and Greif, at age eight, tackled tough Westerners, his face already grayed, his own get oftenest the dogs he had to beat. The year of his finishing his title was 1955. That year, Head took him to the Midwest National, entry of 22 Fld Chs., 2 Duals, a Nat'l F.Ch. and a German import KS. There were plenty to laugh at Stan Head's grayfaced veteran with the jaw-breaker name . . . but Greif carried through to the final series, running the last brace with Dual & Nat'l Ch. Wendeheim's Fritz, but conceding the big win to Field Ch. Gunmaster's Jenta. No matter, he was far from disgraced. He had his title, what more to get, his owner still uninterested in any form of competition.

Time and geography have denied me sight of many Shorthairs it would have been privilege to see. At least I saw Grief, which so few ever did! It was much later, in time of complete retirement, owner Dave Hopkins dead, the dog in Stan Head's kennel as part of the Hopkins' estate. New to USA, a visiting journalist, the interest had been to see the best dog in this then-important FT kennel. It was astonishing to see a grayface come down to the lot . . Sent into the birdfield, his performance was amazing. How old? Oh, about twelve . . . He was posed for my camera for what are quite possibly the only color slides of him in existence. And the report of the performance went under my byline to overseas dog journals . . . the description of the work of the most stylish and energetic hunting dog of my experience. Frank Warner Hill, (English *Dog World* Sporting Editor) thought the California sun had maybe been a little much for me, but the tremendous influence exerted by his three sons down generations verifies the opinion as passed. A great dog . . . but who could have foretold the prepotency passing down through his sons, Yunga, Brunz, Fritz? Now, of course, Greif's name has to all purposes slipped over the back end of all but the most extended pedigrees and even Brunz and Fritz are becoming of the Legion of the Lost of dogs beyond the four-generation compilations. "Now" people will forget them, but indisputable historical fact remains— Where Did You Come From, Baby Dear?

The mating of Field Ch. Von Thalberg's Fritz II to a brace of

Grabenbruch-descended daughters—the Von Bess—clamped near enough mortgage on National Field Trial wins and placings for years. Son Field Ch. Rip Traf v.Bess, in Harden ownership, added National Field to his titles and sired himself a National winner. Son of Fritz—Dual Ch. Zipper Der Orrian—sired the top prepotent bitch of the century in Dual Ch. Dee Tee's Dolly Der Orrian. Another Fritz son, Nat'l Ch. Thalberg's Seagraves Chayne, through *his* son, Field Ch. Ammertal's Lancer D, has provided yet another to come scorching out of the West—1980-81's Nationals winner, Dual Ch. Ehrlicher's Abe.

Old Greif's Dual Ch. son, Oxton's Bride's Brunz v. Greif, also carried the banner, mainly through *his* son, Dual Ch. Oxton's Minado v. Brunz that in repeated mating with Dolly Der Orrian made tremendous breed and historical impact. And not to forget that other conveying medium of Greif inheritances in terms of Dual titling—Ralph Park's Seattle-raised solid liver Gretchen v. Greif that was not satisfied with her own titling as first-ever two-country Dual, but conveyed the qualities that permitted the same doubled-up honors to distinguish her own two children and a grandson.

The same influence was also extended to the East when record-breaking show-producing Ch. Adam v. Fuehrerheim, was honored with a Dual to include in *his* record—Dual Ch. Schatzi v. Balder v. Greif, solid-block Greif breeding all the way back, a daughter of Dual Ch. Brunnenhugel Calder ex Heide Braut v. Greif. Dual Ch. Balder, in his earlier turn, was son of Dual Ch. Oxton's Bride's Brunz v. Greif (ex Ch. Weidenbach Suzette) and Heide v. Braut is full sister to Brunz. Guess there can have been breedings closer, but not by much.

Acquaintance luckily made in Austria, with the then aging Austrian K.S. of the 1960s, Blitz v. Ovilava, featured in a full page picture in an earlier edition of this work, provided interesting discovery that he too was heavily Hundsheimerkogel, with rather more Czech influence than the US import carried. However, the type resemblance was unmistakable, and there was the same familiarity to see in other Czech-bred dogs at the Internationale that year.

Not until late in 1958, when he was dead, did Greif receive national publicity, by then all those Duals surfacing. In life scarcely any dog could have been more obscure, immured in a backyard with the chickens! And then—suddenly he was news as well as dead! *Popular Dogs,* the premier dog publication, had a full page, compiled by Betty Sandberg, of "Kaposia", the then-columnist. There were echoes in other papers and the theme of that old-old Cockney music hall skit was was for recalling—"*Mrs. 'Odkins's Funeral.*"

"Mrs. 'Odkins wuz nuthin', 'ad nuthin', noo nuthin'—
But she was the bloomin' Queen o' Sheba—when she died!"

Nor can it be overlooked that Greif's bitches were chance sorts in the main, Stan Head shepherding the most to the Watsonville yard. The dam of Brunz may have been the best bred. Whelped 1951, she was by Dr Thornton's personal hunting dog, Major V.S., carrying back as he did to early Thorntons—Kamerad v. Waldhausen and Lady Brickwedde. Bridie's dam came from Hjalmer Olsen's Ch. Pagina's Young Lover and a Timm v. Altenau daughter, Sue v. Dusseldorf. The dam of von Thalberg's Fritz was zero for looks, but as a working bitch she was terrific, which may explain why Fritz's get so excelled in Field Trials rather than in shows until his sphere of influence widened and in the course of time, show champions there came to be too.

There was also an extremely attractive Greif son, Field Ch. Feld Jager v. Greif; could easily have been a Dual if the owner had cared to campaign him in the showring. He lived out his days as property of a California hunting club, a popular number with clients.

One thought more—the need to recognize *potential.* As in Greif's own Cinderella story—his *potential* was there, no matter how obscure his life-style—and of course, as in *The Sound of Music* it will always be—"a Bell is No Bell till you Ring It."

* * * * *

So what other great force spread out from the West? Columbia River of course. BIS early-on started falling to Lance McGilbrey's stock down from Tillie and Stormalong, Chs. Lightning, Cochise, Jeepers, Ranger, Vagabond, Thundercloud. Followed in the next generation Moonshine, bred in the Gretchenhof kennels from Ch. Columbia River Jill. Moonshine will be remembered while Shorthair history endures, not only for her intrinsic worth, her great showmanship, but for being the standard bearer that forced the BIS judges to look at her over that fence of prejudice reared with such materials as her breed, her sex . . . From time to time one hears boast of her "record being matched" or "her record being passed." Other times—other circumstances—her record seems likely to stand up to knowledgeable examination—the large entries she bucked—and defeated. Her BISs were at top shows, the nation's best, against competition with the best—and that in the days when showing was still comparatively innocent, as measured in comparison with present day promotional tactics that have the judges' letter-boxes stuffed weekly with blanket-smother publicity to guide the flock of new-fledged adjudicators in the rings.

Columbia River males have over the years paid their homage rather to the big spectacular Stormalong—the bulk—the poster-pretty patterning to catch the eye, the florid showmanship. One feels the distaff side took much rather from Tillie—not even Moonshine could have been described as either florid or showy, nor could have been so described her littermates of the Jill miracle that continues to influence down through the '70s into our present '80s. The color in the males endures in repetition as strongly as—to pick a comparison—the golden-liver of Sussex Spaniels. It goes with the package. Interestingly, quite recently surfaced in this compiler's slides one from the late 1950s, a Columbia River BIS dog now possibly forgotten by most—Vagabond. He could go into present day rings and not strain credulity to gain recognition and praise for his handsomeness.

The Germans have long admired spectacular tick-patch, and lost most of it during the devastation of WWII. The endowment of such as K.S. Kobold Mauderode-Westerholt, K.S. Benno v. Schlossgarten and their slashingly beautiful contemporaries is carried in the main now in memory there, but by no means forgotten. Circumstance of need to make a complete new start in the breed after WWII brought in the search for new foundation blood, settling of course into the wide, blanket employment of Axel v Wasserschling, the solid liver sturdy one that was literally the Father of the New Nation in the rebuilding of the breed. Perhaps the Germans could have used some of the spectaculars out of USA in the rebuilding process carried on the past quarter-century, but there would have needed to be attention to working quality—Tillie's hunting prowess recovered. Most Columbia Rivers are nowadays predominantly show producers. Last letter, now of some years past, from the Klub Kurzhaar then president, Dr. Byhain, he was off to Czechoslovakia to see the young stock there.

Ch. Columbia River Lightning, multiple BIS winner and prepotent sire. Owner, L. V. McGilbrey, Washington.

Tenacity of Type and Jacketing inheritances in Columbia River strain. *Left*, Ch. Columbia River Vagabond, a BIS winner of the later 1950s. Vagabond was by Ch. Columbia River Lightning ex his full sister, Ch. Columbia River Princess. Bred and owned by Lance McGilbrey, Washington. (Photo, *C. Bede Maxwell*, 1961). *Right*, Ch. Bleugras Ramblin' River Tilly (Ch. Gretchenhof Columbia River ex Ch. Cede Mein Gadabout Jill), owned by E. and G. Atkins, Wisconsin. "Tilly" made 1980 Top Producer status with 5 champions, all Bleugras, that include Group and Specialty winners.

There was, of course, that most famous of the strain in modern days here, Ch. Gretchenhof Columbia River. *He* was the one that toppled "Moonshine's record", but he did it much as she had done—with bucking the very top competition, in the top shows, against large entries in the breed—certainly not without the help of considerable promotion and an exhausting show schedule. His BIS at Westminster was of course the high point and, indeed, it has been this compiler's fortune to see the great Westminster BIS cup, now owned in the West by the Irish Setter Club of the Pacific, a legacy from the estate of his owner, the late Dr. Smith. It constitutes an annual award to the club member that has best served the club in practical capacity, and the year this compiler saw the award it went to Jake Huizenga, which was a nice blending of his Irish and Short-hair interests.

It was also coincidence that the great winner—"Traveller" as he was universally known—passed away at the time of compiling this very section of this book revision. He was 12½ years old, and no one doubts Jo Shellenbarger, with whom he lived, will miss his presence in the home.

*   *   *   *   *

Present-day recognition of what's come out of the West must also include reference to that cluster of imports brought into to the Northwest by Bob Holcomb after a second hitch in Germany. These include such as (later) Am/Can. Dual Ch. Arrak v. Heisterholz; (later) Field Ch. Gert v.d. Radbach; (later) Am/Can. Field Ch. Lutz v.d. Radbach, plus a selection of bitches. All have had impact on the breed, Arrak enjoying the longest lifespan and much success as a stud. Gert and Lutz also proved themselves in Dual production, but unfortunately both died very young. It had to have been the sunset years of the Radbachs, long one of Germany's greatest breeding strain. This compiler met Herr Beckman (of the Radbach) at the Internationale, held in the Rhineland in 1967—he then very ill, almost blind, and plainly at the end of his active dog-interested life. Gert was "hyper" to a degree; Lutz arrived with a delicate constitution, to be vividly recalled as he presented himself first to our gaze, a sick puppy of a few weeks of age, arrived by air to California, and Shirley Miner taking over to restore him with care in her kitchen where so many von Thalbergs first made their bond with humans.

112

Gert's influence is preserved down several distinguished Field Trial lines, most successfully perhaps through his two Dual champions ex Am/Can. Dual Ch. Gretchen v. Greif, both taking the title in both countries as well, and one, Dual Ch. Gert's Duro v. Greif, siring a most distinguished representative in three-time National FT winner, Patricia v. Frulord. In the show scene, however, there is also National Specialty Ch. Kooskia's Chief Joseph, sired by Gert's son, Dual & Can. Ch. Radbach's Dustcloud ex a lovely Kaposia-bred—Ch. Red Tail of Kooskia. Now Chief Joseph, in his turn, has kept the ball moving, represented by a successful son in Ch. Kooskia's Chief Timothy, increasingly at the moment the dog to beat in the Northwest, rare though his appearances be.

From the West too, of course, stems that strain which has become braided right through the breed as from Danish import, Field Ch. Moesgaards IB. Imported originally by Hjalmer Olsen, and sold to Ivan Brower of Washington State, IB spearheads the most readily recognizable, often controversial, strain within the breed in this country. It is futile at this late stage, to engage in the long-lived speculation concerning the strain. All his owners are no longer available for questioning; after Brower's death he was resold to Mr. J.A. Karns, no longer engaged in the breed interest. Was there an outcross to the Pointer breed? Was the divergence in breed type—the dimunition of size and the strongly prepotent persistence of the Pointer-type color patterning—merely the result of fantastically-maintained closest inbreeding? Water under the bridge . . .

What can be commented upon however is the radical change over in terms of performance that has accelerated since the spread of the strain, putting highest value on the running dog that is the very opposite to what the idealists of the original breed formation had in mind. There would seem to have burgeoned that fantasy that is by no means restricted merely to some owners of field-trial-oriented German Shorthairs—the vision of the Southern gentleman-planter on his Tennessee Walker, following at best distance the three-hour, horizon galloping Pointers . . . Well, no one is going soon to make a German Shorthair over to a three-hour Southern-bred Pointer with any degree of ease . . . but at least the aspirant owners do have one gain ahead in the game—most of them have their Tennessee Walkers good and fast . . .

The world's only triple-titled German Shorthair. Dual Ch. Frie of Klarbruk, UDT. (Dual and Natl. FT Ch. Kay v.d. Wildburg ex Ch. Gretchenhof Cinnabar, CDX). Owners/Breeders: Joseph and Julie France, Maryland.

Am./Can. Ch. Tara's Command Performance, UDT. (Field Ch. Checkmate's Dandy Dude/Gretchen's Song to Artemis, CD). Carrying the Obedience-titled banner ahead of the competition a generation later than the famed triple-titled Frei of Klarbruck, this multi-titled matron, wh. 1973, was still an active force in competition in 1981, having over the intervening years additionally accumulated distinction as Number One Obedience-titled GSP and a GSPCA Year Book recognition as Top Producing Dam. She currently yields a trifle—no more than that!—to her son, Sure Shot's Country Squire, UD.

7

Nationwide

into the '80s

NATIONWIDE, Shorthairs continue to have strong public support, as up-to-date registrations show, 1980 figures even providing a modest gain when more than one breed in the group was showing decline. The example of the unprecedented drop in Irish Setter registrations could serve as warning that the buying public will make last judgment on a breed, over-promotion and judging preferences notwithstanding. Those with interest in other breeds could afford to examine the process of public rejection of a breed—it is no new thing in dogs. Nor is it any over-night affair—it is a matter of steady building-*down* over many years. Buyers turn to something else. Even Germany has been at need to compound with this long-established truth—buyer choice. There, for most of the 1970s it has been possible—and it was carried out!—to chart the ongoing gain of the Wirehaired over the Shorthair, mainly—as research and examination of registration figures support—a public drift away from the "hyper" type of competitive Shorthair replacing the steady utility type that had for decades fitted so well into the family scene.

Fortunately, USA comes into the 1980s with a rich reservoir of true type dogs to balance the breakaway sorts that cause many dedicates pain to observe, both in terms of structure blatantly variant from type, and performance as foreign to shorthair model as can possibly be assessed. That there should have come about a split between show-oriented and field-oriented is no new thing in any sporting breed. The importance lies in maintaining the basic breeding stock as close to blueprint as possible.

The new decade of the '80s emphasises not only increased registration numbers but also the formation of new clubs during the previous decade. Membership lists have fattened, but many the name that has been taken away. The decade of the '70s may well have seen out the last of those actually connected with breed pioneering. As Hjalmer Olsen, retired to Denmark after the death of his wife, there remarried, and giving ongoing attention to the sending to USA of more of the Danish dogs he had been selecting for years. Perhaps Dean Kerl's Field Ch. Tell may have been the last. Olsen wrote of a 6-months puppy of a great breeding. It was domiciled, however, on a small island and the time was winter, and icefloes were constant and heavy. Who but Hjalmer Olsen would have refused to be thwarted in acquisition of an outstanding dog? He sent a stolid brave boatman out for the puppy, and Field Ch. Tell, in USA, vindicated the exertions of securing him against Scandinavian winter hazards, his 65 US breedings having produced some 500 puppies with two Dual Chs. in the count . . . But Olsen did not live to learn of it . . .

Dr. Clark Lemley? Still listed a GSPCA member though seemingly having relinquished his tremendous, active participation in all spheres of breed engagement and protective club support. George Reudiger—another strong defender of the best qualities in the breed—George is gone but his Big Island strain still crops up behind some great moderns. Joseph and Magdalina Deiss, of the Oakcrests, whose careful breeding provided base upon which Kaposia was solidly built. Past-President Dr. L.L. Kline . . . meshed in the Moesgaards interest, but giving his Nat'l. Fld. Ch. M's Dandy the widest selection of outcross bitches he could find.

A strong representation of those that dominated show and field competition have now moved into judging. Here count Del Glodowski, his "Strauss's" strain name braided into competitive spheres for so long one counts him pioneer, despite his younger years. Dual Ch. Baron v. Strauss (Toby B/Patsy v. Strauss) stands seventh in

Field Ch. Tell (imp. Denmark) (Dan. Ch. Holevgaards C. Kaj ex Sussi), owned by Dean M. Kerl, Minnesota. Historically, seemingly the last dog Hjalmer Olsen shipped from Denmark to the USA, Tell justified the Old Master in the selection made. His get includes two good Dual champions and his tally, totalled at time of his retirement from stud, a total of approximately 500 puppies, good dogs and easy trainers.

Int. Field Ch. Moesgaard's Ib (imp. Denmark), (Holevgaard's Kip ex Nyberg's Rix). Breeder: Niels Hykkelbjerg. Owners: successively, Hjalmer Olsen; Ivan Brower; J. A. Karns. Basic to the well-known, wide-distributed Moesgaard's strain—which in appearance does not resemble him in the slightest, although the inbreeding (on his name?) was fantastic. Clearly, as this rare picture shows, he was a handsome tick-patch, of good shape and substance.

the timewise count of Dual Champions, reaching back in breeding literally to the basics into the Midwest. Del's strain name however carried on most visibly through the exertions of the dog he sold to his neighbors in Sturtivant, Wisconsin, Mr. and Mrs. Serak—the proud holders of "Serakraut" strain name that is dominated by Ch. Strauss's Happy-Go-Lucky (Strauss's Viktor/Strauss's Teora) that keeps the strain name posted high in production tables of this time. It is a steady ongoing stream that "Serakraut" sends out, strongly based on stock from "The House That Del Built."

Also gone to judging are the Sandbergs of "Kaposia" and rather more recently Walt Shellenbarger of "Gretchenhof." At heart, Walt and Jo were exhibitors rather than breeders, so far as their enthusiasms rested, but it was "Gretchenhof" from which came that issue of daughters of Ch. Columbia River Jill that gave such boost to the fortunes of not only immediate first generation issue but ongoing generations of those lucky enough to have the fortune of their participation in breeding programs. One thinks, of course immediately of Tally Ho, the untitled bitch that made first strike for record-making Ch. Adam v. Fuehrerheim, and of sister Ch. Gretchenhof Cinnabar that provided the world's only triple-titled Ch. Shorthair Dual Ch. Frei of Klarbruk, U.D.T., to her mating with famed Kay v.d. Wildburg.

Also to count among those of ongoing association of profitable to-the breed activities is Maxine Collins, of Michigan, who will, one hopes, forgive being counted with the close-to-pioneers. As ongoing Chairperson of the Year Book Committee her dedication has been more than equal to the tremendous task of correlating and steering towards publication the assembled work of all the dedicates that keep statistics for posterity to examine. Those of us with long memories, however, think of her in association with her splendid matron bitch, Am/Can. Ch. Susanna Mein Liebchen, C.D., her produce including among her Duals the produce to Dr. Lemley's Dual & Nat'l Field Ch. Dandy Jim v. Feldstrom, first in the breed to hold both titles and cover boy of this work's first edition. Maxine still breeds an occasional litter and also makes an occasional appearance in the showring as her own handler. All good reasons why some of us continue to think of her as the true "Missus Shorthair."

Also well back there, and still to be glimpsed galleryside at an occasional show, is Lance McGilbrey, of "Columbia River." That the name of his strain will long outlive him seems to be guaranteed by the evidence of the harking back to his basics that can modernly now be discerned in the compilations of the '80s—perhaps not so much through the energies of the males as of the proven prepotency of the females. One guesses he will approve the trend. There is a story this compiler feels should not be permitted to die with either Mr. Gilbrey or myself. It concerns a long-ago time—the earliest 1960s—when this compiler went to Kennewick and the Columbia River kennel to see and to photograph the basic bitch, old Columbia River Tillie—then in her sixteenth year. Up and out from her kennel, no glamorizing, Tillie posed for the incredible picture used in all editions of this work. Her owner looked at her fondly: "Tillie, she doesn't see so good any more . . . and Tillie, I'm afraid she doesn't hear so good any more either. But Tillie eats good and sleeps good and she doesn't hurt any place . . . and she's what I started with . . ." Pride enhanced the big man's smile as he spoke. She had been for all her years his pheasant-dog.

It took longer for breed popularity to catch on in the East than in the West and Midwest, but early-day strains came into being, of which the most importantly noticeable down into the now through the history of the breed in this land has to be that of the brothers Johns, of Benton, Pennsylvania. Do they have a strain name—yes, "Fishing Creek." Did it become a household word in the breed? Never. But say Grabenbruch, and say v.d. Wildburg and identification is instant. In earlier editions of this work it was importantly

Ch. Gretchenhof Moonshine, retiring at the age of 4, compiled 15 BIS and 50 G1, a record in the breed. Top Sporting for 1963 (Phillips System), she was owned by Gretchenhof Kennels, California.—*Photo: C. Bede Maxwell.*

"Grabenbruch" as from the strain based on the smallish, shortlived German import, Sepp v. Grabenbruch. A decade more, and it became the base of Dual & Nat'l Field Champion, Kay v.d. Wildburg (K.S. Pol v. Blitzdorf/Cora v. Wesertor).

Kay went through the years doing what was asked of him magnificently, as his heritage prompted. By his time the "Grabenbruch" strain had been dispersed quite widely, and most of the carriers of the bloodline were in other hands, coast to coast. Nowadays Dick will say, yes, he should have been more active in breeding his great import stock. Why he did not give this the attention their quality merited was mainly because there was so much else in life to interest, his riding, his hunting . . . and in addition, there was his aversion from trumpet blowing in print. If a person wished to use his dogs, would such not come knocking at the door? No shadow of exploitation shadows the ownership of the Benton dogs. They were there, and they were great ones. The satisfaction was to be able to enjoy the gift of field and cover the environment provided, the good sporting days.

Always there have been Shorthair owners, all countries, to set prime value on private hunting interest. My file of 1966 includes a Hamilton Rowan Jr. letter drawing attention to error in my 2nd edition of this work—Dax v. Heidebrink was a show, not a field champion—sweetened with some interesting information besides:

"Dax is a fine dog," wrote Ham, "owned by Bob Johns, Dick's brother, who also lives in Benton. The dog was never field trialed because Bob is an avid grouse hunter and refused to allow the dog to be campaigned in trials because he did not want it to know any game other than grouse. It could easily have finished in field . . ."

So, Dax v. Heidebrink, the grouse dog that could easily have secured his own Dual titling, remains sandwiched between his Dual Ch. sire, Blick v. Grabenbruch, and his Dual Ch. son and Dual Ch. grandson, the Carlson-owned Richlu's Dan Oranian and Ritzie's Oranian Rocco.

As with Bob Johns' Dax, so with Dick's Inge v. Grabenbruch—known to the Benton hunting people as "Missus Woodcock"—another that was valued and restricted solely for use on the game that was to keep her a homebody.

"And a great joy she is to me always when the hills start to color and the woodcock moon is in full, the flights starting down from the north," Dick has written. "She is the witch of the white beech hillside and the black alder swamps—but then, why would she not be? Last of the inbred Grabenbruch line."

Oh well, yes—he should have put more energy into promotion of Kay v.d. Wildburg . . . yes, for the value proven of the stud he should have been mated—so should his earlier hunting bitch, Dual Ch. Valkyrie v. Grabenbruch. Well—defensively—he shrugged— was the dog not always at Benton? Didn't the Shorthair breeders know where to find him? Actually, of course, this is the oldest story in all manner of dog hobby breeding—cattle and horsemen are more practical in their selections, have to be or the sheriff would come put a padlock on the front gate. Dog owners tend to follow wins—show or field—or use the dog that is handiest. Belated realization of this in Germany a few years ago led in the mid-'70s to a novel form of exhibition—a gathering of the available top quality studs from round the nation to let the breeders see—matter discussed in another place in these pages.

Apart from his dedication to his personal hunting sport, Dick Johns has also understanding of historic values. and it is through his discrimination and care that a remarkable historic item has been preserved, an item that establishes beyond all argument that there were Shorthairs in the USA before the time of the Thornton imports. There is this photograph——described as having been picked up in an empty house in Dallas, Pa., and brought to Dick "because he had those kind of dogs." It is a professionally taken, cabinet-size picture, obviously of a family group, with a splendid Shorthair couchant in front. The sole clue to origin is the name of the professional photographer, stamped on the back, Cobb, Binghamton, New York. This compiler's curiosity took her to City Hall in Binghamton to learn that yes, Cobb, Photographer, had been in business there 1890s/1900s. Then how Pennsylvania? Easily Cobb could have traveled in his profession—something much done in those days. Not all emigrants to the US came in condition of destitution, as after the Irish Famine, say, or the Germanic troubles of the 1848, and parallel occasions. There were also newcomers of comfortable situation that brought along the family pet . . . Taking stock of dates, this mature, splendid Shorthair could well have been contemporary with the flowering of the Hoppenrades . . .

121

Pennsylvania also hosted that Father of a Nation in Ch. Adam v. Fuehrerheim, a dog of modest achievement other than in terms of the most remarkable prepotency evidenced in the breed, siring a roster of champion get that, one guesses, not even the famed Axel v. Wasserschling, the patriarch of modern post-war Germanic breed regeneration, can match. A fortune of splendid producing bitches was also his, many with multiple champion get, from which derive some producing dogs with strong influence through in turn their get into these 1980s. Most outstandingly, Ch. Whispering Pines Patos (ex Gretchenhof Tally Ho) who in turn has sired Ch. Fieldfines Count Rambard (ex Fieldfines Tascha) and Ch. Roll On Columbia, (ex Ch. Rudean's Columbia River Katy, a Ch. Gretchenhof Columbia River daughter). Also modernly operative Ch. Rocky Run's Stony (ex Ch. Rocky Run's Poldi) and Ch. Hungerliter's Jug o'Punch (ex Trail Winds Apache) while of bitches, the GSPCA tabulation counts among the productive, Ch. Whispering Pines Francesca (also a Tally Ho daughter). These, and others, are further examined as to production in the production tables elsewhere in these pages.

Interestingly, a late candidate for honors to add to Adam's tally is his on-in-years son, Ch. Adam's Hagen v. Waldenburg, belatedly purchased for Australia, and detained by required quarantine regulations a full year in England. In resident care of the breeder-judge-author, David Layton, of the "Midlanders," this California-bred has newly added the English title to his long held American.

Ch. Whispering Pines Patos, regrettably, did not have a long life. The ongoing maintenance of strain honors therefore now rests with the show-producing Ch. Fieldfines Count Rambard, whose lengthening record is elsewhere examined, topped by a brace of BIS winners in Chs. Fieldfines Lord Tanner (ex Cinnamon Duchess) and Ch. P.W's Challenger v. Fieldfine (ex Ehrick's Jaeger Traum). The rarity of the BIS award to the breed is not to be explained perhaps in other than terms of a current lack of show-dominating spectaculars such as Ch. Gretchenhof Columbia River with his tally of triumphs topped by the BIS at Westminster. No comparable rival to his memory—or the memory of his forerunner, Ch. Gretchenhof Moonshine—appears anywhere within sight at this time, though California-bred Ch. Donavin's Sir Ivanoe (Ch. GeeZee Super Chief ex Plutonian Lady Star Traveller) with several Western BIS awards accumulating, is a very consistent tryer.

Ch. Adam v. Fuehrerheim (Ch. Adam, imp. Sweden ex Tessa v. Fuehrerheim) Breeder: Chas. L. Joran IV. Owner: Robert H. McKowan, Pennsylvania. All-time show-producing stud of the 1960s/70s, whose record as a sire is unlikely to be approached in any forseeable time. His show record counted to 60 BOBs, 7 Group One, 11 breed Specialties and the 1968 GSPCA National Breed Specialty.

Most judges of the breed would concede that the present scene provides considerable disappointment in the judging of Shorthairs in that the Specials class seems everywhere to have become narrowed down to the very minimum—an entry of one Special is by no means unusual—while undoubtedly there has to be a wealth of breed talent just staying home, convinced that trying to buck the modern interpretation of blanket-promotion is just money wasted. The phenomenon is not confined to the Shorthair breed, of course, but no breed ever has been, or ever will be, at benefit from promotion of single champions exerting mortgage on the breed and keeping all the others at home where breeders don't see them.

That the absence of competition in so many Specials classes connotes the lack of good breeding stock in the Shorthairs is simply not true, any more than is the distressing variance of type in so much Field-competitive stock necessarily a spelling out of doomsday for the breed. Betty Sandberg, of the long-maintained "Kaposias," in discussing this matter, concedes that "in my judging experience across the country, I can still find good Shorthairs being shown towards their Dual title, so promising maintenance of basic breed character. As for ourselves, though judging takes up most of our time, we still breed an occasional litter or two each year and this is known to people wanting a good shooting dog. We do here in Minnesota have constant experience of clients getting in touch for replacement after some Old Faithful has lived out its days. Many clients come reporting themselves in shock after looking in on a Field Trial, but people do continue to buy the kind of dog that suits their interest and their purpose, and the hunting people continue to be pleased with what we breed."

Interestingly, this is the self-same theme the Germans have been examining—matter discussed here in the Field Trial Dog chapter.

Kaposia's production, over many years, counts 47 champions listed in the GSPCA Index under the letter "K" alone, give or take those with names starting with any other letter. Neither Betty nor Don can supply a full list of their titleds, but to a researcher it is consumingly interesting to find how many—*how* many!—untitled Kaposia bitches, clearly broods or unshowns, are behind many great dogs of other strains as well.

* * * * *

Through the '70s, there were still those Albrechts out in Kansas, though the '80s finds them in terms of pedigree compilation rather than active participation. Mrs. Albrecht confesses to having "become side-tracked from dog pedigrees these days to become involved with human genealogy," but does not elaborate. But she sent along for this edition a sheaf of her splendidly prepared documentation, dating as from the strain's initiation with 1955-whelped Ch. Katrina v. Albrecht and from Katrina on and down through Ch. Albrecht's Countess Tena to that prideful occasion when the One Hundredth Dual recognition in the breed came to Ch. Albrecht's Tena Hy. It is wholly in character that the photograph that came newly in company shows three 1979 finished Albrecht-descended Field Trial champions that had all finished on the same day at the same Trial!

Nor has retirement of the principals erased the strain name from the Dual-titled list. Dual & AFC Albrecht's Marta's Dino (Ch. Albrecht's Tena Inky/Dual Ch. Dino's Baroness Marta) and Dual Ch. Albrecht's Baron (Jager Albrecht Schlossgarten/Lupkin's v. Skoeps) both make the present edition's updating. Additionally, GSPCA National Ch. of 1979, Dual Ch. Lika Buckskin, is ex Albrecht's Cora Miss. The three Duals finished first as show champions, emphasising Betty Sandberg's observation that true-type Shorthairs are in the showrings in hope to secure Dual titlings.

The present edition updating also emphasises that, while show champions can and do secure Dual titling, many present a Dual titled parent in back. Yet, of course, for every observation there is counter observation, and so we find Dual Ch. Hidden Hollow's Pleasure ex a dam with no title at all, Ceres of Hidden Hollow, but the quality of her get to make additional recommendation. For those interested as to the source of her prepotency, she has no titled forbears for four generations, and in the fifth there are but five titled—but they happen to be Ch. Alnor's Brown Mike (which is back to Thornton), Ch. Windy Hill Sari, Ch. Tell v. Lowin and Chs. Pardner, C.D. and Baba Lin's Ragtime—all names to respect.

Breed inheritance factors, these days of air transport for bitches, are of course widely now distributed. One comes upon the various strengths unexpectedly, as when this compiler, judging at a 1980 Florida show, faced a sizeable Shorthair entry of surprising quality and evennness. It had been major surprise, on eventually checking the catalog, to discover the enormous influence of Ch. Strauss's Happy Go Lucky, half the continent's distance away in his own productive time. The balance was drawn from all over—there was Ch. Moesgaard's Ruffy and even a lesser-light Columbia River stud— Ch. Gunsmoke (Ch. Columbia River Lightning/Helga v. Krawford)—each adding a leg for the Florida three-legged strain.

It is not unusual to find Ruffy behind some good show stock. Though from a litter otherwise wholly to pattern one has learned to recognize as Moesgaard, he was good-sized and well-built, a tick-patch totally unlike his littermates this compiler has seen. Ruffy occupies a warm spot in memory for me, an embarrassing occasion we shared. New to USA, at a Field Trial, asking opportunity to take his photo, it had been astonishment when the handler immediately "WHOA'd" him into classic pointing pose—no bird within miles! Ruffy demonstrated his embarrassment by licking his good

"An episode in the life of"... In the interest of having his "pitcher took", Field Trial Ch. Moesgaard's Ruffy—an honest and successful field trial competitor that interestingly crops up behind some very good show dogs—was whoa'd into a false point by his handler—no bird dog within miles! His embarrassment shows—shouldn't happen to any dog, let along one as good as Ruffy.—*C. Bede Maxwell*

Erdenreich's Marz Wind, CD. Littermate to Dual Ch. Erdenreich's Marz Marsh, this lovely bitch posed a striking picture in work. Breeder/Owners: D. and L. DeGere, Mill Valley, California.

big nose . . . As first, by no means last, of GSP's false-pointed for my camera, he has gone unidentified to many a lecture in company—some shots are lulus! It is, by the way, astonishing how few viewers recognise a pictured dog without its advertised handler, even owners! Ruffy, as sire of Field Ch Moesgaard's Coco, may have helped produce Coco's show champions got from that provenly prepotent showbred bitch in Ch. Callmac's Victory v. Gardsburg. So, Coco is a Dual Producer . . .

As to Ruffy being so different in appearance from his littermates, one is reminded that many folks take for granted that all Danish dogs are white or white and liver patched. It simply is not true. The Danish-breds at home are in the published records identified by color—solid livers, tick-patch, brown'whites. The breed publication which Dr. L.L. Kline was kind enough to lend for the first edition of this work published all pedigrees with color marking— for a solid liver the mark was a blacked-in small circle. For a brown-white (Pointer-patterned) it was a small circle half black half white. The tick-patches, counted the most numerous in the breed, did not carry any marking on the pedigree at all.

That the overwhelming number of Danish imports were predominantly white-brown or even near enough all white may have to do with that it was Hjalmer Olsen who selected most of them— and who in print had confessed long ago that his original love had always been for English Pointers. His eye may well have been affronted by what passed for a Pointer among the folk where he lived, in Georgia, so he came as close as possible to eye-appeal in the other breed—just a thought. The Germans have never liked the white-brown patterning—and one may walk a weary mile to see one there. Most are bucketed at birth—though recognized as authentic recessives from early pioneer breedings, they are unwelcome as constituting a possible screen to cloak what, Heaven forbid, might be enterprise of some unethicals who would try to pass off modern Pointer crosses.

In the US there are buyers, especially among the hunters, who prefer the lighter colors, ticked or patched. Mr. Dean Kerl, a past president of the GSPCA, reports many pre-whelping orders lodged with him for produce of his import, Field Ch. Tell, are favored for this reason. Tell, by the way, through his two good Duals sired Kerlakes Tell's Moonbeam (ex Field Ch. Moesgaard's Ruffy's Mindy, a Ruffy daughter) and Timbertop Tell (ex October's Frost, she a Friend Acres IB's Dex daughter ex the M. Coco daughter Callmac's

Heidi v. Moesgaard) undoubtedly made good on Olsen's tenacity of purpose, haling him off from that ice-girt island all those years ago.

If Show Sire production is dominated, as it is, by Ch. Adam v. Fuehrerheim, be sure the damside honors seem likely to rest for some considerable time to come with Dual Ch. Cede Mein Dolly Der Orrian (Dual Ch. Zipper Der Orrian/Dual Ch. Erdenreich's Jetta Beckum). Mr & Mrs. Dean Tidrick's marvelous Dolly, based in Iowa, seemed well able to help make headlines for her mates. For Dual Ch. Oxton's Minado v. Brunz she was able to whelp three Dual champions, two BIS winners and twelve show champions. Nor did her gifts play themselves out in any single generation. Her son, Dual Ch. and her daughter, Dual Ch. Dee Tee's Dee Tee's Baron v. Greif is at time of writing already sire of a brace of next generation Duals, and her daughter, Dual Ch. Dee Tee's Baschen v. Greif is dam to Dual & Nat'l. Field Ch. Boss Lady Jodi v. Greif, (by Field Ch. Uodibar's Boss Man). Her influence even helped to add a tally of three show champions to the predominantly field-oriented get of the redoubtable Ch. Windy Hill Prince James—making of *him* a Dual Producer as well!

Mention of Dolly invites appreciation of the prefix, "Cede Mein," a constant for years in the show competition of the West. C.D. Lawrence himself handled oftenest his homebreds to good wins over out-of-staters as well. The GSPCA Index lists 34 "Cede Mein" champions merely in the alphabetical "C" columns, but many others scatter among the pages. Then, of course, there was the "Cede Mein" that was Supreme Champion at Westminster a few years ago, a tiny Yorkshire Terrier! Of Shorthair champions, closest to present time may be the intriguingly-named Ch. Cede Mein Chat Nuga Chu Chu! Lawrence had no end of resource in finding names! An earlier winner, Ch. Cede Mein Gandy Dancer, a big broth of a boy, sired a first-class producer in Ch. Cede Mein Brass Badge, ex one of the Columbia River Jill daughters, Ch. Gretchenhof Tradewind, which Lawrence knew how to value. 1974 saw runaway surprise in the taking of the GSPCA National Field Trial with a "Cede Mein" in Georgie Girl—she ex Dolly Der Orrian's dam, Dual Ch. Erdenreich Jetta Beckum, and sired by Field & Nat'l FT Ch. Rip Traf v. Bess, he a Fld Ch. Von Thalberg's Fritz II son ex a Grabenbruch-bred bitch.

Am./Can. Ch. Galileo von Thurber (Ch. Ashbrook's Papageno ex Lori v. Thurber). Breeder/Owner: Robert B. Leach, M.D. "Gally" was at top of the show ratings when he accidentally drowned in August 1981. But it was as a personal hunting dog that he was in his element—the justification of any Shorthair's existence.

In the middle, Ch. Red Tail of Kooskia (Ch. Kaposia's Oconto/Kaposia's Waoke) flanked by her son, Ch. Kooskia's Chief Jospeh (by Dual Ch. Redback's Dustcloud) and (recumbent) his son, Ch. Kooskia's Chief Timothy (ex Kaposia's Princess Owatonna). Breeder/Owners: Noland and Margaret Noren, Julietta, Idaho. Chief Joseph is National GPSCA Specialty winner of 1978. All three serve as practical herd-hunting dogs in Idaho; rare appearances in the showrings are usually well-rewarded.

So—ask again—from where do the proven prepotents come—from the other proven prepotents with carry-on-down-generation capacities.

C.D. Lawrence, presently bowed away, it seems, from dog interest consequent on indifferent health, possessed the indispensable element of flair in his breedings. "Cede Mein" still exercises influence through most excellent bitches as, say, those sitting behind such 1980s strains as Midwest Bleugras, but the little Yorkie that took the Garden seems virtually to serve as Exclamation Point at the end of a good story one would not have wished ended.

Come back, C.D.—wherever you are—Come Back . . .

So many good dogs to leave unnamed—space the compiler's enemy. There needs, however, to be mention of Ch. Ashbrook's Papageno (Ch. Kaposia's Oconto ex Ch. Sieglinde of Ashbrook, a Dual Ch. Biff Bangabird daughter) a top producing stud. This, for recording the tragedy that overtook his son, Ch. Galileo v. Thurber, newly at this very time of compilation. "Galli" had been several years around the shows, doing his share of winning at an employment he didn't so much care for—he was before else a one-dog-family treasure. Mid this year when he had stacked up quite a tally of show wins, having been embarked upon fun-and-games with his owner, Mrs. Leach, of Michigan, he had suffered seizure in the familiar pond, and drowned in front of her eyes! His passing concerns this present book, because we had earlier returned his conventionally stylized show-picture and asked for something more interesting. He had gone then hunting with Dr. Leach, a camera along—so there had resulted splendid pictures, one of which it is privilege here to include. If the original show-win picture had not been rejected for this work, the hunting pictures would never have been taken—Dr. & Mrs. Leach are now so glad that they were!

One contrasts the life of such a family dog as "Galli," excelling in the qualities that are the hallmark of good Shorthairs—utility hunting dogs with a great capacity for companionship as well—with that of others of the breed that are not so fortunate as to escape the pressures of endless campaigning towards aims that are not their own. One does not hold against "Galli's" memory the circumstance that his "show" pictures projected his feeling that, all things considered, he'd much rather be home with his people . . . Taking one consideration with another, that's what, in fact, Shorthairs are all about . . .

130

8

The Field Competitive

German Shorthair

—Aims and Ideals as Internationally Assessed

"It is the great field dogs, the real ones, with noses and heart, style and intensity, that actually carry the whole breed."
                    MCDOWELL LYON *(U.S.A.—1956)*
"Hunde mit denem man jagen kann, so weit der Himmel Blau!"
          KONRAD ANDREAS *(Germany—1956)*

So it was by separate thought assessed in two countries a quarter century ago—the American opinion expressed in favor of the dog that combined qualities deemed essential to field trial competitive performance, such as nose and heart, with the pictorial additives of style and intensity, and the German opinion joyously caroling of the comparison of space and the blue, blue Heaven. And yet . . . and yet . . . in this our time it is the American aim and aspiration to thrust the competitive Shorthair as far as the horizon's blue at speed, and the German opinion that is soberly taking stock in respect of the disastrous effect that over-emphasis on peak performance, fireball style and run, is having on the breed's public reputation and popularity . . . as a breed.

First Shorthairs imported to USA—now more than sixty years back in time—were as the breed's originators had made them, dogs for following on foot, capable on fur or on feather, retrieving from land or water, cold-trailing, able and willing to deal with stray cats, intruding foxes, even to indulge ownerships which might enjoy the music associated with the treeing of a 'coon. There were tall tales told, exaggerated perhaps at times, but exaggeration is the entitlement of any man boasting of the achievements of his dog or the strength of his fishing line. Inevitably, as breed clubs came into being and proliferated, with Competition the aim and Field Trial titles the lure, the tales for telling gradually took on an additional quality. Not only old Tick-patch's hunting skills were subject for boastings, but the additional matter of his speed in getting himself from point A to point B. Not that this early competitive aspect brought about horizon runners, merely there was the proportion of owners, running their Shorthairs, who took pride in the circumstance that their dogs could cover ground faster than bracemates. It was exactly as it has been by someone elsewhere expressed, that by nature the American sportsman preferred to see his property, dog or horse, out in front.

However, not all American owners of Shorthairs were concerned to school their dogs for speed. Joining the breed clubs which proliferated quickly as from the early 1950s, there were many who enjoyed their private hunting sport, and more that had amibtions to win in the showrings, and for such the Field Trial possessed no lure. In many minds nested possibly also the belief that Field Trialing was an expensive, often snobbishly oriented sport—a belief that could have come down to many an American from forebears who had racial memories of the European scene from a less than elevated social level. The sport of the local Great Man—with his handlers and his kennel staff, and his keepers of the preserves of game, and dire woe for the trespassers or the poacher. . .

The hunting buffs sought sport here much as their pioneer forefathers had sought it and the type of Shorthair upon which the Field Trial buffs quite early set their sights had no attraction for such, a dog running so big, so wide, that within another decade a horse to follow would become mandatory. The approach of the owner of a competitive field and show Shorthair in the early 1950s was also still inclined to assess performance by standards closer to those of the hunting man than those of the developing speed buff. The definition was magnificently described by an owner of the '50s, the late Jack Shattuck, proud to have finished the first Dual Champion in the breed, Rusty v. Schwarenberg: "It's a practical gundog," he wrote in a letter to a then-newcomer to the breed, resident in California, young Don Miner of Saratoga, who would make, in the future his strain name one of the best-known in the land, *Von Thalberg*, "retrieving on duck and capably handling upland game. This is what the breed is meant to do. It is not meant to be a wind-splitter, but is as close to the ideal as a man can get with a pointing dog to follow on foot. It is not entered in the Big Trials for Pointing Dogs because it is not bred for that. It is a top shooting dog. That is why its trials are run with birds to be killed and retrieved."

That was written about thirty-odd years ago—thirty *really* odd years when one takes trouble to think back over changes effected. Jack Shattuck's conception of the foot-followed Shorthair has in competition yielded competition in the prestige stakes by which champions are most highly rated to as close an equivalent of the Big Trial Pointers that go racing over those Canadian prairies every season as dog-flesh can be induced to conform. Pointer performance? Even Dr. Thornton, who back in those 1920s, talked the American Kennel Club into recognizing the breed as a Pointer when officially it would have been preferred to recognize it merely as a German Shorthair, would nowadays be astonished at what could have been at the time of his persistence already foreseen— the attempt to ape Pointer performance modernly even if it meant, in some quarters, transforming the dog in the most literal manner, blood and bone and breed type, by means that poorly stand examination but stubbornly refused always to yield proof . . . the reluctance of those with possible information to "become involved."

Re that matter of name by which the breed should be recognized. In Germany already, by Dr. Thornton's time, the German *Klub* had trimmed away the name for which he exerted pressure in USA. The original "German Shorthaired Pointer" had become the "German Shorthair," (*D. Kurzhaar*). While it was conceded that the English Pointer had valuably served to get the Old German Hound's nose up from the ground, the breed developers wanted none of the Pointer's other characteristics, none suited to the makeup of a Utility Dog. Nor, at distance of a couple of decades from breed formation, did they want ambitious "improvers" to be tempted, by the misleading name, to try new incross of Pointer blood. So—away with the designation of *Vorstehhund*-Pointer. Perhaps it was a pity that Dr. Thornton had not known of this . . .

Perhaps it was also his insistence that he had introduced a Pointer that led to the misclassification of the breed here in USA, from which of course, the majority of the breed's present woes probably stem. From that unlucky misclassification—shoving a Utility breed into Pointer/Setter competition—proliferated inevitably the aim and aspiration to develop a dog—call it what you will!—that *could* compete. It was fruitless aim of course, seeking to secure speed by cross-breeding. Cross the Kentrucky Derby winner with a Morgan, however good, and there'll never be another Derby winner among the produce! Even the Shorthair breed's best All-Age speedsters—including the ones that run into the next country and don't come back!—and never a Big Time Pointer classic winner to count among them.

The matter of possible misclassification was one the English Kennel Club dealt with as from near-enough the very beginning of competitive appearance of the breed. A new classification was drafted to suit the work pattern of the Utility breeds (see GSP in British & Commonwealth countries) as soon as officialdom was able to see that the Pointer/Setter classification was unsuitable. Somewhat hesitantly—let us even say tentatively—one does consider the possibility that no American Kennel Club officials ever took trouble to attend in the early days a trial at which the imported Utility breeds were striving to cope with Rule that was so blatantly unsuited to their structure and their inbred skills. In any case, it has never seemed to this compiler that American Kennel Club really set much store by Field Trial competitive affairs. Regulation and rule, of course, but nothing in interests of breed protection. A show dog is subject to the requirements of its breed standard; for gross type or structural inadequacies, for abnormalities present, can be denied the ring. Show judges are—well, so it is claimed!—privileged because of skills suited to their responsibilities. Field Trial judges are under requirement merely to be in good standing with the American Kennel Club, which treats of character, not competences. That there are very capable field trial judges is true, though one doubts such came to the saddle merely by way of ownership of a dog professionally handled, or by faithful service on the breed club committee. Rule governing Trial competition makes no requirement that an entry even conform minimally to breed type. There is certainly no equivalent for the German field trial requirement that an entry must pass conformation examination ahead of field competition. A Shorthair in German trials that cannot pass conformation can just take up and go home. . .

If the governing body, thirty years after permitting Utility breeds to spend themselves frustatingly in Pointer/Setter style trials, has made no move, be sure the owners have not spent thirty years sitting on their hands, watching performances out of tune. If the rules were not for changing—and when WERE Kennel Club rules readily for changing?—was left only to change the dog. Shorthairs cannot as yet outrun top Pointers but they are getting on towards there, this in many instances by grace of radical structural change not always to be counted admirable—but there it is—in front of one's eyes, often the very spit and equivalent of the competitive Pointer stock that suffered hound-cross "improvements" in earlier decades under much the same pressures of competition. And sequentially, with the passing of years, from time to time, some ethical owner of a right-looking, registered Shorthair bitch, presumably purebred, bred to a like-accounted mate, drops into the whelping box something yellow or orange or black-patched and the owner with no resource or compensation, must pick up a bucket of water for indicated usage, meditating meanwhile on the miracle that is the meeting of recessives, generations down the pike. . .

However, the governing body has not overlooked the need to recognize that there has been unethical cross-breeding. Do not the standard's disqualifications, added in January 1976, include one advising judges that "a dog with any area of black, red, orange, lemon or tan, or a dog solid white was for including OUT?"

Shorthairs in all other parts of the world are required in field competition to demonstrate skills suited to the dog for the foot-following utility-minded hunter. Not necessarily a slow-poke—a smart-moving dog is always preferable—but one that does not call for horse-following. In Germany, at the great trials, *everyone* walks. As each dog is provided with a fresh field to work the trial moves over many miles of agricultural land, farm to farm to farm. Handlers walk, judges walk, gallery walks, and be the temperature as it may, the judges walk in beautifully tailored suits, with collars and ties as, indeed, do virtually all hunters.

British and Commonwealth trials are also horseless, putting

Greyhound speed as item for penalizing. The British have their fencing. The Australians, if inclined to watch speedsters, have their Greyhound tracks.

Important in relation to discussion of "run" is the learning that the Germans also have taken to counting this factor in terms of the practical, original blueprint of the breed. There is a most interesting article worth noting, provided in an issue of *Kurzhaar Blätter* towards the close of the 1970s which the writer, Professor Alfons Lemper, Klub Kurzhaar's *Obman fur das Prufungswesen*, (Authority on Field Trial Affairs) has generously made available to this present work. The subject—"whither the GSP?"—deals with the circumstance that during the 1970s the Draathaar (Wirehaired Pointer) has been consistently out-registering the Kurzhaar (German Shorthaired Pointer) two-to-one, year by year.

Analyzing the possible reasons for buyer resistance, the Professor rejects the belief held in some quarters, that the GSP is too big a dog, pointing out that WHP is a "bigger." The market for hunting breeds is never a big one, so it is possible to sell only where market exists, yet the Kurzhaar breeders, who must sell at least two thousand pups a year to break even, can count only on a proportion of their pups going into competitive spheres. The rest must be sold as maybe, and against this operates increasing belief that the GSP is difficult to maintain and to handle.

In a careful survey far too long for these pages, Professor Lemper makes reference to prewar Shorthairs, time of the Golden Age of K.S. Kobold Mauderode Westerholt, Bill v. Hirschfeld, Don v.d. Schwarzen Kuhle and their contemporaries, this by the way reminding American breeders that it was from this era came their own basic pioneer stock. "Where however we stand to-day," continues the Professor, "must be left to the critics. What we know is that old-time breeders wanted quiet, cheerful, versatile retrieving utility dogs for all occasions, to serve one-dog owners. It was Dr. Kleeman's insistence on elegance, dogs with great noses, the distance movers, that generated inbred need for wide spaces to cover and professionals able to handle such fireballs. Kleeman having his way, the breed has developed a type from which the ordinary hunting-sport man turns, buying instead a Draathaar. Times have so changed since Kleeman's day, new industry, spread of housing;

fertilizers bring more land to cultivation, roads that endanger hunting dogs are being everywhere introduced, . . . But still the "Search Fanatics" (literal translation of the professor's term. CBM) have become so indoctrinated in terms of "run" that dogs are bred to the peak of performance such as suggests their mission to be that of running the game to death! There is a forgetting that hunting, apart from running, draws also on use of head and nose. Observe the dog that runs so—does he use the wind? CAN HE? Does he show hunting sense? Can he run—OR MUST HE RUN BECAUSE DRIVEN BY INBRED FORCES? It is the outcome of such breeding that makes the dog useless for the practical hunter—the often-observed senseless running and chasing—five hares in a single afternoon!—*a wild dog* would go to its certain death from starvation. . ."

There are those that claim, continues the Professor, that the Kurzhaar should be only in the hands of professionals but the largest number of pups must be sold to non-professionals. "They go as house dogs, companion dogs, friend-to-children dogs, watchdogs, protectors, such employments as these." (That Professor Lemper does not mention show dogs should surprise no one accustomed to breeder/used thought for the breed in its homeland.)

"Householders cannot cope with a dog making torment for its possession of inherited factors such as an overwhelming hunting instinct that provokes overpowering need to run, along with temperamental instabilities such as fear of thunder or sudden noises or even those greater instabilities that provoke aggression—the fearbiters. Concession must be made to changing times, just as the auto industry had to compound with the realities of traffic and road conditions, so that today's stock car has little in common with the specialized racer. So too, in a dog breed; to prosper it must emphasize livable qualities. Continued existence as a breed can hinge on public favor, and this requires steadier, utility-slanted dogs being produced, Continued straining after peak competitive performance is useless and endangers the breed. And character—so little attention being paid to character, so little known, though the dog has been for centuries mankind's companion. . ."

Space necessitates compression of what is a long, magnificently frank breed study. Worth keeping in mind, too, is the realization that the steadier Draathaar has been consolidating support here in the USA as well. And as to GSP popularity, currently showing increased registrations here rather than diminished, it becomes one to recall that the Irish Setter reached the peak of registration heights even while the public was demonstrating rejection from hyper temperament and structural faults—and as in all breeds that historically have gone into serious decline—the fall came suddenly—in 1980, the registrations plummeted by *six thousand* for the year!

As for the future of the Draathaar here—who knows? Numbers increase, in the showrings they win their proportion of Group awards, and in the Trials they can finish to Dual status—from Gundog Stakes! As for the surgical exactness of the Klub Kurzhaar's official Field Trial mentor's analysis—changing a breed from its inbred patterning to something entirely different has historically always exacted eventual penalty . . . Llewellin Setters, say—or patently crossbred FT Pointers . . . It's why people decades ago switched to the Shorthair . . . But then . . . and then. . .? Let us recall another opinion of about the time of veering away from Utility dog aims . . . Joe Stetson, then the best respected of sporting journalists, writing in *Field and Stream:* "If the German Shorthair is to be used as an ordinary Bird Dog, pushed out further and further, faster and faster, why not a Pointer or a Setter in the first place?"

Since the 3rd edition of this work went to press early in the 1970s, it has become possible to see that the old measure still applies— The Good Ones Come From the Other Good Ones—that apart from the proverbial wisdom it remains true that sow's ears make no one silk purses. The strains importantly prepotent, as the earlier editions noticed, remain in back of the importants of this present time. Give or take the overflow of suspect types that suggest hankypanky somewhere along the breeding processes, there are many hundreds of competent, handsome, companionable Shorthairs in this country, eager to demonstrate in such mediums as the owners might choose, the inbred good that is theirs. As Utility Hunting Breed extraordinary, individual dogs by the dozens can demonstrate their competences wherever the chance is provided. Puppy exposure to game will bring the most consistently-bred show stock to doing what truly comes naturally. Even where the element of run—even within the strains that come down to the now period from forebears recollected as "hyper"—among which count no few modern German imports of the last few decades, fitting exactly into the framework of Professor Lemper's descriptive—the utility skills lurk not too deep for recovery any time breeders and owners should decide to make such fashionable once again. Always remembering, however, that there is also an element of self-interest in so far as some professionals—thankfully not all!—operate. For sure it is easier to school a dog with whip and electronic aids, with horse at its heels or whatever, to run out into the next county than it is to school it to the good manners and the reliable hunting skills that hobby hunters really value. . .

Country to country, a wealth of reportage proclaims the ingrained nature of the breed's instinct to hunt, to track, to protect, even to triumph over questionable breed infusions and recover with the next generation's mending. In this interest, it is worth bringing together a couple of beautifully written reports of Shorthairs at work. One, from the pen of reporter, Mrs. Lynn Hadlock, covers a competitive occasion during the National NGPDA Championships of 1981:

"Conditions were bad. Almost every day the winds ranged in velocity from 25–50 mph. Six of the days the air was gray with dust storms, making conditions very difficult for the dogs. The pheasants were spooky, difficult to pin. The quail were almost impossible to find, as they buried in the heaviest of the woods and cover to escape the wind. Because the winds stayed with us almost the entire time, our winning dogs were not only those with a lot of bird sense under adverse conditions, but also a lot of heart. . ."

During one of these gray, overcast days was contested the National Shooting Dog Championship, winds progressing to over 40 mph throughout the Stake. Mrs. Hadlock mirrors the standard of performance, rated very high. This compiler's interest zeroed in on a brace run between an older, experienced dog, Timberland's Blue Dawn, and a youngster with his reputation still to make. The bracemate took off "very big . . . so big as to be last seen at 10. Blue attended his hunting and had six pieces of bird work. Four times the handler flushed pheasants in front of him. He had two stops to flushes and one non-productive. He was constantly digging into the heaviest cover (where the birds were to escape the wind) and thus at times did not move forward with speed and animation." Named one of the "Dogs of the Day," Blue did not, however, win the Stake . . .

Coincidental with arrival of this fine report of the American Field Championships, arrived from Australia one of that last reports of work of F.T. Ch. South Creek Zachary. He too was braced with a young contender in an All-Age Stake (Report—*New South Wales Field & Game,* which accorded permission for republication here, CBM):

"Australian Trialing, of course, runs under different aims and rules from the American and "speed and animation" are not necessarily of the same over-riding importance. A light breeze blowing on the handlers' backs was by the youngster found difficult to work under, giving him trouble in finding and holding his birds. Old Zac, the experienced, the wily, gave appearance of lifting himself to the challenge, back and forth with his head turned slightly, endlessly testing the wind. Upon scenting the birds he roaded out and nailed them right under his nose. He honored each and every flush, including wild flushing birds. The coveys he located in the same manner, and when flushed the shot birds were marked down with pinpoint precision. His attention was then directed to other birds still on the wing. His handler dropped his bird from every shot fired during the dog's two field rounds, and confidence dog and master held for each other was clearly demonstrated by the relaxed manner in which they worked, a real team effort. When the judges called a halt, clearly the champion had withstood the challenge of the stylish youngster that undoubtedly would have his F.T. title in the not too distant future."

The report concluded with the judge's comment that rapport between handler and dog was such that few commands were necessary. This compiler, reading, recalls the day beside a stream in the Rhineland at an IKP (Internationale) Trial—contenders from six GSP-owning nations, and a Czechoslovakian handler standing to attention, rigid on the bank, while his dog worked through all the complicated routine of a German top Trial Water Exercise, the swim-search, the finding the duck on the opposite bank among thick growth of reeds, the herding it (sheepdog style) back to the water where it would be available to the guns—always excitingly good spectator-fare. And throughout the entire long, long exercise no commands given, no whistle-blowing, not even any arm-waving. NOTHING! A man just standing—while his superbly endowed, trained dog worked out the sequences, eventually bringing the shot duck back to hand. . . The recollection gives lift to yet another, from an earlier German trial attended—the senior judge, irked by some whistle-signals, called handlers together for directive: "If we want music, there are larks in the sky . . . Whistles in your pocket, for use *only* in real emergency. . ."

140

Having overlooked the changing ideals of competitive work in Trialing for the breed, it can never be far from an observer's mind that this changing of a breed is no new story. The great Pointers of the early years of this present century—the fabulous Mary Montrose, Becky Broomhill and the like, multiple National FT winners with show breeding strong behind them all, became "outmoded" in the 1930s as an entirely different kind of "Pointer" emerged, lacking their beauty of structure and their elegance and command of performance that steadily over the intervening years have been changed by suspect type-structure from which, only too often, one inclines to avert the eye. And, in parallel period, the F.T. ownerships, in a very considerable number, slid away from the Pointer interest and became Shorthair people. Even Hjalmer Olsen. . . Whereupon, many efforts were increasingly directed towards bringing a proportion of the new-fancied breed within risk of the very same factors that had downgraded the earlier. One is reminded of parallel enterprises, even in humankind—snare a beautiful young virgin and turn her, over the next few years, into a whore. . .

A great picture of a dog balked in full flight as he picks up scent of a hiding duck. Taken in Germany.—*C. Bede Maxwell*

141

Field & National Field Ch. Patricia v. Frulord (Am/Can. Dual Ch. Gert's Duro v. Greif ex Juliana v. Frulord). Patricia made GSP history by taking both Nationals in 1971, and the AKC National again in 1973. Owner, Mrs. Fred W. Laird, Wash.

At end of a hard-running day, three owners whose dogs, here pictured, had all newly finished Field Titles, discovered further same-day coincidence. All are three-generation descendants of Albrecht's two great producing bitches, Ch. Katrina v. Albrecht (Ch. Jager Valor Albrecht/Susie v. Schwarenberg) and Katrina's daughter, Field Ch. Albrecht's Countess Tena (Ch. Alvin's Blitz, Ger. imp.). The three are Field Ch. Jaablitz Pfefer Albrecht, owned by George Wall; Field Ch. Albrecht's Flaming Arrow, owned by Greg Lamar; and Field Ch. Adolph's Smoky Cid, owned by Ernest Giest. Pictured at Field Trial, October 1979 at Dodge City.

9

Field Trials for German Shorthaired Pointers in America

WORKING towards his title of Field Trial Champion, a German Shorthair may run in the A.K.C.-licensed trials promoted for his breed alone, or in many of those promoted within the same official bracketing: Pointers, Setters, Weimaraners, W.H. Pointing Griffons, W.H. Pointers, Viszlas, Brittany Spaniels.

Rules governing the conduct of the A.K.C.-licensed Field Trials are clearly set out in the manual *Registration and Field Trial Rules and Standard Procedures,* published and copyrighted by The American Kennel Club. It is to be considered a must for novices with Field Trial competition aspirations, and is to be secured on application from The American Kennel Club, 51 Madison Ave., New York, N.Y. 10010.

Field Trials are defined and classified in this Rule book as follows: *"A MEMBER FIELD TRIAL* is a F.T. at which Championship points may be awarded, given by a club or association which is a member of The American Kennel Club.

"*A LICENSED FIELD TRIAL* is a F.T. at which Championship points may be awarded, given by a club or association which is not a member of The American Kennel Club, but which has been specifically licensed by The American Kennel Club to give the specific Field Trial designated by the license.

"*A SANCTIONED FIELD TRIAL* is an informal F.T. at which dogs may compete but not for Championship points, held by a club or association, whether or not a member of The American Kennel Club, by obtaining the sanction of The American Kennel Club."

Competition is further arranged according to age and performance. Material has been reprinted by permission of The American Kennel Club, 1980. The divisions are as follows:

"*OPEN PUPPY STAKE* for dogs six months and under fifteen months of age at the first advertised day of the trial.

"Puppies must show desire to hunt, boldness, and initiative in covering ground and in searching likely cover. They should indicate the presence of game if the opportunity is presented. Puppies should show reasonable obedience to their handlers' commands, but should not be given additional credit for pointing staunchly. Each dog shall be judged on its actual performance as indicating its future as a high class Derby Dog. . . .

". . . if the premium list states that blanks will be fired, every dog that makes game contact shall be fired over if the handler is within reasonable gun range. At least 15 minutes and not more than 30 minutes shall be allowed for each heat."

"*OPEN DERBY STAKE* for dogs six months of age and under two years of age on the first advertised day of the trial.

"Derbies must show a keen desire to hunt, be bold and independent, have a fast, yet attractive style of running, and demonstrate not only intelligence in seeking objectives but also the ability to find game. Derbies must establish point but no additional credit shall be given for steadiness to wing and shot. If the handler is within reasonable gun range of a bird which has been flushed after a point, a shot must be fired. A lack of opportunity for firing over a Derby dog on point shall not constitute reason for nonplacement when it had had game contact in acceptable Derby manner. Derbies must show reasonable obedience to their handlers' commands. Each dog is to be judged on its actual performance as indicating its future promise. At least 20 minutes and not more than 30 minutes shall be allowed for each heat."

"GUN DOG STAKE (OPEN OR AMATEUR) for dogs six months of age and over on the first advertised day of the trial."

"LIMITED GUN DOG STAKE (OPEN OR AMATEUR) for dogs six months of age and over on the first advertised day of the trial which have won first place in an Open Derby Stake or which have placed first, second, third or fourth in a Gun Dog Stake. A field trial-giving Club may give an Amateur Limited Gun Dog Stake in which places that qualify a dog have been acquired in Amateur Stakes only."

The two Stakes above mentioned are bracketed in terms of required performance as follows:

"GUN DOG AND LIMITED GUN DOG STAKES. A Gun Dog must give a finished performance and be under its handler's control at all times. It must handle kindly, with a minimum of noise and hacking by the handler. A Gun Dog must show a keen desire to hunt, must have a bold and attractive style of running, and must demonstrate not only intelligence in quartering and in seeking objectives but also the ability to find game. The dog must hunt for its handler at all times at a range suitable for a handler on foot, and should show or check in front of its handler frequently. It must cover adequate ground but never range out of sight for a length of time that would detract from its usefulness as a practical hunting dog. The dog must locate game, must point staunchly, and must be steady to wing and shot. Intelligent use of the wind and terrain in locating game, accurate nose, and style and intensity on point are essential. At least 30 minutes shall be allowed for each heat."

"ALL-AGE STAKE (OPEN OR AMATEUR) for dogs six months of age and over on the first advertised day of the trial."

"LIMITED ALL-AGE STAKE (OPEN OR AMATEUR) for dogs six months of age and over on the first advertised day of the trial which have won first place in an Open Derby Stake or which have placed first, second, third or fourth in any All-Age Stake. A field trial giving club may give an Amateur Limited All-Age Stake in which places that qualify a dog have been acquired in Amateur Stakes only."

"ALL-AGE AND LIMITED ALL-AGE STAKES. An All-Age Dog must give a finished performance and must be under reasonable control of its handler. It must show a keen desire to hunt, must have a bold and attractive style of running, and must show inde-

pendence in hunting. It must range well out in a forward moving pattern, seeking the most promising objectives, so as to locate any game on the course. Excessive line-casting and avoiding cover must be penalized. The dog must respond to handling but must demonstrate its independent judgment in hunting the course, and should not look to its handler for directions as to where to go. The dog must find game, must point staunchly, and must be steady to wing and shot. Intelligent use of the wind and terrain in locating game, accurate nose, and style and intensity on point, are essential. At least 30 minutes shall be allowed for each heat."

An Amateur Handler is a person who, during the period of two years preceding the trial has not accepted remuneration in any form for the training of a hunting dog or the handling of a dog in a field trial.

No member of the household of a person who does not qualify as an Amateur Handler under this definition can qualify as an Amateur Handler.

Field Trial competition is conducted under basic rules long tested, but is subject to updatings from time to time for clarifications deemed needful. An owner should become possessed of the latest editions, always, of the AKC Rule Book as working from a superseded issue might cause confusion. Stakes at licensed or Member Trials may be run on any of a variety of courses and rules in relation to running and handling are explicitly defined. As too are the Rules governing Drawing and Bracings, attended ahead of the date of the Trial with, however, exception in the case of Limited Gundog and Limited All Age Stakes wherein additional entries may be accepted and drawings occur immediately before the running of the stake, provided such stipulation has been printed in the premium list. There are those holding that the Limited Stake is the Stake for the Stars, but no rule enforces this. In practice champions tend to run in any Stake the owner feels there is chance to win.

Bracing (running dogs in pairs) is in the interest of saving time as well as for permitting judges to assess manners, one dog towards another.

Requirements for a Field Championship, the ten points needed, are exactly defined, along with the additional requirement that a Shorthair, as well as a Wirehaired Pointer or Weimaraner, must have been certified by two approved judges to have passed a Water Test at a licensed or member field trial held by a Specialty Club for one of these three breeds. Amateur Field Championship titles are also subject to the requirement of ten points won under the point schedule operative in regular Amateur Stakes in at least three licensed or member trials,

Discussing briefly some aspects of Field Trial Rule in terms of American Kennel Club Rules, it is also worth mentioning here from Chapter 17, Section 8 (Revision of Jan. 1981): "A National Championship Stake at German Shorthaired Pointer Field Trials shall be for dogs over six months of age, which by reason of wins previously made qualify under special Rules approved by the Board of Directors. This Stake shall be run not more than once in any calendar year by the Parent Association of the Breed. The winner of such Stake shall become a Field Champion of Record (if registered in The American Kennel Club Stud Book) and shall be entitled to be designated "National German Shorthaired Pointer Field Champion of 19--.""

No prouder title for a dog to attain—no prouder designation to attach to his name in tabulations than NFC. Some superb dogs have earned and carried it—*one to a year, as the Rule directs.*

There is a parallel title, carrying similar honor, perhaps—who knows—even somewhat harder to win in terms of the time and terrain. This is the title of National Champion under the Rule of the National German Shorthaired Pointer Association (NGSPCA) of the American Field interests, body that was, in fact, first to promote such competition—already in 1952. Under this Rule, also, some very great dogs have gained the proud national accolade, the title of NFC also carried the one-a-year-triumph, as elsewhere in these pages applauded.

That was the ideal of NGSPCA in 1952, and of GSPCA of 1953— to honor THE Dog of the year. Now, almost thirty years later leaf through the ongoing breed publications and find oneself literally floundering through such a multiplicity of NFC-titleds that the designation promises to rate scarcely a notch above the title of Field Champion for sheer over-use and the disinterest imposed by endless repetition. "National Ch." has been tacked on to just about every Stake considered able to carry it, most of which would seem to be competed for on a twice-a-year basis. Consequently promotion material in the dog press is overloaded with "NFCs" literally by the dozen, reducing all—including the really great Stake winners—to lower common denominator title status.

We are back with that wonderful opinion expressed by the famous Dr. Johnson, as his Boswell reported it: "Sir—your levellers always want to level down. They never want to level up!"

So, for every dog in the game a National Ch. would seem to be the ultimate, forseeable aim, all on the equal mark. . .

There could be possible merit then, as it has become seemingly too late to stem the multiplicity of the "National Champions," to add some further additive to the title which AKC Rule originally approved. To the two Trials designated by the two separate governing bodies, add a further identification—perhaps something along the lines the Germans long ago contrived when they named *their* two top trials respectively after the great pioneer breeders, Prince zu Solms (autumn) and Dr. Kleeman (spring).

American Kennel Club (FT Rule Book) is emphatic in expression of intent that there shall be *one only* National FT Ch. per year. American Field interest may have like thought in mind, but has seemingly yielded to pressure of interests to make the proud title more widely distributed.

There is merit and a capful of pride in owning, or having bred, THE National Field Trial Champion of any given year.

*   *   *   *   *

For its Field Championship a dog must win a total of ten points in regular Stakes in at least three Licensed or Member Club Trials. The only short cut is to win the annual National Field Trial Championship, a route that is as steeply tough as it is short. Of the ten points necessary, three must have been won in one three-point or better Open All Age, Open Gundog, or Open Limited All-Age Stake. Puppy or Open Derby Stakes can count only two points, and Amateur Stakes to four. Points are based on the number of dogs competing, and are scheduled by the Board of Directors of the A.K.C. from time to time, according to the number of dogs usually competing in the various parts of the country.

Water Test: It is now mandatory for a Shorthair (and a Wirehair, or a Weimaraner) aspirant for title honors to be certified by two approved judges to have passed a Water Test at a licensed or member field trial held by a Specialty Club for one of these three breeds.

NATIONAL CHAMPIONSHIP FIELD TRIALS. Two such trials are sponsored annually, one under American Field, one under A.K.C. license. American Field was first to promote such competition, in 1952, when however no dog was held to have shown merit sufficient to be crowned National Champion.

148

National German Shorthaired Pointer Assn. Inc. Champions
(American Field)

Year	Dog	Owner
1952	No Champion Named.	
1953	Field Ch. DIXON'S SKID-DO	Russell Dixon, Michigan
1954	Field Ch. FRITZ V. STRAUSS	Carl Kemritz, Illinois
1955/6	Field Ch. DIXON'S SHIELA	Russell Dixon, Michigan
1957	Field Ch. KAY STARR	Frank Summers, Michigan
1958	Field Ch. DIXON'S SUSY Q	Howard Confer, Michigan
1959	Dual Ch. KAY V.D. WILDBURG (imp. Ger.)	Walter Kogurt, Canada
1960	Field Ch. BROWNIE'S GREIF MCCARTHY	Laurence McCarthy, California
1961	Field Ch. INMAN'S SWISS JAGER	H. & L. Inman, Michigan
1962	Field Ch. REX V. WAGGER	Luther Shockley, Illinois
1963	Dual Ch. BARON FRITZ V. HOHEN TANN	R. Bauspies, Illinois
1964	Field Ch. SUSAN V. HOHEN TANN	T. & M. Schwertfeger, Illinois
1965	Field Ch. DE LONG'S POINTING GABBY	Robert DeLong, Indiana
1966	Field Ch. BUCKSKIN	Claude Butler, Illinois
1967	Field Ch. FIELDACRES SIR JAC	Vincent Laramie, Michigan
1968	Dual Ch. TELSTAR DIRECT	Ralph Laramie, Michigan
1969	Field Ch. MOSEGAARD'S VON SCHMIDT	William Moore, Ohio
1970	Dual Ch. LUCY BALL	Dr. L. Kline, FLorida
1971	Field Ch. PATRICIA V. FRULORD	G. & E. Laird, Washington
1972	Field Ch. PATRICIA V. FRULORD	G. & E. Laird, Washington.
1973	Field Ch. MOESGAARD'S DANDY'S RADAR	L.L. Kline & G. Ostrander. Florida.
1974	Field Ch. TIP TOP TEDDY	R. Brooks, Ill.
1975	Field Ch. AMMERTAL'S LANCER D	J. Reid, Idaho
1976	Field Ch. HUGO VON BERGESKANTE	J. Ullman, Pennsylvania
1977	Field Ch. IB'S HEIR BIFF	E. Caudle, Mich
1978	Field Ch. TIP TOP SAVAGE SAM	E. Arkema
1979	Field Ch. ROMMEL'S BIG SHOOTER S	D. Hillstead, Mich.
1980	Field Ch. EHRLICHER'S ABE	P. & L. Cross, Idaho
1981	Field Ch. EHRLICHER'S ABE	P. & L. Cross, Idaho

National German Shorthaired Pointer Field Champions
(A.K.C.)

Year	Dog	Owner
1953	Dual Ch. DANDY JIM V. FELDSTROM	Dr. Clark Lemley, Michigan
1954	Dual Ch. WENDENHEIM'S FRITZ	Frank Nuzzo, Illinois
1955	Field Ch. GUNMASTER'S JENTA	James M. Howard, Ohio
1956	Field Ch. TRAUDE V.D. WENGENSTADT	Oliver Rousseau, California
1957	Field Ch. B OBO GRABENBRUCH BECKUM	Dr. W. Schimmel, California
1958	Field Ch. DIXON'S SHEILA	Russell Dixon, Michigan
1959	Field Ch. OLOFF V.D. SCHLEPPENBURG (imp.)	Roy J. Thompson, Illinois
1960	Field Ch. DUKE V. STRAUSS III	Steve Molnar, Wisconsin

Year	Dog	Owner
1961	Field Ch. VON SAALFIELD'S KASH	Walter Seagraves, California
1962	Field Ch. MOESGAARD'S DANDY	Dr. L. L. Kline, Florida
1963	Field Ch. MOESGAARD'S ANGEL	D. Prager, California
1964	Field Ch. SHOCKLEY'S PRIDE (previously Fld. Ch. Rex v. Wagger)	L. Shockley, Illinois
1965	Field Ch. ONNA V. BESS	R. G. Froelich, California
1966	Field Ch. FIELDACRES BANANZA	H. & J. Dowler, Pennsylvania
1967	Field Ch. RIP TRAF VON BESS	M. Bess, California
1968	Field Ch. THALBERG'S SEAGRAVES CHAYNE	D. Miner, California
1969	Field Ch. BLICK V. SHINBACK	Cal. Rossi, Jr., California
1970	No Champion Named	
1971	Field Ch. PATRICIA V. FRULORD	Gladys & Fred Laird, Washington
1972	Field T. Ch. WYATT'S GIP V. SHINBACK	W. Palmer
1973	NFC & Fld. Ch. PATRICIA V. FRULORD	Gladys & Fred Laird
1974	Field Ch. CEDE MEIN GEORGIE GIRL	R. A. Flynn & W. P. Troutman
1975	Field Ch. MARK V'S ONE SPOT	R. Rainey, Idaho
1976	Field Ch. FRULORD'S TIM	G. & F. Laird, Washington
1977	Field Ch. JOCKO VON STOLZHAFEN	Dr. J.S. Brown, Pennsylvania
1978	Championship Withheld	
1979	Dual Ch. LIKA BUCKSKIN	G. & H. Short, Iowa.
1980	Field Ch. AMMERTAL'S BOSS RANGER	Gary K. Nehring, Minn.
1981	Field Ch. CHECKMATE'S WHITE SMOKE	S. Lyons, Texas

Field Trial Judging: The best Field Trial judging—like the best Show judging—is based on the recognition of virtues rather than on the mere penalizing of faults, though, of course, mistakes have to be evaluated when summing up the performance of a dog. This country as yet provides no equivalent of the German performance sheet which the judges mark, duty by duty, as the dog dispatches it. These sheets become part of the dog's record, and are often passed over with his papers when he is sold.

In this country, local practices vary. Thus, in some areas judges do make their marking slips available at a place where the owners can collect them after the trials. This is the opposite pole from another recognized procedure, in which the judge fends off dissatisfied owners with a brusque: "That's the way I saw 'em, and that's the way I placed 'em." As a matter of strict fact, there is no official obligation imposed upon a judge to discuss his placings if he does not wish to do so. Incompetents sometimes take refuge

150

under such protection. The philosophy is expressed by the judge who said he knew he placed the dogs right, but if he started giving out reasons, his reasons could possibly be all wrong! So far as the owners are concerned, gracious acceptance of decisions marks not only the good sportsman, but the wise one. He saves his breath to cool his porridge, knowing that there will be another day, another judge, another chance.

Field Trial judges are not subject to licensing by the A.K.C., as Show judges are. It is necessary only that they have their names submitted beforehand by the Trial-giving club for official approval, and that they be persons in good standing with the A.K.C. It is their privilege to run their own dogs in any Stake they are not judging on the same day, with the exceptions to this provided for in Special Rules applying to certain breeds.

A famous handler, who also does his share of judging, recently summarized the responsibilities of a Field Trial judge for the author: "He will forget his friends and his enemies, and any considerations of breeding. He will look for style and class, the way a dog runs the back course. He won't admire a pottering dog, nor one that continually checks back to its handler. He will let handlers make their own pace, ride back of them, never come between the handler and the dog. He will take account of the way a dog searches for game, and also consider the time of day, well knowing that the first and last braces are often in better luck than those running, say, between 11 A.M. and 3 P.M., and make allowance for it. He must remember the Shorthair is a pointing breed, required at all times to be lofty and penalized when not. A judge forgetting that Field Trials are run to improve the breed is not doing his job. It should never be club policy to let two inexperienced judges be braced together. Nor does holding an official position in a club constitute a sufficient reason to consider a person a competent Field Trial judge."

The well-understood requirement in other countries that the dogs should drop, bears hard at times on adult trained dogs imported here from other countries, especially from Germany. Experience seems to vary from dog to dog. Some adapt easily; some never do. The observations of famed trainer Richard S. Johns, of Pennsylvania, who has been associated with many good imported dogs, are valuable in this connection.

"I have imported a good number from Germany and one from France, and experienced difficulty with only one," he advises. "While in Germany, I purchased Nanny v. Lüchseck as a fully trained dog and shot over her for a year. Nanny was trained to stand up on feathered game, but would drop on a hare. Sepp (K.S. Sepp v. Grabenbruch) did not drop to wing and presented no problem, but a bitch I imported from Germany as a trained dog could not be got over dropping to wing and shot. I had no difficulty with the language difference, and all of my imports quickly learned commands in English. However, I no longer import trained dogs from Europe, only pups, and it is my feeling that the majority of people too would be far better off with puppies or early Derby age dogs from Europe. Present National Ch. Kay v.d. Wildburg, imported at Derby age, was not taught to drop in Germany, is very lofty on point, to shot and kill. The Germans, of course, put no pressure on their Derby age dogs, seeking to this age only the proof of inherited working qualities and desirable conformation."

Some owners and trainers have waged terrific, unpublicized battles to re-train adult German dogs to the American style. Stern pressure exerted has too often failed of its aim, resulting only in the complete ruin of the bewildered dog, undergoing heavy punishment for what he was originally taught was the right thing for him to do. The unedifying sight of a once-competent dog false-pointing all over, and going down as soon as he hits scent of any kind, could be as good a text as any for a sermon on the advantages of importing dogs before they have been taught what they do not need to know in this country.

The Germans have always allowed young dogs the privilege of being young, and even some chasing is allowed a Derby there, provided he doesn't turn it into that little bit that is just TOO much. Many of the best American trainers are also of the opinion that all work and no play makes as dull a dog as it makes a boy. If a dog is having fun he'll show it in his eager intensity of style and movement. If he is merely discharging a duty because his ribs will hurt from correction if he doesn't, well. . . .

Bob Holcomb, West Coast trainer, has a useful observation to make: "You cannot force a dog to go find and point a bird *if he does not want to!*" On the opposite side of the country, Joe Murdock, who has trained many great ones, likes to tell his clients who are taking home their promising youngsters he has worked lightly to Derby status: "Go have fun with him for a season or two. Then, when he's grown up, bring him back; all he'll need then will be steadying."

152

All regular Field Trialers have seen the wreckage imposed on promising youngsters by pressure too early applied. From such are recruited the "mechanicals," the "blinkers," the "false-pointers," and all that go in plain fear of punishment—than which no less edifying sight exists—the sad roster of those from whom Too Much was expected Too Soon.

Style: By temperament and by anatomical construction, the truebred German Shorthaired Pointer is of less spectacular working habit than his cousin, the Pointer. He makes, preferably, a cautious approach to his bird rather than a dramatic slam, another characteristic that often involves some grief here now for trainer and for dog. Then, too, there is the proved truth that the working habit of a shrewd German Shorthaired Pointer is influenced by the kind of game on which he is customarily worked. Old Itchy-foot, the pheasant, can develop a foot-scent trailing habit in the local dogs, enough to drive all the trainers crazy, the dog working the bird as his instinct directs. Where the varieties of game tend to stay stolidly put, the dog works more steadily, with a higher stance. Good judges need to know these things as well as the trainers do.

All such hereditary and environmental factors influence style. Most present-day compilers, seeking to define style, take refuge in the definition published in the Gaines Booklet, *Standards of Judicial Practice:*

"*Style:* Loftiness is a desirable characteristic of a dog on point, but intensity is the more desirable characteristic of the pointing dog, and is far more important than the position of head and tail. . . . Joy in hunting is a most desirable characteristic and should always be looked for. This is sometimes indicated by merriness, sometimes by other physical attributes of a dog in motion, but it is always unmistakable. Nor should there be any distinction in the desirability of Style in groundwork or on point between Derby, All-Age, or Championship contenders. . . ."

All the truly great dogs of the breed, their records gleaming brightly in the tables of performance, have been great stylists. It is also true that many useful ones, whose performances never carried them to the giddy heights of National fame, have also had such an eye-catching joy in working as to fix them in the memory of those who have seen them. Such dogs are immediately recognized at a Trial, and their years of competition are often very long, extended into their old age because of the joy they take in running and the joy their owners take in just watching them.

153

THE DUAL CHAMPIONS

RUSTY V. SCHWARENBERG
Owner: Jack Shattuck, Jr., Minnesota

SCHATZ V. SCHWARENBERG
Owners: Dr. H. and Mrs. Zahalka, Minnesota

VALBO V. SCHLESBERG
Owner: Carl Schnell, Michigan

SEARCHING WIND TOPPER
Owner: Hjalmer Olsen, Wisconsin

BLICK V. GRABENBRUCH
Owner: Richard S. Johns, Pennsylvania

VALKYRIE V. GRABENBRUCH
Owner: Richard S. Johns, Pennsylvania

BARON V. STRAUSS
Owner: Del J. Glodowski, Wisconsin

NATIONAL Ch. DANDY JIM V. FELDSTROM
Owner: Dr. Clark Lemley, Michigan

NATIONAL Ch. WENDENHEIM'S FRITZ
Owner: Frank Nuzzo, Illinois

DOKTORGAARDEN'S CARO, imp. Denmark
Owner: Dr. Wm. F. Hartnell, Utah

TRAILBORN MIKE, C.D.
Owner: Carl L. Johnson

JUNKER V. GRABENBRUCH
Owner: J. Lurba, Pennsylvania

FRITZ OF SLEEPY HOLLOW
Owner: F. Z. Palmer, New York

BIG ISLAND SPOOK
Owner: G. Reudiger, Minnesota

CAPTAIN V. WINTERHAUCH (also BIS)
Owner: Millard W. Axelrod, Minnesota

KAPOSIA'S FIREBIRD
Owners: Don and Betty Sandberg, Minnesota

JONES HILL FRIEDRICH
Owner: Dr. Eugene R. McNinch

PETER BRUNER
Owner: E. D. Andrews, Ohio

HEIDIE V. MARVON (also Can. Ch.)
Owner: Charles Puffer, Michigan

(Mars v. Ammertal, imp.
ex Vicky v. Schwarenberg)

(Ch. Fritz v. Schwarenberg
ex Helga v. Schwarenberg)

(Duke v. Rheinberg
ex Heide v. Schlesberg)

(Ch. Searching Wind Bob
ex Fieldborn Katzie Karlwald)

(K. S. Sepp v. Grabenbruch, imp.
ex Nanny v. Luckseck gen Senta, imp.)

(Dual Ch. Blick v. Grabenbruch
ex Ch. Katinka of Sycamore Brook, C.D.)

(Toby B
ex Patsy v. Strauss)

(Ch. Davy's Jim Dandy
ex Ch. Joan v. Feldstrom)

(Fritz v. Pepper
ex Wendy v. Windhausen)

(Fangel's Rolf
ex Holevgaards Kora)

(Erick v. Reffup
ex Trailborn Scholar)

(Dual Ch. Blick v. Grabenbruch
ex Ch. Katinka of Sycamore Brook, C.D.)

(Ch. Donar v. Schlangenberg
ex Susabelle v. Catskill)

(Ch. Rex v. Krawford
ex Graff's Lady Lou)

(Ch. Oak Crest Rick v. Winterhauch
ex Duchess v. Hotwagner)

(Count Snooper v. Dusseldorf
ex Dual Ch. Lucky Lady v. Winterhauch)

(Ch. Pardner, C.D.
ex Ch. Wilhelmia v. Kirsche, C.D.)

(Field Ch. Pheasant Lane Schnapps
ex Hunter's Lady Heflin)

(Necker's Arno
ex Wilhelmina v. Marvon)

RIGA V. HOHEN TANN
Owner: Robert Fletcher, Washington
(Field Ch. Bill's Linzer Boy
ex Ch. Bella v. Hohen Tann, imp.)

GRETCHEN V. SUTHERS
Owner: Paul Putnam, California
(Field Ch. Frederick Wolfgang
ex Paul's Vinkel)

GRETCHEN V. GREIF (also a Dual in Canada)
Owner: Ralph A. Park, Sr., Washington
(Field Ch. Yunga v. Hundsheimerkogel
ex Field Ch. Karen v. Greif)

OXTON'S LEISELOTTE V. GREIF
Owner: E. E. Harden, California
(Field Ch. Greif v. Hundsheimerkogel
ex Ch. Yunga War Bride)

AL-RU'S ERIC
Owner: R. J. Burnand
(Tell v. Grabenbruch
ex Gretchen Barikstettle)

STRAUSS'S WORKING BOY
Owner: Hermann Foss, Wisconsin
(Ch. Otto v. Strauss
ex Rita's Cocoa)

LUCKY LADY V. WINTERHAUCH, C.D.
Owner: A. Frush, Minnesota
(Ch. Oak Crest Rick v. Winterhauch
ex Hephzibah Holzman)

OXTON'S BRIDE'S BRUNZ V. GREIF
Owner: J. Huizenga, California
(Field Ch. Greif v. Hundsheimerkogel
ex Ch. Yunga War Bride)

BARON TURN & TAXIS
Owner: Wm. A. Barth, Colorado
(Heide's Dream
ex Astarte v. Svealand)

ABLE V. ELTZ
Owner: Mrs. K. Metcalf Allen, California
(Ch. Oak Crest Rick v. Winterhauch
ex Duchess v. Hotwagner)

MADCHEN BRAUT V. GREIF
Owner: E. E. Harden, California
(Field Ch. Greif v. Hundsheimerkogel
ex Ch. Yunga War Bride)

TIMBERLANE'S ACE
Owner: Mrs. W. G. Davis, Wash.
also a Dual in Canada
(Fritz v. Sulfmeister
ex Katherine v. Eugen)

FLICK V. HEIDEBRINK
Owner: Not Reported
(Wehrwolf v. Braumatal
ex Dina v. Heidebrink)

SAGER V. GARDSBURG
Owners: R. and L. Sylvester, Georgia
(Ch. Buck v. Gardsburg
ex Ch. Valory v. Gardsburg)

HANS V. ELDRIDGE, C.D. (also BIS)
Owner: R. Eldridge, Wisconsin
(Baron Strauss II
ex Strauss's Pamela)

ALFI V.D. KRONNENMUHLE, imp.
Owner: R. C. Bauspies, Illinois
(K.S. Gernot v.d. Heidehöhe
ex Heide v.d. Emmstadt)

BIG ISLAND RECS
Owner: Duane Petit, Minnesota
(Big Island Skinner
ex Big Island Queen)

ROMMEL V. RUMPELSTILZCHEN
Owner: K. T. Jensen
(Elbing v.d. Forst Brickwedde
ex Karen v. Hesselbach)

GROUSEWALD'S BLITZ
Owners: N. and J. Goodspeed
(Dual Ch. Blick v. Grabenbuch
ex Debby v. Hollabird)

DALLO V. HESSELBACH, C.D.
Owners: C. W. and Mrs. Flinn, Illinois
(Ch. Ace v. Barikstettle, C.D.
ex Calyx v.d. Forst Brickwedde)

WOODY V. RONBERG
Owner: J. Christensen, Wisconsin
(Field Ch. Kim v. Waldheim
ex Strauss' Glamor Girl)

MISS B'HAVEN V. WINTERHAUCH
Owner: R. C. Bauspies, Illinois
(Dual Ch. Captain v. Winterhauch
ex Dual Ch. Alfi v.d. Kronnenmuhle, imp.)

SKID-DO'S BONNIE KAREN
Owners: Mr. and Mrs. J. C. Pope,
California

(Field Ch. Dixon's Skid-Do
ex Field Ch. Dixon's Bonnie)

WAG-AE'S SNOWFLAKE, C.D.
Owner: E. D. Andrews, Akron, Ohio

(Spike of Clover Club
ex Princess Rosie)

FRITZ OF HICKORY LANE FARM

(Dual & Nat'l Ch. Dandy Jim v.
Feldstrom

Owner: William Gill, Michigan

ex Can/Am. Ch. Susanna Mein
Liebchen, C.D.)

GUSTAV MEIN LIEBCHEN

(Dual & Nat'l Ch. Dandy Jim v.
Feldstrom

Owner: Otto Harris, Michigan

ex Can/Am. Ch. Susanna Mein
Liebchen, C.D.)

MARMADUKE MEIN LIEBCHEN
Owner: Maxine Collins, Michigan

(Ch. Fieldborn Tempo II
ex Can/Am. Ch. Susanna Mein
Liebchen, C.D.)

BRUNNENHUGEL BALDER
Owner: Norman Revel, Calif.

(Dual Ch. Oxton's Bride's Brunz v. Greif
ex Ch. Weidenbach Suzette)

SCHOENE BRAUT V. GREIF
Owner: E. E. Harden, California

(Field Ch. Greif v. Hundsheimerkogel
ex Ch. Yunga War Bride)

BRUNNENHUGEL JARL
Owner: N. Revel, California

(Dual Ch. Oxton's Bride's Brunz v.
Greof ex Ch. Weidenbach Suzette)

BIFF BANGABIRD
Owner: Dr. C. P. Gandal, New York

(Chadwick of Hollabird ex
Grousewalds Berta)

ESSO V. ENZSTRAND (imp.)
Owner: D. Glodowski, Wisconsin

(Cato v. Grabenbruch ex
Dina v. Enzstrand)

NAT'L. F.T. CH. MOESGAARD'S DANDY
Owner: Dr. L. L. Kline, Florida

(Field Ch. Moesgaard's Ib ex Field
Ch. Doktorgaarden's Lucky)

ERDENREICH'S EARTHA
Owner: Miss I. Pauly, California

(Erdenreich's Able v. Yankee ex Am.-
Can. Ch. Erdenreich die Zweite, C.D.)

NAT'L. F.T. CH. KAY V.D. WILDBURG
(imp.)
Owners: R. Johns and J. Eusepi, Penna.

(K.S. Pol v. Blitzdorf ex
Cora v. Wesertor)

BEE'S GABBY V. BECKUM
Owner: Donald Briggs, California

(Nat'l F.T. Ch. Bobo Grabenbruch
Beckum ex Field Ch. Skid-Do's Bee)

ALBRECHT'S BARON CID
Owners: M. and L. Albrecht, Kansas

(Ch. Big Island Spotter ex Field Ch.
Albrecht's Countess Tena)

ALBRECHT'S BARONESS CORA
Owners: M. and L. Albrecht, Kansas

(Ch. Big Island Spotter ex Field Ch.
Albrecht's Countess Tena)

DINO V. ALBRECHT
Owners: Happy Hollow Kennels, Md.

(Ch. Big Island Spotter ex Ch.
Albrecht's Apache Breeze)

STREAK'S HERBST VERSPRECHEN
Owners: J. Lee and S. Meredith, Ohio

(Field Ch. Skriver's Streak ex Ch.
Lady Patricia Valbo)

ROBIN CREST CHIP, C.D.T. (and
Canadian champion)

(Ch. Alnor's Brown Mike ex Ch.
Montreal Belle)

NAT'L F.T. Ch. BARON FRITZ V. HOHEN
TANN
Owner: Ray C. Bauspies, Illinois

(Baron v. Heidebrink ex Field Ch.
Sandra v. Hohen Tann)

156

FIELDACRES KATIA
Owner: James R. Jares, Ohio
HEWLETT GIRL PEBBLES
Owner: Herman Levee, New York
ZIPPER DER ORRIAN
Owner: O. L. Borland, Oregon
KAMIAK DESERT SAND
Owners: L. & G. Dorius, California

SATAN V. SCHNELLBERG
Owner: Wilson H. Lufkin, Massachusetts
NAT'L F.T. Ch. LUCKY BALL
Owner: Dr. L. L. Kline, Florida
RADBACK'S ARKO (Also Can. Ch.)
Owner: Alvin Schwager, Washington

JANIE GREIF V. HEISTERHOLZ
Owner: Elaine Stout, Colorado

RITZIE
Owner: George de Gidio, Minnesota
ERDENREICH'S JETTA BECKUM
Owner: C. D. Lawrence, Washington
GRUENWEG'S DANDY DANDY
Owner: Ralph Z. Neff, Ohio
ARRAK V. HEISTERHOLZ (imp. Ger.)
Owner: Ralph A. Park, Sr., Washington
RICHLU'S TERROR
Owners: C. & S. Carlson, Ohio
RICHLU'S DAN ORANIAN
Owners: C. & S. Carlson, Ohio
RAMBLING ROCK
Owner: Hal G. Ward, Virginia
BLITZ V. JAGERSLIEBE
Owner: R. M. Bancroft, Wisconsin
HOCHLANDER'S TITELHALTER
Owner: A. J. Hok, Illinois
CEDE MEIN DOLLY DER ORRIAN
Owner: Dean Tidrick, Iowa
BIG ISLAND SILVER DEUCE
Owner: Robert Smith, Minnesota
HURCKES STEEL VICTOR
Owners: R. & L. Hurckes, Illinois
BO DIDDLEY V. HOHEN TANN
Owner: T. Schwertfeger, Illinois
GERT'S DENA V. GREIF (Also Dual Ch.
in Canada)
Owners: Ralph & Frances Park, Washington
KAJOBAR V. STONY BROOK
Owners: H. & T. Strauss, New York
RADBACH'S DUSTCLOUD (Also a Dual
Ch. in Canada)

(Ch. Boy Howdy ex Fieldacres Geisha)

(Dual Ch. Biff Bangabird ex Field Ch.
Hewlett Girl Greta)
Field Ch. Von Thalberg's Fritz II ex
Zetta v. Fuehrerheim)
(Field Ch. Lutz v.d. Radbach—imp.
Ger.—ex Field Ch. Kamiak Bold
Bark)
(Eros v. Scheperhof—imp. Ger.—ex
Field Ch. Freda v. Schnellberg)
(Dual & Nat'l F.T. Ch. Moesgaard's
Dandy ex Pearl of Wetzler)
(Field Ch. Gert v.d. Radbach—imp.
Ger.—ex Katja v.d. Radbach—imp.
in utero, Ger.)
(Am/Can. Dual Ch. Arrak v. Heister-
holz—imp. Ger.—ex Am/Can. Dual
Ch. Gretchen v. Greif)
Field Ch. Chocolate Chip II ex Big
Island Sheba)
(Field Ch. Stutz Beckum ex Am/Can.
Ch. Erdenreich Die Zweite, C.D.)
(Dual & Nat'l F.T. Ch. Moesgaard's
Dandy ex Ch. Tessa v. Abendstern)
(Lummel v. Braumatal ex Astrid v.
Grossenvorde)
Dual Ch. Sager v. Gardsburg ex Ch.
Richlu's Jan Oranian-Nassau)
(Ch. Dax v. Heidebrink ex Ch. Richlu's
Jill Oranian—Dau. of above)
(Dual Ch. Albrecht's Baron Cid ex
Albrecht's Countess Abey)
(Ch. Kurt v. Osthoff ex Frau v. Jagers-
liebe)
(Field Ch. Mars v.d. Radbach ex
Gretchenhof Tradewind)
(Dual Ch. Zipper Der Orrian ex Dual
Ch. Erdenreich's Jetta Beckum)
(Big Island Junker ex Big Island Lori)

(Ch. Whitey v. Brunnthal ex Hurckes
Gretel v. Becker)
(Nat'l F.T. Ch. Shockley's Pride ex
Field Ch. Susan v. Hohen Tann)
(Field Ch. Gert. v.d. Radbach—imp.
Ger.—ex Am/Can. Dual Ch.
Gretchen v. Greif)

(Dual Ch. Robin Crest Chip, C.D.T.
ex Jodie v. Hohenneuffen)
(Dual & Can. Ch. Radbach's Arko ex
Anka v. Niedersachsen—imp. Ger.)

Dual & Natl. FT Ch. Lika Buckskin (1979), (Fld Ch. Buckskin ex Albrecht's Cora's Miss). Owners: Gary and Harriet Short, Iowa. DC/NFC Lika Buckskin secured his titles under owner-amateur training and handling all the way. This could be counted yet another record on the tally-slate of this great dog.

Dual Ch. Lieselotte von Greif (Field Ch. Greif v. Hundscheimerkogel ex Ch. Yunga War Bride), pictured in a California Specialty Best of Breed win under judge Max Riddle. Breeder: Jake D. Huizenga, California. Owners: Mr. & Mrs. E. E. Harden, California.

FEE V.D. WILDBURG
Owner: Richard S. Johns, Pennsylvania
(Dual/Nat'l F.T. Ch. Kay v.d. Wildburg—imp. Ger.—ex Field Ch. My Ritzie Fer Gitunburdz)

GERT'S DURO V. GREIF (Also Dual Ch. in Canada)
Owners: Ralph & Frances Park, Washington
(Field Ch. Gert. v. Radbach—imp. Ger.—ex Am/Can. Dual Ch. Gretchen v. Greif)

AFC BRIARWOOD'S PEPPERMINT PATTY
Owner: Tom Cross, New Jersey
(Field Ch. Fritz v. Smidt ex Sallie v. Hollabird)

OXTON'S MINADO V. BRUNZ
Owners: K. & I. Clody, California
(Dual Ch. Oxton's Bride's Brunz v. Greif ex Am/Can. Ch. Sorgeville's Happy Holiday)

TIMBERLAND'S FRITZ
Owner: Mes. W. Davis, Washington
(Am/Can. Ch. Lutz v.d. Radbach—imp. Ger.—ex Timberlane's Honey)

TIP TOP TIMBER
Owner: H. Brunke, Illinois
(Field Ch. Tip Top Timmy ex Ute Trail Wild Rose)

FREI V. KLARBRUK, U.D.T.
Owners: Joseph & Julia France, Maryland
(Dual & Nat'l F.T. Ch. Kay v.d. Wildburg,—Ger. imp.—ex Ch. Gretchenhof Cinnabar CDX)

TELSTAR DIRECT
Owner: Ralph Laramie, Michigan
(Field Ch. Zerone Direct ex Trish v. Tess)

RIDGELAND'S FRAULEIN
Owners J. & B. Cuthbertson, Illinois
(Kettle's Fritz ex Chevron Dinah)

AFC DEE TEE'S BARON V. GREIF
Owner: Dr. Stanley W. Haag, Iowa
(Dual Ch. Oxton's Minado v. Brunz ex Dual Ch. Cede Mein Dolly Der Orrian)

DINO'S BARONESS MARTA
Owner: George Gates, Colorado
(Dual Ch. Dino v. Albrecht ex Field Ch. Albrecht's Baroness Freya)

ROGER'S HANS
Owners: Roger & S. Claybaugh
(Claire Junker ex Nestle Bayrer's Alpha)

T.K. EASTWINDS DANDY
Owner: Susan McHugh, New York
(Dual & Nat'l F.T. Ch. Kay v.d. Wildburg, ex Field Ch. Tina of Sleepy Hollow)

BIG ISLAND SASS-A-FRASS
Owner: Mary G. Finley
(Big Island Northaway ex Big Island Chaska)

ALBRECHT'S TENA HY (also Amtr. F.T. Ch.)
Owners: M. & L. Albrecht, Kansas
(Field Ch. Albrecht's Count Gustav ex Field Ch. Albrecht's Countess Tena)

AFC DEE TEE'S BASHEN V. GREIF
Owner: Gary Short, Iowa
(Dual Ch. Oxton's Minado v. Brunz ex Dual Ch. Cede Mein Dolly Der Orrian)

AFC RICKI RADBACH V. GREIF (also Dual Ch. in Canada)l
Owners: Ralph & Frances Park, Washington
(Am/Can/F.T. Ch. Lutz v.d. Radbach—Ger. imp—ex Lulubelle v. Greif)

WALDWINKEL'S PAINTED LADY
Owner: Helen B. Case, Arizona
(Big Island Junker ex Waldwinkel's Gertrude's Joy)

AFC FRITZ V. ZIGUENER (Also Can. Ch.) C.D.
Owner: John Marks, Ohio
(Ch. Fliegen Meister's Gunner ex Gretchen v.d. Ziguener)

EASTWINDS T.K. REBEL
Owner: Franz X. Bentz, New York
(Dual & Nat'l F.T. Ch. Kay v.d. Wildburg ex Field Ch. Tina of Sleepy Hollow)

FRITZ V. TREKKA RADBACH
Owner: Milton Donner, Washington
(Field Ch. Lutz v.d. Radbach—Ger. imp—ex Trekka La Mer)

RITZIE'S ORANIAN ROCCO
Owners: G. & F. De Gideo, New Mexico
(Dual Ch. Richlu's Dan Oranian ex Dual Ch. Ritzie)

GRUENWEG'S DANDY'S BODIE, CDX
Owner: Dean Stanley, Iowa
(Dual Ch. Gruenweg's Dandy Dandy ex Lady von Barenrick)

ERICK von ENZSTRAND
Owners: D. & J. Hill, Wisconsin
(Peron ex Hope b. Luftnose)

NAT'L FLD. CH. LIKA BUCKSKIN
Owners: G. & H. Short, Iowa
(Nat'l Fld. Ch. Buckskin ex ex Albrecht's Cora Miss)

PETER V.D. ZIGEUNER
Owner: T. D. Zaffer, Ohio
(Dual Ch. Gruenweg's Dandy Dandy ex Gretchen v.d. Zigeuner)

PATCHE PRINE JAMES
Owner: D. J. Seabright, Wisconsin
(Field Ch. Windy Hill Prince James ex Her Nibs of Navajo)

AFC ALBRECHT'S MARTA'S DINO
Owners: G. & L. La Marr, Kansas
(Ch. Albrecht's Tena Inky ex Dual Ch. Dino's Baroness Marta)

NAT'L AFC HERR HANS OF THE BARRETTS
Owners: D. & B. Barrett, Illinois
(Ch. Mein Kurtz of the Barretts ex Orland Chocolate Lady)

KERLAKE'S TELL'S MOONBEAM
Owner: Dr. J. Craig, Iowa
(Field Ch. Tell, imp. Den., ex Field Ch. Moesgaard's Ruffy's Mindy.)

JAGER ALBRECHT'S BARON
Owners: D. & M. Damoth, New Mexico
(Jager Albrecht Schlossgarten ex Lupkins v. Skceps)

ESSER'S DUKE V.D. WILDBURG
Owners: T. & A. Mericska, New Mexico
(Esser's Chick, imp. Ger., ex Da Lor's Brandie v.d. Wildburg.)

TIMBERTOP TELL
Owner: J. Corson, Iowa
(Field Ch. Tell, imp. Den., ex October's Frost)

SCHATZI'S ERIC V. GREIF
Owners: E. & G. Harden, California
(Ch. Adam v. Fuehrerheim ex Field Ch. Schatzi's dem Balder v. Greif)

BAR NUTH'N SANDY (also Dual Ch. in Canada)
Owner: B. Matzke, Washington
(Nat'l Fld. Ch. Blick v. Shinback ex Radbach's Carin)

FAGON HAAG V. GREIF
Owner: Dr. S. Haag, Iowa
(Dual Ch. Oxton's Minado v. Greif ex Dual Ch. Cede Mein Dolly der Orrian)

ERDENREICH'S MARZ MARSH, CD
Owners: D. & L. De Gere, California
(Field Ch. Von Der Feld Radbach Jake ex Erdenreich's Neysa)

UODIBAR'S PDQ V. WALDTALER
Owner: L. Soules, Texas
(Field Ch. Uodibar's Boss Man ex Whisky Creek Whirlwind)

AMMERTAL'S CANDY CANE
Owners: D. Ganno & S. Kimball, Washington
(Nat'l Fld. Ch. Ammertal's Lancer D ex Sissy Radbach v. Greif)

BABE'S DRIFTING TOBY V. GREIF
Owner: Don Gyde, New Mexico
(Dual Ch. Dee Tee's Baron v. Greif ex Ritzie's Dan Oranian Babe)

TREFF MARIMAX V.D. WILDBURG
Owners: E. & N. Sardina
(Ch. Deitz v.d. Wildburg ex ex Moesgaard's High Noon)

GOLDEN WEST CHUCKO
Owners: K. & M. Thrasher, California
(Golden West Blick's Fritz ex Waldenburg Chayne's Beasley)

NAT'L FLD. CH. BOSS LADY V. Owners: G & H. Short, Iowa
(Field Ch. Uodibar's Bossman ex Dual Ch. Dee Tee's Baschen v. Greif)

160

ROCCO'S DIAMOND KATE V. BELLE (Dual Ch. Ritzie's Oranian Rocco ex
Owners: G. & F. de Gideo, Minnesota   Deering's Bell Waldwinkel)
HIDDEN HOLLOW'S PLEASURE   (Ch. Warrenwood's Alfie ex Ceres of
Owner: E. B. Gorsky, New Jersey   Hidden Hollow)
EVA V. KIECKHEFER   (Dual Ch. Dee Tee's Baron v. Greif ex
Owner: R. Chisenhall, Minnesota   Adelheid v. Fetterel)
WALKER'S BLUE MOVIE   (Walker's Rip Off ex Amlinn's Dyke Ann)
Owner: Dr. S. Haag, Iowa
EDEN LIGHTNIN SCHNAPPER   (Eden Double Dare ex Jenny IV)
Owners: J. & M. Mueller, Indiana
MILANE CANDYMAN'S BEAU GESTE   (Ch. Milane's Candy Man ex Milane's
Owners: B. & K. Patten, Arizona   Cindy v. Greif)
JB II   (Field Ch. Uodibar's Peter Gunn ex Field
Owner: Joyce E. Olsen   Ch. Hillhaven Cindy)
NAT'L FLD. CH. EHRLICHER ABE   (Nat'l Fld. Ch. Ammertal's Lancer D ex
Owners: P. & L. Cross, Idaho   Missy fer Gitunburdz)
CHECKMATE'S AUGUST DOG   (Field Ch. Tip Top Savage Sam ex Uodi-
Owners:K. & G. Isaacson, Illinois   bar's Sister Brown)

GSHP AKC National Field Trial Championship, 1968—1st, Nat'l Field Trial
Ch. Thalberg's Seagraves Chayne; 2nd, Dual Ch. Richlu's Dan Oranian; 3rd,
Dual Ch. Bo Diddley v. Hohen Tann; 4th, Dual Ch. Tip Top Timber. The
placing of three Dual Champions in National Field Trial competition constitutes a record to that time, deserving the flattery of imitation.

Dual & A.F.C. Hidden Hollow's Pleasure (Ch. Warrenwood's Alfie ex Ceres of Hidden Hollow). Breeder: E. Hollowell. Owner: E. B. Gorsky, New Jersey.

DUAL CHAMPIONS FINISHING FIRST
AS SHOW CHAMPIONS

	Show	Field
RUSTY V. SCHWARENBERG	1942	1947
SCHATZ V. SCHWARENBERG	1948	1949
BLICK V. GRABENBRUCH	1950	1951
SEARCHING WIND TOPPER	1950	1951
VALKYRIE V. GRABENBRUCH	1951	1952
BARON V. STRAUSS	1947	1953
BIG ISLAND SPOOK	1953 (May)	1953 (Oct.)
DOKTORGAARDEN'S CARO	1954 (June)	1954 (Oct.)
TRAILBORN MIKE, CDX	1955 (Aug.)	1955 (Sept.)
JUNKER V. GRABENBRUCH	1955 (May)	1955 (Oct.)
FRITZ OF SLEEPY HOLLOW	1955 (Sept.)	1955 (Dec.)
JONES HILL FREDERICK	1955	1957
PETER BRUNER	1957 (May)	1957 (Oct.)
CAPTAIN V. WINTERHAUCH	1953	1957
GRETCHEN V. SUTHERS	1957 (Feb.)	1957 (Nov.)
STRAUSS WORKING BOY	1957	1958
OXTON'S LEISELOTTE V. GREIF	1957	1958
AL-RU'S ERIC	1956	1958
HEIDIE V. MARVON	1955	1958
TIMBERLANE'S ACE	1957	1960
SAGER V. GARDSBURG	1957	1960
FLICK V. HEIDEBRINK	1960 (Jan.)	1960 (April)
ABLE V. ELTZ	1960 (June)	1960 (Sept.)
MADCHEN BRAUT V. GREIF	1960 (Sept.)	1960 (Dec.)
ROMMEL V. RUMPELSTILSCHEN	1960	1961
HANS V. ELDRIDGE, C.D.	1958	1961
BIG ISLAND RECS	1958	1961
ALFI V.D. KRONNENMUHLE	1956	1961
WOODY V. RONBERG	1961 (June)	1961 (Sept.)
MISS B'HAVEN V. WINTERHAUCH	1957	1961

	Show	*Field*
DALLO V. HESSELBACH	1961 (Feb.)	1961 (Oct.)
SCHOENE BRAUT V. GREIF	1959	1961
FRITZ OF HICKORY FARM LANE	1960	1962
WAG AE'S SNOWFLAKE	1956	1962
GUSTAV MEIN LIEBCHEN	1959	1962
ESSO V. ENZSTRAND	1958	1962
MARMADUKE MEIN LIEBCHEN	1958	1962
BRUNNENHUGEL BALDER	1962	1963
ERDENREICH'S EARTHA	1963	1964
DINO V. ALBRECHT	1963	1964
STREAK'S HERBST VERSPRECHEN	1961	1964
ROBIN CREST CHIP, C.D.T.	1958	1965
BARON FRITZ V. HOHEN TANN	1962	1965
FIELDACRES KATIA	1960	1965
HEWLETT GIRL PEBBLES	1965 (Aug.)	1965 (Sept.)
ZIPPER DER ORRIAN	1964	1965
KAMIAK DESERT SAND	1964	1965
JANIE GREIF V. HEISTERHOLZ	1965	1966
RITZIE	1965	1966
GRUENWEG'S DANDY DANDY	1964	1966
RICHLU'S TERROR	1964	1966
BLITZ V. JAGERSLIEBE	1963	1967
HOCHLANDER'S TITELHALTER	1967 (Aug. 4)	1967 (Aug. 16)
CEDE MEIN DOLLY DER ORRIAN	1965	1967
HURCKES STEEL VICTOR	1965	1968
GERT'S DENA V. GREIF	1967	1968
BRIARWOOD'S PEPPERMINT PATTY	1966	1969
KAJOBAR V. STONY BROOK		1969
FEE V.D. WILDBURG	1969 (July)	1969 (Aug.)
TELSTAR DIRECT	1965	1970
FREI V. KLARBRUK, U.D.T.	1966	1971
ALBRECHT'S BARONESS MARTA	1966	1971
ALBRECHT'S TENA HY (also Amtr. F.T. Ch.)	1966	1972
DEE TEE'S BASHEN V. GREIF	1971	1972
WALDWINKEL'S PAINTED LADY	1966	1972
FRITZ V.D. ZIGUENER, C.D.	1967	1972
EASTWINDS T. K. REBEL	1973 (July)	1973 (Oct.)
RITZIE'S ORANIAN ROCCO	1972	1973
GRUENWEG'S DANDY'S BODIE, C.D.X.	1970	1974
LIKA BUCKSKIN	1973	1974
ALBRECHT'S MARTA'S DINO	1971	1975
HERR HANS OF THE BARRETTS	1970	1975
JAGER ALBRECHT'S BARON	1973	1976
ESSER'S DUKE V.D. WILDBURG	1976 (April)	1976 (May)
TIMBERTOP TELL	1974	1976
BAR NUTH'N SANDY	1975	1978
FAGON HAAG V. GREIF	1973	1978
UODIBAR'S PDQ WALDTALER	1974	1978
AMMERTAL'S CANDY CANE	1977	1978
J.D. BABE'S DRIFTING TOBY V. GREIF	1975	1979
TREFF MARIMAX V.D. WILDBURG	1978	1979
ROCCO'S DIAMOND KATE V. BELLE	1979 (June)	1979 (Aug.)
HIDDEN HOLLOW'S PLEASURE	1976	1979

Dual & AFC Erdenreich's Marz Marsh, CD (Field Ch. Von der Feld Radbach Jake ex Erdenreich's Neysa). Five generations of this accomplished Shorthair's breeding co-opts a fascinating assemblage of California's best known Shorthairs. Breeder/ Owners: D. and L. DeGere, Mill Valley, California.

Dual Ch. Golden West Chucko (Golden West Blick's Fritz ex Waldenburg's Chayne's Beasley). Owner: Kay Thrasher, California. Whelped April '71, Chucko has proved his durability to be as golden as his name. He made Top FT Listings for 1974-5-6-9-1980, and in '81 took BOB away from some prestige-titleds at the Golden Gate KC (San Francisco), competing from the Veterans' class.

DUAL CHAMPIONS FINISHING FIRST
AS FIELD CHAMPIONS

	Field	Show
VALBO V. SCHLESBERG	1949	1950
DANDY JIM V. FELDSTROM	1953 (Sept.)	1953 (Dec.)
RIGA V. HOHEN TANN	1954	1955
WENDENHEIM'S FRITZ	1954	1955
KAPOSIA'S FIREBIRD	1957 (April 7)	1957 (April 13)
GRETCHEN V. GREIF	1955	1958
OXTON'S BRIDE'S BRUNZ V. GREIF	1959 (March)	1959 (May)
LUCKY LADY V. WINTERHHAUCH	1958	1959
BARON TURN & TAXIS	1958	1960
GROUSEWALD'S BLITZ	1960	1961
SKID-DO'S BONNIE KARIN	1961	1962
BIFF BANGABIRD	1961	1963
BRUNNENHUGEL JARL	1962	1963
ALBRECHT'S BARON CID	1961	1963
ALBRECHT'S BARONESS CORA	1963 (Sept.)	1963 (Nov.)
MOESGAARD'S DANDY	1961	1964
KAY V.D. WILDBURG	1959	1964
BEE'S GABBY V. BECKUM	1963	1964
SATAN V. SCHNELLBERG	1964	1965
LUCY BALL	1965	1966
RADBACH'S ARKO	1964	1966
ERDENREICH'S JETTA BECKUM	1966 (March)	1966 (June)
ARRAK V. HEISTERHOLZ	1963	1966
RICHLU'S DAN ORANIEN	1965	1967
RAMBLING ROCK	1964	1967
BIG ISLAND SILVER DEUCE	1967	1968
BO DIDDLEY V. HOHEN TANN	1967	1968
OXTON'S MINADO V. BRUNZ	1967	1969
GERT'S DURO V. GREIF	1966	1969
RADBACH'S DUSTCLOUD	1968	1969
TIMBERLANE'S FRITZ	1969	1970
TIP TOP TIMBER	1969	1970
RIDGELAND'S FRAULINE	1969	1970
ROGER'S HANS	1970	1972
DEE TEE'S BARON V. GREIF	1971	1972
T. K. EASTWIND'S DANDY	1969	1972
RICKI RADBACH V. GREIF	1969	1972
BIG ISLAND SASS-A-FRASS	1971	1972
FRITZ V. TREKKA RADBACH	1969	1973
ERICK VOM ENGSTRAND	1973	1974
PETER V.D. ZIGEUNER	1974	1975
PATCHE PRINCE JAMES	1974	1975
KERLAKE'S TELL'S MOONBEAM	1975	1976
ERDENREICH'S MARZ MARSH	1976	1978
GOLDEN WEST CHUCKO	1975	1979
BOSS LADY JODI V. GREIF	1978	1979
MILANE'S CANDYMAN BEAU GESTE	1980 (Sept.)	1980 (Nov.)
EHRLICHER ABE	1980	1981

The Pointer in England was originally a retrieving dog, too. This picture, by the famed 18th century sporting dog artist, George Morland, is reproduced by permission of the British Museum, London. Note the sitting bitch, still of the heavy "old Spanish" type. In the colored version of this painting she is of recognizable German Shorthaired Pointer color.

10

British and

Commonwealth Shorthairs

In the practical sense, the German Shorthaired Pointer was introduced into Britain immediately after World War II. In the later 1940's, home-returned officers, especially, thought the frustration and expense of the long quarantine period worthwhile to be able to keep the good dogs they had hunted with in Germany. Some dogs came with papers, some without, as modern-day pedigrees attest, but when that matter was evened out, as is possible under English K.C. Rules, some extremely useful sporting dogs began to attract notice, especially where practical hunting men—roughshooters, as the English call them—were concerned.

In a historical sense, though, the introduction of the breed was actually made in England in 1887. That was newly proved in 1961, when, in response to an inquiry initiated by this compiler, the English K.C. delved into its Archives and, through the courtesy of the Assistant-Secretary, Mr. C. A. Binney, made available some most interesting material. The clue had been originally provided by an award made "in London" on the record of a German brood, Holla Hoppenrade, owned by Herr Julius Mehlich, of Berlin.

"1887 records do show that for some reason classes for German Shorthaired Pointers were scheduled at the K.C. event at Barn Elms, London, June 28/29/30 and July 1st. when Herr v. Schmiederberg judged the class. There were at that time no quarantine regulations, and to the best of our knowledge, dogs passed freely between this and other countries. A strong contingent of these dogs was brought over for the show and, I assume, re-exported soon after. A number were registered in June 1887, and as we cannot trace any registrations in previous or subsequent months, they may have been all exhibits at the show. Nor are any subsequent registrations to be traced, nor any records available to show that classes for this breed were scheduled again in this country till after World War II."

Mr. Binney, along with the above explanation, also forwarded the particulars of the 22 exhibits, plus the critique of the judge. As it seems likely that the exhibit comprised a sort of "Show-the-Flag" gesture on the part of the German breeders in that very new stage of the breed's development, the critique is especially interesting. Surely, one may guess that the dogs sent over were the best specimens currently available. Shortly after this English historical matter came to hand, the Danish magazines lent by Dr. Kline also became available, and, in the well-compiled histories of the Hoppenraden and v. Lemgo dogs, provided supporting proof that dovetailed exactly with the records as they were preserved in England—miraculously, one would say, through the years, the wars, the blitz!

The exhibitors included some of the most active of early-day German experimental breeders. Not only Herr Mehlich, of the famed Hoppenraden, was represented, but also Hofjaeger F. Isermann, later known as the breeder of Frigga v. Berry, the dam of the breed pillar, Nidung. With Herr Z. U. O. Borchert, the Hofjaeger provided 14 of the 22 entries. Seven of the entries were sired by the breed basic, Treff 1010. Caro (Mr. W. Schutze's) by Treff ex Diana, is of the same breeding as Hektor 64, sire of the famed Waldin. Edda (Mr. Borchert's) was by Harras Hoppenrade, 312. Feldmann (wh. 1885, so not the caricature-cross Feldman of a decade earlier) was Isermann-owned, ex his Juno 192, and she traceable through the Danish publications as basic to some great German strains. Holla (Hoppenrade) 395, was by (another) Caro ex Cora, 180, a Hektor 65 daughter. Treff II was also ex Juno 192 (by Treff 1010), and Juno's breeding is established as by another unidentified

168

Feldman, and an unidentified Diana. As her surviving photograph shows, Juno 192, wh. 1882, was just such another near-Spanish pointer type as Hektor I, the original studbook entry. One well may marvel at the breeding skill of the Germans in refining all such cloddy material (as Dr. Kleeman later described it scathingly) into the beautiful dogs of the 1890's and onward to our time.

Uncas II and Uncas Bravo were both by Uncas I, whose registration number of 94 places him very close to the starting line. Such may have been also the case with Adda (ex Aunsel), wh. 1886, whose owner, Herr Seydel, stirs interest for us. Unfortunately no one, not even Frau Maria Seydel herself, can now link him with her family exactly—though she thinks he must have been a relative of her deceased husband.

Gaining the B.O.S. placing to Holla Hoppenrade's B.O.B. was Waldo II, 211, also known as Bosco, the property of Herr Mehlich, here listed as from the full brother and sister, Waldo I and Hertha, litter mates of Waldin, 175—particulars at variance with the Danish-published version. Historically valuable as the earliest catalog of the breed in competition that has yet been located, the list is worth re-publishing for the record. (*Courtesy, The English K.C.*)

The Cataloged Entry of German Shorthaired Pointers,
Barn Elms, London, 1887

ADDA	Mr. Seydel's	(Uncas-Aunsel)	Wh. 4/15/1886
CARO	Mr. W. Schutze's	(Treff-Diana)	1/13/1885
CAROLA OF GOTTENBACH	Mr. C. Georg's	(Unknown)	1886
COSAK OF GOTTENBACH	Mr. C. Georg's	"	1886
DIANA	Hofjaeger Isermann's	(Treff-Sally)	8/20/1886
EDDA I	Mr. Z. U. O. Borchert's	(Harras-Colla)	1885
EDDA II	Mr. Z. U. O. Borchert's	(Uncas I-Edda I)	Feb. 1887
FELDMANN	Hofjaeger Isermann's	(Treff-Juno)	4/9/1885
FUTTA	Mr. W. Schutze's	(Uncas II-Wanda)	3/6/1886
HEKTOR III		(Treff-Sally)	8/20/1886
HOLLA (Hoppenrade)	Mr. J. Mehlich's	(Caro-Cora)	4/16/1885
HYDRA	Hofjaeger Isermann's	(Treff-Sally)	8/20/1886
MENTOR	Mr. Saatweber's	(Unknown)	Jan. 1880
NIMROD	Hofjaeger Isermann's	(Treff-Sally)	8/20/1886
TREFF	Mr. W. Schutze's	(Uncas II-Wanda)	3/6/1886
TREFF II	Hofjaeger Isermann's	(Treff-Juno)	5/8/1886
TREFF III	Mr. G. Englestadt's	(Mentor-Zampa)	2/10/1884
TREUMANN	Mr. Z. U. O. Borchert's	(Uncas II-Wanda)	Nov. 1884
UNCAS II	Mr. Z. U. O. Borchert's	(Uncas I-Juno I)	May 1883
UNCAS BRAVO	Mr. Z. U. O. Borchert's	(Uncas I-Edda I)	Oct. 1886
WALDO II	Mr. J. Mehlich's	(Waldo I-Hertha)	5/18/1886
WODAN	Hofjaeger Isermann's	(Treff-Sally)	8/20/1886

We are also indebted to the courtesy of the English Kennel Club for the critique of the judge, Herr v. Schmiederberg, who was at that time a top official of the newly-formed breed club in Germany. This matter is also unique, possibly the only detailed critique of pioneer dogs that still exists in the world:

"*Waldo II* is a strong, powerful dog, just what many German sportsmen want; his color, head, and especially ears are excellent, but his hindquarters not fully developed, and will probably show better next year; the forefeet turn out slightly. *Hektor III* is light in build, his ears set too low, must lay on more muzzle. Of the same description is Wodan. He too has the forefeet outturned, as has Nimrod. They deserved the v. highly commended award however, considering their young age, and that German pointers develop slower than English. *Feldmann* was the best in the class, but he too might have the ears set higher. *Treff II* is very light and shows all the ailings of his brothers. *Treumann* would strike the eye of most German amateurs, he has that stumpy body that is much liked, but lacks quality and his ears are too pointed. A puppy—name not given—won third. I think he will grow into a likely dog, his color and head are promising. *Holla* (Hoppenrade) is an excellent bitch all over. She was without doubt the best of the entry, not too heavy for work. *Diana* resembled her brothers, but showed her shortcomings less and might have been in better condition. *Hydra,* a sister, resembles her. *Edda* is a strongly built bitch, but lacks quality. Her skull is far too broad, but on account of a litter I thought she deserved a commended mark. Her age was stated wrong in the catalog, she is much older. The other dogs of the class were inferior in type and need not be mentioned, though the pluck of their owner, a young breeder, is to be praised."

Many of the faults noted by the German judge are still in the breed today: too broad skulls, outturned feet, lack of muzzle, even sometimes pointed ears. One would like to have had more detail concerning Holla. That she was excellent is proved by her progeny after her return to Germany (Morell and Maitrank Hoppenrade). No picture of this bitch has as yet been located. Maybe some English breed enthusiast, with the above dates to guide him (or her) may now undertake a search through the British Museum newspapers and periodicals of the time. The "Illustrated London News" is a likely source.

English Ch. Midlander Sirius (Ch. & FT Ch. Graff Greif of Praha ex Ch. Midlander Eider). Breeders: Midlander K's, Melton Mowbray, England. Owner: Mrs. J. Roberts. English hunting style, suited to climate and terrain. Note the barbed wire fencing. In England, as elsewhere in the world except USA, Shorthairs are followed on foot. Gunner-handler is David Layton, breeder-judge and author of *All-Purpose Gundog* (1977).

Eng. Sh. Ch. Galahad of Booton (Sh. Ch. Wittekind Happy Harpo ex Anna of Erlescote). Owners: Mr. and Mrs. V. Rusk. Galahad's first Challenge Certificate was won at 17 mos. in 1979. Five Challenges in 1980 took him to runner-up in the breed for the year. A superbly structured, strong dog, his BOB at Windsor 1980, was well-merited. Photo, *McFarlane*.

Seventy years later, and against some opposition from conservative hunting dog interests, the German Shorthaired Pointer returned officially to England, post-war, in 1945. However, Frank Warner Hill points out that isolated specimens actually were in England before that date. Specifically, he refers to meeting with a Mrs. Locker Lampson in 1935, when that early-day German Short-haired Pointer owner was concerned about finding a mate for the bitch she then owned in England (*Dog World,* June 8, 1962).

After the war, the breed had a better chance to take hold in England than it could have had earlier. The new tax structure had whittled away at the guarded hunting privileges of the Squire and His Relations, and the organized shooting drives. Gone were the days when the great Arkwright of the Pointers could fill a *train* with his dogs and kennel help, en route for the shooting in Scotland. The fashion had begun to return to individual hunting, fur and feather, and for this the all-purpose German dog was able to show his worth.

Michael Brander's *Roughshooter's Dog* and *Roughshooter's Sport* (published by MacGibbon & Kee, London) describe how the wheel of hunting sport in England turned full circle over a century and a half. Now, again, it was for the man who went individually and afoot, and his need was for an all-purpose dog. Once again a dog was being asked not only to point game, but to retrieve it when it was down. New? Not really—it was the chore of early-day Pointers too, as the accompanying George Morland picture from the British Museum collection establishes; the period was the later part of the 18th century, as the artist was dead by 1804.

British difficulties with the German dog were first, as Michael Brander describes them, to discover how the breed wished to work, what it could do. He solved his own problem by letting his dog teach *him.* His "Max" actually wrote his *Roughshooter's Dog* for him, he says! Since then, the breed has been taken up by the gamekeepers who neither show them nor run them in trials—they *work* them!

Eng. Ch. Wittekind Igor. A successful Wittekind-bred whose many show wins include the Group at Crufts just before he secured his qualifier for the field which provided his full championship. Breeder, owner, handler: M. Mills de Hoog, Kent.

Sonnenberg Solitaire (England 1981). (Birkenwald Voss ex Birkenwald Sonya). Breeder/Owner: Mrs. Eileen Hughes. Just coming up to his second year, Sage's credentials to date: the sought-after Jr. Warrant at 9 months; BOB at the Gundog Society of Wales at 11 months, plus a Reserve Challenge.—*Freeman*

173

Eng. Ch. Hillanhi Hjordhis, Jun. Warrant (Ch. Midlander Peer Gynt/Sh. Ch. Wittekind Solveig). Breeder/Owner: Mrs. M. J. Bates, Nuneaton, Warks. England. Whelped 1978, Hjordhis has been top winner in her breed 1980/81. Best of Breed and Reserve in Group, Crufts, 1981.

Eng. Sh. Ch. Pittsburgh Argonaut (Qwassinburgh Perseus ex Alexandria of Patterscourt). A strong-bodied, workmanlike, sound-footed one such as the breed in all countries needs when over-emphasis on show elegances whittles the substance a utility breed must have. Breeder/Owner: Mrs. R. Kennedy, Southampton, England. Photo—*Frank Garwood* (Courtesy, Eng. *Dog World*).

No one could say the British hunting folk readily embraced the idea of an introduced German dog that could do EVERYTHING! Tradition was against it, not to mention lingering anti-German feeling so soon after WWII. Hadn't British breeders *made* sporting breeds for all the world—along specialist lines? Pointers were for search and pointing—they *never* retrieved! Retrievers were for retrieving as Spaniels for flushing. If this had always meant extensive kennels and kennel help, well—wasn't a wealthy man's privilege to use his hunting dogs as he used his golf sticks, each individually for specific purposes. And as for extensive kennel help—remember when Arkwright of the Pointers would fill a *train* when he went to Scotland for the shooting? All-purpose hunting dog indeed—the one-man's utility dog? Suggested a dog for a poacher—and poachers had their lurchers! Living down prejudice took time.

Some Shorthairs came with incomplete documentation, some with none. English K.C. machinery included method to deal with obviously purebreds in lack of papers—the process of "listing." Competent persons assess breed status, a separate register received the dog. Over period of time its get could make the stud book and often get provided proof of status, so verifying legitimacy. Example is provided by Eng. Ch. Weedonbrook Elizabeth, a beautiful bitch brought over from Germany by Wing-Commander Godby, R.A.F. Her given dam, "Sara" (GSP Club Year Book, 1968, p.27) becomes "Sara of Sanktvit" (same pub. p.28) her sire as "unknown German wartime." Her descendants, down generations, verify the purity of background. Daughter, Eng. Ch. Brownridge Marga, a notable winner, is dam of Ch. Midlander Eider, even the more notable. Additionally, an Australian pedigree of "Linstan" of Victoria includes an Elizabeth (imp-in-utero) granddaughter in Tainui Gerda (Brownridge Napier/Jan of Walnascar) featured as dam of Aust. Dual Ch. & Ret. Trial Ch. Linstan Kris and littermate, Aust. Ch. & Ret. Trial Ch. Linstan Kathi (subject of the remarkable Ret. Trial picture used in this present work) as well as granddam of Aust. Ch. Linstan Keene.

Attempt to widen Tainui Gerda's background for her impact on Australian breeding of remarkably accomplished stock drew no replies from England. One guesses there had been no awareness of her existence overseas. However, a New Zealand K.C. registration and pedigree attest her whelping in that country, followed by

Eng. Sh. Ch. and Junior Warrant winner, Isara Kurzhaar Hexe (Starlite's Greif v. Kazia ex Eng. Ch. Patrick's Piper of Wittekind). Breeder: Mrs. F. Roberts. Owners: Mr. and Mrs. Gareth Godsall. Ch. Hexe took Challenge Cert. at the GSP Club's Specialty at age 10 months! Her Junior Warrant and Eng. Sh. title followed in her second year. She is by an American-bred that happened to be enroute to Australia, detained in Eng. quarantine.—*Freeman*

Eng. Sh. Ch. Inchmarlo Fodhla (Inchmarlo Ballyragget ex Inchmarlo Markee). Breeder: Mrs. I. Sladden. Owner: Mrs. V. Grant. Having suffered a severed tendon on his left rear leg, this very good dog, in the hands of Professor Vaughan, of the Veterinary College, London, was provided with a carbon fibre tendon which, after a year or so, turned into the real thing! He picked up his interrupted show career and in 1980 secured that always difficult to win English show championship.

Irish Ch. Inchmarlo Ballygar (Karl ex Eng. Ch. Inchmarlo Cora). Breeder: Mrs. N. Sladden. Owner: W. S. Loughlin, N. Ireland. "Otto" won breed at the Golden Jubilee Show of the Irish KC in 1972; judge, C. Bede Maxwell. He has lived golden years since, and in June 1981 took All-Breed Veteran Stake in his homeland. His most successful son, Ch. Waldheim Wehrwolf, is top winner in N. Ireland with (to date) 11 Gundog Groups.

re-export to Australia, as her bona fides. She had been purchased for Australia by pioneer breeder, Jack Thomson of "Dunfriu" who leased her to "Linstan." She appears in other early Australian pedigrees, different States, and her descendants would seem to add further proof of the excellent credentials that must have troubled postwar time. Gerda's breeding is verified by the pictured pedigree.

For the pedigree this work is indebted to Mr. W. Morris, of "Ruvalen" Kennels, Victoria. His interest to take in Tainui Gerda was of course as dam of several of his most distinguished dogs that made such impact in Retrieving Trials especially.

"She was not the handsomest of bitches," Mr. Morris recalls, "but with excellent field qualities and a wonderful love of water retrieving, qualities she passed on to her produce and through those to the next generations. This," he adds, "is much more predominant in our bitches, confirming my belief that the major strength in breeding is to be found in the mother lines."

No linebreeding seems to have been undertaken to preserve Tainui Gerda's qualities, but her litters had wide and interstate dispersal so that those practical endowments that were in her gift can not readily be described as lost.

English Ch. Weedonbrook Elizabeth herself, functioning most importantly as family dog and hunting companion, remained unshown until her fifth year, after which her show successes were exceptional, securing her the hard-won "full" English championship title with passing of her work qualifier, and snaring a BOB at Crufts along the way. Her well-taken photograph survives in David Layton's *All Purpose Gundog* (Eng. 1977) and makes interesting comparison with her contemporaries, none of which approach her pictured quality. Saltus v.d. Brickwedde (German bred) and his successfully prepotent son, Ch. Nevern Jasper, offer type presentation that differs not only from that of the classical Elizabeth, but from that of each other, scarcely to be recognizable as being of same breed, which of course is the common problem wherewith pioneers in any newly-introduced breed anywhere must cope in their breeding programs. In the Shorthair, of course, this divergence has always been, will always be, present, consequent upon the diversity of original material incorporated in the breed at time of formation. There have always been the light-tick-patch, heavier boned, not seldom coarse sorts, as the Brickwedde presents in the English published photographs, and the darker-ticked, rangier, often more

Eng. FT Ch. Sky High Johnny of Wittekind (Wittekind Geoffrey ex Wittekind Katika). Wh. 1976, FT Title, 1981. Breeder, Owner, Handler: Mrs. Mienke Mills de Hoog, Kent, England. Lady owners finishing a field trial dog in England is no common occasion—Mrs. de Hoog is but the second.

Aust. FT & Ret. Ch. Irus v.d. Saaner Mark, imp. Holland. (Pan Rhein Elbe ex Imala v.d. Forst Brickwedde). Owner, J. Thomson, Dunfrui K's, Melbourne, Australia. During quarantine delay in England, en route to Australia, Irus sired four litters in Wittekind K's, Kent, from Dutch-imported bitches. Reverberations throughout the breed in England are still identifiable in the winning lists years after Irus had succumbed to strike of a tiger snake in Australia—too soon, alas, to make his presence felt there.

elegant sorts, along of course, with the solids. The Brickwedde's photograph (Saltus) interests also for the cicumstance that he seemingly carried the elbow fault that travels the generations here in the USA as well, down successive generations from original German import, Bob v. Schwarenberg as *his* preserved picture also established. Oftenest carried unilaterally, and seemingly also oftenest on the "judging" side of a considerable porportion of big tick-patch Shorthairs, it is overlooked by the majority of American judges with cheerful abandon—which is why it is has persisted all these many years and will persist, seemingly into time indefinite . . . There is just a chance that the English breeders and judges, being pickier, managed to eliminate it . . .

Not included in the splendid gallery of English Shorthairs in David Layton's work, is one to interest Americans, Afra v.d. Brille (Afra of the Spectacles) grand-dam of Ch. Springfarm Ben of Cellerhof, he a well-performed one of the later 1950s, bred in Ireland, a 1963 BIS winner when the award fell seldom to the breed. Afra in a Year Book picture, awkwardly posed, and described as owned by the GSP club's first Hon. Secretary, Mr. Vickers, conforms so identifiably to the Donn v.Sulfmeister/K.S. Kobold Mauderode-Westerhold pattern as to look familiar to USA eyes. Whelped 1947, she has been described as *the* earliest in, born in the Rhineland, by Arko v.d.Narrenstadt/Anka v. Neufeld.

Breed acceptance took time, war's end still close. Not that the British ever had stooped to stoning Dachshunds in the streets, such idiot "patriotism" would not have been tolerated in a country where, as the French do say, the word "God" is spelled backwards. Still, an actual German *import* . . . till it became known the Archbishop of Canterbury had one in Lambeth Palace; Prince Philip, Duke of Edinburgh, was hunting over a brace in Scotland, lent him by the Hon. the Lord Ferrier, and with his young son, Prince Charles, was also using one in falconry. In Scotland, Michael Brander was writing his good *Roughshooter* books, and hadn't Major-General de Haviland brought one back as gift to his wife from Herr H. Bollhoff of the famed strain of the Blitzdorfers—Isgo v. Blitzdorf!

Little more than three decades established in England—less in Australia—one can scarcely credit numbers proliferation from a few imports of such variant quality. Basics however were well-picked over by experienced breeders, poor sorts eliminated. It could be interesting, also, to know all the stories of "acquisition." (Navy term!) The late Frau Maria Seydel, of Recklinghausen-Süd, of great breed fame, showed this compiler just where in her yard she had buried her husband's good sporting guns ahead of the arrival of occupational troops from the Ruhr area: "The guns I have," she had sighed, "but my dogs . . . I could not bury . . ." It seems unlikely Seydel-breds were among basic English imports as the solid liver elegances did not make English impact for years. When they did it was with get by a Dutch-bred sire en route to Australia, delayed rather longer than usual in quarantine by a sudden rabies scare. The color encountered considerable prejudice at first—in some quarters it still does, not only in England! Judges complained of "differences"—differences as from tickpatch sorts become by then familiar. Of course the solids are different—different in weight of bone, elegance of structure, texture of coat. Merely, the standards haven't anywhere got round to explaining to the judges that the breed was so constituted in the days of formation a century ago— the welding in tightest individual inbreeding of the available sorts, and the falling into the two types—in Germany described as the *"braun"* and the *"braun-schimmel."* Variant their type then—and now, type so fixed within each grouping as to endure down the centuries, on ahead as in the past. The best of both types are bred to work the same utility pattern, and no amount of prejudice, one way or the other, is going to alter that genetic pattern so firmly fixed a century ago, keeping the inheritance factors continually sorting themselves out, one side or the other. Fashion, and the dominance of some locally-established stud has most to do with the circumstance as to which, at any given time, is most visible as a type. In Germany, for decades, it had been most strongly browns—the result of the enormous use (overuse?) of Axel v. Wasserschling.

A few solids (sort of!) were in this compiler's entry at the 1968 Ch. show of the GSP Club in England, but they were in the main so offtype as to let one doubt status, some even with woolly coats. Top contenders, even then, were however very good; BIS to the then 6-yr-old Ch. Midlander Eider was matched with Reserve BIS to the 8-months-old (future Ch.) Inchmarlo Dunkeld, a son of England's first Dual titled, Ch. & Fld. Ch. Inchmarlo Graff Greif of Praha. Dunkeld went on to a splendid career, a phenomenally long-laster. In 1972, this compiler found (interestingly) a son of

180

Dunkeld's sister, Cora, to take to BOB at the Irish Golden Jubilee show in Dublin.

The German Shorthaired Pointer Club, founded 1951 by Geoffrey Sterne and John Gassman, encouraged utility use of the dogs, most of the period managing to gain the Qualifier to make them full champions. When Kennel Club permission came to compete in Pointer/Setter trials it was soon apparent that this Rule did not suit the utility European breed. In 1958, a new Rule was provided for competition suited to "breeds carrying out the Pointer-Retrieving Schedule," catering expanded nowadays to Shorthairs, Wirehairs, Weimaraners, Vizslas, Large Munsterlanders and Drente Partridge dogs, all utility sorts. As first-ever new Rule provided sporting dogs since 1902 (when Spaniels got their separate Rule) the concession provided for "quartering in the open, in cover, finding of game, the flush, drop to shot, mark and retrieve, land and water, making test of practical hunting abilities that mere quartering at speed against Pointers/Setters could not provide, and no purely 'Trial dog' ought to win." (GSP Club Year Book)

The Rule cancelled out incentive to risk cross-breeding to make speedsters, *protection American Kennel Club has never provided*. It might have been useful, at same time, to have clipped the word "Pointer" from the name, as was early-on done in Germany where "Vorstehhund" (Pointer) designation was cannily counted a possible incentive for some enterprising, off-record breeding. Not that anyone, either country, wanted dull plodding dogs, but neither were speedsters valued in a breed to serve a hunting man afoot; "Our trials are never to be regarded as frightening occasions in which dogs are expected to put up vague and meaningless performance called 'Field Trial Standard,'" warned again the English Club Year Book.

British judges, as judges German, Australian—and all, walk the braces. Hearing that American judges get their Tennessee Walking Horses to ride, there is merely laughing. Trials are held on in-use agricultural land, most countries, fenced quite often, or criss-crossed with roads, cluttered with livestock—it is always interesting to see the disinterest as a Shorthair runs about his business past some startled ewe with her blatting lamb! How is this contrived? "We train them," shrugged a hunter on a Scottish hill.

Numerical breed increase and availability of Challenge Certifi-

First British Dual Ch. Inchmarlo Graff Greif of Praha. His pace, penalized in the breed outside USA, makes necessary running him miles behind a car prior to a trial to slow him down! Tell that around the Chuck Wagon in the USA! Owner: I. E. T. Sladden, MRCVS, Eng.

Show Ch. Appeline Chough, BOB at the first Specialty held by the GSP Club, England. Owners: Mr. & Mrs. D. Appleton, Norfolk.

English Sh. Ch. Midlander Eider, distinguished show champion, field competitor, matron. Out of retirement, BOB 1971 Crufts from F.T. class. Owner: M. Layton.—*Photo, Cooke.*

cates to make champions eventually thinned out much British hunting participation and the majority of British Shorthairs are show dogs. However, there are Dual-titleds finished. and as show competition toughened, poor quality representation dwindled. British breeder skill, taking over, has made much out of very little in terms of basic stock, and imports since war's end have been very few. The most successful was a German-bred solid liver, got out of Holland the turn of the 1960s, that had the rather unusual advantage of being what the Germans call *"Axel-frei"*—that is, his breeding contained no scrap of Axel v. Wasserschling that had been proliferated in Germanic rebuilding of the breed literally from scratch post-war and, by the '60s, had so dominated that outcrosses were difficult to find. That the Dutch dog, Irus v.d. Saaner Mark, was brought out ahead of sharp-searching German breeder's awareness, was due to the enterprise of a remarkable gal in Mieneke Mills de Hoog, Dutch girl, resident of Kent, in England. She secured him for Australian breeder, Jack Thompson, and during his quarantine detention, bred four litters from him. Search now and discover how few—how VERY few!—English bloodlines now lack the influence of Irus . . . even those whose owners, as is usually the case in relation to any import, any country, that had done loudest down-calling while the stud was alive in the country.

There came to be sour onlooking (dog people being human!) when the *allrounder* judges carried Irus get to very eminent placings, son Ch. Wittekind Igor even going off with the Group at Crufts! Many others of the same breeding did extremely well over a space of years, and the next generation still has impact in the English show rings. Thus the two top rated show dogs for 1980, Sh. Ch. Hillanhi, also a BOB winner at Crufts, and Sh. Ch. Galahad of Booton, runner up for the year's honors, are Irus get down through Wittekind—the one. Hjordhis, by Ch. Midlander Peer Gynt ex Ch. Wittekind Solveig, and the other, Galahad, by Ch. Wittekind Gregory/Anna of Erlescote, she with both Ch. Midlander Eider and Ch. Appeline Chough for grandparents.

However, the blood base throughout the country is not particularly wide, and the occasional transient through the quarantine kennels provides seemingly the main source of some outcross blood—this, of course, to the same bedeviling that greeted Irus—the new boys in town . . . 1978 saw the temporary residence and quarantining of the first-ever American bred to be en route to Australia, a matter that involves first a long year's delay in England, the 6-months-old Starlite's Greif v. Kazia, with a fantastic 5-generation muster of American producers behind him. (Dual Ch. Schatzi's Eric v. Greif/Ch. Schatzi v. Heiligsepp. CD). A gawky adolescent, the young dog, becoming universally known in reportage as "Hank the Yank", managed to leave behind him a litter that included several very useful ones and one flyer—the bitch, Isara Kurzhaar Hexe (ex Sh.Ch. Patrick's Piper of Wittekind). She secured her first C.C. at age 10 months at the breed club specialty, and her Junior Warrant and show title by age two. In Australia, to date, the now mature stud has had better fortune—better fortune too than Irus— so far escaping snake encounter. His daughter, Aust/New Zealand Ch. Kazia Pay the Piper, is a useful representative there, plus a granddaughter that made spectacular debut in field trial competition, with a Certificate of Merit at her first-ever trial—Sedgefield Georgia.

At time of this compilation, a second American stud en route to Australia has completed his English quarantine requirements, an on-in-years American show-champion, Adam's Hagen v. Waldenburg (Ch. Adam v. Fuehrerheim/Ch. Fraylene's Maybe, a National FT Ch. Rip Traf v. Bess daughter), which adds another contribution of famed F.T. Ch. Greif v. Hundsheimerkogel bloodline into the mixture that was earlier brought in by the younger dog. The older dog has also been able to pick up his English Championship—which will be another title to add to the Adam v. Fuehrerheim collection—and has sired at time of this writing his first English litter. The two additives, following so close onto one another, cannot fail to add some useful boost to the English bloodlines pool. The Adam son is destined for West Australia, the ownership of Burnbrook Kennels of Mr. & Mrs. Byrne, which spells out as the width of the continent in miles' distance from the location of the younger that preceded him.

Which brings us to the continent-wide development of the breed in Australia—a country that twenty-five years ago could have been combed across its three thousand miles width and never a Shorthair to find. The first brace, in 1962, included a dog that would have the burden of "showing" the Australian hunting folk the worth of his breed. He was Heathman of Fruili, and he stemmed from top working stock in a Dunpender sire—Dunpender Kim—from Michael Brander's breeding, and a bitch that for several years dominated early-day English field trialing—Littlestat Seidlitz. With Heathman came a Dunpender bitch, both for the pioneer kennel

Show Dog of the Year, 1981 (GSP Soc. NSW,) Australian Ch. Bergen Schatten (Ch. Wildheart Namisch ex Ch. Wildheart Saite.) Breeder/Owners: K. & M. Donald, Annangrove, NSW. Best of Breed, Sydney Royal Show, 1981—Judge, R. James, England.

of Jack Thomson of Melbourne. His inspiration to import had been as that of Dr. Thornton in the USA—the wish to possess such a utility breed as the Germans described their breed to be. Heathman secured his titles in Australia, and managed to break down some of the opposition, if anything more solid than that which the breed encountered in England. With his curiosity satisfied, Thomson began to bring in other dogs, including dogs from France and other countries, and of course the luckless Irus.

The rivalry between the States of Victoria and New South Wales is a constant as from days of the pioneers, so if the Victorians were going to have Shorthairs soon, too, the New South Wales folk would follow suit. New South Wales stock was differently based, this on imports out of New Zealand that were there whelped from early imported British breds . . . There would seem to be acceptance of the circumstance that Mrs. Sally Hartley brought in first to make impact for her strain she would name "Wildheart" in future Ch. Vorstehhund Skylark, C.D., one that had been imported in utero

185

to New Zealand, along with a brace mate in Vorstehhund Decoy. Both were ex an English-bred dam, Arodel Wren, a Ch. Nevern Jasper daughter. This was influence that was typewise widely at variance with the big ones that came by way of Dunpender. The accompanying production tables spell out the future developments.

For a two decades time span, the strength of the breed in the country has been amazingly contrived. As with the English scene, the breed base has been of necessity narrow—nothing under the Dog Star Sirius shines upon hurdles placed more obstructively than those placed for the negotiation by importers of livestock to Australia. However, the reason is simple. The island continent has no rabies (and, by the way, is free of quite a few other stock diseases that trouble other lands) and there is firm intent that rabies there shall never be. So far, the score is Quarantine authorities, 100—opposed to Quarantine, nil. There is no way to get around the laws involved—and in the case of the occasional optimist that has tried to smuggle in some small pet . . . there is the drastic penalty that involves taking the animal concerned and destroying it forthwith.

GSP Soc. Award-winning Show Dog of the Years 1979, 1980—Aust. Ch. Limburgia Chock-daw, CD, (Arawang Chockdaw ex Dunvernor Linda.) Breeders: Mr. and Mrs. Gielen. Owners: S. Rudd & B. Burke, NSW. Bred from unshown working Shorthairs of best English breeding in back, this dog of natural presence combines the genes of Nevern, Dunpender, Wittekind, Littlestat and Appeline. A most beautiful dog in an unmatchable self-taken pose.

Aust. Ch. Gergen Seltsam (Ch. Wildheart Namisch ex Wildheart Saite.) Owners: R. & M. Howarth, NSW. His wins include BIS at the GSP Soc. Ch. show, 1978, in addition to many all breed BIS awards.—Photo, *Michael Trafford*.

Aust. Ch. Kazia Liebling Liesl (Ch. Wildheart Namisch ex Ch. Birdacre Kara, CD.) Breeder/Owners: L. & C. Butler, NSW. Whelped 1976, Liesl was top NSW GSP show bitch for 1977-78.–Photo, *Michael Trafford*.

Starlite's Greif v. Kazia ("Hank the Yank"), by Dual Ch. Schatzie's Eric v. Greif ex Ch. Schatzi v. Heiligsepp, CD. Breeder, M. Desmond, California. Owners, L. & C. Butler, NSW, Australia. The first Am-bred Shorthair to be imported to Australia, Greif survived almost two years of quarantining processes after leaving California as a 6-months puppy. His litter in England was topped by a bitch taking Challenge at the GSP Club Specialty before she was out of puppy class.—Photo, *Lynn Butler*, 1981.

How hamperingly the law, reasonable as is its intent, operates can be learned from the nearest dog-importer. Of the California dog that came to Lynn and Caroline Butler in New South Wales a couple of years ago—"Hank the Yank—Carolyn Butler confesses that "there went her new car in prospect" to cover expenses involved over more than 18 months of the quarantine sequence of two-country detentions, first England, then Australia.

Why Shorthairs, one would have said, knowing that Australia had never been really Pointer country. Of the six (huge) Australian States, three count as hosting a proliferation of upland game: New South Wales, Victoria, South Australia. The tropical north is as another world, so far as upland game is countable. The southern States however have an explosive quail population in season, six varieties, with Stubble the most numerous, the very mainstay of Trials as the Rule Number One provides that, unless the bulk of the game throughout any FT is Quail, the Trial must be either postponed or abandoned. Shooting and Game Laws of each State must be observed and will govern the conduct of all Trials in conjunction with the Rules and Regulations of each State's governing kennel body.

188

"Hank the Yank's" daughter, Australian and NZ Ch. Kazia Pay the Piper (Starlite's Greif v. Kazia ex Kazia Liebling Liesl), bred and owned by L. & C. Butler, NSW, Australia. Won her first Challenge Certificate at only 14 mos. under a visiting German judge. Was Puppy of the Year, 1980/81.—Photo, *Lynn Butler.*

Another Hank the Yank's daughter, Sedgefield Georgia (Starlite's Greif v. Kazia ex Birdacre Gold Dust), bred and owned by Kevin Walshaw, A.C.T., Australia. Georgia is pictured (top) at 7 weeks and (below) grown up and at her first Field Trial, spring 1981. She came home runner-up to a top Ch., and with—for the first time ever by a GSP—a Certificate of Merit in her first FT competition.

Snipe come from Japan in September, returning in April (Spring and Fall—seasons topsy turvy Down Under!) Pigeons and duck are also plentiful, pigeons being acceptable in the conduct of Water Trials, and of course there is no lack of rabbits and those, with the somewhat less plentiful hares are also Trial-useable game.

Little differentiates English from Australian trials, distance perhaps the most important. The Englishman may cover 25/200 miles of travel to a Trial, the Australian (even as the American) between 150/1000 (or more!) The English use elected gunners, handlers do not shoot. Australians gun for themselves, with a backstop gunner if needed. Waterwork is of high standard, and the ability of Shorthairs to compete for title in Retrieving Trials is great breed advantage. (Little real encouragement is given the American Shorthair to excel in water-competitive occasions, though waterwork is, as it has long been, the greatest draw the breed has exerted on the practical hunting folk as purchasers and users, as the Midwesterners especially, well know). Hunting range is determined by terrain and the conditions of the day, but under good conditions the average Shorthair in Australia works at between 70-100 yards either side of the gunner, zigzagging back and forth between 50/100 yards in front. Walking pace permits a full day's hunt without stress.

"This paragon of gundogs will handle without reproach the wiliest of quail in natural habitat of thistles or native grasses, wheat stubble or, as occasionally they will be found, in marshy areas while snipe hunting," explains Kevin Walshaw, dedicated, literate enthusiast among practical hunting men. "Shorthair ability to locate and station itself on point over these great little birds leaves nothing to be desired. Used on waterfowl, swim-ability and skill to mark fallen game are outstanding. Snipe give the Australian hunter the most exacting bird hunting, but a good snipe dog will stand up to any testing, stamina, nose, ability to recover the bird under marshy conditions. In the main, snipe will flush, but sometimes sit tight hoping to be undetected. A good nose and plenty of experience become the dog's best assets. With wounded birds in tussock the difficulties will show up any deficiencies in training. Hard hunting tests a dog's construction and if inadequate will soon show it . . . good dogs produce good dogs and rubbish breeds rubbish . . . with the food bill the same! There has to be the physical and mental equipment, and Shorthair, as a breed, is in lack of neither."

Aust. Field Trial Ch. South Creek Zachary
(Ch. Dunfriu Hansel ex South Creek Zane.)
Breeder: Mrs. N. Jessop-Smith, NSW.
Owner: Kevin Walshaw, NSW. Australia's
first NSW registered FT champion (any
breed) was whelped 1968, died 1979.
Trained and field trialed by his owner,
Zachary was unplaced only once in seven
years of competition. GSP Soc. NSW Year
Book 1981 identifies Zachary as the dog
against which the performances of other dogs
are, and will be, judged.—Drawing, *Lynn
Harwood*, GSP Society member.

The classic employment for which the Shorthair breed was formed—the Hunter and his all-purpose
Utility-Working dog. Australian Kevin Walshaw with his great Field Trial Champion and personal
hunting dog, Field Ch. South Creek Zachary. "I'm certainly not about to buy a horse . . ." muses
Kevin, the day on snipe having provided new memories to treasure with the old.—Photo by *Alan
H. Fox*: Presented with compliments of the Director, National Parks and Wildlife Service, New South
Wales, Australia.

Kevin Walshaw's own splendid F.T. Ch. South Creek Zachary, bought as a baby puppy from the breeders, held in high esteem over seven years in competition, holding his own with the country's best, left his owner a scale by which to measure future dogs in ownership: "his burning desire to work, the countless magic of the days afield with him, his affection, courage, tireless energy, coupled with his deadly accuracy . . ."

Death of his great dog at age eleven inspired a poignant tribute from Walshaw: ". . . with a quail under his nose, I buried him. I figured he would find that rabbit we had so often seen hereabouts. As I patted the earth quiet down and brushed my eyes with the back of my hand, some ducks landed on our dam, a short distance away. It seemed as though the game had come to pay its respects to the master. I felt we were together again—he is just eleven weeks old, his little head held high, his body frozen rigid from under a tussock . . . Zac sits—the rabbit races away . . . and I realize I have ten and a half more years to go . . ." (From: GSP Society of New South Wales's *Pointer View*)

Age-old wisdom has always advised that the cure for loss of a dog hurt is acquisition of a new. Now Kevin Walshaw has "Hank the Yank's" daughter Sedgefield Georgia; already her debut has been made, runner up to a top champion in the FT award of Certificate of Merit—"1982 will be her year," he forecasts.

Aust. Ch. Burnbrook Atlas, CD (Ch. Dunfriu Plutu ex Wittekind Persephone.) Owners: G. & M. Byrne, West Australia. A GSP of versatile achievements, holding his own in show, obedience, and in Retrieving Trials. His sire's background reaches to strong German lines—Hanstein, Wasserschling.

The Producers

Long-extended tabulations such as the American scene presents cannot be expected from the British and Commonwealth countries where registration figures are but fractional compared with the American, and where championships—especially English championships—are infinitely so much more difficult to obtain. The British tabulations also honor the concept of a "full" title, in that a dog must have demonstrated hunting ability to qualify.

CH. NEVERN JASPER
Breeder: W.K. Simpson
Owner: D. Atkinson
 Ch. Springfarm Sandpiper
 Ch. Ferrier Jager
 Ch. Mordax Morning Mist
 Ch. Larberry Link
 Show Ch. Larberry Fern
 Fld. T Ch. Littlestat Susie
 Ch. Littlestat Condiment
 Fld. T Ch. Littlestat Salamander of
  Cellarhof

(Saltus v.d. Forst Brickwedde ex Nevern Jenny)

(Niccola of Stockhill)
(Bramble of Windlehill)
(Weedonbrook Wunder)
("   ")
("   ")
(Show Ch. Decima Octava)
(" " " ")
(" " " ")

CH. LARBERRY LINK

Breeder: W. Wade
Owner: Miss J. Farrand
 Ch. Midlander Eider
 Ch. Midlander Marcasite
 Show Ch. Midlander Moonstone
 Ch. Midlander Sioux
 Show Ch. Danpoint Artillery
 Show Ch. Gormire Adam
 Show Ch. Madresfield Hawthorn
 Show Ch. Mandy of Alton Hill

(Ch. Nevern Jasper ex ex Weedonbrook Wunder)

(Ch. Brownridge Marga)
(Ch. Midlander Eider)
(" " ")
(" " ")
(Madresfield Thuya)
(Horkesley Mitzy)
(Madresfield Sitka Spruce)
(Alton Sall)

CH. & F.T.CH. INCHMARLO GRAFF
 GREIF OF PRAHA.
Breeder: H.B. Meissener
Owner: Mrs. N. Sladden
 Ch. Inchmarlo Cora
 Ch. Inchmarlo Dunkeld
 Ch. Midlander Sirius
 Show Ch. Midlander Carina
 Fld T.Ch. Inchmarlo Tuscan

(Fritz of Praha ex Deanslane Daystar of Praha)

(Inchmarlo Tamara)
(" ")
(Ch. Midlander Eider)
(" " ")
(Inchmarlo Heidi)

193

SHOW CH. APPELINE CHOUGH

Owner/Breeder: Mrs. C. Appleton.
  Ch. Midlander Mark Anthony
  Show Ch. Appeline Auk
  Show Ch. Linklander Lippizaner
  Show Ch. Linklander Caspian
  Show Ch. Firhouse Midlander Rinda
  Show Ch. Carrigtemple Little Auk

(Ch. Springfarm Ben of Cellerhof ex Appe-
line Lorelei of Walnascar)

(ex Ch. Midlander Eider)
(Appeline Chaffinch)
(Ch. Midlander Marcasite)
("   "   )
(Midlander Shawnee)
(Appeline Wittekind Francine)

AUSTRALIAN F.T. & RET. TRIAL CH.
  IRUS V.D. SAANER MARK
Owner: Jack Thomson (Australia)
  Ch. Wittekind Gregory
  Ch. Wittekind Igor
  Ch. Wittekind Erica
  Show Ch. Wittekind Edelstein
  Show Ch. Wittekind Felicity
  Show Ch. Wittekind Frederick
  F.T. & Ret. T. Ch. Dunfrui Nicholas
    (Australia)

(Ger. imp to Aust. siring Eng. get en route)

(Connie v.d. Arriervelden-Dutch imp.)
("   "   "   ")
(Kleiner Helga)
("   ")
(Appeline Juniper)
("   ")
(Dunfrui Naomi)

CH. WITTEKIND GREGORY

Breeder/Owner: Mrs. W. Mills de Hoog
  Ch. & F.T. Ch. Maltham's Dark
    Claret of Trolanda
  Show Ch. Wittekind Hannibal
  Show Ch. Wittekind Happy Harpo
  Braz. Ch. Wittekind Shirley's Jolyan
  Aust. Ch. Axel of Kenstaff
    Wittekind
  Irish F.T. Ch. Affra of Kenstaff
  Can. Ch. Stockhull Peepers

(Aust. FT & Ret T. Ch. Irus v.d. Saaner
Mark/Connie v.d. Arriervelden)

(Inchmarlo Dark Damsel)

(Appeline Juniper)
("   ")
(Kleiner Helga)
(Birkenwald Korta)

("   ")
("   ")

Note: Compilation source, (Eng. titles only) *All Purpose Gundog,* by David Layton, Standfast Press, Gloucestershire, 1977.

New South Wales—where the club long since honored this compiler, has available, and carefully compiled for this work by Mrs. Judy Marshall of Austinmeer, *Gesellighund* Kennels, has a most interesting tabulation of basic breed establishment, as counting from the original importation of Ch. Vorstehhund Skylark, C.D.—she having made impact with her Bests of Breed at successive Sydney

194

K. S. Elk vom Hege-Haus, D.I., S.I., mS, WGP. Whelped 3/16/76.
(K.S. Caesar v. Uphuser-Kolk ex Unda v. Hege-Haus.) Breeder:
Karin Stramann, Germany. Owner/Importer: A. Cosolets, Victoria,
Australia. Elk's distinguished winning includes Derby and Solm
firsts. Sire Caesar is a tightly linebred Wasserschling—interweav-
ings of Axel and Imme v. Wasserschling.

Aust.Ch. LINSTAN RAQUEL.   Owner: Ruvalan Kennels,Vic.
                                                  Wh. 2/12/69.

PARENTS	GRAND PARENTS	GREAT GRANDPARENTS	GREAT GREAT GRANDPARENTS
Australian Champion Unfriu Kurt Reg.no.1.V.63	Sire Ch.R/T.Ch. Heathman of Fruili(Imp. Reg.no. 72666/62 U.K.	Sire Dunpender Kim(Imp.U.K)	Sire Dunpender Attila
			Dam Dunpender Bess
		Dam Littlestat Seidlitz	Sire Blits of Lonsutton
			Dam Octava (UK)
	Dam Dunpender Eva(Imp.U.K.) Reg.no. 69275/62	Sire Dunpender Danial	Sire Dunpender Ben
			Dam Dunpender Weedonbrook Weera
		Dam Dunpender Fredika	Sire Nevern Bruce
			Dam Fredika of Kieva
Australian Champion Unfriu Klara Reg.no. 12.V.65	Sire Nevern Norrey(Imp.U.K) Reg.no.7891/65	Sire Haregrove Bryntegryd	Sire Nevern Artus
			Dam Linda of Bockelheide
		Dam Navern Feldjaegerinfanny	Sire Bruce Von Muglitztal
			Dam Nevern Jaegerin Heide
	Dam Tainui Gerda(Imp.N.Z.) Reg.no. L61/2391	Sire Brownridge Napier	Sire Aber Max
			Dam Weedonbrook Elizabeth
		Dam Jan of Walnascar	Sire Primus
			Dam Jan.

Australian pedigree that combines documentation of first Australian imports with that
of first post World War II imports into England.—Courtesy, Linstan Kennels, Australia.

Royal Shows 1966/69 inclusive, period when the breed was considered in rare status indeed. Her son, Ch. Wildheart Jager, started the ball rolling, and the bracketed bitches kept it on the move. As under:

CH. WILDHEART JAGER   (*Ch. Wildheart Gunther ex Ch. Vorstehhund Skylark, CD (imp. Brit.*)

Breeder/Owner: Sally Hartley

Ch. Wildheart Jacke	(*ex Ch. Wildheart Just Gerda*)
Ch. Wildheart Jammer	(" " " ")
Ch. Wildheart Jaspis	(" " " ")
Ch. Wildheart Gerda Too	(*ex Ch. Wildheart Sturmvogel-sister to W. Just Gerda*)
Ch. Wildheart Lager	(*ex Wildheart Liebchen*)
Ch. Wildheart Natasha	(*ex Ch. Dunfrui 11 Abegail*)
Ch. Wildheart Namisch	(" " ")
Ch. Wildheart Nennen, C.D.	(" " ")
Ch. Wildheart Nicholas	(" " ")
NZ Ch. (FT) Wildheart Neben	(" " ")
Ch. Wildheart Sattler, CD	(*ex Waidmann Sassa (imp. Brit.*)
Ch. Wildheart Saite	(" " ")
Ch. Arcturahunde Anna	(*ex Ch. Bernadel Elsa, C.D.*)
Ch. Gunnawarra Kaffka, CDX	(*ex Lachienvale Pia*)

From these basics—and yet the back count is of so few years actually—Namisch and Nennen became standout studs, spearheading a cluster of next-generation producers several now behind present day breedings. It was also interesting to uncover Ch. Dunfrui 11 Abigail. Ex English imported Wittekind Anna Marie, owned by Dunfrui kennels, Victoria, and bred at Wittekind (Eng) by Eng. Ch. Appeline Chough ex Connie v.d. Arriervelden (Holland) a brace of good-lookers, little Anna Marie came into this compiler's ring in Australia from her few days' old litter, heavy in milk, totally unkempt, and yet it was impossible to deny her the Challenge for her basic type, that contrasted to the point of violence with a tall and beautifully presented tick-patch that took the breed. It was however the overwhelming quality of the daughter of Chough/Connie that made it impossible to do other than excuse her post-maternal presentation, she having been brought to pay me a compliment, being present. She remains in memory, but the Best of Breed. . .? There have been in the years of judging, so many tall, beautifully presented tick-patch males—how to remember them all?

196

Australian Dual Ch. & Retriever Trial Ch. Markheim Debonair, UD (Aust. Ch. Linstan Keene ex Rockfield Clara Cindy, CDX.) Breeders: Markheim Kennels, So. Australia. Owners: R. & A. Smith, So. Australia. This beautiful bitch's triple-titled achievements will not easily be duplicated.—Photo, *K. Barkleigh Shute.*

Aust. Ch. Jinfrau Jubal. Breeders: B. K. and N. J. Campbell, Queensland, Aust. Owners, J. & C. Sawers, Queenland. Steadily climbing, Jubal's wins at time of this compilation already counted to 5 BIS all-breeds; 26 Group 1; BOB at three of Australia's well-supported prestige shows, including Sydney 1979, this under Mrs. Anne Clark (USA).—Photo, *Trafford.*

Aust. Ch. Burnbrook Hamilcar (Ch. Burnbrook Castor ex Ch. Burnbrook Aphrodite.) Breeder/Owners: Burnbrook Kennels, West Australia. Grandson, both sides, of tickpatch Eng. Ch. Wittekind Gregory, although both parents were solid livers.

CH. WILDHEART NAMISCH

(Ch. Wildheart Jager ex Dunfrui 11 Abigail-
she ex Wittekind Anne Marie by Arko
v.d. Feldkampen (imp. Ger.)

Breeder/Owner: Sally Hartley
    Ch. Wildheart Segler   *(ex Waidman Sassa (imp. Brit)*
    Ch. Wildheart Selten, C.D.   ("   "   "   "   )
    Ch. Wildheart Selig   ("   "   "   "   )
    Ch. Wildheart Geben   *(ex Ch. Wildheart Gerda Too)*
    Ch. Wildheart Gemme   ("   "   "   "   )
    Ch. Wildheart Grazzie   ("   "   "   "   )
    Ch. Wildheart Grafin   ("   "   "   "   )
    Ch. Wildheart Gratin   ("   "   "   "   )
    Ch. Wildheart Skylark   *(ex Wildheart Skyline, she ex a Ch. V. Skylark*
                                             daughter)

    Ch. Bergen Schatten   *(ex Ch. Wildheart Saite)*
    Ch. Bergen Seltsam   ("   "   ⌐ "   )
    Ch. Bergen Sardelle   ("   "   "   )
    Ch. Birdacre Heine, C.D.   *(ex Ch. Birdacre Senta)*
    Ch. Kazia Kleeman, C.D.   *(ex Ch. Birdacre Kara, C.D.)*
    Ch. Kazia Liebling Liesl   ("   "   "   "   )
    Ch. Kazia Gretchen   ("   "   "   "   )
    Ch. Kazia Mein Madchen   ("   "   "   "   )
    Ch. Kazia Nijinsky   *(ex Ch. Kazia Gretchen)*
    Ch. Moruada Liebe Ziggy   *(ex Ch. Wildheart Grafin)*

CH. WILDHEART NENNEN, CD

(Ch. Wildheart Jager ex Ch. Dunfrui 11
Abigail)

Breeder: Sally Hartley
Owners: Peter & Judy Marshall
    Ch. Gesellighund von Adel   *(ex Ch. Wildheart Selten, C.D.)*
    Ch. Gesellighund Abende   ("   "   "   "   )
    Ch. Gesellighund Bote   ("   "   "   "   )
    Ch. Gesellighund Bote   ("   "   "   "   )
    Ch. Gesellighund Bringen   ("   "   "   "   )
    Ch. Gesellighund Bruder   ("   "   "   "   )
    Ch. Gillbrae Nice 'n Easy   *(ex Klugerhund Siegi (imp. Brit)*
    Ch. Gillbrae Mi Masquerade   ("   "   "   )
    Ch. Sutherlarach Tardis   *(ex Ch. Blitzdorf Hexe)*
    Ch. Sutherland Cassie   ("   "   "   )

GSP Number One! New South Wales
(Australia) license plate, owned by Lyn
Butler of the GSP Club of New South
Wales. His wife's automobile carries GSP
002.

11

Showing Your German Shorthaired Pointer

A SHOW Dog is essentially a production to delight the eye, a presentation, as is a piece of theatre. While it must be of good basic quality, it must also be well raised, well fed, sufficiently exercised, carefully groomed, handled to its best advantage. Nothing is more sure than that the Show Dog, like the Field Trial Dog, is *produced* rather than merely born to triumphs. The stars in the heavens are not more numerous than good prospective show dogs that have been ruined by poor management.

The belief is held among the owners of long-haired breeds especially that the owners of smooth-haired breeds have no show problems; that all a smooth-hair needs to be ready to show is a bath. Actually, the show smooth-hair presents more acute problems than the long. He has no "bib" to screen such faults as a wide front, loose shoulders, paddling gait; no "bracelets" to mask slack pasterns; no breach "feather" to keep the secret of poor hind movement. If he has faults, the judge can see them. Of course, if he has many virtues those are equally clear and on parade.

The claim that smooth-hairs "don't go out of coat" is just plain nonsense. They have the same seasonal ups and downs. Bitches go through the same cycles as do longhairs, their coats go out and their coats come in as their hormones dictate. Early in your show experience you should learn to recognize the "out-of-coat" condition in your German Shorthaired Pointer, male or female. This isn't merely a matter of a few loose hairs on the living-room rugs. The entire jacketing of an "out-of-coat" dog becomes harsh and dry to the feel. All-liver, or liver-patched, coloring bleaches out as a rusty, spilt-iodine shading.

What sometimes escapes the novice is that when the coat is "out" the dog's body tone, flesh and muscle, and also its spirit are influenced as well. When the coat comes back, the flesh firms, the muscles harden, the dog is gayer. Renewal is usually from for'ard to aft—the head, neck, shoulders, will be sleek with new hair while the loins and quarters are still harsh and dryly covered with jacketing thin enough to let the daylight through. The important truth to cling to is that this condition will pass.

The bitch usually suffers much more noticeably than the dog. Smooth-hair or long, she will likely start her shedding about fourteen weeks after the onset of season, the time corresponding to that of pregnancy and lactation—whether she has been bred or not. If expensively doctored, she will get a new coat in due course. If not expensively doctored she will also get a new coat in due course— and as soon. No doubt, some veterinarians have gained reputation and bought Cadillacs on the strength of this predictable cycle. Susy comes to the office, out of condition, shedding, maybe scratching the irritation of loosening hair. The doctor prescribes this and that. In a few weeks, Susy's flesh is firm, her spirits lift, her coat comes new and shiny. Wonderful doctor—wonderful treatment! The point is, she'd have her coat new and shiny if she'd never gone to the office, and dabbings of camomile or some such soothing application had taken care of the local irritation. The best treatment of all is to get rid of the old hair as quickly as possible, either by brush or by hand massage. (There are, of course, pathological conditions quite different from the mere cyclical shedding, and these need professional attention!)

This cycle is well understood by the experienced. They learned the hard way, learned to watch for the spearing of the new coat as it makes, and to keep away messy potions, to work with nature.

200

They learned, too—also the hard way—that taking Susy to shows in her "down" period was merely wasting entry money to win points for someone else. One of England's most respected dog authorities, Vernon Hirst, has wrapped up a lifetime of experience in his direction: "If your dog is out of coat, there is nothing you can do but wait till it grows again."

The glow of a top-conditioned German Shorthaired Pointer's coat is not merely a matter of spraying on hair-oil. It is best produced by the combined factors of top condition (cyclical), good keeping in terms of food, housing, exercise, and the work of your own two hands. Following regular daily brushing, nothing puts on such a finish as hand massage. Your dog will love the attention, look forward to it, relax under it, and the actual work can even do something for your own waistline as well. One way is to stand behind the dog, bend forward, stroke rapidly and rhythmically with both hands down from the occiput, along his neck, back, flanks. Five minutes is plenty, which is usually all your wind will stand, anyway. A wipe over with a slightly-dampened rag before beginning the massage brings up even a brighter glow. This procedure does wonders for any smooth-haired breed.

Even with such regular daily conditioning, you will want to wash your dog before the Big Day. The best way is to do it a couple of days early, to allow natural oils time to seep back into the coat. *Where* you bathe him depends, of course, on facilities available. If you have no prejudice, the family bath tub will do. The tiled walls and floor make mopping up so much easier. One argument against the family bath tub is the crick that locks your spine after you've been bending down at the job—especially if more than one dog has to be washed. The old-style, waist-high laundry tubs were great—but who has them any more? (Large kennels, as a rule, have such a back-saving installation.) Automatic washing-machines are not recommended. This compiler has a recollection of helping get seven English Setters ready for a country show in Australia. All were dunked successively into the family's backyard washboiler, a big copper container over a slow coal fire that kept the water comfortably tepid. Which brings us back to where we came in—you use what comes handiest.

Any shampoo good enough for you is usually good enough for your dog. He will need very thorough rinsing to be sure all the

Ch. Kaposia's Tucumcari (BIS & Specialty BOB Kaposia's Waupun II ex Ch. Kaposia's Star of the North). Here, as in virtually all stock from this strain, is the strong, balanced, utility type that can discharge tasks as the owners might require. Precisely this classic structure is the endowment a top Kaposia dog is able to bring to combine as advantages to matings even with completely unrelated lines. Breeder/Owners: Kaposia Kennels, Minnesota.

Ch. Kaposia's Oconto (Ch. Kaposia's War Lance ex Ch. Kaposia's Star Dancer). Last of the long sequence of outstanding Kaposia-breds personally campaigned by Don and Betty Sandberg. These days, both are committed to judging.

soap film is out of his coat. Plug his ears with cotton wool before starting, but don't forget to take it out later and swab the ear canals. A grubby inner-ear won't look well. Watch the soap around his eyes, he doesn't like the sting, either.

Thorough drying is important. Never leave your dog damp, day or night. An electric hair-dryer does the job fastest, but a rough towelling and a final hand-drying often does it better, allowing the coat to lie flat and sleek. Trial and test and your own inclination have to provide the answer here. It takes more energy to hand-dry a dog than to hold a dryer over him—more time, too.

You will trim his whiskers, of course, and if any minor fringing fuzzes his outline you could snip that away as well.

If you have taken care of his teeth there should be no tartar. If there is it needs to be scaled away. His toenails should have been having regular care too, not left till a few hours—or a few minutes!—before he goes into the ring. When they have been cut, be sure to file the sharp edges. Now and again, he enjoys a little scratch, and it is tough on him to be carrying razor-blades at the ends of his toes. Those unfiled toenails can give you a nasty cut too if you happen to bump against them. To leave them to the last minute, then have them guillotined by some hasty operator—you or anyone else—can bring a sound dog into the ring limping. That, of course, may then involve you in the embarrassment of a veterinary examination, called for by the judge. When the toenails have been filed, a dab of oil smoothed over gives them a nice shiny finish. Such a dab can go on a dry nose too—especially if photographs are to be posed.

Select a lead for efficiency rather than for showiness. The less conspicuous a show lead, the better it becomes your dog. A metal choke collar looks glamorous but seldom gives the result achieved by a soft leather show lead handled by someone who knows how to use it—which is loosely. However, your dog can only go prettily on the loose lead if he has been trained to gait. The world of dog shows is full of people who take pride in telling everyone that "this is the first time he was ever on a lead!" One notes, by and large, that such dogs do not figure high in the winning lists. As numerous are the people who talk about a good performing dog being, *of course,* just "a natural shower." To hear these "experts," one would think that the great show stars went unschooled from their whelping boxes. That some dogs have better show temperament than others is quite true, but when the art of the handler is added to such a dog's inclination to show himself, the most important partnership is achieved—and the result brings applause from the watching gallery, and the all-important nod from the judge.

At the ring entrance, you can rub him over to get rid of any last stray specks of dust. Use a soft cloth in a stroking motion. This employment will do marvels for your nerves as well as his. He will come to associate such a pleasant stroking with waiting around the entrance to the ring, and be all ready for what you want him to do. If you watch a good handler, you'll see that he isn't just wasting his time, *just standing there*. He is waiting for the right moment to make his entry. There is no reason why you shouldn't try to do the same. If you have a big-striding, prettily-moving dog that can make a prima-donna's entrance into the ring, hold it back till the judge is looking. Don't waste all that motion on a judge who has his back turned, jotting down the numbers of the last class winners. If some eager beaver jostles to get ahead of you, let him go. But find some way to delay your own entrance a second or two, long enough to let him get ahead so you won't have your good-striding dog falling over his dog's heels. There are ways and ways—you have to work out these things for yourself, play it along by ear. But at one of these shows, stay back to watch the groups, even if your own dog isn't eligible. See how the show-wise competitors time their entrances wherever and whenever they can. They don't blunder after some other dog as a small page-boy after the bride moving up the aisle of the village church. They make sure they get *their* share of everyone's attention—including the judge's. Sometimes you'll hear such tactics criticized by the acid gallerites whose dogs didn't make the group. You can play it much smarter—don't fight the good handlers, join them!

You'll hear it said that the professional handlers know all the tricks, and use them. Granted. If they didn't they wouldn't have much of an income. But the professional can be challenged in the ring by the amateur with a good dog—PROVIDED THE AMATEUR HAS TAKEN THE TIME AND THE TROUBLE TO SCHOOL HIMSELF TO THE PROFESSIONAL'S STANDARD OF GROOMING AND PRESENTATION. Handling showdogs in the ring is not a gift that good fairies give to babies in their cradles.

It is a skill that must be learned—like playing the piano or speaking French. That's what the professional handler had to do—learn.

Your best investment on your way to matching yourself with the professionals could be a big old mirror, maybe one you'll find in a junk shop. Prop it against the wall outside the house and set up your dog in front of it. Looking across his back you will see him reflected exactly as the judge sees him in the showring. You can check up on how he looks, and how you are presenting him. You should be able to see his faults and his good points, and then it's up to you to figure out how, in partnership with him, you can minimize the one and enhance the other. Practice till you are a team, you and your dog. Again, it needs to be only a matter of a few minutes a day.

In setting up a dog it is usually easier to get his front lined up if you lift him up off his front legs, one hand under his jaw, the other under his chest. Watch that his legs are in a naturally straight position, then let him drop down with them so. In this way you can avoid that awkwardly conspicuous "placing" of front legs that most amateurs (and surprisingly many professionals) seem to do. Such "fiddling" with a dog's front is undesirable for two reasons; first, the dog's natural reaction is to pull back his leg from the position in which you are trying to set it, and he can do it because his weight isn't on it while you are moving it; Second, if he has a faulty front, the more you fiddle with it, the more likely you are to draw the judge's attention to it.

A useful trick is to press slightly forward and down on a dog's withers—at the top of his shoulder blades. It tends to "set" him in an attractive, forward-leaning pose. Another trick is to give a slight tap near the base of the tail (not a haymaker, the gallery will think you are walloping him!) to a dog that tenses behind. The tap will relax him sufficiently to let his rear-end muscles slacken, to the benefit of his outline and his rear-end angulation. Tensing of the hindquarters makes many a well-angulated dog look straight as a stick behind, and props his rump in the air quite often as well. This is a tendency your mirror-mirror-on-the-wall-outside should be able to show you, and how your tap on his tailbutt relaxes it.

Of course, you know that one about never getting between the judge and the dog. If you want to get a line on this exercise, stroll over to the junior handling rings and watch. Those kids really work at not getting between the judge and the dog. Some of them revolve like moths around a street lamp. You needn't expend quite so much energy as that, but the general principle is one to observe.

In gaiting, obey the judge's direction. If he asks you to go THERE, and return from THERE, try and do what he asks. He has his reasons. The gaiting of big sporting dogs in tiny indoor rings is usually something of a farce anyway. No big dog can get into his true stride in three-steps-this-way-and-turn, three-steps-that-way-and-turn, and back to the judge. Just do the best you can. *You* know, if the judge doesn't, how your dog can move if only someone would give him a chance and a few extra yards of space. The only chance a big show dog ever has to show his gait is in the Groups, so concentrate on getting your good-mover into that select assembly as quickly as you can.

The important factor in gaiting a dog in a show ring is to move with a rhythm that he can match. If you waddle flat-footed like a duck, or like any one of that group of arthritic old gentlemen who once shared a showring with me and my best-moving English Pointer, to our sad hindrance, hire yourself a handler. A show dog positively cannot move correctly, let alone showily, with a bumble-footed handler. Gaiting is also something you can practice with advantage a few minutes every day. Learn your dog's best speed, and practice those turns at the end of the line. Then your dog knows what you want him to do, and is prepared to make his turns with you.

And one last factor of successful showmanship. In front of that mirror-mirror-on-the-wall, practice how to smile—smile if it kills you! Smile nicely when you win, and ten times more nicely when you lose. As we said at the beginning of this chapter, showing a dog is a presentation, like a piece of theatre. And in the theatre everyone learns to smile, no matter what.

There are, of course, the necessary preliminaries to entering a dog for show. The best way to catch on to these is to give your name to the local show superintendent. Then you will receive premium lists of forthcoming shows, plus entry blanks. The blanks are self-explanatory—you fill in the dog's name, sex, breed, sire and dam, breeder, date of birth, registered number, the class in which you are entering it. Then you sign to the effect that you will not exhibit a dog that has had any infectious disease, or has been in contact with any such. You include your check for the entry fee, and that's all there's to it. Some time later, before the show, you will receive tickets and advice as to judging times, etc., from the show superintendent, and your obligation, of course, is to have your dog there at the time specified. In a benched show he will have to stay all day—in some few shows, even two days. In unbenched shows he need be there only in time for his judging, and you can leave as soon as he is no longer in competition; that is, when he has been beaten either in his breed or, later, if he is a breed winner, when he is beaten in his group. If he's a group winner, of course, he stays on for Best In Show competition.

Show equipment can be as elaborate—or as plain—as you care to make it. A crate for your dog is always a good investment. A leash is a necessity, as are brushes and a drinking bowl. For benched shows you will need a bench chain. From there on you can follow your own inclinations. Most dog shops and pet dealers have their shelves and showcases crammed with the most exciting additional wares, and you'll have all the fun in the world browsing and buying.

If possible, get your dog to move his bowels before you leave home. If time does not permit, or if he just won't oblige, consider a suppository—baby-size will usually do the trick. Or, if the show day is to be long, and the road is long to reach the showground, so there's a gap of hours between the time you leave home and the time he goes into the ring, take the suppository with you. Anything, *anything* to avoid having him attend to his function in the ring. It unsettles you, it unsettles him, if he "goes," and if he doesn't "go" when he wants to because his gentlemanly (or her maidenly) instinct tells him it's neither the time nor the place, the restraint will show in his gait. He'll have his mind on other things rather than on the free-striding you know he can command when he's feeling comfortable.

It is also necessary for a dog to have the opportunity to empty its bladder before going to the ring. The desperate dog using its handler's trouser leg as a hydrant is no ring rarity, nor is the bitch that squats to void a pool wide enough to float the Queen Mary. Such performance always draws acid criticism from the gallery, based on speculation as to how long the "poor thing" had been cooped up in its crate without a chance to "go." Professional handlers' dogs seldom offend in this way, it being fairly well understood that such exhibition has a tendency to rebound against the good name of the handler concerned. However, professional or amateur, a real headache is represented by the bitch (invariably it *is* a bitch!) that refuses to "go" away from home or on the lead. Such a one is often overtaken by sheer necessity at the most awkwardly conspicuous time. The *miles* we have walked with some like that—the operettas we have whistled all the way through—the cajolings, the prayers, the—Oh, what's the use! She just *won't GO!* To encourage your show bitch, then, to attend to her functions while *on the lead* any time and anywhere you take her to a suitable place for this, is a very important part of her show training. In campaigning her there will be many occasions when it will be impossible to let her run off-lead for the purpose—busy highway areas, or the environs of a city show, for example.

Now you are in there pitchin'. Take in there with you a tidbit to make your dog feel happy—just as the handlers do. Otherwise, what has a dog to feel happy about in a showring? This is standard practice the world over—except in Australia, where they have funny rules on the subject: no tidbits, a dog has to "show naturally." "Naturally" includes being strung out like a lizard, topped and tailed, and having his head set just *so,* often with heavy traction on his lip. But no tidbits or out of the ring you go! Well, you aren't showing your German Shorthaired Pointer in Australia. Anything you can find to make him happy in the ring, slivers of dried liver, cheese, a squeaky mouse, A.K.C. regards with a benign and kindly tolerance. Try, if you can, to take also with you a feeling of confidence in yourself and your dog. That's worth a bushel of tidbits to you both. And keep your ears closed to the "well-wishers" who tell you you can't win with a German Shorthaired Pointer in the showring unless he's oversized and almost white. The list is simply *crammed* with the names of hundreds upon hundreds of German Shorthaired Pointer champions that are neither big *nor* almost white. They include all the colors there are. Every one of them had sufficient nods from sufficient judges to make the grade, dark-ticked ones, liver ones, even the white-and-liver pointer-patterned ones. Whether a dog goes up or down usually depends on factors other than color. In most cases, ascribing the success of a good show dog to its color is merely overlooking all the *other* qualities it brought into the ring. Very often these "other qualities" have in-

Ch. Weidenbach Bridget, type-true, magnificently moving, winning three Specialties, BOS at two more including the 1971 GSHP National, plus 8 BOBs,—and all without any promotion at all, which may count among her items of pride. A great one! Pictured in win under the author, 1973. Owners: N. and M. Revell, California. *Photo: Henry Schley.*

Am. & Can. Ch. Jillard of Whispering Pines, CD, ("The Beanie"). Winner of 7 Groups and 90 BOBs, including 1975 National Specialty. Dam of 3 show champions. Owned and handled by Patrick Nannola and Salleyann Meier.

cluded superb presentation in terms of conditioning and handling—and this, for sure, is right where YOU come into the picture with YOUR dog.

BEST IN SHOW-WINNING GERMAN SHORTHAIRED POINTERS

Ch. SPORTSMAN'S DREAM
Owner: V. E. Lantow, Colorado
(Astor v. Fischtal, imp., ex Sieglinde v. Meihsen)

Ch. FLASH V. WINDHAUSEN
Owners: C. and S. Nussbaum, Utah
(Ch. Rex v. Windhausen ex. Lady Waldwinkel

Ch. SIR MICHAEL OF HANSON MANOR
Owner: L. W. Linville, Colorado
(Ch. Sportsman's Dream ex Bugle Ann Waldwinkel)

Ch. PHEASANT LANE'S STORM CLOUD
Owner: Mrs. J. W. Gordon, New York
(Ch. Pheasant Lane's Stormalong ex Ch. Pheasant Lane's Deborah)

Ch. COLUMBIA RIVER LIGHTNING
Owner: L. V. McGilbrey, Washington
(*MULTIPLE B.I.S.*)
(Ch. Pheasant Lane's Stormalong ex Columbia River Tillie)

Ch. COLUMBIA RIVER COCHISE
Owner: B. K. Maxson, Wash.
Washington (*MULTIPLE B.I.S.*)
(Ch. Pheasant Lane's Stormalong ex Columbia River Tillie)

Dual Ch. CAPTAIN V. WINTERHAUCH
Owner: Millard W. Axelrod, Minnesota
(Ch. Oak Crest Rick v. Winterhauch ex Duchess of Hotwagner)

CH. CORA V. WINTERHAUCH
(bitch)
Owner: John R. Hutchins, Texas
(Ch. Oak Crest Rick v. Winterhauch ex Duchess of Hotwagner)

Ch. GUNMASTER'S RICKI
Owner: Ricaviling Kennels, Ohio
(Dual Ch. Doktorgaarden's Caro ex Gunmaster's Super Speed)

Ch. COLUMBIA RIVER RANGER
Owners: E. D. and Mrs. Andrews, Ohio
(Ch. Columbia River Lightning ex Helga v. Krawford)

Ch. COLUMBIA RIVER JEEPERS
Owner: L. H. Barnett, Texas
(*MULTIPLE B.I.S.*)
(Ch. Columbia River Lightning ex Helga v. Krawford)

Ch. COLUMBIA RIVER VAGABOND
Owner: L. V. McGilbrey, Washington
(Ch. Columbia River Lightning ex Ch. Columbia River Princess)

Ch. BUCK V. GARDSBURG
Owner: D. D. Williams, California
(*MULTIPLE B.I.S.*)
(Ch. Red Velvet ex Zukie v. Gardsburg)

Ch. ERDENREICH'S BEAU V. GARDSBURG
Owner: Mrs. J. Greer, California
(Ch. Buck v. Gardsburg ex Can/Am. Ch. Erdenreich die Zweite)

Ch. RICEFIELD'S JON
Owner: Miss Camilla Lyman, Mass.
(Ch. Beaver of Hollabird ex Ch. Ricefield's Brown Bomber)

Dual Ch. HANS V. ELDREDGE
Owner: R. S. Eldredge, Wisconsin
(Ch. Baron Strauss II ex Strauss's Pamela)

Ch. HUNTSMAN'S DRUMFIRE
Owners: P. F. and M. Winger, Colorado
(Field Ch. Dan-d Leyba ex Rocky's Reign)

Ch. LUDWIG V. OSTHOFF
Owners: C. and F. Weckerle, Wisconsin
(*MULTIPLE B.I.S.*)
(Gunar v. Alf ex Ch. Ermgard v. Osthoff)

Ch. Strauss's Happy Go Lucky, a BIS-winning showdog and outstanding producer, whose influence on modern-day breeding is still strong and good. Owned by Serakraut Kennels, Wisconsin.

Ch. Serakraut's Anxious (Ch. Serakraut's Tailor-Made ex Serakraut's Stardust). Breeder-Owner: Mrs. Ann Serak, Wisconsin. Whelped December 1978, this youngster is obviously the next-in-line of descendants of Ch. Strauss's Happy-Go-Lucky to take the judicial eyes.—*Olson*

Ch. ROBIN CREST CHIP, C.D.T.
Owners: Robert Crest Kennels, N.Y.
Ch. GRETCHENHOF MOONSHINE
Owners: Gretchenhof Kennels, Calif.
  (*MULTIPLE B.I.S.*)
Ch. COLUMBIA RIVER THUNDERCLOUD
  (MEX.)
Owners: Gretchenhof Kennels, Calif.
  NOTE: This B.I.S. was won in
  Mexico.
RICHLU'S BECKY ORANIAN (bitch)
*Owner:*W. V. Rawlins, Georgia
Ch. GRETCHENHOF WHITE FROST
Owner: John Hutchins, Texas
Ch. GUNHILL'S MESA MAVERICK
Owner: P.C. Tuttle, Va.
Ch. IRE JA'S STARLITE GUNBEARER
Owner: Irene Stapp, Ohio
Ch. STRAUSS'S HAPPY GO LUCKY
Owner: Serakraut Kennels, Wisc.
AM/CAN. CH. CEDE MEIN SIR GANDY
  DANCER
Owner: Cede Shorthairs (Reg.), Wash.
Ch. WEIDENBACH ARIC TEUFEL SKERL
Owners: S. K. & B. Topliss, Calif.
Ch. KAPOSIA'S WAUPUN II
Owner: Helen Case, Ariz.
Ch. KAPOSIA'S OCONTO
Owners: Kaposia Kennels, Minn.
Ch. OTTO V. OSTHOFF
Owner: Charles Weckerle, Wisc.
Ch. GRETCHENHOF MOONSONG
Owners: Gretchenhof Kennels, Calif.

Ch. NESSETHAL'S BROWN MIKE
Owners: Mrs. Rose Ann Scully, New
  York
Ch. BENWICK KRONNENMUHLE BECKUM

AM/CAN. CH. CEDE MEIN CHAT NUGA
  CHU CHU
Owners: C. D. Lawrence, Mill, and
Davidson, Wash.
Ch. GRETCHENHOF COLUMBIA RIVER
Owner: Dr. R. Smith, Calif.
Ch. ROCKY RUN'S STONY
Owner: R. L. Arnold
Ch. FAUTAIX'S HAPPY O, CD
Owner: W. Fauteaux, Alaska.
Ch. WETHERLING WINDCLOUD, CD
Owner: R. Miller, Pennsylvania

(Ch. Alnor's Brown Mike
ex Ch. Montreal Belle)
(Ch. Columbia River Thundercloud
ex Ch. Columbia River Jill)

(Ch. Columbia River Lightning
ex Ch. Columbia River Princess)

(Ch. Richlu's Jeffson
ex Ch. Richlu's Jan Oranian-Nassau)
(Ch. Columbia River Thundercloud
ex Ch. Columbia River Jill)
(Ch. Tasso Fran Hallam
ex Manchaps Alaska)
(Ch. Fliegen Meister's Gunner ex Ira Ja's
  Starlite Kippy Karen)
(Strauss's Viktor
ex Strauss's Teora)
(Am/Can. Ch. Columbia River Moon-
  watcher
ex Zeugencarl's Duchess v. Aho)
(Ch. Weidenbach Kamiak Snoe Shoe
ex Weidenbach Bo Calypso)
(Ch. Kaposia's Otsego
ex Ch. Kaposia's Blue Chinook)
(Ch. Kaposia's War Lance ex Ch. Ka-
  posia's Star Dancer)
(Ch. Ludwig v. Osthoff
ex Baroness v. Freckles)
(Dual & Nat'l. Ch. Baron Fritz v. Hohen
  Tann
ex Ch. Gretchenhof Blue Moon)
(Baba Lin's Ima Fancy Flash
ex Elaine's Ginny)

(Baron Kronnenmuhle Beckum
ex Lucas McCaine's Sue)
(Ch. Cede Brass Badge
ex Ch. Cede Mein Gadabout, C.D.)

(Ch. Gretchenhof Moonfrost
ex Columbia River Della)
(Ch. Adam v. Fuehrerheim
ex Ch. Rocky Run's Poldi)
(Ch. Timberlines Ruff & Tuff
ex Blitzkreig's Mlor CDX
(Ch. Grousemanor Sindstorm,
ex Ch. Whispering Pines Francesca)

Ch. Dee Tee's Flambeau v. Greif
Owner: J. Whitfield & J. Sener, Ill.

(Dual Ch. Oxton's Minado v. Brunz ex Dual Ch. Cede Mein Dolly der Orrian)

Ch. Beauregard Ix, CD
Owner: P.W. Barron, Hawaii

(Golden West Bebel ex Keinan Cho-Cho)

Ch. Geezee Super Chief
Owners: D. & D. Gilliam, Calif.

(Charisma Columbia River Fame ex Geezee Missy)

Ch. Herr Bodo of the Barretts
Owners: B. & D. Barrett, Ill.

(Ch. Strauss's Happy Go Lucky ex Die Ilsa of the Barretts)

Ch. Birdacres Aruba
Owner: Betty Jane Smith, Ill.

(Ch. Adam v. Fuehrerheim ex Birdacres Amber Doll)

Ch. Nock's Chocolate Chip
Owner: K. Lytle, Florida

(Ch. Baron Marquis of Ashbrook ex Wild Winds Mitzi)

Ch. Conrad's Brio
Owners: G. & N. Conrad, Penna.

(Ch. Mika v.d. Gartensteole ex Ch. Missy v. Nevins)

Ch. Dee Tee's Grandee v. Greif
Owners: B. & G. Hochnadel, Colo

(Dual Ch. Oxton's Minado v. Brunz ex Dual Ch. Cede Mein Dolly der Orrian)

Ch. Donavin's Sir Ivanhoe
Owners: D. & D. Gilliam, Calif.
(*MULTIPLE B.I.S.*)

(Ch. Geezee Super Chief ex Lady Plutonian Star Traveller)

Ch. P.W.'s Challenger v. Fieldfine
Owner: L. Berg, NY

(Ch. Fieldfines Lord Rambard ex Ehrichs Jaeger Traum)

Ch. Fieldfines Lord Tanner
Owners: L. & M Shulman, Vermont

(Ch. Fieldfines Lord Rambard ex Cinnamon Duchess)

Can/Am. Ch. Robin Crest Little John
Owners: J. & J. Remondi, NY

(Can/Am. Ch. Robin Crest Achilles ex Can/Am.Ch. Robin Crest Color Me Cocoa)

Ch. Donavin's Sir Ivanhoe (Ch. Geezee Super Chief ex Lady Plutonian Star Traveller). Multiple BIS winner, 1980/81. Owners: D. and D. Gilliam and Valerie Nunes, California.—*Ludwig*

12

The A.K.C. Standard

AS approved for the purebred dog breeds recognized by The A.K.C., Standards blue-print the ideal—the physical, and often the mental, characteristics that distinguish one breed from the other. The breeder should aim to produce dogs as close to this ideal as possible. The judge is obligated to accept its direction, a knowledge of the Standard being, of course, a prerequisite to gaining a license.

To support such an aim, such an obligation, there must be Rule. Briefly, and to quote: "When the banks are removed, the stream becomes a swamp." (Mary Gilmore, D.B.E.) In any activity, the alternative to Rule is chaos. In dogs, specifically, it is degeneration.

The present Standard for the German Shorthaired Pointer was compiled by the Parent Club (The German Shorthaired Pointer Club of America, Inc.) and approved by the Directors of the American Kennel Club in 1975. Though there has been considerable agitation over many years for overhaul, the actual work was belatedly undertaken only in the later 1960s, when some clarifying language was grafted to the original, imposing no drastic changes but attempting a clearance of obscurities, defining aims and, where possibly some adverse trends were recognizable, in drawing up remedial requirements to help the judges. The better compiled of modern breed

Standards, incorporating the scientific findings in respect to dog movement, specifically those of the late McDowell Lyon (*The Dog In Action*), have prompted also an interest to define Shorthair Gait, merely skimmed over in the original compilation of 1946.

Whenever a modern-day revision is undertaken, there is necessarily a good deal of work involved. Inevitably, there must in such cases be clashes of interest; especially as most regional groups tend to put most emphasis on the problem recognized as most acute within their own territory. That, of course, means compromise—as all Committee work necessarily must mean compromise. Yet, however involved may have been the processes by which these various Standards were modernized, wherever the work was attended to, high aims seem to have been favored. Best brains are hopefully enlisted and basic attention paid to the breed's reason for existing.

THE BREED STANDARD OF THE GERMAN SHORTHAIRED POINTER
(As approved by the Board of Directors of the American Kennel Club, to be effective January, 1976.)

The Shorthair is a versatile hunter, an all-purpose gun dog capable of high performance in field and water. The judgment of Shorthairs in the show ring should reflect this basic characteristic.

GENERAL APPEARANCE: (A.K.C. Standard)
The overall picture which is created in the observer's eye is that of an aristocratic, well-balanced, symmetrical animal with confirmation indicating power, endurance and agility and a look of intelligence and animation. The dog is neither unduly small nor conspicuously large. It gives the impression of medium size, but is like the proper hunter, "with a short back, but standing over plenty of ground."

Tall leggy dogs, or dogs which are ponderous or unbalanced because of excess substance should be definitely rejected. The first impression is that of a keenness which denotes full enthusiasm for work without indication of nervous or flighty character. Movements are alertly coordinated without waste motion. Grace of outline, clean-cut head, sloping shoulders, deep chest, powerful back, strong quarters, good bone composition, adequate muscle, well-carried

215

tail and taut coat, all combine to produce a look of nobility and an indication of anatomical structure essential to correct gait which must indicate a heritage of purposefully conducted breeding. Doggy bitches and bitchy dogs are to be faulted. A judge must excuse a dog from the ring if it displays extreme shyness or viciousness toward its handler or the judge. Aggressiveness or belligerence toward another dog is not to be considered viciousness.

SYMMETRY: (A.K.C. Standard)
Symmetry and field quality are most essential. A dog in hard and lean field condition is not to be penalized. However, overly fat or poorly muscled dogs are to be penalized. A dog well-balanced in all points is preferable to one with outstanding good qualities and defects.

AUTHOR'S COMMENT: If the novice in the breed up and asks that "unduly small" and "conspicuously large" be rather more exactly defined, he deserves at least a hearing. If he mentions the requirement that the dog should "give the impression of medium size," he is probably within his rights when he asks: "Medium size, as compared, say, with what?" And in a day when the automobile rules the road, not everyone that reads a dog Standard really gathers the import of the long-familiar, older-day comparison with the "proper hunter, with a short back, standing over a lot of ground." It's dollars to doughnuts that many who read that for the first time picture the "hunter" with two legs, not four, and wonder what exact gymnastic exercise the guy is actually up to, by golly! As for the opening sentence of the second paragraph, think how much wordage could be saved by just setting down that fat dogs are out—period. Cold-blooded analysis can find more excess wordage, but for now, let it go.

We are all on much firmer ground when reviewing the demand for "an aristocratic, well-balanced, symmetrical animal with conformation indicating power, endurance, agility . . ." The best minds within the breed, from the great German experts, such as Dr. Paul Kleeman, to the most knowledgeable of our own judges, have always applied such a measure to the German Shorthaired Pointers

216

that come within their sight. They ask for a dog that looks right because it is built right to move right. Mere flashiness may catch the judges who don't know—"mug-catchers," we call dogs of such a flashy description where I hail from—but it never catches the ones who do know. The ones who know look for elegance in all-over appearance, the sloping shoulders that shape the short back, the long upper arms that facilitate movement, the rib cage that makes place for heart and lungs, the clean legs that provide the movement, and the sound, thick, arch-toed feet that carry the load. They look for the kind, wise eyes of a temperamentally sound dog, and the tail that emphasizes what the eyes have said. These indicators, fore and aft, are the proof of "intelligence and animation."

Dr. Kleeman has pointed out that the rules of structural engineering are also the rules of nature. To work right, a dog must be built right. To be built right, it has first to be born right. Mighty simple, if one comes to think of it. . . .

HEAD: (A.K.C. Standard)

Clean-cut, neither too light nor too heavy, in proper proportion to the body. Skull is reasonably broad, arched on side and slightly round on top. Scissura (median line between the eyes at the forehead) not too deep, occipital bone not as conspicuous as in the case of the Pointer. The foreface rises gradually from nose to forehead. The rise is more strongly pronounced in the dog than in the bitch as befitting his sex. The chops fall away from the somewhat projecting nose. Lips are full and deep, never flewy. The chops do not fall over too much, but form a proper fold in the angle. The jaw is powerful and the muscles well developed. The line to the forehead rises gradually and never has a definite stop as that of the Pointer, but rather a stop-effect when viewed from the side, due to the position of the eyebrows. The muzzle is sufficiently long to enable the dog to seize properly and to facilitate his carrying game a long time. A pointed muzzle is not desirable. The entire head never gives the impression of tapering to a point. The depth is in the right proportion to the length, both in the muzzle and in the skull proper. The length of the muzzle should equal the length of skull. A pointed muzzle is a fault. A dish-faced muzzle is a fault. A definite Pointer stop is a serious fault. Too many wrinkles in forehead is a fault.

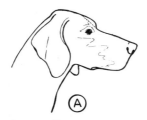

GOOD HEADS
"A" AND "B"

POOR HEADS
"C" AND "D"

"B"

"C" HAS A COARSE EAR, TOO MUCH CHOP AND A FLEWY LIP.

"D" HAS EARS THAT ARE TOO LONG AND POINTED, A POINTED SNIPY MUZZLE, IS TOO ROUNDED IN SKULL AND HAS A POOR EYE SET.

BOTH LACK BALANCE, ARE SHORT IN MUZZLE, HAVE TOO MUCH STOP.

AUTHOR'S COMMENT: In the practical sense, as is to be observed, the variation of head type within the German Shorthaired Pointer breed is extremely wide, not only in American-bred dogs, but also in the dogs imported from overseas. There appears here to be a variation from the widest of "Pointer" skulls to the finest of "Setter"—to quote the extreme opposites. Between, one finds every possible variation on those themes, adding up to the reasonable belief that head type in the breed is not as yet exactly fixed, and that each line-bred strain tends to favor a head type of its own. Actually, most heads seem to sit suitably on the front ends of the dogs that own them, so that the vagueness of the opening sentence of the Standard, as it applies to this part of the dog, reasonably caters to them all. "Neither too light nor too heavy, in proper proportion to the body" . . . "skull should be reasonably broad," leaves much to the discretion of a judge. How little is "too light"? How much is "too heavy"? What is "reasonable breadth"? In the listing of the faults, further along, heads are held less desirable if they are "too large, with too many wrinkles in forehead, dish-faced, snipy muzzle." But how *many* wrinkles are too many? How large *is* too large? Certainly, such wordage presents some good arguments for the compilation of dog breed Standards in a pictorial medium rather than in words.

With the head the seat of character and intelligence, inevitably it can make or mar a dog. It is the first thing looked at, by the buyer in the yard, the trainer at the kennels, the judge in the show ring. If the head displeases in that first going-over, the rest of the dog may even be dismissed without any great amount of further consideration—it happens. The bitterest wrangling of the pioneer German breeders was in respect to the head the developing utility breed should have. The first direction to prevail was for a head described as "Grecian" in profile, as near as could be a straight line, nose to occiput. In the view of many strong supporters of this type of head, it was considered to favor trailing-keeping (which meant hound) abilities, as distinct from the dished profile of the high-scenting Pointer. Many of the best of the early-day dogs, pillars of the breed such as Wodan Hektor II v. Lemgo, and Tell aus der Wolfsschlucht, had definitely Roman-nosed heads. The tendency to a "bump" on the bridge has come down the generations with a persistency that not even the disapproval of the original Standard here has been able wholly to thwart. One still sees many a German Shorthaired Pointer with the same bumpy profile as, say, K.S. Michel v.d. Goldenen Mark had in his prepotent day. Such inheritances are not lightly scotched.

Over the years intervening since such dogs as Tell and K.S. Michel, there came to be emphasis on the signs of working qualities, such as a skull really broad enough to contain brains and the ole-factory (scenting) nerves; a lower jaw long, deep and strong enough to bite to kill when necessary, as well as to bear heavy weights over long-distance carries. It is just such a head that the present-day Standard seems to define, the good honest head of a useful working dog. However, the wording could possibly be made clearer for the novices. One useful way would be to delete references of comparison with the Pointer. The modern American field trial Pointer is not the familiar sight in Shorthair competition that he was when the first breed Standard was compiled in 1946. Many novice Short-hair owners may never actually have seen a true Pointer-type head, though modern resurgence in show competition has brought many classic examples to the fore. But the average Pointer seen at Field Trials may have a head in which any resemblance to classic breed type is purely coincidental. For these reasons, the comparison as worded provides little help in making the definition clear to German Shorthaired Pointer novices.

EARS: (A.K.C. Standard)

Ears are broad and set fairly high, lie flat and never hang away from the head. Placement is just above the eye level. The ears, when laid in front without being pulled, meet the lip angle. In the case of heavier dogs, the ears are correspondingly longer. Ears too long or fleshy are to be faulted.

K.S. Kara v. Hohenfeld at Kleeman Au slese Prufung, 1968. This superbly beautiful Axel v. Wasserschling daugh ter was refused top rating in confor mation for low ear placement, a fault German judges never overlook. Many U.S. judges would not give it a thought! All standards ask for Shorthair ears to be "broad and set fairly high, never hang away from the head."—C. Bede Maxwell

AUTHOR'S COMMENT: Now, *there's* some dog Standard writing at its very best. Every word means exactly what it says, and no confusing comparisons dragged in—nor any comparisons needed.

The Germans, perhaps still influenced by the preoccupation of the pioneer breeders with ear shape, spell the requirements right out—ears shall be neither too thick nor too fine, and lower ends shall be blunted and round. Well, the A.K.C. Standard takes care of that description as well, bracketing it in the fault column, spelling out exactly what German Shorthaired Pointer ears shall *not* be.

Closer to home, a writer in the A.K.C. *Gazette* has truthfully described the ear as "the one part of the dog that cannot tell a lie." In many animals, as a matter of fact, the ears are the barometers of emotion. Who doubts the message conveyed by the flattened ears of the horse, or those of the family tomcat? Similarly, the dog can convey his feelings by the movement even of such pendant lugs as grace the heads of the sporting dogs as a group.

Ears in this breed, as in all smooth-coated, pendant-eared breeds, are cruelly vulnerable. Flaps suffer in cover, get chewed in fights, are prey to flies. Absence of feather helps the entrance of grass seeds, foreign bodies. Blows can produce painful, bulging hematomas, and allergic reactions do the strangest things. I am reminded of a fine young bitch greeting me one morning with her ears swollen literally inches thick through, and heavy as lead—a condition (oedema) that vanished as rapidly and as mysteriously as it came, within a few hours.

Looking over the ears of the German Shorthaired Pointer breed, one may discover them to be as varied in type as heads—ears long, ears short, sometimes even folded. However, the Standard directions are excellently plain, so no confusion should be experienced by breeder or by judge as to how those ears *should* be.

EYES: (A.K.C. Standard)

The eyes are of medium size, full of intelligence and expressive, good humored and yet radiating energy, neither protruding nor sunken. The eye is almond shaped, not circular. The eyelids close well. The best color is dark brown. Light yellow (Bird of Prey) eyes are not desirable and are a fault. Closely set eyes are to be faulted. China or wall eyes are to be disqualified.

AUTHOR'S COMMENT: The Germans are more detailed in their definition of German Shorthaired Pointer eyes. They ask for as little as possible—none at all they hold better—of the conjunctiva tumica showing, not wanting the haw of the hound. They reject a deepset eye, and define a "bird of prey" eye as light yellow. No doubt, a German breeder could not visualize, even in nightmare, a "china" or "wall" eye coming up. There does not seem to be, in the purebred German Shorthaired Pointer, any source from which such an eye could legitimately be derived. Breeds permitted such an eye—such as harlequin Great Danes, say, or the varied breeds of merle or "dappled" color—just don't seem to have come into allowable genetical contact with the dog from Germany—in its purebred representation, at any rate.

Otherwise, in Germany as here, breeders have their troubles keeping to a desirable dark eye. In the Summer, 1961, issue of *Kurzhaar Blätter,* the German breed magazine, a judge's critique of the *Sonderausstellung* (Specialist Show) of the *Südwestdeutscher Klub Kurzhaar,* in June, 1961, is spotted through with two complaints: loose elbows and light eyes. Both faults meet the judges here, too. However, many new imports from Germany to the United States *are* bringing in nice dark eyes.

In the breed monograph, *Deutsch Kurzhaar,* on pages six and seven, the famed German expert, E. v. Otto, makes an interesting observation concerning problems of eye color. He points out that in the early days the brown coat color, with or without white, was held to be the only genuine color for a Kurzhaar (judges who penalize solid livers please note!), and a too-close adherence to this belief resulted in a loss of pigmentation and the prevalence of ugly, light, staring eyes. As a counter-measure, experimental breeding was undertaken, using black pointers from England, notably Killian v. Kanatsche, bred by Wm. Arkwright, and the bitch, Beechgrove Bess. These founded strains of black-brindled (or dark gray) dogs, that for a time were given a seperate registration in Germany as "Prussian Shorthairs." From these there was gained an improvement in eye color throughout the breed generally, and they no longer have a separate registration.

American breeders with stubborn problems of light eyes in their strains can take no hope from this experimentation of fifty years ago. First, where would they find their black pointers? Well, Scandinavia has some still but in any case, prevailing American registration rules would not sanction such cross-breeding, and the Standard, as we shall presently see, lists any black pigmentation as a fault. Those fortunate enough to gain dark eyes through some of the newer German imports here should perhaps budget to take good care of them, for they are so easily lost in all breeds!

One other thing is necessary to know about eyes: what particular *shade* of light eyes does a puppy have? In English Pointers, for example, the greenish-yellow eye of a pup will remain undesirably light for the lifetime of the dog. The honey-yellow eye, on the other hand, continues to darken as the dog matures, so that at two years of age, the light-eyed pup will have a nice hazel eye. It is an observable process, the pigment darkening inward from the iris rim to the pupil. Breeder-trainer Bob Holcomb was told in Germany that a well-bred, dark-colored German Shorthaired Pointer pup does not get his true eye color till two years. The same rule, then, would seem to apply in this breed as in Pointers. German breeders also hold that the lighter colored a well-bred German Shorthaired Pointer's jacket is, the darker should be those well-pools of his spirit, his eyes.

This German teaching holds well with what prevailed in the old-time requirement for English Pointers here. Long-time breeders will recall the one-time requirement of the Standard in America that an orange-and-white Pointer should have—well, didn't the Standard actually ask for a *black* eye? Only the liver-and-white was permitted a hazel eye by the old Pointer Standard, now discarded for a 1968 revision. This wiping-out of a rigid eye-color requirement could be a coming to terms with the realities of the present day, the once-desirable eye-color having become virtually lost to the breed. The new Pointer Standard requires of an eye only that it be "the darker the better." This could represent a compromise to which the German Shorthaired Pointer Standard might never be reduced if breeders take care with keeping eyes right. Worth mentioning here is the observation that experience in sporting breeds generally opposes what one often hears at the ringside: "Maybe his eyes *could* be a bit darker, but I wouldn't call them *light*—they match his coat." In truth, such eyes *are* light. The requirement seems to be rather that the lighter the jacketing, the darker the eye. Pointers, Springers, English Setters, etc., all come within this rule, as well as German Shorthaired Pointers.

Also widely held, is the belief that light-eyed dogs are uncertain of temperament. Experiment and experience do not support the belief. In English *Dog World* (February 24, 1961), E. Sandon Moss points out that eye color is unimportant in Border or Working Collies, the only breeds that rely on their eyes to impress or force the dominance of their personalities. "Contrary to general belief, one can rarely estimate character, fidelity, or any other quality in the dog by the expression of its eyes," he writes. "It would be difficult for Labradors, or Spaniels, for example, whatever their feelings, to convey anything but ready and willing compliance and abounding good nature by their eyes alone. Other breeds . . . have a consistently hard expression that is certainly no real indication of their frame of mind or attitude to life generally."

Mr. Frank A. Longmore, of the kennel-governing Executive of Victoria, Australia, also had a most important observation to make concerning eyes and the dog. Dogs, he held, can suffer severely from eye-strain—"the strain of your eyes and mine!" he clarified. "Often, when judging, I find it necessary to turn my eyes away from a dog under review, finding it restless, even resentful, under a too-concentrated stare."

Based on wide judging experience, Mr. Longmore's is an observation to be digested by the type of judge who makes a performance of "going through the motions" in the show ring. Such often stand and stare at a dog, acting the part of being in the deepest judicial thought. Presently, visibly, the dog goes to pieces. Some back away. Some glare in resentment, ready to defend their persons against such psychological intrusion.

NOSE: (A.K.C. Standard)
Brown, the larger the better, nostrils well-opened and broad. Spotted nose not desirable. Flesh-colored nose disqualifies.

AUTHOR'S COMMENT: Nothing there that doesn't make best sense. The German view seems to be that the outward sign of good scenting is a big, moist nose with flaring nostrils, prominent, movable. Those among us with interest in history know that one of the features of the Old Spanish Pointer was that "double nose" the engravers always depicted so faithfully at the end of his face. "Double," of course, merely describes the visual effect—as of two circles, back to back.

TEETH: (A.K.C. Standard)

The teeth are strong and healthy. The molars intermesh properly. The bite is a true scissors bite. A perfect level bite (without over-lapping) is not desirable and must be penalized. Extreme overshot or undershot bite disqualifies.

AUTHOR'S COMMENT: The "scissors bite," as the Standard asks, is a neat fitting of the front teeth of the upper jaw over the front teeth of the lower, with no space between. Any variation of this pattern is not desirable. An *overshot* (or pig) jaw is one in which the upper teeth protrude beyond the lower. An *undershot* jaw is one in which the bottom teeth protrude beyond the upper. Either fault, if at all severe, makes a dog's head look wrong, especially in profile. In their more serious manifestations, such mal-formations make it hard for a dog to pick up an object. Cosmetic considerations apart, hunting men will not want a dog so handi-capped.

In assessing puppies' mouths, it should be remembered that the lower jaw grows out more than the upper. If a youngster shows you his erupting second toothy-pegs with the top ones jutting out a bit in front, don't start worrying for a while. In most cases, natural jaw development takes care of it, and at maturity such a pup will usually have a good scissors bite. But if the *lower* jaw sticks out beyond the upper, chances are not usually good. The lower jaw will likely grow out further still and the mouth of the mature dog will look worse than that of the pup.

Many dogs have a completely level mouth, upper teeth sitting neatly on top of the lower in front. Owners tend to be annoyed if a judge looks hard at a mouth of this kind and, indeed, most judges let it pass. Yet experience shows it to be less than desirable. Those "riding" teeth on top wear down the lower. Long before such a dog is middle-aged he will have a mouth full of ground-down shards. Some breeders of wide experience also hold that level "riding" mouths of this pattern can in one generation be the source of really faulty undershot mouths in the next. Then, of course, there is the school of thought that believes faulty feeding practice, rather than inheritance, imposes bad mouths. That, of course, is only to be proved by a carefully controlled experiment that is beyond the hope of an ordinary breeder to put into practice.

NECK: (A.K.C. Standard)

Of proper length to permit the jaws reaching game to be retrieved, sloping downwards on beautifully curving lines. The nape is rather muscular, becoming gradually larger towards the shoulders. Moderate houndlike throatiness permitted.

AUTHOR'S COMMENT: Anatomically, there are the same number of vertebrae in the neck of a dog that appears short-necked as in that of a dog that appears long-necked. The factor of length, then, is something of an illusion. It is wholly influenced by lay of shoulder. The steep-fronted dog's shoulder blade imposes the "start" of the neck inches further along the string of vertebrae than does the shoulder blade that is desirably and obliquely sloping.

Reasonably, one may believe that correct shoulder assembly and a general front-end flexibility count for more in making it easy for a dog to retrieve game than any mere illusion of length his neck may present to view. (If he has this correct anatomical construction, then of course his neck *does* look desirably long.) Something along these lines may possibly be given consideration as expressing the requirement rather better in terms of strictly practical breeder concern. After all, the recognized retriever breeds, all whizzes at scooping up game, are not usually considered remarkable for swanlike length of neck. But they ARE, in all their A.K.C.-recognized varieties, required to have good sloping shoulder assembly wherein, the anatomists tell us, are located those mechanical aids that favor the designated work. The dog with the tied-in, straight shoulder, his short upper-arm forming with that shoulder a straight line that runs right down his leg to his toes, as one sees quite often, is the dog likely to have his troubles getting his jaws down to his game. And the apparent "length" of his neck, plus or minus, has no more to do with his awkwardness than the length of his tail, also plus or minus.

It is beyond argument that an elegant neckline sloping into correctly-placed shoulders benefits not only the show dog, but the

The neck elegance of the prepotent pioneer import, Arta v. Hohreusch, has come down as inheritance to her Dual- and BIS-winning descendants.

field dog as well. Nothing contributes more style to the stance of a dog on point. Nothing furthers the beauty of a show pose so unmistakably.

CHEST: (A.K.C. Standard)

The chest in general gives the impression of depth rather than breadth; for all that, it should be in correct proportion to the other parts of the body with a fair depth. The chest reaches down to the elbows, the ribs forming the thorax show a rib spring and are not flat or slabsided; they are not perfectly round or barrel-shaped. Ribs that are entirely round prevent the necessary expansion of the chest when taking breath. The back ribs reach well down. The circumference of the thorax immediately behind the elbows is smaller than that of the thorax about a hands-breadth behind elbows, so that the upper arm has room for movement.

AUTHOR'S COMMENT: The requirement of an oval, rather than a round, chest formation has been long understood in the case of dogs required to exert themselves in action. As the Standard points out, round ribs hinder expansion for extra breathing needs. The reason is mechanical—a circle cannot be further expanded. The relationship between round (barrel) ribs and a wide (bulldog) chest; the forcing apart of upper-arms that are oftenest short, and shoulder blades ditto; the bull-neck coarseness imposed by the wide gap between the tops of the shoulder blades—all are clearly demonstrable. These are very commonly seen anatomical faults in the German Shorthaired Pointer. Dogs come into sight with such a width between their shoulder blade tops that one may be pardoned for guessing a cup of coffee could be balanced there, as on a table, with no trouble at all!

Oval ribbing facilitates the expansion imposed by stress in breathing, thus helping endurance. It is most often matched anatomically by long upper arms and long shoulder blades lying with their tops desirably close. Instead of the bulldog front of the barrel-chested dog, with the awkward far-apart placing of the front legs that imposes a choppy gait, the oval-chested dog will be able to stand on legs much closer together, to stride out cleanly. This is the fore-chest formation, as just mentioned, that lets a dog get his nose down. Herr v. Otto, as quoted by Dr. Kleeman, draws attention to the ability of Foxhounds, big-bodied as they are, to get their noses down, even at the gallop, because their legs are set well beneath them in the proper forehand assembly. (Check back to Columbia River Tillie, Chapter 6.)

That the circumference of the chest should be slightly less just behind the elbows is also easy to understand. There has to be clearance for the upper-arm, working along the same lines as the piston-rod of a railway engine. In the round-ribbed, wide-fronted dog, the upper-arm get forced right out, and awkward movement results. In the tied-in shoulder, equally undesirable, the opposite prevails, with equal effect on easy gait. The pointing breeds, caught by the camera racked-up on a bird, can usually provide a good object lesson in respect to the inter-relationship of rib and front assembly generally.

The wide front too often seen in the German Shorthaired Pointer, unwelcome as it is, has been with the breed rather too long. It is

Connie v.d. Arriërvelden (imp. Eng. from Holland). Owned by Wittekind Kennels, Eng. Why the Standard asks for "the circumference of the breast to be slightly less just behind the elbows." There must be clearance for the shoulder mechanism to function.

Columbia River Tillie, at age 16, exhibits correct slope of (long) shoulder and a well-angled (long) upper arm which set the dog's forelegs well beneath her. In Shorthairs, the good ones are forever. *Photo: C. Bede Maxwell*

not only a local problem. It has caused concern to breeders in most parts of the world, perhaps as successfully as anywhere in England where high popularity has brought experienced breeders into the Shorthair interest and considerable attention has been paid to elimination of defects of coarseness.

BACK, LOINS and CROUP: (A.K.C. Standard)
Back is short, strong and straight with slight rise from root of tail to withers. Loin strong, of moderate length and slightly arched. Tuck-up is apparent. Excessively long, roached or swayed back must be penalized.

AUTHOR'S COMMENT: In the dog, where length of body sufficient to contain the vital organs is asked for in the same breath as a short back, the length of back is measurable from the highest point of the withers to the first of the lumbar vertebrae. The back is the member that spans the distance between the forehand assembly and the hindquarters as a bridge, supports the head and the neck, the weight of the down-hanging ribs, the body organs contained below. For this, it needs to be taut and strong. For this, most judges look away from swampy-backed (dippy-backed) dogs with their backbones sagging between shoulders and hips like a garden hammock between two trees. The opposite curve, known as a roach, is also undesirable and usually penalized, though preferable to a dippy-back as less suggestive of a structural weakness. Old engravings seem usually to depict the Old Spanish Pointer as roached, but modern breeding practices have long since done their best to eliminate this not-so-handsome outline from German Shorthaired Pointers.

As does the neck, the back owes its "length" or, in this case, shall we say its "shortness," to the lay of shoulder. Again, there are the same number of vertebrae in a long-backed dog as in a short. Thus, a steep-shouldered dog will appear longer in back than one with a correctly placed shoulder. An interesting game to play with a view to understanding this is to place an imaginary saddle on the dog's back, as though he were a horse. If the saddle rides up towards his ears, his shoulders are steep, his back is long (and his neck correspondingly short). If the saddle sits where saddles on horses are supposed to sit, the dog is shortbacked, with correct shoulder placement.

The Germans, who will not countenance a long-backed German Shorthaired Pointer, ask for a taut back to further such energetic movements as, say, jumping. In loin, they ask for a short, slightly-curved area, holding that too strong an arch here hinders action and speed.

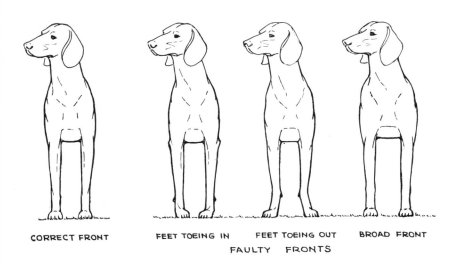

CORRECT FRONT   FEET TOEING IN   FEET TOEING OUT   BROAD FRONT

FAULTY   FRONTS

FOREQUARTERS: (A.K.C. Standard)
The shoulders are sloping, movable, well-covered with muscle. The shoulder blades lie flat and are well laid back nearing a 45° angle. The upper arm (the bones between the shoulder and elbow joints) is as long as possible, standing away somewhat from the trunk so that the straight and closely muscled legs, when viewed from the front, appear to be parallel. Elbows which stand away from the body or are too close indicate toes turning inwards or outwards, which must be regarded as faults. Pasterns are strong, short and nearly vertical with a slight spring. Loose, short-bladed or straight shoulders must be faulted. Knuckling over is to be faulted. Down in the pasterns is to be faulted.

AUTHOR'S COMMENT: In connection with the Standard's requirement of an upper arm to be as long as possible (how long IS possible?), Dr. Paul Kleeman has also observed in his German discussion that the further back a dog can move its elbows, the more easily it will be able to drop its torso between its upper shoulder-blades. Seeking the dog that can take its elbows furthest back, he directs, look for the one with the longest upper-arm, and to find it, look in turn for the dog with the longest shoulders and the most usefully developed withers.

The ability to drop and elevate the body between the shoulder-blades, especially while in motion, has served the best hunting dogs for centuries, maybe since the beginning of time. It is a first instinct, carried along from the era when men hunted birds with nets, when the dog's low-to-ground creeping was in the essential nature of its work. It is amazing with what tenacity the instinct clings within the mentality of the sporting breeds, as may be rapidly learned of most dogs themselves when they have not been receiving training to be lofty. Present-day field trial performance in America, of course, definitely discards much movement; the drop-to-shot requirement of the European and English trials is not permitted here. However, practical hunters in any part of the world, including here, seldom quarrel with it, the movement having its useful application to their service. On the other hand, to eradicate it can cost a field trial trainer plenty of sweat when some individual dog, otherwise a good field trial prospect, makes up a stubborn mind that the way his fore-bears hunted clear through the centuries, feather or fur, is good enough for him.

HINDQUARTERS: (A.K.C. Standard)
The hips are broad with hip sockets wide apart and fall slightly toward the tail in a graceful curve. Thighs are strong, well-muscled. Stifles well bent. Hock joints are well angulated and strong, straight bone structure from hock to pad. Angulation of both stifle and hock joint is such as to combine maximum combination of both drive and traction. Hocks turn neither in nor out. A steep croup is a fault. Cowhocked legs are a serious fault.

AUTHOR'S COMMENT: Here, too, the Standard presents an exact word-picture of what is required in the after-end of a good German Shorthaired Pointer. It disallows narrow, weak-looking hips and the straight-stick back legs increasingly seen. In the show-ring, by the way, there are times when a judge should exactly satisfy himself whether the apparently straight, stuck-out hindleg of a dog

232

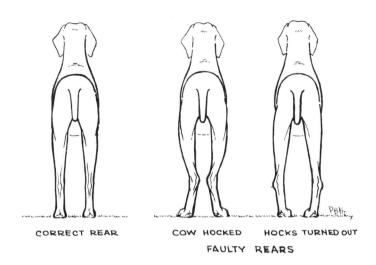

CORRECT REAR   COW HOCKED   HOCKS TURNED OUT

FAULTY REARS

is the result of poor construction or showring tenseness. Many a correctly-built dog will mulishly or nervously straighten out his backlegs in the showring, and no amount of persuasion on the part of his handler can coax him to relax and stand normally. (A sharp little tap near the tail-butt will effect the relaxation in many cases, perhaps operating on a nerve-center. Don't know why, but it seems to work.) On the other hand, it is also necessary for a judge to discover whether the dog with a sharply-sloping topline (which the Standard doesn't ask for, anyway!) really is as over-angulated as he appears, or whether his handler is contriving a crouching pose in the interests of outline. Pulling the legs unnaturally far back will correct a "dippy" back at times—till the dog moves. Spreading the legs wide apart at the rear will counteract a tendency to "high behind." Both methods are used consistently by handlers in posing dogs in the show ring, but the contrivances do not work when the dogs are required to move. The "dippy" back shows, and so does the "high behind." A "high behind" is also masked quite often in action by a good handler who will bring back a dog in an exact straight line to the judge in gaiting—then the head and neck mask the fault. All these smart tactics are fair in love and war, so far as the show ring is concerned, but they do not help in producing good pups in the breeding pen. Old Mother Nature is never bamboozled by such.

233

The requirement that hocks shall turn neither in nor out is also clear. No uglier sight exists than the cow-hocked dog, especially in tall breeds. The term applies to hock joints that lean in together, as opposed to equally faulty hocks that lean out the opposite way and turn the back legs into a pair of parentheses, as viewed from behind.

FEET: (A.K.C. Standard)

Are compact, close-knit and round to spoon-shaped. The toes sufficiently arched and heavily nailed. The pads are strong, hard and thick. Dewclaws on the hind legs must be removed. Dewclaws on the forelegs may be removed. Feet pointing in or out is a fault.

AUTHOR'S COMMENT: Here is another paragraph of the Standard that may possibly lend itself better to pictured explanation than to that of words. What is a novice to make of "sufficiently arched"? Sufficiently for what? The description of the foot itself as "round to spoon-shaped" could also bother anyone not versed in some elementary knowledge of a dog's foot construction. Taking for granted that the "round" foot refers to what most dog folk call the "cat" foot; that the "spoon-shaped" refers to the "hare" foot, obviously the Standard is here saying that any shape of foot goes. For, presumably, as boys and girls are the only two kinds of babies the stork can bring, "cat" and "hare" are the only kinds of sporting-dog feet. These are recognized also in Pointer and Setter breeds, with those who don't like a "cat" foot on the Pointer charging it to the inheritance from the Foxhound. Well, for the German Shorthaired Pointer, any shape of foot. . . . No problem.

GOOD FOOT

The Germans add a further requirement that the dewclaws be removed. This is usually done at a very early age in the pup, within a few days of birth. The removal guards against one annoying form of hunting field accident. Front leg dewclaws are very susceptible to laceration, they catch on this or that out in the field, causing ugly tearing wounds. Also, when the nails on dew claws are left untrimmed, as so often they tend to be, it can often be the *owner* that suffers a nasty tearing wound when the friendly dog reaches over to give his boss a love pat.

There is no lack of those, among the old-time Field Trial men especially, who are strongly opposed to the removal of dewclaws. As one expressed it not so long ago, he holds these dewclaws to be necessary to the German Shorthaired Pointer. Necessary for what? "For climbing trees!" he claimed in all possible seriousness. Cats, yet! But even cats don't use dewclaws to climb!

In general, the toenails of sporting dogs—of *all* dogs!—deserve more care than they usually get. While hard-run dogs tend to grind their own, a little extra help is seldom amiss. Nothing destroys the "compact, close-knit" formation of the German Shorthaired Pointer foot so completely as do neglected nails that enforce a loose spreading of the toes. Kenneled dogs especially need regular toe-nail care. Often such dogs present a grievous sight to dog-minded visitors, which reminds the author of two German Shorthaired Pointers once seen in a kennel—the matron with her toenails left so long they were curving back under her feet! On the other hand, there is no need to go to the extremes being currently practiced among many of the poodle fraternity, where even the handlers themselves often feel a little squeamish over the close guillotining imposed on their charges. "One starts it, and the rest of us have to follow," is the limp explanation for bloodied little feet. Perhaps, in this connection, the forthrightness of an overseas judge is worth recalling. He eliminated one of the nation's top-winning sporting dogs from his final consideration for B.O.B. for just such closely-guillotined nails. Speaking of this later, following the judging, he spread his own hands on the table. "If my fingers were chopped right back to the first knuckle, would you call this a sound hand?" he asked, not unreasonably.

The desirable state of a sporting dog's foot pad is that of hardness and strength, as the Standard requires. To the searching fingers of the experienced judge, the sandpaper roughness of a pad tells an agreeable story of good conditioning. Nothing, but NOTHING, feels worse than a foot composed of thin pads, slippery smooth as rubber.

COAT AND SKIN: (A.K.C. Standard)

The skin is close and tight. The hair is short and thick and feels tough to the hand; it is somewhat longer on the underside of the tail and the back edges of the haunches. It is softer, thinner and shorter on the ears and the head. Any dog with long hair in body coat is to be severely penalized.

AUTHOR'S COMMENT: The German Standard makes specific objection to any extra length of hair on the underside of the tail. Any resemblance to a "brush" is also rated a fault with them as, too, it would be rated here. However, it is interesting to turn back to appearance of the Talbot Hound (p. 17). If his tail were to be lopped where a German Shorthaired Pointer's tail is nowadays lopped, he would be going his way with a tail much as the present Standard describes—with the hair a little longer on the underside. He has that hair on the back of his haunches as well. No comment. Merely an observation.

That the skin be close and tight-fitting is most important. Nothing looks less attractive than a German Shorthaired Pointer whose tailor has done nothing for him, his coat slopping loose on his frame.

TAIL: (A.K.C. Standard)

Is set high and firm, and must be docked, leaving 40% of length. The tail hangs down when the dog is quiet, is held horizontally when he is walking. The tail must never be curved over the back toward the head when the dog is moving. A tail curved or bent toward the head is to be severely penalized.

AUTHOR'S COMMENT: A thick tail is also held objectionable in the same way as is a dewlap, or loaded shoulders and thick ears, faults that seem to lean together.

236

Cutting the tail of a German Shorthaired Pointer pup is not much as surgical operations go, but it requires doing with the very greatest of care. It involves estimation of the eventual size of the dog, and what will be an eye-pleasing, balancing length for him to carry aft. The majority of opinion would seem to hold that leaving the tail a mite long is better than cropping it a mite short. A smidgin could be shaved off later if necessary, but no one has yet worked out a way to stretch an extra inch onto a tail that's too short. Many a good German Shorthaired Pointer's appearance has been improved by re-docking an overlong tail. As Dr. Kleeman has pointed out, this can provide an illusion of strengthened hindquarters. He quotes the horse-dealer practice of bundling up a tail to provide a like illusion.

Apart from looks, a reason for docking the sporting dog is to save it from injury. Not only in the field, either; long wagging tails in the house, or in the kennel, can do themselves dire hurt against the walls, and such tail-tip injuries are stubbornly resistant to healing. Dr. Thornton, in his early-day Kennel Brochure, gruesomely warns of the injuries that can result from uncut tails. He also adds another reason for docking: "It adds greatly to the appearance of the dog, as most of them have large, heavy tails carried over from their hound ancestors. Docking serves to remove this hound appearance."

One thing more before leaving the subject of German Shorthaired Pointer tails. Just turn back the page and read again the Standard's description of the placing of a tail—*down* when the dog is quiet, *horizontally* when he is walking, *never* turned over the back! The breed could use some firm-minded judges who will walk over to a German Shorthaired Pointer being ring-posed like a Boxer, in respect of his tail, and require the handler to allow the tail to assume its natural position. Such a judge might even then discover a long back that otherwise he might easily have missed.

BONES: (A.K.C. Standard)
Thin and fine bones are by no means desirable in a dog which must possess strength and be able to work over any and every country. The main importance accordingly is laid not so much on the size of bone, but rather on their being in proper proportion to the body.

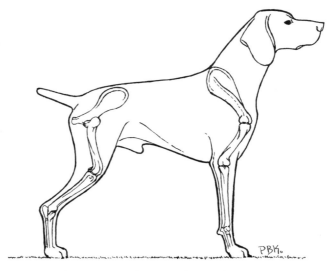

GOOD ANGULATION

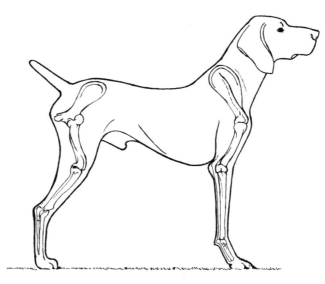

POOR ANGULATION

Bone structure too heavy or too light is a fault. Dogs with coarse bones are handicapped in agility of movement and speed.

AUTHOR'S COMMENT: The German Standard further points out that when breeding is carried on with the breed's advancement in view, the skeletal shape will be refined, its bone texture become closer and firmer, as opposed to the porous, spongy texture of bone that is too bulky. Checking *puppy bone,* it should be remembered that it *is* porous and spongy. Anyone acquainted with the fantastic rate of growth in well-reared pups in the larger breeds within their first six months, understands this very well. The pup that has flourished like a green bay tree stalks around on leg bone that looks—and is—enormous. It is also full of air cavities because of its quick growth. As the pup matures, the spongy baby bone consolidates into a good hard strength to support him for the rest of his life. So, if your otherwise promising six-months' pup is stomping around on young tree trunks rooted in enormous feet—don't sell him down the river for that. The one to discard would be rather the one with the fine underpinnings. Fine bone in a pup consolidates into finer bone still in the adult.

WEIGHT AND HEIGHT: (A.K.C. Standard)
Dogs, 55 to 70 pounds. Bitches, 45 to 60 pounds. Dogs, 23 to 25 inches. Bitches, 21 to 23 inches at the withers. Deviations of one inch above or below the described heights are to be severely penalized.

AUTHOR'S COMMENT: There has always been squabbling on the subject of height, especially, and there have always been those fanciers who would like to see a disqualification clause added, it seems, specifically to control *the show judges,* against some of whom is held a belief in their tendency to lean towards overlarge dogs. Such disqualification clauses do operate in several breeds, including some within the sporting group. Where a disqualification clause applies, a judge *must* check the measurement where it seems to be necessary. Certainly, most will do so only where such an obvious necessity does exist, though there is always the chance that some disgruntled exhibitor will over-readily employ that bane of show superintendents and officials generally—the protest. It can even happen that in the hurly-burly of the showring confusion, a very good dog can be tossed out over the chance of a fraction of an inch incorrectly measured against him. It can also happen that judges subconsciously penalize a dog that is possibly close-up to a standard size burdened with a disqualification because of reluctance to make waves or bring about delay caused by necessity to measure.

Doubtless, it is just such a consideration that has influenced compilers of some modern revised Standards to shy away from including any such disqualification clause, realizing that good dogs come in a range of sizes. The Irish Setter Standard (revised, 1960), for example, is one such, holding that over-all balance is a more important consideration than inch-fraction measurement. The exact same reasoning could possibly be behind the reluctance of many German Shorthaired Pointer breeders to support any revision in terms of disqualification for reasons of height and/or weight.

In the current clamor, by the way, it is notable that the most noise and heat seem to be generated in field trial circles where, so far as it is possible to establish, such a disqualification, based on measurements up or down, would have no bearing. Dogs in field trial competition would not expect to be measured. Therefore, the claim that agitation for "locking up the Standard" in terms of disqualification clauses governing height and weight is being made to "protect the breed" would seem to ring rather hollowly. By and large, the show exhibitor breeds with an eye close to the requirements of the Standard, his dog being judged by these. The field trial owner is subject to no such discipline. If, then, the claims arising in these quarters for imposing height and/or weight qualifications are honestly advanced for the benefit of the breed, it should be required that the measurements be applied to dogs within both spheres of activity, and that measurings operate in both directions, up *and* down. ("Sir!" thundered Dr. Johnson. "Your levellers always want to *level down*—they never want to *level up!*"—*Boswell.*)

In breeds that possess varieties distinguished by size, as in Poodles, Beagles, Dachshunds, etc., a measurable Standard requirement is, of course, arbitrary. But where no such division applies, there could be a case made for finding good in the big ones *and* the little ones, one tendency counterbalancing the other. Breeders opposed to "locking up" the Standard, hold the view that the most important qualities in a German Shorthaired Pointer are those of sound conformation plus the desire to hunt. An inch or two, or a pound or two, more or less, makes no great matter, these feel. Be that as it may, and even granting that there may be danger in over-size or under-size, in actual and practical breeding, these qualities appear to cancel each other out. Most German Shorthaired Pointers seen in the showrings and the field trials fit very nicely into the (desirable) middle range. Those predicting ruin to the breed when a big one (or small one) has a win in their area do not have statistics on their side. The only persons competent to assess the true trend would be the busier judges that officiate clear across the country. To date, none seems to have been moved to air an opinion or to forecast the prospect of breed ruin.

To draw again on the wisdom of the German breeders, it is also understood by these that size and weight are often relative, influenced by other factors. A dog with a bulky skeleton and sloppy-fibred fleshing may weigh less than a dog of smaller build with firm flesh and muscle.

COLOR: (A.K.C. Standard)
The coat may be of solid liver or any combination of liver and white such as liver and white ticked, liver spotted and white ticked, or liver roan. A dog with any area of black, red, orange, lemon or tan, or a dog solid white will be disqualified.

AUTHOR'S COMMENT: Wide color tolerance of Shorthair color and patterning is restricted in the USA only by a disallowance of blacks and tricolors. As elsewhere in the world, the tick-patch dog is the most numerous, hair-for-hair stitching of brown and white, with or without patches. Lightly-ticked dogs are liked in the show-ring and the hunting field, mainly for being more conspicuous. Solid livers have many friends and the color has often been carried by exceptionally good dogs of versatile worth. The field trial scene here accepts a proliferation of clear white-brown Pointer-patterned which the rest of the world does not favor. The main criticism of such color is that it can serve to cloak possible irregular breeding practice.

German Klub Kurzhaar recently published color analysis in that country: Liver-ticked, 66%; Solid liver, 28.4%; Black-ticked, 4%; Solid Black, 0.6%; white-brown patched, 0.4%. (*Kurzhaar Blätter, May 1971.*)

One does not see clear white-brown patched in Germany. Black-

241

ticked are few. Two appeared under my eye at 1967 Solms and one at the Kleeman (1968). The two at the Solms (Dortmund) were sired by Maniz v.d. Forst Brickwedde, a strong source of modern black factor. The Kleeman K.S., Anke v. Ichenheim was ex a black-tick dam also carrying Brickwedde, by Esser's Chick, the Axel v. Wasserschling son. No solid blacks appeared anywhere I gallery-sided.

In May, 1966, Dr. Byhain, then president of Klub Kurzhaar, reported club concern over a young solid black male at the breed Specialty. He asked through *Kurzhaar Blätter* pages, that persons that could throw any light on this dog's background factors to please pass this on to Herr F. Bollhöff, who dealt with statistics in this realm. A percentage of solid black breeding still to report in 1971 suggests a channel of conveyance still exists in Germany.

It is then entirely possible that a *legitimate* black-ticked whelp could crop up in a purebred Shorthair litter in the U.S., but one would reserve judgment in respect of solid black. Almost a century ago, German experimentation introduced black Pointer in hope to darken pigmentation, eye color especially. The strain resultant, known as *Prussian Kurzhaar,* was for a time given separate stud book recording, but the practice fell into disuse long since—Shorthairs are Shorthairs! However, the circumstance of the black Arkwright Pointer introduced for this purpose has been used for decades since as justification of any black that crops up in Shorthair litters. USA is the only country where anyone really worried about a black-ticked, but solid black is a dog of another color, literally as well as figuratively.

Of course, not only black Pointer blood put such ticking into Shorthairs ages past. Many European Pointing types (universally known as Braques) carry the blue-tick (i.e. black-speckled).

In any "patched" breed, a very good show dog can occasionally be handicapped by markings in an unfortunate location. Thighs and necks are especially vulnerable. A ticked dog with an elongated solid patch on his thigh bordered by ticking can, at a slight distance, especially if the lighting is poor, appear to have a thin, stringy thigh that the judge will hold against him. Patching that runs the length of the neck can similarly make it appear thin and scraggy. This is one of the things an owner may discover while practicing by posing his dog in front of a mirror. Once discovered, it is up to

242

him to figure out how to show his dog to counteract such a disadvantage.

It seems to be the perversity of fate that such undesirable markings are usually located on the "judging side" of a good dog. Within my own experience, my own best show Pointer was so handicapped, a slash of solid liver down one side of her neck being bordered by white, top and bottom. From a distance, especially in a poor light, her neck looked ewe. Her "other side" was clear white, showing the correct and elegant shape that took her to several B.I.S. awards. Figuring that no K.C. rule, in any country, says that a dog MUST stand with head pointed in any particular direction, I made it a rule to pose her first-up with her "good side" to the judge. So, he received his first so-important impression to her advantage. Turned the "other side" he may quite likely have gained a totally different one. All her ring-photos show her standing the opposite way to the rest of the class. This was an extremely good bitch, well deserving of her many wins. It would have been a sad waste to sacrifice her quality and show career to what is, after all, a convention.

If the mirror-mirror-on-the-wall shows your German Shorthaired Pointer similarly handicapped, consider turning it around in the ring. The judge may wonder why you stand the dog so. Even if he asks you to turn it the same way as the others (which many do not bother to do, as my experience showed), he will have gained his first impression usefully, and then of course will understand why you turned your dog about. His function is to find the best dog in the class. Anything that will help towards that end deserves his appreciation.

GAIT: (A.K.C. Standard)
A smooth lithe gait is essential. It is to be noted that as gait increases from the walk to a faster speed, the legs converge beneath the body. The tendency to single track is desirable. The forelegs reach well ahead as if to pull in the ground without giving the appearance of a hackney gait, and are followed by the back legs which give forceful propulsion. Dragging the rear feet is undesirable.

13

Gait

IN no sphere of dog interest is more errant, utter nonsense talked around the show rings than in connection with dog gait. By and large, it would seem, undesirable gait is the gait that the other fellow's dog employs. This is the more damnable in that the gait of a fast-moving big dog, especially (in which category place the German Shorthaired Pointer, of course), is not to be assessed by the human eye at high speed. It is only possible to *deduce* what happens—which is the reason McDowell Lyon had to employ his slow-motion camera tactics to catch what goes on. In the same way, it long since became apparent to me that my eye could not serve me well enough either. I took to collecting *still* pictures of gaiting dogs in various free-moving breeds of the sporting, working and hound groups. This proved better than using movies, as the movie, like the human eye, moves too rapidly for accurate comprehension.

The stills freeze action so that the exact placings of the legs can be seen. It quickly became apparent to me that the best-moving dogs are those that are balanced—whose hind and front quarters are in tune in terms of substance and angulation. It also became obvious that the major factor in smooth fast going is forehand assembly which permits reach. A dog with a correct forehand, having a long upper arm (as the Standard asks for) set at an angle to permit freedom, can take a stride as much as three times as long as that of a straight-shouldered dog with a short upper arm. This means that a

Contrary to belief publishing media tend to provide, a gaiting dog does not come under the judges' eyes only in stylized, paste-flat-on-paper passing line. Here, circling the ring, 9-yr. old Ch. Weidenbach Bridget is approaching head on, but it has taken the famed camera of Callea, action-photographing specialist from Davis, California, to catch the power and the precision drive. Owner: Weidenbach Kennels, Cotati, California.

Another exciting shot that has caught a strong moving Shorthair in the process of circling. . . Pat v. Hanstein (Axel v. Wasserschling ex Iris v. Hanstein) had reputation as a Fireball, and manages to convey the quality with his driving strength as he circles past the camera. Photo, courtesy *Gustav Machetanz*, "Wasserschling", Germany.

straight-shouldered animal has to work three times as hard and take three times as many steps to cover the same distance. Additionally, his construction produces a short, high step—a prance that looks well in the hackney horse ring, and that has been known to delight the dog show galleries and judges of lesser knowledge, but which imposes restraint and weariness of muscle on the dog.

The use of the long upper arm for which the GSP Standard asks (and too few people take the trouble to find out why it does!) may be better understood by the novice by noting its like employment in fast-moving horses, both trotters (standard breds) and gallopers requiring a construction that permits extended forward reach. Only insofar as a horse is not a dog is there any real difference. The operating principle is exactly the same, and dog owners could do worse than clip out and study newspaper action pictures of great race horses. It's all there to see, fore and aft. Don't expect to see this kind of picture at horse show rings, either. There the showy action is secured not only by breeding for such short, high-stepping construction of the forehand as would literally cripple a dog, but by "mechanical" aids under which dogs would lie down and die.

In regard to forehand construction in the dog, it is very important to understand that this is something a dog is born with. Exercise won't develop it nor prayer command it. It is apparent in the baby puppy as soon as it gets up on its legs—for better or for worse. And it stays with the dog for as long as it lives, even into such fantastic old age as was granted Columbia River Tillie.

The camera can also tell us a great deal about the way a dog uses its rear assembly in free and fast going. Too many people "learn" gait from standing around dog show rings or standing up with the gallery, half-a-mile away, watching field trial dogs run. Here again we need the camera's eye, as our own only produces confusion. There has been great recent interest in gait in England where sporting dog judges are demanding that an end be put to the too-common "rear-end movement." Pointer expert, Mr. John Garnett, describes this as "hind legs swinging from the hips like pendulums." It is, of course, the typical and always ugly, stilted action of a straight-stifled dog. This is all he can do—swing his straight legs like broomhandles. Mr. Garnett calls for insistence on the requirement that a "dog shall bring his hocks well up behind him," an action that must surely astonish the many who have only watched at ringside where dogs may be moved by sluggish, often aged, handlers within a small area. To see a dog that brings up his hocks stupefies them. It must be wrong, they comfort each other. The others don't do it! In this connection we have another illuminating comment from a great international judge, Leo C. Wilson: "Any dog that is expected to work over rough terrain should be able to pick up his hocks behind him, but too many of our current crop would trip over a candy wrapper left lying in the ring!"

With camera in hand, I found that indeed, the majority of our best Shorthairs *do* pick up their hocks, if only they can get the chance. The "chance" means a ring large enough to get going, and a handler who can step. Some very interesting pictures illustrate this truth, of which the excellent ones of the East Coast dog, Ch. Gunhill's Mesa Maverick, are as graphic as any. This is a good dog, well put together, and blessed with an agile handler. Forward striding, and usefully picking up his hocks after him as he goes, Maverick pleases knowledgeable judges with his smooth and fast gait.

The novice GSP owner should be thoroughly on his guard against the lofty briefings that are delivered on the subject of gait by self-proclaimed "experts." The most destructive words are: "It wouldn't do in the field." For this statement, the novice should have a good laugh ready. A dog in the field, whatever breed, has no special gait. He just goes the way he is built, using the same levers that he was born with for faster or slower. Many fine field trial dogs of exceptional performance, go in spite of their construction, not because of it. Handicapped by imbalance or faulty construction fore and-or aft, they go on heart and will-to-please to get from A to B. But dearly do they often pay for the extra exertion imposed by the faulty construction. The number of "practical" field trial dogs that fold with heart trouble is not to be disregarded by those with breed interest at heart. Such dogs are not found commonly among the long-lasters, nor do they shine in the sphere of production. A dog must be correctly equipped in his body for what we ask him to do, and the death of a dog from heart strain is a reflection on the owner's lack of discernment in working a deficient animal.

It cannot be too often or too clearly stated that the novice should at all times be leary of the person who tries to sell him the idea that it is of minor importance how a dog is built. It is of primary importance, indeed. The poorly constructed dog of good performance does show up continually, but his glory is often short-lived and his fate not always enviable. Nor is there any reason to doubt that he would have been an even better performer if his construction had matched his great heart, his burning will to hunt, his good nose, or his desire to please.

In the show ring, it is impossible for a big sporting dog's gait to be accurately measured during a brief sally across a small enclosure. Seldom is there scope for such a dog to get into his stride before he and his handler are falling into the ropes across the way. It is certain that a big sporting dog cannot demonstrate gait properly in a constricted area where he has to hold himself against the chance of landing right out of the auditorium, into the street. That the judging of gait (sound or unsound) under such conditions is little better than farcical could be one of the reasons why so many show dogs get by with such poor movement. Not until the big rings are cleared for Group judging does a naturally fast-moving dog in any breed get a chance to display his true gait.

Around the ringsides, some amazing interpretations appear to be read into the brief reference made to gait in the Standard of the German Shorthaired Pointer, in which even the adjective employed is merely "desirable," and in no way obligatory. Strangely enough, these appear to be directed not at the dogs with the ugly, stilted gait imposed by undesirable hind member assembly, but rather at the dogs able to demonstrate a fast, smooth going with such a flexible hock movement as delights the judges.

How a dog places his legs in movement, as opposed to how some folk *think* he does, is not the whole story of sporting dog gait, either. If a dog has not been reared right, fed right, and properly exercised over the important periods of his growth, he is likely to do all manner of peculiar and undesirable things with his legs in adulthood. The several breed Standards directing that hocks shall "turn neither in nor out" refer to a disability that is perhaps the most common of all in the sporting dog rings—hocks that sag, one way or the other, for lack of muscle to support them; no thighs, certainly no second thighs. The long legs of the taller sporting breeds, especially, are no better engineered to stand unbraced than is a tent pole. Fortunately, the German Shorthaired Pointer, with his accepted status as a utility dog, gets rather more running and for this reason, this type of unsoundness is far less prevalent with him than in some other breeds within the Group.

248

14

Breeding Your German
Shorthaired Pointer

---

*Honoring the many great producing bitches of this breed that
have over decades. built up so many credits for their partners
in production. They remind us all that the Ancient Wisdom
is still operative as when, five hundred years ago, the Master
Falconer told his noble patrons: "If You Would Have a
Fayre Hound, You Must First Have a Fayre Bitch."*

cbm

To breed for less than the best is to waste time,
trouble, money, and the birthpangs of the bitch. The new breeder
might heed the warning that the current winner is not necessarily
the best mate for his bitch. This one's name might sell you a pup
or so, but cannot guarantee their quality. Many big winners—in any
breed—become so because of wide campaigning across the country
with top handlers. Such winning records prove no prepotency. The
measure of a stud is still that applied by the great Dutch geneticist,
Hagedoorn: "The value of a stud is proved only by the quality of his
get."

Since cross-country campaigning costs lots of money, many spank-
ing good dogs never get an opportunity to compete coast to coast.
There could be such a one in your own area—one with much to
give the breed. Among the top-producing studs in German Shorthaired Pointers, many are known to us less by their own winnings
than by the brilliant comet's tail of their get. Such was Field Ch.

Greif v. Hundsheimerkogel. Treu v. Waldwinkel was never shown. Timm v. Altenau, with 15 champion get, did not finish for his title. Ch. Rick v. Winterhauch, though a successful winner, was no circuit star. This, of course, is matched with the other side of the picture. Ch. Buck v. Gardsburg, several times top winner for the year in the breed, very widely shown, proved a very fine sire. So, Dr. Hagedoorn's measure yet applies—what has a dog produced?

Great dogs, as the various tables in this book attest, can come from competitively obscure but demonstrably good parents. Horses, too. The 1961 Derby winner, Carry Back, got heart and speed from an unfashionable sire and a dam seemingly valued at little more than on-the-hoof value as meat, yet the qualities must have been there. Perhaps Europeans come near the truth in describing breeding as an art, and the clever breeder as an artist. Such can always explain the use of a sire: "He suited my bitch."

Several reasons for using a stud do not stand scrutiny. One is using him because he happens to be *there*. In other words, you own him or he's a close auto drive away. Your own dog may be your heart's pride and a good winner. That doesn't necessarily make him the right mate for your bitch. Both may have the same faults—wide front, say, or short, thick heads. Another poor reason for using a stud is that he happens to be owned by a friend. Equally bad is by-passing the right dog because you don't like the guy who owns him. So you don't like the guy? You pay your check to get what you may possibly need—the complementing qualities to help your bitch.

What "complementing qualities" means is that you hope to gain from the dog something your bitch may lack. If your strain lacks something, the only way to get it is to go out for it. It won't generate spontaneously. In the same way, if your strain is plagued by a persistent fault, you must by-pass your dog, his parents, his get. It can involve time and leg work, or a few more gallons of gas, but results often justify all this.

The strangest things happen in breeding, which is why the graph-and-chart characters so often come to grief. Take litter brothers— one's a fine producer; the other, maybe with more opportunities, maybe the better winner, show or field, in production is a nothing. It happens in all breeds. Hagedoorn's research, of course, was carried out in the sphere of farm animals where aims were limited to milk and/or meat. Flock and herd owners listened because they knew they had to be practical. Such do not become emotionally involved with herd or flock sires as do dog owners with their kennel prides. The breeding duds go to the butcher, their faults thus siphoned away. *Raus mit!*

Many dog breeders go by the opposite rule. They cull *nothing!* They breed *everything*, faults and all. Kennel blind, they blink at the stud reproducing his own faults—they will even breed him to his daughters! The bitch unsuited to show or field will "do" for a brood!

Ringside, or at the trials, one hears: "Who's he by?" Less often: "Who's he out of?" Yet many a stud owes his reputation to the luck of linkage with one or more great producing bitches. Never embark on the heartbreaking process of "grading-up" from a poor bitch. Even to screen out one fault can take years. The only shortcut is to buy the best bitch you can afford from the best-bred strain available to you. Long experience seems to have made clear that even a moderate one from a good strain is a better buy than a flyer, chance-got from a poor. In buying the best bitch you can afford from the carefully bred stock of a successful strain, you make your start at the point at which the breeder has arrived after years of hard work.

For such a bitch, your responsibility to pick the best mate becomes heavy. One wrong mating throws you back to where that good breeder started, perhaps ten or fifteen years ago. The view of breeding as *continuity* is a valuable one. The best expressed view of this I ever heard was that of a Great Dane breeder who started with moderates and had reached the commendable heights. Praised for this, he observed thoughtfully: "Yes, I've come a long way. But there's still a ways further to go. *I've got to run the pups through a few more bitches yet.*" With each breeding, he hoped to make his strain a little better, and a little better still.

It is poor breeding practice to attempt the cancellation of a fault by introducing its opposite. Two wrongs make no right in breeding, either. If your bitch is straight behind, breeding her to a grotesquely overangulated dog only multiplies your problems. You then have *two* kinds of poor rear ends instead of only one. A big, coarse, football of a head is not corrected in the next generation by introducing the equivalent of Minnie Mouse's. Short legs in your bitch will not be stretched in her produce by a sire too tall. It is much safer to use the dog that is as close to the Standard as you can find

—and try to discover if his parents are as well. Nor should you hope to correct all faults in a single mating. You, too, will likely have to "run the pups through a few more bitches yet" to reach your ideal.

When your stud is chosen, come to an agreement with his owner. Reserve a booking, give an idea when you expect her in season. When she shows signs, such as swelling of the vulva, the presence of color, notify the stud's owner. Don't appear on his doorstep unannounced, claiming your bitch to be ready right now! It could even happen that the dog has an engagement for that same time. What financial arrangements you make are between you and the stud owner. If it's anything more than handing over a check, have the agreement in writing. If you give choice of litter, have a written agreement as to when the stud's owner is to make his choice. Otherwise, you could find yourself holding the litter weeks and weeks past the best selling time. The older the pups when he makes his pick, the better end of the deal he gets, even if only in terms of board and lodging. Choice of litter can involve other disadvantages. It takes experience, as a rule, to discover them.

If your bitch misses, the stud owner usually extends the courtesy of a repeat mating—to the same bitch. Actually, this *is* a courtesy, not any legal obligation. You buy a mating, you don't buy pups. Some stud owners do advertise "Pups guaranteed," and that could ensure your free return service. However, sometimes the most guarantees issue from the owners of the least desirable studs. A guarantee is fine—good pups are better.

The owner of a good bitch (maybe even a not-so-good bitch!) will sometimes be approached by the owner of a stud looking for business, show or field. As you gather in your winning bitch after an event, you may find this character at your elbow. You should *breed* that bitch, you really should, he'll tell you. You should breed it to his champion! He'll leave his card. Very often—VERY OFTEN—he owns the one stud you should by-pass for your good bitch. The aftermath of such salesmanship can be seen in several breeds: a much touted—therefore much used by novices—stud, who has put his own faults through and through the breed in some certain locality. Novices are this promoter's all-time prey. He seems able literally to smell them out. Brush off such promotion. Take your time. Look around. Talk to everyone. Learn and observe. Seek out the best opinions available to you. Nothing but the very best is ever right for that good bitch you took so much care to select in the first place.

If you own a good, well-bred male, you doubtless hope he will have opportunity at stud. An owner of a stud has, of course, different problems from those of the owner of a bitch. Yet, basically, he, too, has grave responsibilities if he has the welfare of his breed at heart. He will at times recognize that his dog is not suited to some proposed bitch with whom, perhaps, he shares a fault of some gravity. Where, for any reason, you feel a mating may not help your dog's reputation, it would be wise to refuse his service.

Experience seems to prove the advisability of some early matings for a dog intended to use for stud, choosing, where possible, an older, experienced bitch to help him learn the Facts of Life. Breeding kennels seem to prefer to use a dog at least once before he is a year old. The most harrowing tales of frustration seem to come from those breeders who seek to get the co-operation of some middle-aged dog that has till then lived a bachelor life. Often enough he has the desire, but just doesn't know the drill.

Often times the tendency, in such cases, is to seek the boon of artificial insemination. Here, by the way, the novice with a good dog might accept a word of warning. Be wary of the "modern-minded" owner of a bitch that is inclined to think artificial insemination is *the* way to go about the contrivance of a mating. Give nature a chance first, being sure that the bitch is actually ready for service. Especially, if your dog is a proved stud, view with reservation the owner who comes to you and says "his bitch can only be mated artificially." Quite often this is not strict truth, but opinion derived from attempts to mate a bitch before she is ready.

However, there are certainly times when some artificial aid may be needed, and if so, be very sure of the capacity of the veterinarian who is entrusted with the job. Some glaring examples of mishandling in this respect are seen from time to time—male dogs who have resented the means by which semen was taken, and thereafter retain some deep suspicions of any person (especially strangers) who may put a hand near their after parts. So far as a show dog is concerned, it could mean the end of his career if he will not allow a judge to handle his rear end. It has happened.

As the function of a breed definitive book cannot possibly be considered the equivalent of—or the substitute for—a stud book, the requirement of selection immediately faces any compiler who must tailor coat to cloth—or records of production to space available. Selection there had to be, and the one basis for selection that made any sense at all was in terms of the dogs and bitches that had proven themselves able to provide stock that could win recognition in the sphere both of conformation and of performance. That is, in brief, stock that could acquire field *and* show titles. In many lands it is not necessary to spell out this requirement as a "champion" (per se) is automatically a dog that *has* proven itself both in terms of bodily conformation and working ability.

There have been many fine producing studs and broods that have operated here in but one sphere of endeavor—this of course not necessarily by *their* decision, but by that of the owners. Often enough, in the case of the get of some one dog shining *only* in show sphere, this is because those who owned his stock had no interest in the work sphere. In the case of the working dog it may also be that the interest to have assessment of conformation is lacking. These reasons for one-sphere performance are entirely valid, but for such a work as this present edition of the breed definitive book, where some measure *must* be applied to fit material between the covers, the restriction of the tabulations to the dual-sphere producers has proved mandatory.

However, in assessing production, must *also* be taken into consideration the time factor—the time in which the studs and broods were active. Thus, in the period prior to AKC licensing of Field Trials for Shorthairs, there was no chance for any stud to be honored with F.T. Ch. get. In an earlier time still, say that of the great bitch import, Arta v. Hohreusch, there was not even any recognizable show venue for the breed.

Further, the factor of registration figures adds also to the difficulty of assessing the production records of Shorthairs over the decades. Thus when F.T. Ch. Greif v. Hundsheimerkogl was compiling *his* record, Shorthair registrations were down under 5000 annually, and the interest in the production of Dual Chs. was scattered and somewhat lukewarm. Now, such an aspirant to the crown of production versatility as the late F.T. Ch. Lutz v.d. Radbach (among others!) is free of the production figures of near enough 15,000 per annum—and an ever-growing aspiration of owners towards the distinction of the Dual title. Over and over have been heard the expressed aims of stud owners to have their dogs compile a record "to beat Greif's." It would take a better mathematical brain than that of your present compiler to assess figures in accurate relationship to the differing numerical status of the breed of the '70s as compared with the '50s.

No breed definitive work can omit the productions of the early studs and broods that in their competitive venues made the fame of the Shorthair in this country. Their influence still sits in back of so many of our very best contemporary dogs, as the Dual Champion tabulations accurately portray. Even when subjected to less than wise management, even at times to deplorable waterings down with less valuable contributions, the genes seem to have the ability again and again to assert themselves. The Germans have a proverb about "the Apple that Never Falls Far From the Stem." Apples and Short-hairs, Cabbages and Kings, the same rule would seem to apply. So, let's honor the Old 'Uns. But for the luck of their introduction to the United States at a difficult time in the history of this old world we might well be lacking those great qualities they sped on and down into this time that is momentarily our own.

First, then, some of the numerically-strongest of the producers of the 1940s, by which time competition in the show-rings had built up from the fairly general one-dog-to-a-class, and three, maybe four dogs to a breed, of the 1930s. Let us start with Treu v. Waldwinkel and Fritz v. Schwarenberg, and please don't overlook the presence of the mama they shared:

TREU V. WALDWINKEL
Breeder: L. C. Cori, New York
Owner: Joseph Burkhardt, Minnesota
  Ch. Searching Wind Bob

  Ch. Thalbach Waldwinkel Hans
  Ch. Searching Wind Cita

  Ch. Fritz v. Schlossgarten

(*Hallo Mannheimia ex Arta v. Hohreusch, German imports both*)
(*ex Maida v. Thalbach—his grand-daughter*)
(" " " ")
(*ex Dual Ch. Schatz v. Schwaren-berg*)
(*ex Bessie v. Winterhauch—a Fritz v. Schwarenberg daughter*)

Ch. Glanz v. Winterhauch	(" " " " " " ")
Ch. Senta v. Waldwinkel	(*ex Feldjager's Grisette (German import*)
Ch. Prince v. Waldwinkel	(" " " " ")
Hans v. Waldwinkel	(*ex Berg's Choice—ex Arta v. Hohreusch*)
Ch. Heinrich v. Karlwald	(*ex Senta v. Karlwald*)
Ch. Jack v. Schoen	(*ex Susie Dee Waldwinkel*)

Ch. FRITZ V. SCHWARENBERG	(*Bob v. Schwarenberg ex Arta v.*
Breeder: Joseph Burkhardt, Minnesota	*Hohreusch, his half-sister. Ger-*
Owner: Jack Shattuck Jr., Minnesota	*man imports both*)
DUAL Ch. Shatz v. Schwarenberg	(*ex Helga v. Schwarenberg*)
Ch. Tell v. Schwarenberg	(" " " ")
Ch. Kraut v. Schwarenberg	(*ex Lena v. Dreschler*)
Ch. Trae v. Schwarenberg	(*ex Hun v. Dusseldorf*)
Ch. Sporting Butch	(*ex Braunne v. Schmeling*)
Ch. Dreaming Sweetheart	(*ex Jäger's Pagina—German import*)
Ch. Pagina's Young Lover	(" " " ")

Now, see Mars v. Ammertal and his Dual Ch. son, Rusty v. Schwarenberg, a brace adding wealth to the tally of studs and broods to be found in the pedigree hinterlands of many best dogs of later years.

Ch. MARS V. AMMERTAL (German import)	(*Heros v. Ammertal ex Asta v. Rohrhalde*)
Owner: Jack Shattuck Jr., Minnesota	
DUAL Ch. Rusty v. Schwarenberg (first SHP Dual Champion)	(*ex Vicki v. Schwarenberg, she ex Feldjager's Grisette imp. Ger.*)
Ch. Cora	(*ex Vicki v. Schwarenberg—above*)
Ch. Rex v. Brecht	(*ex Senta v. Karlbach*)
Ch. Madchen v. Karlbach	" " " ")
Ch. Karl v. Schwarenberg	(*ex Dixie v. Schwarenberg*)
Ch. Heidi v. Ammertel	(*ex Heidie v. Schwarenberg*)

DUAL Ch. RUSTY V. SCHWARENBERG	(*Mars v. Ammertal ex Vicki v. Schwarenberg*)
Breeder/Owner: Jack Shattuck, Jr. Minnesota	
Ch. Hal	(*ex Dutchy v. Schleswig*)
Ch. Hanover Hills Hansel	(*ex Hanover Hills Kitrena*)
Ch. Rusty of Min o'Wash	(*ex Heidi v. Ammertal*)
Ch. Iron v. Schwarenberg	(*ex Bess v. Schleswig*)
Ch. Thor v. Schwarenberg	(*ex Sue v. Schwarenberg*)
Ch. Vesta of Penray	(" " " ")
Ch. Pixie v. Ritter	(*ex Dixie v. Waldwinkel*)
Ch. Pheasant Lane's Schnapps	(*ex Ch. Four Winds Gretchen*)

256

Ch. Jo Jo v. Schwarenberg	(ex Waldewinkel's Mahogany Flash)
Ch. Rex v. Forst Ammertal	(ex Heidi v. Forst Ammertal)
Ch. Tustav v.d. Schwarzwalder	(ex Lady Golden Mark)

Ch. Pheasant Lane's Schnapps, of course, made a name as a producer with his son and grand-daughter Duals. Ch. Cora, the daughter of Mars, founded the Winterhauch line. Iron v. Schwarenberg, in a more modest way, was a valuable promotional force and early-day stud on the West Coast.

Though he did not finish to his title, Timm v. Altenau, a grandson of the great German prepotent, K.S. Kobold Mauderode-Westerholt, by way of the Kobold son, imported Donn v. Sulfmeister, provided a tremendous influence that survives down to our time, to be found behind many distinguished Duals. He was out of Dr. Thornton's breeding entirely, and his virtues have been preserved by clever management of close breeding by his owner.

TIMM V. ALTENAU (9 points) *
Breeder: Dr. Charles Thornton, Mont.
Owner: William Ehrler, Michigan

(Donn v. Sulfmeister (imp. Ger) ex Dreizenheim v. Brickwedde)

Ch. Bella v. Rheinberg	(ex Distel v. Rheinberg)
Ch. Hilda v. Rheinberg	(" " " ")
Ch. Karl v. Rheinberg	(" " " ")
Ch. Tillie v. Rheinberg	(" " " ")
Ch. Timmy v. Rheinberg	(" " " ")
Ch. Treu v. Rheinberg	(" " " ")
Ch. Madel v. Rheinberg	(ex Dixie v. Rheinberger—sister to Distel above)
Ch. Treff v. Rheinberg	(" " " ")
Ch. Bea v. Dee	(" " " ")
Ch. Ford v. De	(" " " ")
Ch. Alsedda	(ex Tillie v. Rheinberg Distel daughter, as above)
Ch. Rita v. Rheinberg	(" " " ")
Ch. Sweet Tillie Too	(" " " ")
Ch. Rhoda v. Rheinberg	(ex Wanda Gale Altmark, dam of Distel and Dixie. Wanda is a granddaughter of John Neuforsthaus, first Thornton stud of pioneer note)
Ch. Loal's Dot	(ex. Zest v. Horstig)

* As Timm did not finish his title in those days of little interest in show competition, neither did his son, Duke v. Rhenberg (ex Wanda Gale Altmark) who later sired Dual Ch. Valbo v. Schlesburg. Timm's strong bitch production tally has operated to lace so much K.S. Mauderode-Westerholt inheritance into early-day American Shorthair stock that still serves so usefully.

Mention of imported Donn v. Sulfmeister, the K.S. Kobold-Mauderode Westerholt son, brings us also within hail of his grandson, Ch. Davy's Jim Dandy, and here we are pitchforked again into the heart of Dr. Thornton's Missoula enterprise.

Ch. DAVY'S JIM DANDY	(*Fritz ex Freda v. Waldhausen*)
Owner: L. McGilbrey, Washington	
DUAL & NAT'L FIELD Ch. DANDY JIM v. FELDSTROM	(*ex Joan v. Stolzenfels*)
Ch. Pheasant Lane's Stormalong	(*ex Krautina v. Stolzenfels*)
Ch. Jim Dandy v. Roger	(" " " ")
Ch. Sistie Frau	(" " " ")
Ch. Hunter's Moon Jemima	(*ex Boots Etta v. Schwarenberg*)
Ch. Cupid Casador	

Now, in strict and tidy sequence, we look first at Dual & Nat'l Ch. Dandy Jim v. Feldstrom and then at Ch. Pheasant Lane's Stormalong, which adds up to being busy for the next few minutes. First the Dual . . .

DUAL & NAT'L FIELD Ch. DANDY JIM v. FELDSTROM	(*Ch. Davy's Jim Dandy ex Ch. Joan v. Feldstrom*)
Breeder/Owner: Dr. Clark Lemley, Michigan	
DUAL Ch. Fritz of Hickory Lane Farm	(*ex Am/Can. Ch. Susanna Mein Liebchen*) *
DUAL Ch. Gustav Mein Liebchen	(" " " " " ")
Sth/Am Dual Ch. Jaime Mein Liebchen	(" " " " " ")
Ch. Gentleman Joe of Crescent	(*ex Dark Pattern of Crescent*)
Field Ch. Grand Discovery of Crescent	(" " " " ")
Field Ch. Eric v. Zelon	(*ex Bee-Coo of Zelon*)
Field Ch. Gussie v. Feldstrom	(" " " " ")

* Am/Can. Ch. Susanna Mein Liebchen, C.D. is also the dam of DUAL Ch. Marmaduke Mein Liebchen, to a mating with Ch. Fieldborn Tempo II, a Timm v. Altenau grandson, a legacy shared by Susanna, who was all Old American breeding, at long range. The concentration of the Donn v. Sulfmeister blood is here very strong.

Still with the descendants of imported Donn v. Sulfmeister, through son Fritz and grandson Ch. Davy's Jim Dandy, we have Ch. Pheasant Lane's Stormalong who slips under our barrier requirement of versatility of production with a Field Champion plus the great producing bitches that helped him make the pioneer impact he did.

AM/CAN. Ch. PHEASANT LANE'S STORM-
  ALONG
Breeders: Mr. and Mrs. W. H. Warren,
  S. Dak.

(*Ch. Davy's Jim Dandy ex Krautina
  v. Stolzenfels*)

Ch. Columbia River Lightning (B.I.Ss)	(*ex. Columbia River Tillie*)
Ch. Columbia River Cochise (B.I.Ss)	(" " " ")
Ch. Columbia River Chief	(" " " ")
Ch. Columbia River Princess	(" " " ")
Ch. Rena Cazadora	(" " " ")
Ch. Grand Columbia Chilli	(" " " ")
Ch. Pheasant Lane's Storm Cloud (B.I.S.)	(*ex Ch. Pheasant Lane's Deborah*)
Ch. Pheasant Lane's Tomahawk*	(" " " " ")
Ch. Pheasant Lane's Lightning	(" " " " ")
Ch. Pheasant Lane's Liesel	(" " " " ")
Ch. Mustang v. Derer	(*ex Ch. Heddy v. Holly Lane*)
Ch. Pheasant Lane's Treu	(*ex Ch. Four Winds Gretchen*)
Ch. McElroy's Cates	(*ex Pat v. Cates*)
Ch. Cates' Pat of Millvale	(" " " ")
Ch. Dutchess Beverly	(*Ch. Hedda of Hollylane*)
Field Ch. Schlosser's Dusty Jack	(*ex Spottie v. Brickwedde*)

* Sire of 9 show champions.

The Stormalong tabulation provides prelude to a sequence of distinguished producers that relayed his prepotency. Predominantly, this is a show strain, but the inclusion of Dual and exceptionally high-rated obedience titleholders passes our requirement of versatility. Herein, the K.S. Kobold inheritance is braced with the K.S. Artus Sand inheritance through Columbia River Tillie. The Stormalong/Tillie weld was rich in productive sons, Chs. Columbia River Lightning, Cochise, Chief. Lightning sired sixteen show champions, seven of them ex Helga v. Krawford (Ch. Rex v. Krawford ex Lady Golden Mark). Cochise sired ten show champions and a field champion. Chief sired only two show champions, but proved himself the most important in the long-term sense—that to be described as More by his Good Luck and Enterprise than by anyone's Good Management. He found Helga v. Krawford one day before his brother, Lightning the nominated stud. The result of that happy accident—which was likely deplored at the time—was a neat, beautifully constructed bitch, later Ch. Columbia River Jill. With the assist from a full brother to her sire (Ch. Columbia River Thundercloud) Jill really started something. So, first to look at her produce and then what stems from it:

Ch. COLUMBIA RIVER JILL

(Ch. Columbia River Chief ex Helga v. Krawford)

Breeder: L. McGilbrey, Washington
Owners: Gretchenhof Kennels,
    California.

Ch. Gretchenhof Moonshine (Multiple BIS)	*(by Ch. Columbia River Thundercloud)*
Ch. Gretchenhof Cinnabar, CDX	(" " " ")
Ch. Gretchenhof White Frost (BIS)	(" " " ")
Ch. Gretchenhof Stormy Weather	(" " " ")
Ch. Gretchenhof Snowflake	(" " " ")
Ch. Gretchenhof Thunderbird	(" " " ")
Ch. Gretchenhof Cimarron	(" " " ")
Ch. Gretchenhof Thunderbolt	(" " " ")
Am/Can. Ch. Gretchenhof Trade Wind	(" " " ")
Gretchenhof Tally Ho	(" " " ")

As a vehicle for prepotency, Ch. Columbia River Jill has her place in record. First, honored by her sparkling, multiple BIS winning daughter, the famous bitch Ch. Gretchenhof Moonshine that

Ch. Columbia River Jill (Ch. Columbia River Chief ex Helga v. Krawford), a main conveyance of prepotent factors behind Gretchenhof; her daughters ex her Ch. Columbia River Thundercloud litter backstop several of the most famed strains in USA. Breeder: L. V. McGilbrey. Owners: Gretchenhof Kennels, California.

taught the show judges to look at Shorthair bitches in Group and Best-in-Show competition. Her record of 15 BIS and 50 Group One held during her lifetime, was passed by a great grandson whose record as a winner presently stands seemingly beyond challenge, Ch. Gretchenhof Columbia River. Moonshine's own production was modest—a daughter, Ch. Gretchenhof New Moon, that did well in her showing, and another that is to be found safely tucked behind the production of some very useful get whelped to Dual Ch. Baron Fritz of Hohen Tann, Ch. Gretchenhof Blue Moon, through which is established the link between the great show bitch of the 1960s and the great showdog of the 1970s, Ch. Gretchenhof Columbia River.

It was however through her daughters of far less striking successes in the showrings that Columbia River Jill is assured of her place in history.

Ch. GRETCHENHOF CINNABAR, CDX
(Ch. Columbia River Thundercloud ex Ch. Columbia River Jill)

Breeders: Gretchenhof Kennels, California
Owners: Joseph & Julia France, Maryland
    DUALCh. Frie of Klarbruk, U.D.T.   *(by Dual/Nat'l Ch. Kay v.d. Wildburg)*
    (only triple-titled Shorthair to this 1981 tabulation)
    Ch. Heide of Klarbruk, U.D.T.   ("   "   "   "   "   "   )
    Jillian of Klarbruk, U.D.T. (Nat'l   ("   "   "   "   "   "   )
    Obed. winner, '68)
    Ch. Moonshine Sally of   ("   "   "   "   "   "   )
    Runnymeade
    Ch. Neckar v.d. Klarbruk, U.D.T.   *(by Radback v. Lowin —he by Ger. imp. K.S. Ulk v.d. Radback)*

AM/CAN. Ch. GRETCHENHOF   *(by Ch. Columbia River Thundercloud ex Ch.*
    TRADEWIND   *Columbia River Jill)*
Breeders: Gretchenhof Kennels
Owner: C.D. Lawrence, Idaho
    DUAL Ch. Hochland Jaeger's   *(by Mars v.d. Radbach)*
    Titelhalter
    Ch. Cede Brass Badge   *(by Ch. Cede Mein Gandy Dancer)*
    Ch. Cede Mein Featherbedder   ("   "   "   "   "   )

Ch. Cede Brass Badge proved also in his turn to be a strong producer of show stock; the 1979 GSPCA Year Book tally credited him with 13 show champions.

It was however Tally Ho, the untitled member of the sisterhood owning Jill for dam, that proved the most distinguished of the producers, her fourteen champions from her matings with Ch. Adam v. Fuehrerheim providing him initially with that early boost towards fame which is the greatest of all fortunes that can come the way of a stud, and compared with which the production to Field Ch. Tip Top Timmy of four show champions on Bruha prefix by the fourth of the quartet of prepotent sisters, Ch. Gretchenhof Snowflake, appears even modest.

Ch. GRETCHENHOF SNOWFLAKE	(*Ch. Columbia River Thundercloud ex Ch. Columbia River Jill*)
Breeders: Gretchenhof Kennels, Calif.	
Owner: Tony Gwinner	
Ch. Bruhas Mission Flying Wheel	(*by Field Ch. Tip Top Timmy*)
Ch. Bruhas Mission Hex Wheel	(" " " " ")
Ch. Bruhas Ring Wheel	(" " " " ")
Ch. Bruhas Buck v.d. Gwinnerwheel	(" " " " ")

That Gretchenhof Tally Ho remained untitled was seemingly an accident of fortune, and not as has at times been suggested, heavy preoccupation with maternal duties. As the story goes, her owner lost interest in show business when she was within grasping distance of her last points, a matter that must remain as it rests, so far as history is concerned, her owner long gone to his eternal reward. However, lack of show title does not rob her record as a producer of one smidgin of its luster.

GRETCHENHOF TALLY HO	(*Ch. Columbia River Thundercloud ex Ch. Columbia River Jill*)
Breeder: Gretchenhof Kennels	
Owner: Robert Jordan	
Ch. Whispering Pines Patos	(*by Ch. Adam v. Fuehrerheim*)
Ch. Whispering Pines Tally Hi	(" " " ")
Ch. Whispering Pines Francesca	(" " " ")
Ch. Whispering Pines Ranger	(" " " ")
Ch. Whispering Pines Daquiri	(" " " ")
Ch. Whispering Pines Dark Secret	(" " " ")
Ch. Whispering Pines Orissa	(" " " ")
Ch. Wetherling Whispering Pines	(" " " ")
Ch. Wind Song's Whispering Pines	(" " " ")
Ch. Whispering Pines Tanja	(" " " ")
Ch. Grouse Manor Windstorm	(" " " ")
Ch. Adam's Fan Tan	(" " " ")
Ch. Adam's Happy Warrior	(" " " ")
Ch. Lax's Gretchen Monkey Shines	(" " " ")

The prepotency was carried along by several of the company. Ch. Whispering Pines Patos, credited in 1979's GSPCA tabulations with 20 show-titleds, tops his own descendants with Ch. Fieldfines Count Rambard (ex Fieldfines Tascha) as an exclusively show-titled producer. Of the bitches, Ch. Whispering Pines Francesca made a mark, including production of an eventual BIS winner in Ch. Wetherling Windcloud, sired by her litter brother, Ch. Grouse Manor Windstorm. Ch. Tally-Hi kept the name further forward, and most of the balance of the get did well. If there was hope in other owners that the "Columbia River thing" would end with these, there was to be disillusion. Lance McGilbrey came up with another daughter of Ch. Columbia River Chief, Columbia River Della. In mating to the Moonshine grandson, Moonfrost, Della brought forth the big, handsome, flashy Gretchenhof Columbia River to demolish all records, Moonshine's included. To date, no other Shorthair approaches the record of this Chief grandson, not even within that mythical distance the Australians measure as "within coo-ee," which deals with distance beyond the scope of the eyes.

Ever since breeder interest has been stirring in the production of dogs, hopefuls have seized upon some demonstrated success of close inbreeding and plunged to match this with belief in the mere mechanics of putting parent to get. Bare accumulation of names in each generation has never provided of necessity the delivery of good stock. While knowledgeable (and lucky?) inbreeding is behind some of the great dogs of this wide world, the magic of such directed prepotency in successive generations has always stemmed from well-proven, outstandingly good individual basics. Failures are much more common than successes—the rate of difference is geometrical (as in astronomy!) but success siphons in tremendous breed gain.

The initial requirement, of course, is to find the vehicle of prepotency that produces gains, not losses. There have been times when the discovery of such prepotents have been accidental—as in Ch. Columbia River Chief, with that one chance mating providing greater boon to his breed than have the activities of his much-used litter brother. This of course is not unique to the Shorthair breed, that one brother may prove a producer of enormous value, the other merely average or so-so.

Trouble is, the value of a stud or brood is too often measured in terms of competitive successes and promotional advertising, neither of such activities influencing actual production. Too much of a dog-breeding success then is in terms of happenstance—Chief snatching his brother's bride—Greif having the interest of a field trial trainer to rustle a backyard dog a few bitches. Many valuable inheritances fritter away from lack of promotion.

The Grabenbruch name here is one of the many strain names borrowed out of Germany from whence, after World War II, Dick Johns, on service in Germany bought little K.S. Sepp. One Dual, two show champions, was all the short-lived little fellow left behind him. The strain name here was made instead by his son, and mighty has been the contribution in terms of background stock to find in so many of our present-day compilations.

DUAL Ch. BLICK V. GRABENBRUCH
Breeders/Owners: Grabenbruch Kls,
    Penn.
	(K.S. Sepp v. Grabenbruch, he by
	    K.S. Odin v. Weinbach ex Leda
	    v. Grabenbruch)

DUAL Ch. Valkyrie v. Grabenbruch	*(ex Ch. Katrina of Sycamore Brook,*
	    C.D., she by Ch. Dallo v.d. Forst
	    Brickwedde)

DUAL Ch. Junker v. Grabenbruch	(" " " " " ")
Field Ch. Dirk v. Grabenbruch	(" " " " " ")
DUAL Ch. Grousewald's Blitz	*(ex Debby v. Hollabird)*
Field Ch. Tricia v. Baab	*(ex Asta v.d. Schwarzwaldforte* *(imp))*
Field Ch. Dax v. Heidebrink	*(ex Betsy v. Heidebrink)*
Ch. Dixie v. Heidebrink	(" " " ")
Ch. Donar v. Schlangenberg	*(ex Susie v. Schlangenberg)*
Ch. Tuxa v. Schlangenberg	(" " " ")
Ch. Gamecock Hallmark	*(ex Adda v. Assegrund (imp))*
Ch. Sue v. Krupp	(" " " " ")

The years of the early 1950s, providing the introduction of National Field Trial competition under American Field and American Kennel Club rules, generated increasing interest in the German breed, with the production lists of studs and broods mirroring this with faithful precision. Early in the public eye during this decade were the well-performed field trial dogs of Dixon breeding. This strain provided three National Field Trial champions over a very short span of years, all out of Dixon's Starlite (Shot v. Falkenhorst ex Field Ch. Dixon's Belle). They were the Field & AmField National champions Dixon's Skid-Do and Kay Starr, and the immensely brilliant Dixon's Sheila who collected the title in both spheres of competition under both American Field and A.K.C. license.

264

Ch. REX V. KRAWFORD   (*Schnapps v. Waldwinkel ex Katrina*)
Breeder: John F. Crawford
Owner: W. A. Olsen, Minnesota
  DUAL Ch. Big Island Spook   (*ex Graff's Lady Lou*)
  Ch. Baron v. Fuehrerheim   (*ex Gretchen v. Fuehrerheim*)
  Ch. Senta v. Fuehrerheim   ("   "   "   "   )
  Ch. Waldwinkel Lisa   (*ex Roxy v. Waldwinkel*)
  Ch. Waldwinkel's Nutrena Heini   (*ex Judy of Ettendorf*)
  Ch. Will o' the Winds Greta   (*ex Sandra*)

Interesting contribution at this period was made also by an imported German K.S.—Franco Beckum—a German-trained that managed to adjust to American F.T. rule, changeover that not all finished K.S. proved able to make. His mating to Kenwick's Diana Beckum (by Ch. Tell v. Grabenbruch, a Franco Beckum son, to Dual Ch. Valkyrie v. Grabenbruch) produced the strongly influential F.T. sire, F.T. & Nat'l F. Ch. Bobo Grabenbruch Beckum whose daughter brace, Patsy and Mitzi, made National F.T. history.

FIELD & NAT'L FIELD Ch. BOBO   (*K.S. & Am.Fld. Ch. Franco Beckum*
  GRABENBRUCH BECKUM   *ex Kenwick's Diana Beckum*)
Breeder: Dr. Kenworthy, Vermont
Owner: Dr. Wm. Schimmel, California
  DUAL Ch. Bee's Gabby v. Beckum   (*ex Field Ch. Skid-Do's Bee*)
  Field Ch. Bee's Beau v. Beckum   ("   "   "   "   "   ")
  Field Ch. Rebecca Grabenbruch Beckum   ("   "   "   "   "   ")
  Field & Nat'l Fld. Ch. Von Saalfield's Kash   (*ex Von Thalberg's Belle*)
  Field Ch. Von Saalfield's Jill   ("   "   "   "   )
  Field Ch. Stutz Beckum   (*ex Thornton's Princess*)
  Field Ch. Mitzi Grabenbruch Beckum   (*ex Becky v. Luven*)
  Field Ch. Patsy Grabenbruch Beckum   (*ex Duchess of California*)
  Field Ch. Michael Kane of California   ("   "   "   "   )
  Field Ch. Gretchen Grabenbruch Beckum   (*ex Pacific Wind Penny*)
  Am/Can. Ch. Rappa Ringo Feldstrom Beckum   (*ex Field Ch. Gussie v. Feldstrom*)
  Ch. Tammy Grabenbruch Beckum   (*ex Flikker v. Windhausen*)
  Ch. Rocky Road v. Jonesdorff   (*ex Feldunbach Von Sue Ann*)
  Ch. Von Flecki's Bo Beckum   (*ex Miss Pepperoni v. Sudwald*)

The tremendous pioneer strength of the Minnesota import bloodlines was running steadily through many fine dogs as from the 1940s onward. A representative stud with ability to produce field and show dogs into the '50s was Ch. Oak Crest Rick v. Winterhauch, a very fount of versatility and prepotency. His get includes three Duals and a bitch that was first of her sex in Shorthairs to take a Best in Show.

Ch. OAK CREST'S RICK V. WINTERHAUCH Breeder: Dr. E. Berg, Minnesota Owners: J. & M. Deiss, Minnesota	(Ch. Glanz v. Witnerhauch ex Chimes Girl who were respectively grandson and granddaughter of Arta v. Hohreusch)
DUAL Ch. Lucky Lady v. Winterhauch*	(ex Hephizibah Holzman)
DUAL Ch. Captain v. Winterhauch (BIS)	(ex Duchess v. Hotwagner)
DUAL Ch. Able v. Eltz	(" " " ")
Ch. Oak Crest Cora v. Winterhauch (BIS)	(" " " ")
Ch. Northern Flights Cash v. Eltz	(" " " ")
Am/Cub/Mex. Ch. Clipper v. Eltz	(" " " ")
Ch. Blitz v. Oak Crest	(ex Smocky v. Treuberg)
Ch. Tell v. Lowin	(ex Heidi v. Lowin)
Ch. Oak Crest's Arno v. Winterhauch	(ex Maida v. Thalbach)
Ch. Rudolph Ammertal	(ex Velvet v. Ammertal)
Ch. Wag Inn's Mistress	(ex Miss Lace the Ace of Windy Hill)

* Dual Ch. Lucky Lady v. Winterhauch was dam of Dual Ch. Kaposia's Firebird.

The legacy that is the double endowment of the great Arta v. Hohreusch in the above compilation carried on also in Dual Ch. Captain v. Winterhauch and also in due course in Ch. Oak Crest Cora v. Winterhauch, both slanting towards show stock in the main. However, Captain's Dual Ch. daughter, Miss B'Haven v. Winterhauch represents a very early example of that always impressive happening, a Dual with Dual parents—her dam having been the German imported Dual Ch. Alfi v.d. Kronnenmuhle, whose sire line stems from her grandfather, great prepotent German stud, K.S. Axel v.d. Cranger Heide.

A different pattern began increasingly to be woven, however, as the continued infiltration of Danish breds came to be in turn combined with the best of Old American. An outstanding example of such is Ch. Sobol's Pointing Jay Mer, whose get includes no Dual Champion but titled dogs in both field and show spheres.

Ch. SOBOL'S POINTING JAY MER	(*Skriver's Jens (Danish imp.) ex Cocoa Queen*)
Breeder/Owner: Oscar Sobel.	
Field Ch. Sobol's Pointing Pepper II	(*ex Sobol's Pointing Snow Ball*)
Field Ch. Sobol's Pointing Argus II	
Field Ch. Marko v. Lindenwald	(*ex Am/Can.Ch. Fraulein Gretel v. Lindenwald*)
Am/Can. Ch. Katrina Radbach v. Lindenwald	(" " " ")
Am/Can. Ch. Kristen Radbach v. Lindenwald	(" " " ")
Can. Ch. Jens Radbach v. Lindenwald	(" " " ")
Ch. Our Gal Sally v. Grabenbruch	(*ex Our Sal*)
Ch. Gruenweg's Binger	(*ex Gretchen Gruenweg*)
Ch. Kristi v. Lohengrin	(*ex Heidi v. Lohengrin*)
Can. Ch. Colonel Dennis Moflame	(*ex Fieldborn Heinrich Villaricos*)
Ch. Sobol's Pointing Jens	(*ex Gunmaster's Sohio Supreme*)
Ch. Gruenweg's Minda	(*ex Ch. Tessa v. Abendstern*) *
Ch. Gruenweg's Graf	(" " " " ")
Ch. Gruenweg's Emilie	(" " " " ")

* Ch. Tessa v. Abendstern is further the dam of Dual Ch. Gruenweg's Dandy's Dandy and Can. Ch. Gruenweg's Ib, both by Dual & Nat'l Field Ch. Moesgaard's Dandy, representing a doubling of Danish blood as Tessa was a grand-daughter of Ch, Skriver's Jens, and her maternal line stemmed clear back as a great grand-daughter of the first Danish imported dog to here, Gelsted's Bob. Bob's mating to a Treu v. Waldwinkel daughter, ex Bessie v. Winterhauch, however, provided a powerful addition of Old American bloodlines to balance the Danish.

Perhaps this is as good a place as any to examine the record of that truly magnificent bitch, Am/Can. Ch. Erdenreich die Zweite, C.D., that stubbornly held her high place so long in the tabulation of modern producing bitches. This one owed as good as nothing to modern importation. Her background stems solidly from Old American lines, no import closer in her pedigree than the fourth generation where we find imported Aar v.d. Wengenstadt in a mating with that magnificent Old American solid liver prepotent, Little Gretchen's Brownie.

"Cissie" is important for more reasons than one. First, to the student of bloodlines, as the dam of Dual Ch. Erdenreich's Jetta Beckum, dam of the fabulous producing Dual Ch. Cede Mein Dolly

Der Orrian (elsewhere discussed) and second, and so *very* importantly, because she was a big strapping bitch—perhaps the biggest presently lodged in this compiler's color slide file. That her arch rival at that time was the *smallest* bitch of quality the slide file holds—Am/Can. Ch. Gretchen v Greif—forever firmed in this compiler's understanding the folly of using inch-measurements in terms of identifying top producing Shorthairs. The good ones come in all the sizes there are, even of course as does the rubbish—but the inch-fractional measure is unreliable indication of breeding worth.

AM/CAN. Ch. ERDENREICH DIE ZWEITE, C.D.
Breeder:
Owner: Miss Irene Pauly, California
DUAL Ch. Erdenreigh's Eartha

    DUAL Ch. Erdenreich's Jetta Beckum

    Ch. Erdenreich's Beau v. Garsburg (BIS)
    Ch. Erdenreich's Buck v. Gardsburg
    Ch. Erdenreich's Bea v. Gardsburg
    Ch. Erdenreich's Jim Dandy Beckum
    Field Ch. Erdenreich's Ginger v.d. Yankee

(Ch. Yankee Tim's Kurt ex Ch. Yankee Sal)

(by Erdenreich's Able v. Yankee, he by Ch. Yankee Tim, double grandsire of Die Zweite)
(by Field Ch. Stutz Beckum)

(by Ch. Beau v. Gardsburg)
(" " " "   ")
(" " " "   ")
(by Field Ch. Stutz Beckum)
(by Ch. Erdenreich's Aar Von Yankee)

Can. & Am. Ch. Erdenreich die Zweite, C.D., distinguished show bitch and unique producer (left). When this was taken, only one of her two Duals had finished, but the entry includes here a Dual, a BIS, two show champions (one with a C.D. additionally), a bitch with 8 FT points, and a puppy.

268

There are still those in California who remember a day when Little Gretchen's Brownie was braced with an old tick-patch import with a jawbreaker name. No one who watched them seems to have forgotten the thrill of the performances. Now Brownie is long ago dead, and so too her bracemate. Brownie lives on in the hinterland of pedigree compilations, but great fame attends the name of her bracemate of that day. Fourteen years after his death in 1958 we still find Old Greif the dog to beat in terms of versatile production and a prepotency that defies the weight of the generations. It is surely time that, in these pages, we took a look at what was in gift of Brownie's obscure bracemate that long ago day . . . Field Ch. Greif v. Hundsheimerkogl, imported Austria.

FIELD Ch. GREIF V. HUNDSHEIMERKOGL   (*Alf Gindl ex Berta Spiessinger v.*
Breeder: Viktor Rohringer, Austria   *Pfaffenhofen-Ilm*)
Owner: D. H. Hopkins, California
   DUAL Ch. Oxton's Leiselotte v. Greif   (*ex Ch. Yunga War Bride*)
   DUAL Ch. Oxton's Bride's Brunz v.   (" " " " ")
     Greif
   DUAL Ch. Madchen Braut v. Greif   (" " " " ")
   DUAL Ch. Schoene Braut v. Greif   (" " " " ")

   Ch. Lisa v. Greif   (" " " " ")
   Field & Nat'l Ch. (Am. Field)   (*ex Field Ch. Brownie's Pat*
     Brownie's Greif McCarthy   *McCarthy*)
   Field Ch. Yunga v. Hundsheimerkogl (*ex Bettina v. Schwarenberg*)
   Field Ch. Karen v. Greif   (*ex Freida v. Schoenweide*)
   Field Ch. Konrad Christenson v.   (*ex Lily Marlene v. Greif his daugh-*
     Greif   *ter*)
   Field Ch. Katy v. Hundsheimerkogl   (" " " " " " ")
   Field Ch. Hanne Lore v. Greif   (*ex Hella v. Yunga, his grand-*
                                              daughter)
   Field Ch. Della v. Hundesheimerkogl (" " " " ") -
   Field Ch. Feld Jager v. Greif   (*ex Toni Marlene*)
   Ch. Baron Rudiger v.d. Heide   (*ex Ch. Royal Victrix v. Kurt II*)
   Ch. Bissen v. Flieger   (*ex Frau Jill*)
   Ch. Bote v. Flieger   (" " ")
   Field Ch. Von Thalberg's Fritz II   (*ex Von Thalberg's Katydid—his*
                                              grand-daughter)

First indication of the prepotency extant here was given with the maturing of the oldest son, Field Ch. Yunga v. Hundsheimerkogl, the solid liver, by way of his v. Schwarenberg background.

Dual Ch. Cede Mein Dolly Der Orrian (Dual Ch. Zipper Der Orrian ex Dual Ch. Erdenreich's Jetta Beckum). Breeder: C. D. Lawrence, Idaho. Owner: Dean Tidrick, Iowa. Dolly is the runaway top in GSP production—the dam of dual champions that now, in turn, are producing Duals. Her grandparents included—on the sire's side, Field Ch. Von Thalberg's Fritz II, and on the dam's side— Am./Can. Ch. Erdenreich Die Zweite, CD.

Dual Ch. Oxton's Minado von Brunz (Dual Ch. Oxton's Bride's Brunz v. Greif ex Ch. Sorgeville's Happy Holiday). Out from retirement to win Veteran Class (and FT Class!) at the 1973 National Specialty. Owned by K. and I. Clody, and handled here by Laura Clody, age 14.

FIELD Ch. YUNGA V. HUNDSHEIMEROGL	(*Field Ch. Greif v. Hundsheimerkogl ex Bettina v. Schwarenberg*)
AM/CAN. DUAL Ch. Gretchen v. Greif	(*ex Field Ch. Karen v. Greif above*)
Field Ch. Fritzel v. Greif	(" " " " " ")
Field Ch. Kristen v. Greif	(" " " " " ")
Field Ch. Rex v. Hundsheimer	(*ex Ch. Freida v. Schoenweide, dam of Karen, above*)
Ch. Chula Hundweise Galli	(" " " " ")
Field Ch. Carol v. Hohen Tann	(*ex Ardy's Judith of Hohen Tann*)
Ch. Ricefield's Eric	(*ex Ch. Ricefield's Brown Bomber*)
Ch. Ricefield's Maja	(" " " " ")
DUAL Ch. OXTON'S BRIDE'S BRUNZ V. GREIF	(*Field Ch. Greif v. Hundsheimerkogl ex Ch. Yunga War Bride*)
Breeder/Owner: J. Huizenga, California	
DUAL Ch. Brunnenhugel Balder	(*ex Ch. Weidenbach Suzette*)
DUAL Ch. Brunnenhugel Jarl	(" " " ")
Ch. Brunnenhugel Brock	(" " " ")
DUAL Ch. Oxton's Minado v. Brunz	(*Am/Can. Ch. Sorgeville's Happy Holiday*)
Ch. Oxton's Liese v. Brunz	(" " " " ")
Ch. Holiday's Wendi v. Greif	(" " " " ")
Ch. Holiday's Sieglinde v. Greif	(" " " " ")
Ch. Aintree Dyna-mite v. Brunz	(" " " " ")
Ch. Jody Radbach v. Greif	(*Ch. Becky Radbach v. Greif*)
Ch. Greta Radbach v. Greif	(" " " " ")
Ch. Merry Maker's Extra Special	(*Ch. Merry Maker's Cherub*)
Ch. Ricefield's Sohn v. Greif	(*ex Bellshon de Kristine*)
Ch. Oshabere Kibou	(*Dual Ch. Bee's Gabby v. Beckum*)
Ch. Castlecrag Bonnie Lassie	(*Heidi Niedersachsenhoff*)
Field Ch. Hulcy's Bailey v. Greif	(*ex Hulsey's Brownie*)
Field Ch. Oxton's Gretta Lore v. Greif	(*ex Field Ch. Oxton's Hanne Lore v. Greif*)

If, as philosphers and biblical scribes have preserved to us, a good woman is above the price of rubies, then the stud that has the fortune of alliance with a specially good bitch is also to be counted the recipient of favors most valuable. As Dual Ch. Oxton's Minado v. Brunz had the luck of Dual Ch. Cede Mein Dolly Der Orrian, so had his father before him the luck of an outstanding mate in the Canadian-bred, Am/Can. Ch. Sorgeville's Happy Holiday, owned by John and Gertrude Dapper of Sacramento. Despite the congratulatory breast-beatings of the owners of the studs, in all congress of the sort it still takes two to tango. The Canadian background of Ch. Sorgeville's Happy Holiday is not readily to

Dual & AFC Dee Tee's Baron v. Grief (Dual Ch. Oxton's Minado v. Brunz ex Dual Ch. Cede Mein Dolly Der Orrian). Baron already has to his credit two Duals of his own, extending the so-well-proven lineage yet another generation along the way of distinction. Breeder: Dean Tidrick. Owner: Stanley Haag, M.D.

Dual Ch. Fagon Haag v. Grief (Dual Ch. Oxton's Minado v. Greif ex Dual Ch. Cede Mein Dolly Der Orrian). Breeder: Dean Tidrick, Iowa. Owner: Dr. Stanley Haag, Iowa.

Dual Ch. Dee Tee's Baschen v. Greif (Dual Ch. Oxton's Minado v. Brunz ex Dual Ch. Cede Mein Dolly Der Orrian). Breeder: Dean Tidrick. Owners: Gary and Harriet M. Short. Baschen is in turn the dam of Dual Ch. Boss Lady Jodi v. Greif.

hand for analysis, but this compiler remembers—and cherishes good color slides—of her constructional elegances. Additionally, which no pedigree form could possibly ever convey, there was her exuberance—Happy Holiday, indeed, all fire and git up and go! With advantage, she might have been used more, one feels. But she does represent a valuable prelude to the production of Dolly and deserves not to be forgotten.

Dual Ch. Cede Mein Dolly Der Orrian—what to say of her that her record does not clarify. All those champions to Minado were not the full tally of her production—she could even coax show champions out of so strong a Field Trial oriented producer as Fld. T. Ch. Windy Hill Prince James. Her dam, as a daughter of Erdenreich Die Zweite—Dual Ch. Erdenreich Jetta Beckum, has already been mentioned elsewhere. Her sire, Dual Ch. Zipper Der Orrian, was a Field Ch. Von Thalberg's Fritz II son. And it is worth mentioning here that Dual Ch. Zipper had a full sister—Dolly's aunt—Am/Can. Ch. Zeugencarl's Elsa v. Ida—that additionally adds to the illumination of what was stored up in this inheritance. Elsa's own production was to a count of nine, half Am/Can. champions,

Ch. Dee Tee's Flambeau v. Grief (Dual Ch. Oxton's Minado v. Greif ex Dual Ch. Cede Mein Dolly Der Orrian). Best in Show winner. Breeder: Dean Tidrick. Owners: J. Whitfield and J. Sener.

half just plain Am. champions. She lived to extraordinary old age—extraordinary in terms of more than time. At something around age thirteen she appeared at a Specialty in this compiler's judging ring—outstandingly the best mover of the day. Energy! Would anyone wonder—scanning back over the names, sire side and dams, that Minado proved to be the producer that he was?

DUAL Ch. OXTON'S MINADO V. BRUNZ

(Dual Ch. Oxton's Bride's Brunz v. Greif ex Am/Can. Ch. Sorgeville's Happy Holiday.)

Breeders: John & Gertrude Dapper, CA.
Owners: K. & I Clody, CA.

DUAL Ch. Dee Tee's Baron v. Greif	*(ex Dual Ch. Cede Mein Dolly der Orrian)*
DUAL Ch. Dee Tee's Baschen v. Greif	(" " " " " " ")
DUAL Ch. Fagon Haag v. Greif	(" " " " " " ")
Ch. Dee Tee's Grandee v. Greif (BIS)	(" " " " " " ")
Ch. Dee Tee's Flambeau v. Greif (BIS)	(" " " " " " ")
Ch. Dee Tee's Buc v. Greif	(" " " " " " ")
Ch. Dee Tee's Benedict v. Greif	(" " " " " " ")
Ch. Dee Tee's Blitz v. Greif	(" " " " " " ")
Ch. Dee Tee's Britta v. Greif	(" " " " " " ")
Ch. Dee Tee's Trey v. Greif	(" " " " " " ")
Ch. Dee Tee's Fanny v. Grief	(" " " " " " ")
Ch. Dee Tee's Flash v. Greif	(" " " " " " ")
Ch. Dee Tee's Fan Cede v. Greif	(" " " " " " ")
Ch. Dee Tee's Garbo v. Greif	(" " " " " " ")
Ch. Dee Tee's Gaea v. Greif	(" " " " " " ")
Ch. Dee Tee's Gypsy Rose v. Greif	(" " " " " " ")
Ch. Dee Tee's Fasan Jagerin v. Greif	(" " " " " " ")
Ch. Minado's Sassy Sadie	*(ex Callmac's Mona Lisa)*
Ch. Jubilant Jenny v. Minado	(" " ")
Ch. Westfield's Cara Mia v. Minado	(" " ")
Ch. Minado's Faith, Hope, and Love	(" " ")
Minado Mona Lisa's Chukar, U.D.T.	(" " ")
Ch. Callmac's Mariah v. Minado	*(ex Ch. Callmac's Victory v. Gardsburg)*
Ch. Moesgaards Helga v. Waldenburg	*(ex Callmac's Katrina v. Moesgaard)*
Ch. Uberaschung v. Greif	*(Gina Braun v. Greif)*
Ch. Oxton's Minado Mark	*(Kleine Flag v. Greif)*
Ch. Minado's Doc Holiday	*(Von Flecki's Holiday)*
Ch. Clsambra's Mister Minado	*(Ch. Clsambra's Lucky Domino)*
Ch. Weidenbach's Miss E. v. Minado	*(Ch. Weidenbach Brunhilde)*
Ch. Freida Miss E. von Minado	*(ex Lilla Bella Foreiglian (imp. Italy)*
GRANDGET:	
DUAL Ch. Babe's Drifting Toby v. Greif	*(Dual/AFC Dee Tee's Baron v. Greif ex Ritzie's Dan Oranian Babe)*
DUAL Ch. Eva von Kieckhafer	*(Dual/AFC Dee Tee's Baron v. Greif ex Ch. Adelheid von Fetterell)*

Acknowledging the strength of feminine influence in producing fine stock to good studs, please not to count this as other than a convenient way of making clear the Italian Court's great Falconer's directive of five hundred years ago—the one about having a Fayre Bitch if one would have a Fayre Hound. Breeding, is *never* a one-sided affair, nor ever will be. . . The complacency wherewith some stud promoters labor to overlook this truth is long overdue for disturbance.

FIELD Ch. VON THALBERG'S FRITZ II   (*Field Ch. Greif v. Hundsheimerkogel ex Von Thalberg's Katydid*)

Breeder/Owner: Don Miner, Calif.

DUAL Ch. Zipper der Orrian*	(*Zetta v. Fuehrerheim*)
Am/Can. Ch. Zeugencarl's Elsa v. Ida	(" " ")
Field & Nat'l Field Ch. Thalberg Seagraves Chayne	(*Field Ch. Patsy Grabenbruch Beckum*)
Field & Nat'l Field Ch. Rip Traf v. Bess	(*Field Ch. Mitzi Grabenbruch Beckum*)
Field & Nat'l Field Ch. Onna v. Bess	(" " " ")
Nat'l Am/Fld Ch. Heinrich v. Bess	(" " " ")
Field Ch. Marga v. Bess	(" " " ")
Field Ch. Missy v. Bess	(" " " ")
Field Ch. Rip v. Bess	(" " " ")
Field Ch. Blitzkreig v. Bess	(" " " ")
Field Ch. Blitz v. Bess	(" " " ")
Field Ch. Jake v. Bess	(" " " ")
Field Ch. Rusty Grabenbruch Beckum	(" " " ")
Field Ch. Bo Jack v. Bess	(" " " ")
Nat'l Am/Fld Ch. Andora v. Hokenborn	(*Centa v. Bornefeld (imp. Ger*)
Field Ch. Von Thalberg's Redbach X-cell	(" " " " ")
Field Ch. Von Thalberg's Wurtze v. Greif	(*Yunga's Heide*)
Field Ch. Fritzi v. Grief	(" ")
Field Ch. Maxine v. Heidelberg	(*Field Ch. Schatzi v. Heidelberg*)
Field Ch. Von Thalberg's Greif II	(*Patti v. Greif*)
Field Ch. Lucky Ducate	(*Hildy v. Beckum*)

*Sire of Dual Ch Cede Mein Dolly Der Orrian (ex Dual Ch. Erdenreich's Jetta Beckum, initiating a distinguished modern production).

"Old Fritz" proved most prepotent of Greif v. H's own get-with strength also in his untitled bitches that became broods. He was a

Field Ch. Von Thalberg's Fritz II (Field Ch. Greif v. Hundsheimerkogel ex Von Thalberg's Katydid). Progenitor of great field performers. Bred and owned by Don Miner, Von Thalberg K's, California. The ever-lasting recurrence of Fritz's daughters behind current champions is not the least of his credits.

Natl. FT Ch. Thalberg's Seagraves Chayne (Field Ch. von Thalberg's Fritz II ex Field Ch. Patsy Grabenbruch Beckum), owned by Don Miner, California.

1975 NGSPA All-Age Ch. & Fld Ch. Ammertal's Lancer D (NFC & Field Ch. Thalberg's Seagraves Chayne ex Field Ch. & AFC Ammertal's Kitt v. Shinback). Owner, Jim Reed, Idaho. Well-performed, Lancer was also, as his breeding suggests, a successful sire with dual-titled get.

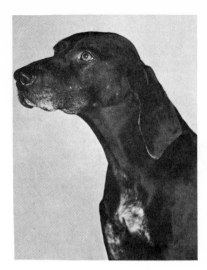

Dual Ch. Gretchen v. Greif; her Dual title individually in both U.S. and Canada a unique record. At the age of nine she could still make her presence felt in the nation's top competition. Owner, Ralph Parks, Sr., Washington.

most companionable, clever dog in the sense that the German pioneer breeders valued, a hunting man's all purpose dog. One recalls this, standing by his sleeping spot in a Saratoga, Calif. camellia grove, son Chayne to his one side, son Greif II the other.

In this ongoing saga of Greif inheritance, fits in also another fine producing bitch, Am/Can. Dual Ch. Gretchen v. Greif, first of any breed to hold the Dual title in both countries. She was basic to the breeding program of the late Ralph A. Park, Sr. of Washington, used with two German imports brought in at this time, Am/Can. Dual Ch. Arrak v. Heisterholz and Field Ch. Gert v.d. Radbach, As follows:

AM/CAN. DUAL Ch. ARRAK V. HEISTER-
    HOLZ (Ger. imp.)
Breeder: Carlheinz Herwegh, Germany
Owner: Ralph A. Park Sr., Washington
    DUAL Ch. Janie Greif v. Heisterholz

    Field Ch. Kreig Heisterholz v. Greif
    Field Ch. Heisterholz's Helga v. Greif
    Ch. Eckener Heisterholz v. Greif
    Ch. Greif v. Heisterholz CD
    Bal Lakes Felecka v. Greif, UD
    Field Ch. Wolfwiese Radbach Eric
    Field Ch. Augustine v. Holkenborn

    Field Ch. Duke Radbach v. Heister-
        holz

(*Lummel v. Braumatal ex Astrid v.
    Grossenverde*)

(*ex Am/Can. Dual Ch. Gretchen v.
    Greif*)
("   "   "   "   "   "   )
("   "   "   "   "   "   )
("   "   "   "   "   "   )
("   "   "   "   "   "   )
("   "   "   "   "   "   )
(*ex Mara v. Hanstein*)
(*ex Heisterholz Shooting Star, she
    an Arrak g-daughter &
    Gretchen g-g-daughter*)
(*ex Tammy O'Shea*)

277

FIELD Ch. GERT V.D. RADBACH (Ger. imp.)	(*K.S. Zeus v. Blitzdorf ex Ruth v.d. Radbach*)
Breeder: Ernst Bleckman, Germany	
Owner: Ralph A. Park Sr., Washington	
AM/CAN. DUAL Ch. Gert's Duro v. Greif*	(*ex Am/Can. Dual Ch. Gretchen v. Greif*)
AM/CAN. DUAL Ch. Gert's Dena v. Greif	(" " " " ")
Field Ch. Tarzan v.d. Radbach	(" " " " ")
Ch. Greif v. Radbach	(" " " " ")
AM/CAN. DUAL Ch. Radbach's Arko	(*ex Katja v.d. Radbach (Ger. imp.)*
Ch. Radbach's Asco	(" " " " " ")
Ch. Ulda Amber v. Offa	(*ex Tamm v. Grabenwald*)

* Duro is sire of Nat'l Field Trial Ch. Patricia v. Frulord, for whom 1971 was a banner year, she taking both AKC and Am. Fld licensed Nationals in the same season—a record to date.

Am/Can. Dual Ch. Radback's Arko carries the qualities on and down through his son, also a Dual Ch—Radbach's Dustcloud. Dustcloud, in his turn, faithfully carries the flame, as sire of an outstanding quality show dog in Ch. Kooskia's Chief Joseph, owned in the Idaho mountains and much employed as a hunting dog, that from time to time during the 1970s, would emerge to be the dog to beat in any ring he graced, his record embracing breed and group wins, as well as the 1978 GSPCA National breed specialty. Chief Joseph is also at benefit of a strong line, solid Kaposia back line for generations, carried by his dam, Ch. Red Tail of Kooskia (Ch. Kaposia's Oconto ex Ch. Kaposia's Waoke) and has in his turn a son also at benefit of Kaposia—Ch. Kooskia's Chief Timothy (ex Kaposia's Princess Owatonna). Sparsely as they are campaigned these dogs provide conveyance for the bloodlines of Germany's very best—K.S. Zeus v. Blitzdorf, K.S. Pol v. Blitzdorf, K.S. Duro v. Braumatal. Interestingly, though seemingly "Axel-frei" (free of Axel v. Wasserschling) in his breeding background, Chief Joseph bears uncanny resemblance to the great stud.

As with Arrak and Gert, a third stud selected in Germany by Robert Holcomb in the early 1960s and brought into Washington, (later) Am/Can. Field Ch. Lutz v.d. Radbach, had also much in gift. His life was very short, but his total production count of 15 titled get includes four Dual Champions, representing a percentage that must give the thoughtful matter for consideration and all got from bitches of wide diversity of background.

278

AM/CAN. FIELD Ch. LUTZ V.D. RADBACH (Ger. imp.)	(*Xot v.d. Radbach ex Fitz v.d. Radbach*)
Breeder: Ernst Bleckman, Germany	
Owner: R. L. Holcomb, Washington	
DUAL Ch. Timberlane's Fritz	(*ex Ch. Timberlane's Honey*)
Am/Can. DUAL Ch. Ricki Radbach v. Greif	(*ex Lulubelle v. Greif, she ex Dual Ch. Gretchen v. Greif*)
Field Ch. Arraka v. Greif	(" " " ")
DUAL Ch. Kamiak Desert Sand	(*ex Field Ch. Kamiak Bold Lark, she a Ch. Buck v. Gardsburg daughter*)
Ch. Kamiak Desert Dawn	(" " " " " ")
Field Ch. Kamiak White Lightning	(" " " " " ")
Ch. Radbach's Karin	(*ex Katja v.d. Radbach (Ger. imp.*)
Am/Can. Field Ch. Radbach's Chips	(*ex Glucka v. Greif, she ex Dual Ch. Gretchen v. Greif*)
Field Ch. Von Thalberg's Radbach Queen	(*ex Centa v. Bornfeld (Ger. imp daughter K.S. Vito v.d. Radbach*)
Field Ch. Radbach's Kniff	(*ex Wolfsjaeger's Anka*)
Field Ch. Radbach's Luke	(" " ")
Field Ch. Radbach's Krip	(" " ")
Can/Field Ch. Wolfjaeger's Dax v. Spee	(" " ")
Can/Field Ch. Wolfjaeger's Don v. Spee	(" " ")
DUAL Ch. Fritz v. Trekka Radbach	(*ex Trekka v. La Mer*)

Brief period of production of Lutz is matched in an earlier time by that of another German import—Ch. Alvin's Blitz, in the ownership of the late George Reudiger of Minnesota. Blitz, who appears to have become lost—maybe in hunting?—lives on in his get, Mr. Reudiger's great producing stud, Ch. Big Island Spotter (Ch. Alvin's Blitz ex Field Ch. Big Island Dancer) and through his daughters ex Ch. Katrina v. Albrecht, Chs. Albrecht's Countess Tena and Sandy v. Albrecht especially.

Again the picture is of the welding of pioneer American bloodlines with latter-day German imports. Through her grandsire, Dual Ch. Valbo v. Schlesburg, Katrina draws on the thoroughly proved Timm v. Altenau—Donn v. Sulfmeister—K.S. Kobold Mauderode Westerbolt strength. Ch. Big Island Spotter's dam, Big Island Dancer, was ex Dual Ch. Big Island Spook, a daughter of prepotent Ch. Rex v. Krawford whose untitled daughter, Helga v. Krawford, provides such fantastic strength to Columbia River.

Ch. BIG ISLAND SPOTTER   (*Ch. Alvin's Blitz ex Field Ch. Big*
Breeder: George Reudiger, Minnesota   *Island Dancer*)
Owner: Houston Carter, Missouri
  DUAL Ch. Albrecht's Baron Cid   (*ex Field Ch. Albrecht's Countess*
     Tena)

  DUAL Ch. Albrecht's Baroness Cora   ("   "   "   "   ")
  Ch. Albrecht's Baroness Cora   ("   "   "   "   ")
  Field Ch. Albrecht's Baroness Freya   ("   "   "   "   ")
  Field Ch. Albrecht's Baron Cy   ("   "   "   "   ")
  DUAL Ch. Dino v. Albrecht   (*ex Ch. Albrecht's Apache Breeze*)
  Ch. Apache Breeze Pride   ("   "   "   "   ")
  Ch. Apache Belle Starr   ("   "   "   "   ")

DUAL Ch. ALBRECHT'S BARON CID   (*Ch. Big Island Spotter ex Field Ch.*
Breeders/Owners: M & L Albrecht,   *Albrecht's Countess Tena*)
  Kansas
  DUAL Ch. Rambling Rock   (*ex Albrecht's Countess Abey*)
  Field Ch. Albrecht's Ruff & Tuff   ("   "   "   ")
  Field Ch. Albrecht's Van Joker   ("   "   "   ")
  Field Ch. Albrecht's Count Gustav   (*ex Ch. Katrina v. Albrecht*)
  Ch. Cimarron's Cracker Jack   (*ex Trudel Turn & Taxis*)
  Ch. Cimarron's Cannonball   ("   "   "   ")
  Ch. Baron Cid's Best Bette   (*ex Ch. Fieldwood Britta*)
  Ch. Zandor Smoki v. Greif   (*ex Bebita Lohman v. Greif*)

FIELD Ch. ALBRECHT'S COUNT GUSTAV   (*Dual Ch. Albrecht's Baron Cid ex*
Breeders: M. & L. Albrecht, Kansas   *Ch. Katrina v. Albrecht*)
Owner: Thomas C. Bowman, Kansas
  DUAL & Amtr. Field Ch. Albrecht's   (*ex Field Ch. Albrecht's Countess*
    Tena Hy (*Dual Champion One*   *Tena*)
    Hundred)
  Ch. Albrecht's Tena Inky   ("   "   "   "   "
  Field Ch. Marshall v. Braun   (*ex Pepper's Pride*)

The consistency of this strain in the production of Dual champions and the versatile titled in both field and show competition, studs and greatly prepotent broods included, is likely unrivalled within the breed in USA—which makes all the more satisfying the accidental fall of the time factors that permitted an Albrecht to slip into the One Hundred slot in the Dual tabulation.

The comments of the breeders at this period of sustained endeavors is interesting: "We've always preferred the Dual type dog, although in stubbornly persisting with such, have had also to accept the sacrifices that go along with it.

We have found our reward in the holding-up of the strain through the generations. We certainly have not produced the 100% perfect dogs—nor did we expect to. Few have completely satisfied us—and when the perfect animal is produced anywhere, we will be the first to acknowledge it. Our production however has pleased us in terms of *all-over* quality."

Myron Albrecht has never been a professional, but trains, handles, shows all their dogs. His further dedication is to the continued improvement of his strain and the retention of its consistency in reproduction. Beyond those aims, he devotes much time to schooling club members to make the best of their own dogs, conceding that often enough it is harder to train owner than dog. This is a discovery known to the sport as far as a century back.

History of the introduction and braiding into the prevailing strains of the Danish importations remains to be written as some separate venture but whenever, or by whom undertaken, the start will have to be made with that solid rock of breed integrity, Hjalmer Olsen, who confessed that to give up his original interest in English Pointers had not been easy. Doubtless this explains the circumstance that of the many dogs he routed as from Denmark into USA—a count believed to approach seventy—the majority had the color inheritance factors that so closely paralleled that of the English Pointer. Several of his imports had strong influence—as count importantly Field Ch. Moesgaard's IB and his mate Field Ch. Doktorgaarden's Lucky, whose management—perhaps in terms of inbreeding carried beyond the reasonable—have carried the strain-name coast to coast and border to border—and to the tune of many questions asked and never answered. However, judging by his surviving picture, no questions would seem to have been reasonably asked of IB, and his appearance was no ways unusual in terms of breed type.

The influx is far too large to enumerate herein, as from first impact made by (later) Dual Ch. Doktorgaarden's Caro (imp); Field Ch. Skriver's Streak (by Field Ch. Skriver'd Jesper ex Lady Lydia Swift) who sired the handsome Dual Ch. Streak's Herbst Versprechen; as Ch. Skriver's Jens; as Field Ch. Skovmarken's Sep; as Skriver's Sofus, who sits in behind that distinguished show dog, Ch. Buck v. Gardsburg.

Ch. Buck v. Gardsburg, repeatedly the nation's top show-winning German Short-haired Pointer till his retirement in 1961. Buck and his handler, the late Roland Muller, always made an eye-catching team. A prolific stud, with versatile get. Owner: D. D. Williams, California.

Ch. BUCK V. GARDSBURG (BIS)
Breeder: A. Alvin
Owner: D. D. Williams, California
　DUAL Ch. Sager v. Gardsburg*

　　Ch. Pepsie v. Gardsburg
　　Ch. Erdenreich's Beau v. Gardsburg
　　　(BIS)
　　Ch. Buck v. Gardsburg
　　Ch. Erdenreich's Bea v. Gardsburg
　　Ch. Atun of Janley Acres

　　Ch. Briarwyn's Buckskin
　　Ch. Briarwyn's Bootjack
　　Ch. Timm v. Lohengrin
　　Ch. Heidi v. Lohengrin
　　Ch. Paglo's Frivol
　　Ch. Konig v. Gardsburg
　　Ch. Callmac's Victory v. Gardsburg*+
　　Field Ch. Kamiak Bold Bark
　　Field Ch. Kamiak Cloudy Weather

(Ch. Red Velvet ex Zukie v. Gards-burg, Ch. Red Velvet by imp. Skriver's Sofus)
(ex Ch. Valory v. Gardsburg, with Timm v. Altenau 3rd genera-tion both sides)
("　　"　　"　　　　")
(ex Am/Can. Ch Erdenreich die Zweite, CD)
("　"　"　"　　"　　")
("　"　"　"　　"　　")
(ex Ch. Oak Crest Cora v. Winter-hauch, (BIS)
("　"　　"　　"　　"　")
("　"　　"　　"　　"　")
(ex Copper's Kam)
("　　"　　"　)
(ex Ch. Paglo's Cindy)
(Ch. Heidi v. Waldhausen)
("　　"　"　　"　　)
(ex Kimlet of Cayest Meadow, CD)
("　　"　"　"　　"　　")

282

DUAL Ch. SAGER v. GARDSBURG
Breeders/Owners: R. & L. Sylvester,
   Pennsylvania
DUAL Ch. Richlu's Terror

Ch. Richlu's Stormy Gale
Ch. Richlu's Tara*
Ch. Richlu's Jeffson
Ch. Mobe's Dapper
Ch. Waidmann's Ingwer

(Ch. Buck v. Gardsburg ex Ch.
   Valory v. Gardsburg)

(ex Ch. Richlu's Jan Oranien-
   Nassau)
("   "   "   "   "   )
("   "   "   "   "   )
(ex Thora v. Assegrund)
(ex King's Lady II)
(ex Ch. Kristi v. Lohengrin)

The Gardsburg influence holds fast down through another couple of generations through the Sager granddaughter, Ch. Richlu's Jill Oranian, passing to her son, Dual Ch. Richlu's Dan Oranian (by Ch. Dax v. Heidebrink.)

DUAL Ch. RICHLU'S DAN ORANIAN

Breeders: R. & L. Dylvester, GA.
Owners: C. & S. Carlson, Ohio
   DUAL Ch. Ritzie's Oranian Rocco
   Ch. Shircle's Twig Oranian
   Ch. Shircle's Dax Oranian
   Fld Ch. Betsy v. Braumatal
   Field Ch. Ben v. Almenbruce
   Field Ch. Richlu's Hewlett Sandy
   Field Ch. Skyliner Hannah Belle
   Ch. Mitchell's Ohio Belle
   Ch. Crossing Creek Kate
   Ch. Bond's Bruno v. Kieckhefer
   Ch. Shady Dell's Satin Gretchen
   Can. Ch. E.F. Fox's Fienie

(Ch. Dax v. Heidebrink ex Ch. Richlu's Jill
   Oranian)

(ex Dual Ch. Ritzie)
(" *Dual Ch. Richlu's Terror)*
(" *Alfie v. Braumatal)*
(" *Alfie v. Braumatal)*
(" *Dual Ch. Richlu's Terror)*
(" *Hewlett's Lady Bess)*
(" *Ch. Sleepy Hollow Rollo's Nosey)*
(" *Mitchell's Anka)*
(" *Ch. Crossing Creeek Molly Pitcher)*
(ex Ch. Adelheid v. Fetterell)
(Ch. Rochlin's Broun's v. Satin)
(Ch. Field Ch. E.F. Fex's Blind)

Sale of imported Field Ch. Moesgaards IB to Washington breeder, the late Ivan Brower, preluded a complete change of type within the ranks of the Field Trial competing dogs out of this strain. How it was contrived has been matter of speculation for decades, Brower resisting all attempts to secure information that would explain the metamorphosis of the German Shorthair Field Trial competing dogs in such wide percentage into dogs of a completely alien cast of appearance and, indeed, habit of work. There is a school of thought that believes that the system of fantastically locked-up close inbreeding is responsible, matter to which none can say yea or nay in the absence of the man that contrived the matings. There is equivalent, perhaps, in the destruction of the Llewellin English Setter strain at the turn and earliest years of this present century. There the breeding—the stud book—was locked against any additional blood strain whatsoever—"dirt in the veins" was the descriptive the "purists" applied to any suggestion of outcross. The outcome, of course, as history establishes, was end put to the strain in toto. There are, yes, still those who claim to have "Llewellins" but the historical truth is that the Llewellins just faded away—La Besita, National Ch. of 1915, is counted the last of the "straight-breds" of the strain (*A.F. Hochwald, Bird Dogs & Their Achievements, p. 80*).

No one can guess what course the ongoing Moesgaards' breeding may have taken if the original entrepeneur had not lost his life (a plane accident, as was reported). However, in the main, since then a considerable amount of incrossing on the strain has been undertaken, and one finds Moesgaards in some most unexpected combinations behind some very interesting Shorthairs indeed. As for the original inbreeding process, it was as follows:

FIELD Ch. MOESGAARD'S IB (imp. Den)   (*Holevgaard's Kip ex Nyberg's Rix*)
Breeder: Niels Hykkelbjerg, Denmark
Owner: Ivan Brower, Washington

  Field Ch. Doktorgaarden's Lucky (imp. Den)   (*ex Field Ch. Doktorgaarden's Bunny*)
  DUAL & NAT'L Field Ch. Moesgaard's Dandy   (*ex Field Ch. Doktorgaarden's Lucky (above, sire-daughter breeding)*)

  Field Ch. Moesgaard's Doktor   ("   "   "   "   )
  Field Ch. Moesgaard's Sis   ("   "   "   "   )
  Field Ch. Moesgaard's Ruffy   (*ex Moesgaard's Arta (and she already a M. Ib daughter out of his daughter Lucky)*)

  Field Ch. Moesgaard's Lucky II   ("   "   "   )
  Field Ch. Fieldacres Ib   (*ex Moesgaard's Girl (again a daughter of M. Ib and Lucky, as above)*)

  Field Ch. Fieldborn Ib   (*ex Lady Windsor—she of course outside the above pattern*)

Continually is raised in Shorthair discussion the opinion that a Pointer cross was resorted to at Friday Island, which would—if true—invalidate the above pedigrees. However, no acceptable proof in the legal sense has ever been provided to support the opinion. It may as likely be merely that the admittedly off-type appearance of so many dogs from this breeding, tending to complete negation at times of Shorthair breed appearance represents merely the inevitable degeneration imposed by the mechanics of their production. Where a saving cross of different blood was shackled to Moesgaard inheritance, as in the Dual Ch. get of M. Dandy and the show champion get of M. Coco, some very good dogs resulted.

DUAL & NAT'L F.T. Ch. MOESGAARD'S DANDY
(Field Ch. Moesgaard's Ib ex Field Ch. Doktorgaarden's Lucky)

Breeder: Ivan Brower, Washington
Owner: Dr. L. L. Kline, Florida

DUAL Ch. Gruenweg's Dandy Dandy
(ex Ch. Tessa v. Abendstern, g-daughter of Skriver's Jens plus an Am. pioneer dam line)

DUAL Ch. Lucy Ball
(ex Pearl of Wetzler, who stems back to Schlossgarten/Ammertal lines)

Field Ch. Big Red
(" " " ")

Field Ch. Moesgaard's Judy
(" " " ")

Field Ch. Erdenreich's Major
(ex Field Ch. Erdenreich's Hecla v. Greif, a Greif v. Hundshermerkogl granddaughter)

Field Ch. Erdenreich's Maisie
(" " " " ")

Field Ch. Erdenreich's Maxie
(" " " " ")

Field Ch. Von Holster's Calli
(ex Kay of Hollabird)

Ch. Moesgaard's Dandy's Old Smokey
(ex Gunsmoke's Comanche Squaw)

Field Ch. Moesgaard's Dandy's Mark
(ex. Babs v. Dakona, his daughter ex Fieldborn Bessie, Danish but not Moesgaard)

Field Ch. Southview's Count Dandy
(ex Skriver's Shovaard's Clove)

Field Ch. Moesgaard's Dandy Ian
(ex Fieldborn Flighty Sonja (she from Ch. Doktorgaarden's Fiks and Skriver's Jesper get))

Field Ch. Moesgaard's Dandy's Buck
(ex Fieldborn Flighty Glenda)

Field Ch. Moesgaard's Dandy's Pixie
(ex Moesgaard's v. Pyroberg Pix a Fld Ch. M.Ruffy/M.Sis daughter)

Field Ch. Moesgaard's Dandy's Benno
(ex Moesgaard's Pat (daughter of M/Ib ex M.Girl, she by M./Ib ex his daughter Lucky))

Field Ch. Moesgaard's Dandy's Cruiser
(ex Field Ch. Moesgaard's Lucky II (she by M.Ib ex his daughter Arta)

Ch. Moesgaard's Dandy Orlando
(" " " " " ")

Possibly the most inbred of all Moesgaard's produce that has made a place in these tabulations was Field & Nat'l FT Ch. Moesgaard's Coco. Coco's impressively long production list was made in the main with the assistance of two amazingly prepotent bitches. His field champions stem in terms of a batch of eleven from the equally inbred Nat'l FT Ch. Moesgaard's Angel, plus a quartette also from inbred Moesgaard's bitches, most of the produce generally swinging wide of classic Shorthair appearance. His show champion production was bolstered by the tremendous strength of one of the great prepotent bitches of our time, the Ch. Buck v. Gardsburg daughter, Ch. Callmac's Victory v. Gardsburg, of whom it was said that mate her as one might, she could be relied upon to throw good ones. She honored Coco with no less than eight show champions.

AMT'R NAT'L FIELD Ch. MOESGAARD'S COCO (*Field Ch. Moesgaard's Ruffy v. Field Ch. Moesgaard's BIS*)

Breeder/Owner: M. L. Sanders, California

Field Ch. Moesgaard's Alamo (*ex Field & Nat'l FT Ch. Moesgaard's Angel whose 4 g-parents were M. IB (twice) Arta and Lucky.*)

Field Ch. Moesgaard's Angel's Peppy (" " " " " ")
Field Ch. Moesgaard's Alicia (" " " " " ")
Field Ch. Moesgaard's Angel's Bart (" " " " " ")
Field & Amtr. FT Ch. Moesgaard's Angel's Bonnie (" " " " " ")
Field Ch. Angel's Rambling Danny (" " " " " ")
Field Ch. Moesgaard's Angel's Dee Jay (" " " " " ")
Field Ch. Moesgaard's Starlite (" " " " " ")
Field Ch. Moesgaard's Angel's Tambora (" " " " " ")
Field Ch. Moesgaard's Kurt (" " " " " ")
Field Ch. Moesgaard's Baron (" " " " " ")

Amtr. Nat'l Field Ch. Pentre Bach Coco (*ex Pentre Bach Pepper, she a Dual Ch. M. Dandy daughter of pioneer Am. background*)

Field Ch. Pentre Bach Erika (" " " ")
Field Ch. Moesgaard's Stylish Ib (*ex Moesgaard's Pat (M.Ib ex M Girl, she by M.Ib ex his daughter, Lucky)*)
Field Ch. Pentre Bach Dolly (*ex Moesgaard's Ruffy's Dolly*)
Field Ch. Moesgaard's Siegfried (*ex Field Ch. Saxony Sue*)
Ch. Callmac's Flecken Moesgaard (*ex Ch. Callmac's Victory v. Gardsburg, she by Ch. Buck v. Gardsburg*)

Ch. Callmac's Frederick Moesgaard (" " " " ")

286

Am/Mex Ch. Callmac's Fraya v. Moesgaard	(" " " " ")
Ch. Callmac's Franz	(" " " " ")
Ch. Callmac's Hank Moesgaard	(" " " " ")
Ch. Callmac's Kurt v. Moesgaard	(" " " " ")
Ch. Callmac's Kapitan v. Moesgaard	(" " " " ")
Ch. Charnet's Geronimo	(" " " " ")
Ch. Coco's Candy Cane	(*ex Lady Sandra v. Hohen Tann*)
Field Ch. Erdenreich's Sadhy	(*ex Field Ch. Erdenreich's Hecla v. Greif*)

Whether a Shorthair turns to show or field is matter of owner choice at all times, but in the tide of new Trial fashion that now dominates the sport in other than Gundog Stake competition, many good and useful breeding stock has gone into eclipse one hopes will be temporary. Surely will be, for always and always there have been owners with understanding and mind to preserve the qualities that gave the breed world popularity in the first place. Clearer assessment of true values, as trends threaten to swamp certain qualities, could restore priority to the dual-producing potential that manifests itself in ongoing generations, not in some mere Numbers Count petering out in single generation appearance after help of some useful opposite-aim matings. Studs and broods with true dual-producing ability do not lack in the breed—the two following providing useful examples:

FIELD Ch. TIP TOP TIMMY	(*Duke v. Jager ex Rexann v. Stolzhafen*)
Owner: Fred Z. Palmer, New York	
DUAL Ch. Tip Top Timber	(*ex Ute Trail Wild Rose*)
Ch. Broha's Mission Flying Wheel	(*ex Ch. Gretchenhof Snowflake*)
Ch. Bruha's Ring Wheel	(" " " ")
Ch. Bruha's Mission Rex Wheel	(" " " ")
Ch. Bruha's Buck v.d. Gwinnerwheel	(" " " ")
Ch. Guerda of Sleepy Hollow	(*ex Hedwig of Sleepy Hollow*)
Field Ch. Tanzer of Sleepy Hollow	(" " " " ")
Field Ch. Tina of Sleepy Hollow	(" " " " ")
Field Ch. Rollo of Sleepy Hollow	(" " " " ")
Ch. Taffy Town Tara	(*ex Duchess of Lorkin*)
Field Ch. Sepa-Fetchit	(*ex Grousewald's Dot*)
Field Ch. Wylde Wood Gus	(*ex Fizcre's Wendy*)
Field Ch. Tip Top Beau Brandy	(*ex Fieldacres Vesta*)
Field Ch. Fauna v. Stine	(*ex Field Ch. Maltese Wanderer*)
Field Ch. Molnar's Gamble	(*ex Field Ch. Ute Trail Lore*)
Field Ch. Mr. Tuff of Jagershof	(*ex Ute Trail Cocoa*)
Field Ch. Hewlett Engelchen Nutmeg	(*ex Field Ch. Hewlett Girl Greta*)

287

Field Ch. Timmy's Chocolate Chip	(*ex Ute Trail's Bonnie*)
Field Ch. Uodibar's Boss Man	(*ex Field Ch. Heide v. Uferwald*)
Field Ch. Hugo v. Bergiskante	(*ex Mountain Lea*)
Field Ch. Tip's Lady Nip	(*ex Field Ch. Maltese Wanderer*)
Field Ch. Rexford's Zip	(*ex Heidelberg Gretchen*)
Field Ch. Rexford's Elsa Baby	(*ex Field Ch. Rexford's Zip*)
Field Ch. Blaze v. Donner	(*ex Tanzer's Little Min of Sleepy Hollow*)

Identification of Field Ch. Uodibar's Boss Man in Timmy's production—demonstrating ongoing prepotency—helps clarify the
point. Timmy was dead by 1970, and Kay did not long outlast him,
both operative as studs during a period when registrations were
but fractional as compared with the present. The oft-used comparison offered by owners anxious to elevate the honor of their
producing dogs, the claim that such-and-such a notable's record
has been passed in this our time of highest-ever registrations and
competitive opportunities, frequently seen in the 1970s/80s re-em-
phasize the futility of assessing breed or performance stock worth
by numbers' count alone. How assess number count in relation to,
say, Am/Can. Field Ch. Lutz v.d. Radback, pitifully shortlived, from
a most famous German strain, whose 15 titled get include four
Duals? As against some Old-Promoted that lived a long life, handily-
domiciled, with high count of run-of-the-mill get punctuated by

Dual and Natl. FT Ch. Kay v.d. Wildburg (imp. Germany), by KS Pol v. Blitzdorf
ex Cora v. Wesertor. Owners: Richard S. Johns & J. Eusepi.

288

some few of other than transient importance—the breed has always had such, not to any notable benefit in the long range sense. And how to assess—where Numbers are predominantly the Aim—such a one as the *world's* only triple-titled GSP—Dual Ch. Frei of Klarbruk, U.D.T. whose owner has shared with this compiler the written initiative he was at need to take to get his Triple-titled brought even to consideration for Honors Roll inclusion! Numbers yet! Mathematical Nonsense!

In true assessment of production, the *untitled* get spells out as much, often enough, as the titled—all the great broods by famed sires that were too busy to earn their show titles. Long past time their recognition was provided. . .

DUAL & NATIONAL FIELD Ch. KAY V.D. WILDBURG (imp. Ger)   (*K.S. Pol v. Blitzdorf ex Cora v. Wesertor*)
Owner: Richard S. Johns & Joseph Eusepi
  DUAL Ch. Frei of Klarbruk, U.D.T.   (*ex Ch. Gretchenhof Cinnabar, C.D.X.*)
  Ch. Heidi of Klarbruk, U.D.T.   ("   "   "   "   ")
  Jillian of Klarbruk, U.D.T. (spayed)   ("   "   "   "   ")
  Ch. Moonshine Sally of Runnymede   ("   "   "   "   ")
  DUAL Ch. Fee v.d. Wildburg   (*ex Field Ch. My Ritzie fer Gitunburdz*)
  Field Ch. Kay fer Gitunburdz   ("   "   "   "   "   "   ")
  DUAL Ch. Eastwinds T,K. Dandy   (*ex Field Ch. Tina of Sleepy Hollow*)
  DUAL Ch. Eastwinds, T.K. Rebel   ("   "   "   "   "   "   ")
  Field Ch. Eastwinds T.K. Caesar   ("   "   "   "   "   "   ")
  Field Ch. Eastwinds Bourbon King   ("   "   "   "   "   "   ")
  Field Ch. Wynyard Apollo Lobreda   (*ex Seydel's Lottchen (Ger. imp)*)
  Field Ch. Maltese Wanderer   (*ex Field Ch. Ute Trail Lori*)
  Field Ch. Trinka Sam's Girl   (*ex Field Ch. Xilla Oranian-Nassau*)
  Field Ch. Budweiser v.d. Wildburg   (*ex Field Ch. Albrecht's Baroness Freya*)
  Ch. R.B.'s Heidi v.d. Wildburg   ("   "   "   "   ")
  Field Ch. Jinx v.d. Wildburg   (*ex Field Ch. Wag-Ae's Helga v. Radbach*)
  Ch. Kay v.d. Wildburg Bud   ("   "   "   "   "   "   ")

  Ch. Luftnase to Bar-Hardy Kay   (*ex Ch. Wag-Ae's Sheba Bruner*)
  Ch. Luftnase the Caisson   ("   "   "   "   "   ")
  Ch. Hope v. Luftnase   ("   "   "   "   "   ")
  Ch. Wildburg's Pointriever   (*ex Ch. Heity v. Grabenbruch*)
  Ch. Vermar's Cindy Wildburg   (*ex Ch. Richlu's Becky Oranian*)
  Ch. Deitz v.d. Wildburg*   (*ex Gruenweg's Bonnie*)

  *Ch. Deitz v.d. Wildburg is in turn of Dual Ch. Treff Marimax v.d. Wildburg (*ex. Moesgaard's High Noon*)

As change of location of from West and Mid-West, Texas makes 1980s appearance with clarion call . . . Field Ch. Uodibar's Boss

Field Ch. Uodibar's Boss Man (Field Ch. Tip Top Timmy ex Field & NFC Heide v. Uferwald). Three times selected as GPSCA Sire of the Year, Boss Man's production includes Dual-titleds, National Field Trial Chs, Field Chs, AFC Chs, Show Chs, and Obedience-titleds, got from a very wide selection of bitches. Breeders: H. and R. Meyer. Owner: John Rabidou, Texas.

Field & Natl. Field Ch. Ammertal's Boss Ranger (Field Ch. Uodibar's Boss Man ex Field & AFC Ammertal's Kitt v. Shinback). A "tireless All-Age dog, running with class and desire," Ranger is in tune with modern American FT style. Distinguished son of distinguished sire, his record includes 1980 GSPCA National. Already represented by young winning get. Breeder, Gary L. Stevens. Owner, Gary L. Nehring, Minnesota.

Man, tick patch veteran still around, with tally of get to include Dual Chs; Nat'l Field Chs; AFCs; Show Chs., Obedience Chs..

FIELD CH. UODIBAR'S BOSS MAN (*Field Ch. Tip Top Timmy ex Field Ch. Heide v. Uferwald*)

Breeder: H. & R. Meyer
Owner: John Rabidou, Texas.

DUAL & NAT'L Fld Ch. Boss Lady Jodi v. Greif (*Dual Ch. Dee Tee's Baschen v. Greif*)

DUAL CH. Uodibar's PDQ v. Waldtaler (*Ch. Whiskey Creek Whirlwind*)

Field & AFC Hillhaven's Whoopsy Daisy (" " " ")

Field & AFC Hillhaven Cindy (" " " ")

DUALCH. Glenmajor's Dunkas Top Boss (*Seiger's Farina (imp. Ger.)*)

Field Ch. Glenmajor's Dunkas Boss Woman (" " " ")

Field Ch. Uodibar's G. M's Booker T Brown (" " " ")

Field & NAT'L Fld. Ch. Uodibar's Rachel (1978 GSPCA All-Age Dog of the Year) (*Wyoming's Gretchen*)

Field & GSPCA NAT'L Fld Ch. Ammertal's Boss Ranger (1980) (*Field Ch. Ammertal's Kitt v. Shinback*)

Field & AFC Lyon's Tiger v. Ammertal (" " " ")

Field & AFC Uodibar's Mouse (*Fieldacres Candoit*)

Field Ch. Uodibar's Peter Gun (" ")

Field & AFC Silly Sally Seashell (" ")

Field Ch. Quarry Hill Mr. Mike (" ")

Field Ch. Uodibar's Nikkers (" ")

Field & AFC Uodibar's Barney Brown (*Heisterholz Lulu v. Greif*)

Field Ch. AFC Uodibar's Willow Chip (" " " ")

Field Ch. Randa's AC-DC Duke (" " " ")

Field Ch. & AFC Blazer VIII (*Colonial Missy*)

Field Ch. Sky Pilot (*Field Ch. Tip's Lady Nip*)

Field Ch. Tiffany von Cap (" " " " ")

Field Ch. Nip's Pride (" " " " ")

Field Ch. Boss Man's Busch (*Cindy v. Wasserschling*)

Field Ch. Fleeta v. Boss Man (" " ")

Field & AFC Moesgaard's Dee Jay's Dirk (*Moesgaard's Angel Dee Jay*)

Field Ch. Wrenegade's Mordecai v. Boss (*Fld & NAT'L Field Ch. Moesgaards Wrenegade*)

Field & AFC Skyliner Duchess v. Uodibar (*Moesgaard's Ruffy Petite*)

Field & AFC Voglein's Remarkable Butch (*Checkmate's Sister Sara*)

Ch. Uodibar's Raven of Hillhaven (*Uodibar's Pigeon*)

Ch. Jimandee's Son of a Gunrunner (*Field Ch. Jimandee's Kelly Jo*)

Boss Man blazing the trail, the 1980s scene expanded with a cluster of distinguished dual-producing studs firmly entrenched for the most part in the Field Trial scene though able, each in his area, to provide representation in show competition as well. The count includes such as Field Ch. Windy Hill Prince James (Tri State Trooper ex Windy Hill Whylimina); Field & Nat'l Field Ch. Blick v. Shinback (Esser's Chick, imp. Ger. ex Melissa v. Greif) and Field Ch. Ammertal's Lancer D (Field & Nat'l Ch. Thalberg's Seagraves Chayne ex Field Ch. Ammertal's Kitt v. Shinback).

Taking the youngest of the trio first, Idaho-owned Field Ch. Ammertal's Lancer D, still currently active, has already two Duals in credit, one of which carries additionally National Field titles of 1980/81.

FIELD Ch. AMMERTAL'S LANCER D	*(Field & Nat'l Ch. Thalberg's Seagraves Chayne ex Field Ch. Ammertal's Kitt v. Shinback)*
Owner: Jim Reed, Idaho	
DUAL Ch. Ammertal's Candy Cane	*(Cissy Radbach v. Greif)*
DUAL & NAT'L Fld. Ch. (1980/1) Ehrlicher's Abe	*(Ch. Misty fer Gitunburdz)*
Ch. My Shotgun fer Gitunburdz	(" " " ")
Field & NAT'L Ch. Frulord's Tim	*(Frulord's Frau Doktor)*
Field & Can Ch. Radbach's Savage v. Greif	*(Cissy Radbach v. Greif)*
Field Ch. Lancer's Homermann	*(Mayfield's Wurtzina v. Greif)*
Field Ch. Little Joe Dan	(" " " ")
Field & AFC Uodibar's Pigeon	*(Field Ch. Heide v. Uferwald)*
Field Ch. Lancer's Royal Scot	*(Gertrude fer Gitunburdz)*
Field Ch. Lancer's Jagermeister v. Greif	*(Cissy Radbach v. Greif)*
Field Ch. Babe's Moonshadow of Cariblu	*(Babes Tree v. Greif)*

The interesting discernment of versatile production on the part of some of the top contemporary field trial studs leads to the swift discovery, checking backlines, that these are themselves the product of true-type breeding untouched by any suggestion of unethical practices, bearing out the belief that this breed, with its specially-recognizable inbred endowments that permit the balance to swing whichever way an ownership inclines to favor, possesses innate capacity for preserving basic heritage. Against proven abilities of show-oriented breeding stock to produce useful hunting or gundog trial Shorthairs to work or field-oriented partnerships, is again and

Dual & Natl. Field Ch. Boss Lady Jodi v. Greif (Field Ch. Uodibar's Boss Man ex Dual Ch. Dee Tee's Baschen v. Greif). A very distinguished lady indeed, with a record in competition that will keep her name honored for a long time to come. Breeders/Owners: Gary & Harriet Short, Iowa.

Dual Ch. Uodibar's PDQ von Waldtaler (Field Ch. Uodibar's Boss Man ex Ch. Whiskey Creek Whirlwind). Owner, L. Soules, Texas.

Field & Natl. Field Ch. Uodibar's Rachel, owned by Lynn T. Hadlock, Illinois. Her credits include GSPCA Field Dog (All Age) of 1978; NGSPCA National (All Age) 1978 and 1980 NGPDA 1980 All Age. Her "Boss Man" heritage is enhanced through her dam, Her Nibs of Navaho, with solid-block "Big Island" breeding in back.

again demonstrated the ability of the field-slanted to seize upon the proffered advantage of the show-breds. Both sides of breeding ventures provide examples. Thus, against show-oriented Ch. Adam v. Fuehrerheim's ability to get a Dual to his credit from a bitch that was solid-block Greif v. Hundsheimerkogel both sides of her breeding, plus a Field trialer out of a Tip Top Timmy bred, there is the interesting circumstance of Field Ch. Windy Hill Prince James, a Field-trial producer of considerable note and success, having become honored by a trio of show champions—whence? Dual Ch. Cede Mein Dolly Der Orrian!

FIELD Ch. WINDY HILL PRINCE JAMES	(*Tri State Trooper ex Windy Hill Whylimina*)
Breeder: A. Dax.	
Owner: John Urso, Wisconsin.	
DUAL Ch. Patche Prince James	(*Her Nibs of Navaho*)
Ch. Dee Tee's Catrina v. James	(*Dual Ch. Cede Mein Dolly Der Orrian*)
Ch. Dee Tee's Corky v. James	(" " " " " ")
Ch. Dee Tee's Corky v. Timber	(" " " " " ")
Field Ch. Heide V. Uferwald	(*Jimmie's Joy Kosy*)
Field Ch. Otto v. Windyborn	(*AFC, Nat'l Fld Ch. Andora v. Holkenborn*)
Field & AFC Oak Creek Weekend Widowmaker	(*Dual Ch. Ridgeland's Frauline*)
Field & AFC Char-Don's Prince Jager	(*Tip Top Taffy*)
Field Ch. Windy Hill's Toby	(*Saxony's Brandy*)
Field & AKC Erik's Rum Runner	(*Field Ch. Hurckes Katrina Kontrary*)

Updated count credits this stud with around at least 30 Field Champions more to the last, the 1979, published count available at this time. In presenting merely a compression owing to considerations of space in such a publication as this, selection has not been made on any particular basis as to suggested merit, one dog over another. Just as they surfaced in the records . . . and every gunner knows how it is when aim is taken at the flight overhead— some fall to the gun and the rest fly by. . .

Same consideration applies to the presentation of most of the top producers in these times of enormously expanded registration figures.

Field & National Fld Ch. Blick v. Shinback, running brace with Prince James so far as production count is concerned, is also noteworthy in that he was the medium of providing another stud with a splendid boost in terms of his competitive performances—he, the son of German import Esser's Chick and a grandly prepotent bitch of name that proclaims her background—Melissa v. Greif, who

294

comes down the pike by way of a dam that was a granddaughter of Am/Can. Dual Ch. Gretchen v. Grief. Sire side Melissa was a Field Ch. Von Thalberg Fritz II daughter, and a welter of best German breeding takes up the fourth generation in back. For Esser's Chick the mating was fortune itself—and as has been the case with other sires, the fame attaching to the occasion brought him a succession of other good bitches to consolidate his fame. Field Ch. Blick, National Field Trial winner in 1969, has made the very best of his stud opportunities, though but brief documentation can be in these pages accommodated:

FIELD & NAT'L FIELD Ch. BLICK V. SHINBACK	(*Esser's Chick* (*imp. Ger*) *ex Melissa v. Greif*)
Breeder: John Hulcy	
Owner: Bradley M. Calkins, Colorado	
DUAL Ch. Bar n' Sandy	(*Ch. Radback's Carin*)
Field & NAT'L Field Ch. Wyatt's Gip v. Shinback	(*Ch. Ginger v. Bess*)
Field & AFC Blick v. Shinback's Shaun	(*Sierra Apollo Rae*)
Field & AFC Blick's Sierra Hondo	(" " ")
Field Ch. Duchess v. Shinback	(" " ")
Field Ch. Blick's Miss Sierra Dawn Jill	(" " ")
Ch. Hoofer's Enough	(" " ")
Ch. Schatzi v. Jango	(*Val's Heide v. Schmoldt*)
Ch. Jamocha von Jango Cando	(" " " ")
Field & AFC Blick v. Shinback's Ace High	(*Moesgaard's Maggie*)
Field Ch. Shilo v. Hessenwald	(*Field & AFC Jetta Liz Fesmire*)

Field Ch. Blick, too, will greet the official tabulations of numbers in the next-issued Year Book with a vastly expanded count of his get.

For Esser's Chick, the fortune of the Melissa v. Greif encounter which had so much modern impact—the siring not only of Fld/NFC Blick (above) but also of a superbly proven prepotent bitch in Blick's litter sister, Field & Nat'l Field Ch Ammertal's Kitt v. Shinback, *her* produce including 1980's GSPCA National winner, sired by Field Ch. Uodibar's Boss Man, being Ammertal's Boss Ranfer)—was partnered also with another stroke of best fortune. His Dual Ch. Esser's Duke v.d. Wildburg came onto his record through the contribution offered by Da Lor's Brandie v.d. Wildburg, an inbred Kay produce, Kay to his daughter, Dual Ch. Fee v.d. Wildburg (ex Fld Ch. My Ritzie Fer Gitunburdz).

With credentials so presented, the fortune of Esser's Chick went steadily forward, show and field champions sired, and in back, of course, he had the support of his own famed sire, Axel v. Wasserschling.

ESSER'S CHICK (imp. Germany)   (*Axel v. Wasserschling ex Jager's Nana*)
Breeder: Ludwig Esser (Ger)
Owner: Colonel Darwin Brock, Virginia

K.S. Anka v. Ichenheim (Germany-blk-ticked) (Kleeman Auslese Prüfung, 1968)	
DUAL Ch. Esser's Duke v.d. Wildburg	(*Da-Lor's Brandie v.d. Wildburg*)
Field & NAT'L Fld Ch. Block v. Shinback	(*Melissa v. Greif*)
Field & NAT'L Fld Ch. Ammertal's Kitt v. Shinback	(" " ")
Field & AFC Rieko v. Shinback	(" " ")
Field & AFC Schling v. Shinback	(" " ")
Field & AFC Arno v. Shinback	(*Hulcy's Katie v. Shinback*)
Field & AFC Kleine Schelle v. Heiligsepp	(*Field Ch. Kleine Bombe v. Heiligsepp*)
Field Ch. Lutz v. Heiligsepp	(" " " " ")
Ch. Crystalwood's Daisy v. Esser	(*Crystalwood's Katrina*)
Ch. Crystalwood's Stormy v. Esser	(" ")
Ch. Crystalwood's Tanya v. Esser	(" ")
Ch. Crystalwood's Zero v. Esser	(" ")
Ch. Misty Morn of Sigma Tau Gamma	(*Watrous Sugar Joy*)

. . . *und so weiter und so weiter,* as Chick might have heard it expressed in the land of his birth, his production cover at least a couple of dozen more, show and field.

There was—for years *and years!*—that California stalwart, Field & Nat'l Field Ch. Rip Traf v. Bess, owned by the Hardens, Gene and Ercia, one of the sequence of Von Thalberg's Fritz II get that came out of the Von Bess breedings with their mortgage for years on National Field Trial placings, Field Ch. Mitzi Grabenbruch Beckum his dam. He sired a National Field Ch. for his own reputation, Cede Mein Georgie Girl (ex Dual Ch. Erdenreich's Jetta Beckum which, as we all know by now is back again to old Fritz II through his son, Dual Ch. Zipper der Orrian.) Credited with 21 Field Chs. and two show champions besides, Rip Traf is by numbers tabulated a notch above his sire in the 1979 GSPCA Year Book—provoking again the thought that the more one studies numbers-ratings, the less sense do they make!

296

Rip Traf also impressed in terms of longevity, siring a litter at age 15 which, of course, would have required AKC approval. He ran his first Field trial in 1963 and his last in 1975 to a count of 50 FT wins, 143 placements, the winning of a National F.T. championship and the placing in two others, plus 47 All-Age Stakes won. If it is records are to be sought, this is one not to miss.

Records? Well, there are in all breeds records and records—in Shorthairs it is Adam v. Fuehrerheim's show championship get— not to forget his couple of field trial titleds as a bonus. As no equitable arrangement can position a hundred-and-a-quarter titles to the credit of one dog in this present work, considering that space restriction would thereby cancel out one or two others not quite so spectacular in the numerical sense but equally notable in terms of value to the ongoing breed, it seems cross-sectioning of get in terms of the most outstanding ladies in Adam's life might be at least one fair way.

So, one looks first to Gretchenhof Tally Ho, already tabulated in the bracketings of the sensational inheritance down from Ch. Columbia River Jill. This union yielded Adam's son exerting the greatest on-going influence in terms of present-day breedings, Ch. Whispering Pines Patos. *His* modernly operative sons, Ch. Fieldfines Count Rambard (ex Fieldfines Tascha) and the strikingly photogenic Ch. Bleugras Roll-On Columbia (ex Ch. Rudean's Columbia River Katy, she a Ch. Gretchenhof Columbia River daughter ex Columbia-River-loaded Ch. Cede Mein Gadabout Jill (ex Ch. Cede Mein Gadabout CD) both haul interest back to source—basics.

From the same union (Adam/Tally Ho) comes also Ch. Whispering Pines Ranger that has triggered another ongoing prepotence though a splendid show and usefully prepotent bitch in Ch. Lieblinghaus Snowstorm. Snowstorm's dam, Ch. Mein Liebchen von Werner, C.D., carries us back again to Square One in that she results from a mating of yet another Adam/Tally Ho son, Ch. Grouse Manor Windstorm, with a very usefully-proven brood in Ch. Harkin's Hi-Dee-Ho, a Ch. Fleigen Meister's Gunner daughter. Snowstorm's breeding record, presently to be examined, shows the same owner-breeder inclination to reach back behind Tally Ho to strongest possible Columbia River influence.

Ch. Whispering Pines Patos, a handsome, successful show dog as well as prepotent sire was not overly long-lived, which would seem to have been regrettable, as the ongoing eminence of his get suggests. Assessing some trends in present-day breeding, one guesses his strong body, good-muscled, properly angulated thighs—neither over nor under—as his photographs preserve, could be with advantage utilized in some parts of the country.

Next lady of importance in Adam's life, Ch. Traveler v. Waldtaler, presently top producing dam in GSPCA records—after, of course, that runaway first Dolly Der Orrian!—is presently credited with 17 champion produce, of which 12 are Adam v. Fuehrerheim sired. Her own breeding owes to yet another provenly prepotent strain—Albrecht—down by way of Dual Ch. Dino v. Albrecht who had all that Big Island show inheritance in gift. Her dam presents an unexpected welding of Columbia River (by way of Ch. Columbia River Gunsmoke) with Moesgaard through my old friend, Field Ch. Moesgaard's Ruffy. All her champions carry Arawak prefix:

CH. TRAVELER VON WALDTALER   *(Ch. Pati-Lyn's Silver Bullet ex Link's Patty of Rockin-Pas)*

Breeder: Patricia L. Toner
Owners: S. & R. Abel, Florida

Ch. Arawak Bummin' Around	*(Ch. Adam v. Fuehrerheim)*
Ch. Arawak Vagabond	(" " " ")
Ch. Arawak King of the Road	(" " " ")
Ch. Arawak Rambling Rose	(" " " ")
Ch. Arawak Wanderlust	(" " " ")
Ch. Arawak Anheuser Busch	(" " " ")
Ch. Arawak Explorer	(" " " ")
Ch. Arawak St. Pauli's Girl	(" " " ")
Ch. Arawak Miller's High Life	(" " " ")
Ch. Arawak Carling	(" " " ")
Ch. Arawak Olympia von Jordan	(" " " ")
Ch. Arawak Sentimental Journey	(" " " ")

To spare chance of confusion with the ongoing strain name, it would seem wise here to interpolate this bitch's get by another stud—Ch. Conrad's Brio—also a good strong-winning dog in his own right.

AM/CAN. CH. CONRAD'S BRIO   *(Ch. Mika Mika v. Gartensteole ex Missy v. Nevins)*

Breeder/Owners: G. & N. Conrad.

Ch. Arawak Foxy Lady in Blue	*(Ch. Traveler von Waldtaler)*
Ch. Arawak Blue Angel	(" " " ")
Ch. Arawak Blues in the Night	(" " " ")
Ch. Arawak Misty Blue	(" " " ")
Ch. Arawak Blue Bayou	(" " " ")

Ceres of Hidden Hollow, 1979 Dam of the Year (Field). (Knight ex Middleton's Girl). Breeder: L. Middleton. Owner: E. Hollowell, New Jersey. Ceres, with an interesting backline of pedigree that draws upon a batch of splendid dogs of the '50s and '60s, has proven her prepotency with her direct get of eight that includes Field and AFC titled as well as a Dual Ch. Her grandget is carrying on the endowment in which equable temperament proper to a personal hunting dog predominates.

Ch. Warrenwood's Kandy Kane, a next producing mate, shares sire with Ch. Adam v. Fuehrerheim, both by Swedish import, Ch. Adam, with Kandy Kane claiming Cindy of Warrenwood for dam, Cindy having been sired by Dual & Nat'l Ch. Dandy Jim v. Feldstrom ex Am/Can. Ch. Susanna Mein Liebchen C.D. Her best son, Ch. Warrenwood's Alfie, earns accolade by in his turn siring a daughter Dual Ch. in Hidden Hollow's Pleasure (ex Ceres of Hidden Hollow).

CH. WARRENWOOD'S KANDY KANE	(*Ch. Adam (imp. Sweden) ex Cindy of Warrenwood*)				
Ch. Warrenwood's Alfie	(*Ch. Adam v. Fuehrerheim*)				
Ch. Warrenwood's Nutmaker Blaze	("	"	"	"	)
Ch. Warrenwood's Lollypop	("	"	"	"	)
Ch. Warrenwood's Brickel, C.D	("	"	"	"	)
Ch. Warrenwood's Kandy Klown, C.D.	("	"	"	"	)
Ch. Warrenwood's Honey Nougat	("	"	"	"	)
Ch. Warrenwood's Kandy Kane II	("	"	"	"	)
Ch. Warrenwood's Magic of Murpheus	("	"	"	"	)
Ch. Warrenwood's Major Hoops	("	"	"	"	)
Ch. Pop's Judson of Warrenwood	("	"	"	"	)

Interesting contributing force comes in terms of the dam of Ch. Warrenwood's Alfie's Dual ch. daughter, Hidden Hollow's Pleasure. She is Ceres of Hidden Hollow, owned by Hidden Hollow Kennels—E. & H. Hollowell, New Jersey. She has a most interesting and ongoing-by-generation record of production, crowned most recently by her whelping Field Ch. Hidden Hollow's Go Go Girl to her grandson, Field & AFC Ch. Hidden Hollow's Ronlord Ruler, She has enjoyed being featured in the GSPCA Year Book as a Dam of the Year, and is reported now, at age 13, to be still the ruling matriarch, teaching the young 'uns at home how to conduct their trade. She represents, as do so many of her unpromoted like, that produce without which a breed cannot function, the steadily-on-going matron able to endow her get with on-going quality.

Ch. Harkins HiDi-Ho, the Fleigen Meister's Gunner daughter just mentioned, her sire a notable producer of a couple of decades ago, honored in GSPCA tabulations with 37 show champions, has also produced well to Ch. Adam v. Fuehrerheim, a total of 6 champion get. In like bracketing is to find the California-domiciled Ch. Machtoloff's Chukar Hill Pride (Ch. Blitzkreig v. Weltmeister/Ch. Burgen v. Grabenbruch) of background close matched with that of basic Erdenreich breeding at Sonoma. The Machtoloff bitch has produced four of her six champions to Adam, the other two are from Ch, Bangabird Link of Hi-Hollow.

Continuing the count of bitches with multiple Adam get, there is Ch. Rocky Run's Poldi (Ch. Rocky Run's Rascal/Deda v. Fuehrerheim) with 6 champions topped by that other strong producing Adam son, Ch. Rocky Run's Stony, to date with a credit of 8 of his own. Count also Ch. Birdacre Amber Doll (Ch. Johelsie's Kraft of Hoyne/Ch. Kaposia's Dancing Wind.) The Amber Doll addition to the record roll call was also 6—of which Ch. Birdacre's Aruba has made most next-generation impact, sharing parentage with Ch. Amber Ace—Bit of Amber—Moonshot—Chantilly Lace—Windstorm, all of which carry the Birdacre strain name.

The overflow—and there are so many—come in production tallies of twos or perhaps as singleton champions from a wide range of bitches. Now, a second generation is present, of which Ch. Field-fines Count Rambard is the most actively before the public—not only as a successful show stud but even, at advancing age, still a factor in show competition, carrying off major trophies, bests of breed, even from veteran classes.

Third generation representation is also being honored by the produce of Ch. Lieblinghaus Snowstorm; in retirement from show successes this beautiful bitch was put back to Ch. Whispering Pines Patos, full brother to her sire. Ch. Whispering Pines Ranger, producing from the inbreeding a brace of champions in Chs. Lieblinghaus Starshine and Lieblinghaus Storm Trooper. Her owners, thereafter, plainly made choice to throw in their luck with Columbia River, first in a mating with Ch. Gretchenhof Columbia River, from which resulted also a brace of titleds, Chs. Lieblinghaus Storm Hawk CD and Ch. Lieblinghaus April Snow and subsequently with Ch. Gretchenhof Columbia River's son, Ch. Gretchenhof Westminster (ex Gretchenhof Moonsong.) At time of this compilation,

Ch. Lieblinghaus Snowstorm (Ch. Whispering Pines Ranger ex Ch. Mein Liebchen von Werner, DC). A top show bitch, "Stormy" has also proven herself a good producer. Breeders/Owners: Dennis and Ruth Ann Ricci, New Jersey.—*Ashbey*

the latter mating had already fielded five titleds, with several others on the way.

In the time of her show career, Snowstorm had many admirers. Her production record will not disappoint the expectations of those that take time to examine it.

Undoubtedly, Am/Can. Ch. Fieldfines Count Rambard, however, is the one steadily making his way to the peak of the prevailing production scene. further carrying along the Whispering Pines Patos influence in step with Lieblinghaus Snowstorm and the on-going champions from Bleugras. As for Rambard's production, exclusively show in the manner of his grandsire, it has to be subjected also to trimming in interest of space.

AM/CAN. CH. FIELDFINES COUNT RAMBARD *(Ch. Whispering Pines Patos ex Fieldfines Tascha)*

Breeder/Owners: R. & D. Vooris, N.Y.

Am/Can. Ch. Fieldfines Lord Tanner (BIS)	*(Ch. Cinnamon Duchess)*
Ch. Rutlan's Dusty Dan of Sheridan	(" " ")
Ch. Challenger v. Field Fine (BIS)	*(Ehrick's Jaeger Traum)*
Can. Ch. Field Fines River Shannon	*(Shaas River Risque)*
Ch. Wilhelm Augustus v. Steuben	(" " ")
Ch. Fieldfines Foxey Lady	(" " ")
Ch. Fieldfines American Beauty	(" " ")
Ch. Fieldfines Winterweed	(" " ")
Ch. Fieldfines Little Feather	(" " ")
Ch. Fieldfines Pride of Kingswood	*(Am/Can. Ch. Wentworth's)*
Ch. Kingswood's Shady Lady	*(Happy Wanderer, C.D.)*
Ch. Kingswood's Lusty Lucas	(" " ")
Ch. Kingswood's Happy Hunter	(" " ")
Ch. Kingswood's Chocolate Chip	(" " ")
Ch. Kingswood's Night Tide	(" " ")
Ch. Kingswood's Gilda	(" " ")
Ch. Wentworth's Benchmark, CD	(" " ")
Ch. Fieldfines Dawn of Stillwater	*(Fieldfines Lady of Stillwater)*
Ch. Fieldfines Lady Luck	(" " " ")
Ch. Fieldfines Summer Breeze	(" " " ")
Ch. Fieldfines Top Choice	*(Fieldfines Jillard)*
Ch. Sheridan's Brandy of Fieldfines	(" ")

Am./Can. Ch. Fieldfines Count Rambard (Ch. Whispering Pines Patos ex Fieldfines Tascha). Breeder/Owners: D and R. Vooris, New York. This distinguished stud seems likely to hold the fort against all contenders for the honor of being named Top Producer within the show dog sphere for the 1980s.

Count Rambard's production stretches far past this brief resume, and with many ongoing champions still likely to honor him, will positively have more to boast about when next GSPCA's ratings are published.

Also of interest, overlooking Rambard production, is one of his partners, Am/Can. Ch. Wentworth's Happy Wanderer, C.D. Seemingly bound for the heights, glimpse of her ongoing production to another stud has interest:

AM/CAN. CH. WENTWORTH'S HAPPY WANDERER, C.D.   (*Jaeger v. Langstadt ex Northview's Lady*)
Owner: J. Burns, New York
  Ch. Kingswood Our Sportsman   (*By Ch. Nock's Chocolate Chip*)
  Ch. Kingswood's Royal Flush   ("   "   "   "   ")
  Ch. Kingswood's Encore   ("   "   "   "   ")
  Ch. Kingswood's Rolling Thunder   ("   "   "   "   ")

Follows the stud that seemed likeliest to challenge Rambard for the production throne of the '80s, Ch. Gretchenhof Columbia River, known the continent across as "Traveller," and the close to home kept pride of Jo Shellenbarger who shared his triumphs. It is sad to be at need to report that at the time this material was being put together, the super show dog being 12½ yrs old, has just left the scene. Undoubtedly, there are many of his get yet to become added to the eventual tally of the titleds.

Am./Can. Ch. Fieldfines Lord Tanner (Am./Can. Ch. Fieldfines Count Rambard/Cinnamon Duchess). This elegant, dark-tick-patch dog has usefully demonstrated the lasting qualities of the breed, having his best successes when well along in years, including BOB at the 1980 GSPCA National Specialty and following with all-breed BIS honors at a period when (late '70s, early '80s) the honor was become increasingly rare in the breed. Owners: L. and M. Shulman, Vermont—*Ashbey*

Ch. Fieldfines Ribbons, wh. 1978, (Ch. Fieldfines Rocky Run ex Ch. Fieldfines River Shannon). This lovely Count Rambard granddaughter is compiling a standout show record that includes BOB at Westminster 1982. Owned by Joyce Oesch and Kathleen Plotts (Pa.) she was bred by Allen Vooris and Debra Strnad, and is handled by Dot Vooris of the Fieldfine Kennels.

CH. GRETCHENHOF COLUMBIA RIVER   *(Gretchenhof Moonfrost ex Columbia River Della)*

Breeder: L. V. McGilbrey, Washington
Owner: Gretchenhof Kennels,
   California.

Ch. Bleugras Rambling River Tilly	*(Ch. Cede Mein Gadabout Jill)*
Ch. Rudean's Columbia River Katy	(" " , " " ")
Ch. Columbia River Britches	(" " " " ")
Ch. Columbia River Domino	(" " " " ")
Ch. Royal River Ms G's Fancy Me	*(Ch. Cede Mein Mizzen Royal)*
Ch. Marlene Schoene Diana	(" " " " ")
Ch. Royal River Spectrum	(" " " " ")
Ch. Columbia River Super Star	(" " " " ")
Ch. Royal River Misty Morn	(" " " " ")
Ch. Country Acres Columbia Jac	(" " " " ")
Ch. Von Dunwyck Rosie	(" " " " ")
Ch. Shaas River Reflection	*(Ch. Shaas Haas v. Franzel)*
Ch. Shaas River Traveller	(" " " " ")
Ch. Shaas River Racer	(" " " " ")
Ch. Shaas Von Chances Are	(" " " " ")
Ch. Shaas River Boat	(" " " " ")
Ch. Gretchenhof Westminster	*(Gretchenhof Moonsong)*
Ch. Gretchenhof Windjammer	(")
Ch. Gretchenhof Fredericus Rex	(" ")
Ch. Gretchenhof Damfino	*(Gretchenhof Moonwalk)*
Ch. Jamohr's Moonriver	(" ")
Ch. Jamohr's Harvest Moon	(" ")
Ch. Jamohr's Moon Shot	(" ")
Ch. Hollyhof Colonel Shaas	*(Gretchenhof Moondance)*
Ch. Gretchenhof Hussong	(" ")
Ch. Hollyhof Dancer's Circle	(" ")
Ch. Hollyhof Dark Town Strutter	(" ")
Ch. Cedarpark Bold Venture	*(Ch. Wetherling Whispering Pines)*
Ch. Cedarpark Brandywine	(" " . ")
Ch. Lieblinghaus April Snow	*(Ch. Lieblinghaus Snowstorm)*
Ch. Lieblinghaus Storm Hawk	(" " ")
Ch. Minado's Travelling Salesman	*(Ch. Callmac's Mariah v. Minado)*
Ch. Xavier's Darth Vade	*(Geezee Coronet Brandy Chaser)*
Ch. Xavier's Free Spirit	(" " " ")
Ch. Xavier's Holland's Mischief	(" " " ")
Ch. Jagerstraum's Bound for Glory	*(Ch. DeeTee's Flambeau v. Greif)*
Ch. Moonraker's Here I Am	*(Maggie v. Wildburg, CD)*
Ch. Shellbrook's Merry June	*(Ch. Shellbrook's Megan)*
Ch. Shellbrook's Silver Dollar	(" " ")
Ch. Wing King of Bradenburg	*(Ch. Heidie v. Bradenburg, C.D.)*
Ch. Princess of Brandenburg	(" " " ")
Ch. Indian Country Columbia Moon	*(Ch. Columbia River Moon Mist)*

*   *   *   *   *

Am. & Can. Ch. Gretchenhof Columbia River making breed history with win of Best in Show at Westminster in 1974 under judge Len Carey. "Traveller's"AKC record included 29 BIS, 102 G1, 44 other Group placings, and 182 BOBs including 3 independent Specialties. Bred by L. V. McGilbrey, owned by Dr. Richard Smith and handled by Joyce Shellenbarger.

C.D. Lawrence, having for health reasons bowed away from the show and breeding scene to which he contributed so much thoughtfully-arranged welding of basic lines, it would seem that the most dedicated retention—the gathering, the using—of the Columbia River inheritance may now be in the hands of a tireless student of pedigree and its application in Mrs. Eve Spanic Atkins, of Wisconsin, building up her Bleugras strain with some very solid-grained Columbia-River-breds that trace not only to rock-basic Columbia River, but add in Fld. Ch. Von Thalberg's Fritz II, through daughter Am/Can. Ch. Zeugencarl's Elsa v. Ida (9 chs.-most Am/Can. titled). Elsa's daughter, Ch. Cede Mein Gadabout, C.D., is the pipeline—as under:

CH. CEDE MEIN GADABOUT, C.D.	(*Am/Can. Ch. Columbia River Moon-watcher/Am/Can. Ch. Zeugencarl's Elsa v. Ida*)

Breeder: C.D. Lawrence, Wash.
Owner: G. & N. Hoenig, Idaho

Am/Can.Ch. Cede Mein Chat Nuga Chu Chu (Multiple BIS)	(*Am/Can. Ch. Cede Mein Brass Badge*)
Am/Can. Ch. Zede Mein Denali Stormcloud	(" " " " " ")
Am/Can. Ch. Cede Mein Charo of the Bastion	(" " " " " ")
Ch. Cede Mein Gadabout Jill	(" " " " " ")
Ch. Cede Mein Thundercloud, C.D.	(" " " " " ")
Ch. Cede Mein Red Baron	(" " " " " ")
Ch. Cede Mein Cash Flow plus Winsome	(" " " " " ")
Ch. Cede Mein Sally	(" " " " " ")

It was a daughter of Ch. Cede Mein Gadabout Jill of this breeding that drew attention of Mrs. Eve Spanic (now Atkins) who had been spending much time examining the compilation of pedigrees she had put together over a long period in preparation for establishing a strain of her own. With intended emphasis on Columbia River, she had acquired the Gadabout Jill daughter she named Bleugras Ramblin' River Tilly. Pleased with Tilly, she had made the tremendous plunge of buying in three of Tilly's littermates! They were (later Chs.) Rudean's Columbia River Katy; Columbia River Britches; Columbia River Domino.

"I chose Columbia River for the carefully inbred generations that would save me years of time," Mrs. Atkins explains. "The elderly gentleman in Idaho who owned Gadabout Jill told me he knew nothing of pedigrees; that Jill was his personal hunting dog and that when it came time to breed her he decided nothing but the best for her. When he was told "Traveller" (Ch. Gretchenhof Columbia River) was the best—that's where Jill went!"

Could be this will prove to be major Columbia River conveyance to end of the century—a tremendous venture of building back from four close-bred littermates.

"It seems to be working out," the dedicated student concedes as 1981 draws to a close. "There had been the inevitable heartaches and false starts and wrong directions over earlier years, but now the plan is solidifying and a definite strain emerging."

Ch. Geezee Super Chief (Charisma Columbia River ex Geezee Missy). 1975 BIS winner. Breeder: D. L. Padie. Owners: D. and D. Gilliam, California.

As to the definite strain: when the four littermates were safe in her yard, she sent Ch. Rudean's Columbia River Katy to Ch. Whispering Pines Patos (Adam/Tally Ho) recalling that Katy's grandam, was Ch. Gretchenhof Tradewind, Tally Ho's littermate in that fabulous dam production, the Col. River Jills . . . Though Adam represented complete outcross, the tireless student was able to dig from her papers, that way back on his dam's side was Ch. Rex v. Krawford, sire of Ch. Columbia River Jill's dam, Helga v. Krawford. . .

All very complicated, makes the ears buzz in the relation. . .

From Patos/Katy came Ch. Bleugras Roll On Columbia, with already 12 titled get, of which the most successful to date would be Ch. Bleugrass Hi-Rolling Huntabird (wh. Feb. '79) whose everlengthening win-list, at this time of compilation, counts the Chicago International K.C. and GSPC of Illinois Specialty double, Oct. 1981, as latest honors to include. Ch. Bleugras Ramblin' River Tilly, the original purchase, reaches Top Producing Dam status this same year with a count of 5 titled, Group and Specialty winning produce.

Of course, pedigree unravellings notwithstanding, it still takes two to tango—even the most prepotent of bitches can't do it all . . . any more than can the most prepotently assesed of sires.

Ch. Whispering Pines Patos (Ch. Adam v. Fuehrerheim ex Gretchenhof Tally Ho). Owners: A. and F. Stephanatos, Eatonton, Georgia. "Monarch" they called him, and well they might—with his outstanding get of 21 keeping him still high in the GSPCA tabulations though he had gone early to his rest. He counts among his get Ch. Fieldfines Count Rambard, Ch. Bleugras Roll-on-Columbia and Ch. Lieblinghaus Starshine.—*Gilbert*

Ch. Bleugras Roll-on-Columbia (Ch. Whispering Pin Patos ex Ch. Rudean's Columbia River Katy). Breede Owners: Eve and Gordon Atkins, Wisconsin. Throug his dam, he brings together the influence of two fro the famous Ch. Columbia River Jill litter, Ch. Ka coming through Ch. Cede Mein Gadabout Jill dow from Ch. Gretchenhof Tradewind.—*Olson*

Ch. Bleugras Hi-Rollin' Huntabird (Ch. Bleugras Roll-on-Columbia ex Ch. Huntabird Last Chance). Owners: Eve and Gordon Atkins, Wisconsin. Wh. 2/6/79, by end of 1981 Huntabird had already garnered 50 BOBs and 4 Specialty awards, demonstrating additionally intention to Keep A'Goin'.

15

Picking Shorthair Pups

THE litter safely in the nest, check first for abnormalities, happily rare in this breed. Salvage attempts are usually ill-advised. If the litter is very large, at least consider reduction. Six or so, sharing the cafeteria, do fine, make no trouble for anyone; twelve or so can be an intolerable burden to the novice with no facilities. It is also one of the facts of dog-breeding life that novices unknown in the dog world often have trouble selling their pups. Big kennels can cope—what's a few more pups when you're already feeding fifty? The one-bitch owner, of moderate means, working at something else all day, can find a large litter expensive, and unrewarding, too.

When picking over whelps it helps to know the background of your strain. For example, some strains are male-producing, some produce better bitches. Why? No one seems to have the answer. In such cases, it is usually better to work with, rather than against, Nature. If you own a dam from a strongly bitch-producing line, say, don't set your heart beforehand on getting from her a male to set the show world afire. The chances are you won't get him.

Sorting whelps by size alone can also lead you into steel-jawed traps for young players. The snap decision to eliminate all little ones or all big ones could be costly. If you are inexperienced, you could use the help of a breeder who knows the score. Size is trickily comparative. Not long ago, in another breed, we were shown a litter of four. One was tiny; two, medium-sized, were a pair; the fourth looked like the cuckoo in the nest. Now the litter is grown, the tiny is a freak, and the medium pair are undersized. Only the "cuckoo" is correct for size.

In situations like this, value the help of an experienced breeder, especially one who has kept records, weighed and measured pups at birth, checked figures against the size of the dogs when adult.

Many experienced breeders like to check the litter within 24 hours or so after birth. From then on, pups change almost hourly. A newborn can show a fair preview of eventual conformation. Hold it up in the air between your two hands, supporting the head and the hindquarters. The legs will drop down into what would be standing position. This lets you see shoulder lay that governs length of neck, back, loin. Depth of chest you will see (and perhaps better than you will be able to see it again for many a month), and you can see if the ribs are barrel or desirably curved. Out-turned "Charlie Chaplin" feet will show, and a wide forechest, and tail-set.

One of the finest breeders of my acquaintance schooled me in this method. Plucking a new pup from its dam she'd hold it out: "See? See that back, loin, shoulder? If they're not there now, Sister, believe me, they're NEVER going to be!"

German Shorthaired Pointer heads are inclined to be less informative at the new pup stage than are the heads of some other breeds. Yet, all things being equal, the big coarse head on the whelp can be expected to sit, later on, in front of a big coarse dog. Head tendency seems always to be towards more in growth rather than less.

At a later stage, good bone is a must, always remembering that pups "grow up" to their legs and feet. Skin can be difficult for a novice, saggy all over and draped under the chin; but apart from plainly throaty ones, most German Shorthaired Pointers seem to grow into their skins.

The stages-of-growth frights that bedevil all who rear pups come a little later on. Pups never seem to grow all over at the same time, but push up first one end, then the other. These heavings-aloft cancel each other out by maturity, but in the meantime they can give an inexperienced owner fits.

310

It's a lucky dog breeder that goes along without letting a flyer pup slip through his fingers. Many have the bad luck to sell the litter pick. Many have the good luck to buy it back again. Picking pups successfully calls for luck and the wind with you, as the sailors say. But even if it is your incredible luck to pick out the best one, don't forget that that's just the starting point. The transient world of dog showing is full of people who expect their untrained, unshaped, unpolished dog to do great things just because he is well-born.

In picking an older pup—say in another kennel, with a view to purchase—make your first measure temperament. No matter how good the conformation, how *pretty* the dog, how fast or how stylish, if his temperament isn't good, you are buying only frustration. If he comes to you bouncing, with tail wagging, that's at least one guarantee that temperament is right. If he runs off with his tail tucked, you'd best remember an engagement somewhere else.

If you have mastered your Standard and looked over some good dogs, you should have at least a good idea what to look for. You want bone and balance, a head with a big nose and flared nostrils. You'll turn from a snipy muzzle—*that's* not for picking up fine fat pheasants! You'll look at the bite, remembering that a pup's mouth is not an adult's. Very *slightly* overshot—time will usually fix that. Undershot, *no matter how slightly,* reject. Eyes? Don't take a pup with greeny-yellow eyes. Honey-yellow—yes. Up-ended quarters shouldn't worry you much in adolescence, if the rear-end assembly angulation is right. But if his hocks are overlong and his thighs straight sticks, you won't like what he has later on. Wide chests remain wide chests (they get wider!). Barrel ribs remain barrel ribs. Feet? You can't overlook feet. Pups' feet in these big sporting breeds are *big* feet. But *good* big feet have thick pads in a compact foot, high-arched toes, not spread toes, wide like a duck's.

His parents will be your safest guide. Contrary to the fairy tales, no-goods produce no-goods. One good pup in a mess of rubbish is not for you, either. If that's the one you take home, somewhere along the line the law of averages will catch up with you.

TRAINING THE PUP: The training of your German Shorthaired Pointer is not within the scope of this book. That a training manual for German Shorthaired Pointers is long overdue is self-evident, and the breed in America has suffered for decades because of it. The necessary use of Pointer and Setter manuals for training instruction has not helped to form the breed ideal correctly in the minds of new German Shorthaired Pointer owners. There are many extremely fine and capable professional trainers operating in the breed, and it would be grand if one (or more) would get down to the job of providing a guide for new owners.

Meanwhile, a few observations: First, it is oftenest most important that the *owner* be trained before he attempts to train the pup. If wholly incompetent, especially in terms of a hasty temper—don't try. If you do have the temperament, and you *do* try, and you make a good hunting or field trial dog out of your pride and joy, it will prove one of the most satisfying achievements of your life. If you don't feel competent, shop around before committing yourself to a trainer. There are lots of good ones—and a few bad ones, too!

If you plan to train your bird dog, remember, a first essential is *birds*. If you plan to make him your duck dog, introduce him to water at an early age. It must be wide water, running water; the pan in his run won't do. In the same way, planted birds are poor substitutes for wild ones—but that is often a local problem. You may live where there *are* no wild birds—most of us do. Then you have to settle for the next best.

Don't be sold on fancy methods to get him used to gunfire. The way that is as good as any is to fire off your lighter artillery while he's chasing around, having fun—he'll be too preoccupied to be scared. It is important to protect him from hoodlum mischance. A thrown firecracker has ruined many a young sporting dog forever. And if you're a sucker for gadgets, wait a bit, wait till you've properly learned the score in respect to elementary training practice before you load up on the electronics. There are some ruined dogs to show for those, too. You're in the kindergarten class, right? Well, leave the college stuff till you've graduated.

16

German Titles,
Vocabulary, etc.

E VEN with a working knowledge of German, and the help of a dictionary, it can prove hard work translating pedigree information and the show and performance ratings on the papers of imported dogs. The German dog world, like the English or American, has its own language, and words do not always carry the exact dictionary meanings. Abbreviations, much used, make the job even tougher. Names of dogs, as a rule, translate easily, helped by the tendency of German breeders to use their home locality as a strain name. Awards are more complicated, especially in abbreviation. The historically-minded, too, can blunder into confusion because of a re-organization of the canine government that was enforced after 1934 by the Nazi government.

The pre-1934 governing body was the *Deutsches Kartell Für Hundewesen* (DKH). Dogs imported before that time were so sponsored. After 1934, the re-organization brought the body into new being as the *Reichsverband Für Das Deutsche Hundewesen* (RDH), which translates as the Reichs Organization (or Club) for German Dog Affairs. The new body created some confusion by making a retrospective re-issue of pedigrees originally issued by the DKH. Some early-day American imports have certificates from both. The first Nebraska imports (Claus v. Schleswig-Konigsweg and Jane v. grünen Adler) arrived in 1931, were American-registered in 1932. Both have German pedigrees under RDH headings that are dated in Stuttgart (Germany) in 1936. The second brace to Nebraska, several years later, had RDH pedigrees dated 1934. Researchers who have wondered whether there were *two* German canine governing bodies seemingly did not know about the re-organization.

With the establishment of RDH, Specialist clubs catering to various breeds were absorbed as *Fachschafts* (Sections). Each was required to keep a stud book for its breed under the strict supervision of the RDH. In 1937, there came into being the *Reichsverband Deutscher Kleintier Züchter* (Reichs Organization of German Small Animal Breeders), which sponsored the rule that breeding should be permitted only from dogs rated "excellent" or "very good" by approved judges.

Working breeds were required also to have at least one parent possessed of a Training Certificate—an *Ausbildungkennzeichen*—to ensure that the desired working qualities for the individual breeds were within the gift of sire or dam, preferably both. Along with all the re-organization, most of the Specialist Clubs went along as they had been doing, in individual strength. This was and is true of the *Fachschaft Deutsch Kurzhaar* (Klub Kurzhaar), the Parent Club of the German Shorthaired Pointer, with headquarters in Berlin.

Awards are fairly well understood by most importers. *Sieger* and its feminine counterpart, *Siegerin,* denotes champions that have fulfilled the requirements for the title. At first it was sufficient for a dog to have won three First Prizes with a rating of *Vorzüglich,* (Excellent) under three different approved judges at recognized shows. Later it became necessary for sporting or working breeds to qualify by performance as well as conformation.

Early day dogs earned a *Klub Sieger* (K.S.) title, as many of them as could qualify, with a *Jahressieger* (Champion of the Year) to the winner of the annual Specialist show, provided it had the necessary Vorzüglich rating. After the 1934 re-organization, *Fachschaftsieger* became useable for *Klub Sieger,* and the *Jahressieger* title became *Reichssieger* (R.S.) with, of course, the feminine equivalent where the rule of gender applied. Further, at a designated European show, annually, was made the award of *Welt Sieger* (W.S.)—World Champion—to be won in competition with breed representatives from other countries.

ABBREVIATIONS:

D1 or D1A	*Dienst,* or *Dienstsuch Hund* with a rating of 1 or 1A in performance. (*Working Dog or Working Search Dog.*)
S1 or S11	*Such Hund* with a rating of 1 or 11. (*Search Dog.*)
G.H.St.B	*Gebrauchshund Stammbuch.* The general studbook for Field and Working breeds. It was originated in 1902 as the *Gebrauchsund-Luxushunde* (*Utility and Toy Dog*): *Stammbuch,* catering for the 17 breed specialist clubs then publishing their own studbooks.
Z.K.	*Zuchtbuch Kurzhaar,* the Studbook of the German Shorthaired Pointer breed in Germany.
m.S.	Sharpness Test (killing a cat or a fox under the inspection of two judges.)
F.W.	*Formwert.* (*Conformation marks.*)

Adult imports usually bring the record of their field performances as abbreviations entered on their registrations, and often as separate sheets of performance rating, signed by the judges. Each aspect of the dog's work is separately rated .

To comply with the rules of the *Jagdebrauchshundverband* (Hunting Dog Club), performance is assessed, as in the top left-hand corner, by numbers:

0	*Ungenügend*	Insufficient
1	*Genügend*	Sufficient
2	*Ziemlich Gut*	Fairly Good
3	*Gut*	Good
4	*Sehr Gut*	Very Good
4h	*Hervorragend*	Distinguished/Outstanding

A. *Fährtenarbeit*

B. *Feldprüfung* ratings are for *Nase* (Nose), *Suche* (Search), *Vorstehen* (pointing), and *Gehorsam* (Obedience), in all of which this particular young dog (later imported to America) did very well. In *Hasenhetzen* (coursing—hare-chasing) he was marked on voice—*spurlaut* (trail-loud), *sichtlaut* (sight-loud), or *stumm* (silent—dumb). Cosak's combined markings earned him his *Erteilter Preis* (awarded Prize) of 1 d and 4th place in his Prize-class (*Preisklasse*).

Club Utility Search work is assessed on the *Zensurenformblatt für Verbands-Gebrauchsprufüngen* (Assessment Sheet for Club Utility Search). This is divided into four sections: *Waldarbeit* (Forest work), *Wasserarbeit* (Water Work), *Feldarbeit* (Field Work) and *Bringen* (Retrieving). These sections are subdivided and separately marked. *Waldarbeit* alone totals 10 sub-sections, later to be totaled as the *Summe der Urteilsziffer von Sec. I* (Total of Judges' Markings for Sec. 1). *Wasserarbeit* totals 3 sub-sections: Search, Search for Duck in the Reeds, and Retrieving from Deep Water. *Feldarbeit* totals 9 sub-sections, including Nose, Search, Staunch Pointing, Obedience, Steady to Shot, Hare-clean. *Bringen* includes retrieving fur and feather, dealing with beasts of prey (fox or cat), and a final retrieve over an obstacle carrying a fox.

By the time all these separate exercises have been assessed and marked, the judges have compiled a very thorough record of an individual dog's work. What is more, the sheets on which the markings are made are available to the owners, who can take them home to study. There is education as well as satisfaction in such records of performance. However, judges who must so commit themselves to a written record that anyone may scan must be highly competent.

ABBREVIATIONS used in other countries:

F.C.I.   *Federation Cynologique Internationale* (The International European Canine Governing Body).

CACIB   Int. Bench Champion Award made by the F.C.I. Requirement is 3 firsts with the mark of Excellent under 3 different judges. This is the only true "International Championship." This title is often applied to dogs that have won in both America and

Canada, but is not recognized as an International Award by the A.K.C. or elsewhere.

SH. CH.   A British award, applied by the English K.C. to Sporting Dogs that have won the titles on the Bench by accumulating 3 Challenge Certificates under 3 different judges at recognized Championship shows. To gain a full championship title a Sporting dog in this country must first gain his "qualifier" under approved Field Trial judges, proving that he possesses the basic qualities of nose, search, steady to shot, etc.

ABBREVIATIONS used in America:

FIELD CH.   Field Champion.
CH.   Show Champion.
DUAL CH.   Field and Show Champion.
C.D.   Companion Dog (Obedience—1st Stage).
C.D.X.   Companion Dog Excellent (Obedience—2nd Stage).
U.D.   Utility Dog (Obedience—Final Stage).
T.   Tracking Dog.

The first Sporting Dog to hold all the above Titles, and for long the only one, is an Irish Setter, Dual Ch. Red Arrow Show Girl, U.D.T., owned by L. Heist, of Fontana, California. The feat was matched in 1961 by a Weimaraner.

A brief vocabulary, covering much of the information likely to come with dogs from Germany:

Ahnentafel	Pedigree
Ausbildungskennzeichen	Training Qualifications
Ausstellung	Show (Exhibition)
Ausstellung von Hunden Aller Rassen	All-Breed Show
Beachtung	Notice
Besitzer	Owner
Besitzwechsel	Change of Ownership
Beglaubigungen	Certifications
Bewertung	Rating
Bewertungs-karte	Qualifications Card
Breit	Broad
Decken	To cover—to mate
Decktag	Date of Service
Deckurkunde	Certificate of Mating
Dienstssuchhund	Police Tracking Dog
Dientsuchhundprüfung	Police Tracking Trial
Eintragen (im Stammbuch)	Registered (in Stud Book)

Eltern	Parents
Farbe und Abzeichen (als unter)	Color and Markings (as under)
Braun	Brown
Braunschimmel	Brown-ticked
Dreifarbig	Tri-color (lit. Three-colored)
Dunkel (Augen)	Dark (eyes)
Gelb	Yellow
Schwartz	Black
Weiss	White
Führer	Handler
Geschlect	Sex
Gebrauchshund	Utility (Working) Dog
Gewörfen	Whelped (Thrown)
Glaathaar	Smooth (or Short) Hair
Grosseltern	Grandparents
Haar	Hair
Hals	Neck
Hund	Dog (any dog, not specifically Hound)
Hundin	Bitch
Kupiert	Cut
Kurz	Short
Lang	Long
Laufen	Running
Mangelhaft	Mediocre (in Performance, etc.)
Ohren	Ears
Ohrbehang	Ear Carriage
Paarsuche	Brace (in Trials)
Platten	Patches (body color)
Quittung	Receipt
Rassekennzeichen	Breed Standard (Characteristics)
Reichsverband für Deutsche Hundewesen (RDH) (Auslandstelle)	Foreign Dept. of the German Kennel Governing Body
Richtig	Correct
Rüde	Male Dog (Stud)
Rute (Schwanz)	Tail (both words)
Schweisshund	Scenting Dog, Trail Dog—ANY Breed
"Schweisshund"	Bloodhound—when specifically used to describe this breed
Sekundierte	Backed (on a Point)
Siegeraustellung	Championship Show
Stammbuch-Führer	Keeper of the Stud Book
Suchhundprüfung	Tracking Test
Urgrosseltern	Great-grandparents
Wurftag (Wurfdatum)	Whelping Date
Wurfmeldung	Litter Registration
Wurfstärke	Size of litter (number of whelp)
Zimmerrein (also Stubenrein)	Housebroken (lit. Room-clean)
Zuchtbuch	Stud Book
Züchter	Breeder
Zuchtbuch No.	Studbook Number
Zuchtbuch Führer	Studbook Keeper
Zuchthundin (Stammutter)	Foundation bitch

318

Zuchtbuchstelle .... Club Pedigree Register
Zuchtverein .... Specialty Club
Zwinger .... Strain (Strain Name)

Some of the old-style documentation that came in with the earliest imports included an observer's word-picture of the dog. Such a description survives among the Forwarding Documents of Treu v. Saxony, the big dog imported by Dr. Thornton in 1926. As the examining veterinarian, Dr. Albrecht, saw Treu, he was:

"In schöner weiss und braun gefleckter Farbe, kurz und knapp edel im Haar, mit edlen, ausdruckvollen Kopf, langen breiten Ohrbehang und vorschriftsmässig kupierter Rute, gut auf den Läufen gestellt, kräftig entwickelt."

(*Trans.:* "Handsome white and brown flecked color, coat short and excellently close of hair, with an excellent, expressive head, long and broad ear-hang, tail cut according to regulation requirements, well established on his running-gear, strongly developed.")

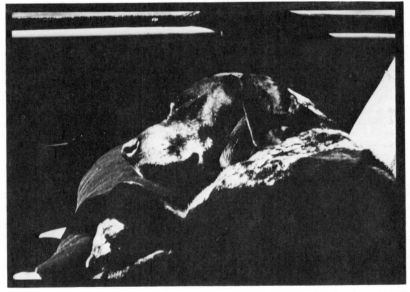

Field Trial Ch. Von Thalberg's Fritz II. Truly, the father of a Nation in terms of his stud work, his get and grandget, titled and untitled, supports some of the greatest prepotencies of our time. Riding home from a day's hunting up in Bitter Root Valley, Montana, be sure his dreaming was sweet.

319

BIBLIOGRAPHY

ALL OWNERS of pure-bred dogs will benefit themselves and their dogs by enriching their knowledge of breeds and of canine care, training, breeding, psychology and other important aspects of dog management. The following list of books covers further reading recommended by judges, veterinarians, breeders, trainers and other authorities. Books may be obtained at the finer book stores and pet shops, or through Howell Book House Inc., publishers, New York.

Breed Books

AFGHAN HOUND, Complete	Miller & Gilbert
AIREDALE, New Complete	Edwards
ALASKAN MALAMUTE, Complete	Riddle & Seeley
BASSET HOUND, Complete	Braun
BEAGLE, Complete	Noted Authorities
BLOODHOUND, Complete	Brey & Reed
BORZOI, Complete	Groshans
BOXER, Complete	Denlinger
BRITTANY SPANIEL, Complete	Riddle
BULLDOG, New Complete	Hanes
BULL TERRIER, New Complete	Eberhard
CAIRN TERRIER, Complete	Marvin
CHESAPEAKE BAY RETRIEVER, Complete	Cherry
CHIHUAHUA, Complete	Noted Authorities
COCKER SPANIEL, New	Kraeuchi
COLLIE, Complete	Official Publication of the Collie Club of America
DACHSHUND, The New	Meistrell
DALMATIAN, The	Treen
DOBERMAN PINSCHER, New	Walker
ENGLISH SETTER, New Complete	Tuck, Howell & Graef
ENGLISH SPRINGER SPANIEL, New	Goodall & Gasow
FOX TERRIER, New Complete	Silvernail
GERMAN SHEPHERD DOG, Complete	Bennett
GERMAN SHORTHAIRED POINTER, New	Maxwell
GOLDEN RETRIEVER, Complete	Fischer
GREAT DANE, New Complete	Noted Authorities
GREAT DANE, The—Dogdom's Apollo	Draper
GREAT PYRENEES, Complete	Strang & Giffin
IRISH SETTER, New	Thompson
IRISH WOLFHOUND, Complete	Starbuck
KEESHOND, Complete	Peterson
LABRADOR RETRIEVER, Complete	Warwick
LHASA APSO, Complete	Herbel
MINIATURE SCHNAUZER, Complete	Eskrigge
NEWFOUNDLAND, New Complete	Chern
NORWEGIAN ELKHOUND, New Complete	Wallo
OLD ENGLISH SHEEPDOG, Complete	Mandeville
PEKINGESE, Quigley Book of	Quigley
PEMBROKE WELSH CORGI, Complete	Sargent & Harper
POMERANIAN, New Complete	Ricketts
POODLE, New Complete	Hopkins & Irick
POODLE CLIPPING AND GROOMING BOOK, Complete	Kalstone
PULI, Complete	Owen
SAMOYED, Complete	Ward
SCHIPPERKE, Official Book of	Root, Martin, Kent
SCOTTISH TERRIER, New Complete	Marvin
SHETLAND SHEEPDOG, The New	Riddle
SHIH TZU, The (English)	Dadds
SIBERIAN HUSKY, Complete	Demidoff
TERRIERS, The Book of All	Marvin
WEST HIGHLAND WHITE TERRIER, Complete	Marvin
WHIPPET, Complete	Pegram
YORKSHIRE TERRIER, Complete	Gordon & Bennett

Breeding

ART OF BREEDING BETTER DOGS, New	Onstot
BREEDING YOUR SHOW DOG, Joy of	Seranne
HOW TO BREED DOGS	Whitney
HOW PUPPIES ARE BORN	Prine
INHERITANCE OF COAT COLOR IN DOGS	Little

Care and Training

DOG OBEDIENCE, Complete Book of	Saunders
NOVICE, OPEN AND UTILITY COURSES	Saunders
DOG CARE AND TRAINING FOR BOYS AND GIRLS	Saunders
DOG NUTRITION, Collins Guide to	Collins
DOG TRAINING FOR KIDS	Benjamin
DOG TRAINING, Koehler Method of	Koehler
GO FIND! Training Your Dog to Track	Davis
GUARD DOG TRAINING, Koehler Method of	Koehler
OPEN OBEDIENCE FOR RING, HOME AND FIELD, Koehler Method of	Koehler
SPANIELS FOR SPORT (English)	Radcliffe
STONE GUIDE TO DOG GROOMING FOR ALL BREEDS	Stone
SUCCESSFUL DOG TRAINING, The Pearsall Guide to	Pearsall
TOY DOGS, Kalstone Guide to Grooming All	Kalstone
TRAINING THE RETRIEVER	Kersley
TRAINING YOUR DOG TO WIN OBEDIENCE TITLES,	Morsel
TRAIN YOUR OWN GUN DOG, How to	Goodall
UTILITY DOG TRAINING, Koehler Method of	Koehler
VETERINARY HANDBOOK, Dog Owner's Home	Carlson & Giffin

General

COMPLETE DOG BOOK, The	Official Publication of American Kennel Club
DISNEY ANIMALS, World of	Koehler
DOG IN ACTION, The	Lyon
DOG BEHAVIOR, New Knowledge of	Pfaffenberger
DOG JUDGE'S HANDBOOK	Tietjen
DOG JUDGING, Nicholas Guide to	Nicholas
DOG PEOPLE ARE CRAZY	Riddle
DOG PSYCHOLOGY	Whitney
DOG STANDARDS ILLUSTRATED	
DOGSTEPS, Illustrated Gait at a Glance	Elliott
ENCYCLOPEDIA OF DOGS, International	Dangerfield, Howell & Riddle
JUNIOR SHOWMANSHIP HANDBOOK	Brown & Mason
MY TIMES WITH DOGS	Fletcher
OUR PUPPY'S BABY BOOK (blue or pink)	
RICHES TO BITCHES	Shattuck
SUCCESSFUL DOG SHOWING, Forsyth Guide to	Forsyth
TRIM, GROOM AND SHOW YOUR DOG, How to	Saunders
WHY DOES YOUR DOG DO THAT?	Bergman
WILD DOGS in Life and Legend	Riddle
WORLD OF SLED DOGS, From Siberia to Sport Racing	Coppinger